Political Decision-makers

CONTRIBUTORS

William Buchanan, UNIVERSITY OF SOUTHERN CALIFORNIA

Daryl DeBell, M.D., PALO ALTO, CALIFORNIA

Mattei Dogan, C.N.R.S., PARIS, FRANCE

Heinz Eulau, STANFORD UNIVERSITY

LeRoy Ferguson, MICHIGAN STATE UNIVERSITY

W. L. Guttsman, LONDON SCHOOL OF ECONOMICS
   AND POLITICAL SCIENCE

Harold D. Lasswell, YALE UNIVERSITY

Dwaine Marvick, UNIVERSITY OF CALIFORNIA AT LOS ANGELES

Renate Mayntz, FREE UNIVERSITY, BERLIN, GERMANY

Lucian W. Pye, MASSACHUSETTS INSTITUTE OF TECHNOLOGY

Charles R. Nixon, UNIVERSITY OF CALIFORNIA AT LOS ANGELES

Edward A. Shils, UNIVERSITY OF CHICAGO

John C. Wahlke, VANDERBILT UNIVERSITY

INTERNATIONAL YEARBOOK
OF POLITICAL BEHAVIOR RESEARCH

GENERAL EDITOR: HEINZ EULAU STANFORD UNIVERSITY

Political

Decision-makers

EDITED BY *DWAINE MARVICK*, UNIVERSITY OF CALIFORNIA

THE FREE PRESS OF GLENCOE

A DIVISION OF THE CROWELL-COLLIER PUBLISHING COMPANY

Preface

THE VITALITY of an intellectual enterprise may be judged by the number and the intensity of attacks it invites. As one who came to behavioral political science with training in traditional political theory and institutional analysis, I am rather pleased by recent laments over "the behavioral challenge to political theory." Though these complaints are ill-conceived and based on a misreading—deliberate or not—of behavioral research in politics, they suggest that what behavior-oriented political scientists and sociologists are doing can no longer be ignored by students of political theory.

This is as it should be. If systematic behavioral inquiry has an effect on the study of political theory—whether conceived as a "challenge," as by the critics, or as "fulfillment," as by its advocates—the consequences, intended or not, are likely to be salutary. I hope that it may bring about that necessary unity of theoretical and empirical research which was lost after the turn of the century, when political theory declined into historicism and political research into brute empiricism.

In short, I do not think that behavioral research "challenges" political theory, if by "challenge" is meant "threat"—as, I have reason to believe, it is meant by some. The research reported in this volume is ample enough proof. If behavioral research challenges anything, it is the comfortable assumption that theory is the same thing as knowledge. Whatever the plausibility of theoretical speculations and intuitive understandings, and no matter how valid they may be, they are not truths—full, partial or probable. For theory is not knowledge but a necessary tool on the road to knowledge; just as facts, as such, are not knowledge, but only the raw materials that must be molded, through theoretical and experiential manipulation, into statements acceptable as probably true because they have been tested in the crucible of empirical investigation.

If theory is a tool, like all tools it periodically tends to wear out and needs replacement. I don't think that any behavioral political scientist has ever maintained that political theory is expendable. He might say that some particular theory or proposition is worn out, because, on being tested, it just does not seem to yield worthwhile knowledge. If political theorists feel challenged by behavioral research, therefore, let us hope that they will respond by producing better theory for a cumulative science of politics, and not by confirming their suppositions and presuppositions.

This second volume of the *International Yearbook of Political Behavior Research,* like its predecessor, is dedicated to the proposition that formulating theories, manipulating empirical data, and inventing methods constitute a single intellectual enterprise. Three further volumes, devoted to the same effort, are now under way. Volume III, edited by Samuel P. Huntington, of Columbia University, will present theory and research on "Frontiers in Civil-Military Relations." Volume IV, edited by two members of our Advisory Board, Seymour M. Lipset, of the University of California (Berkeley), and Stein Rokkan, of the Institute for Social Research, Oslo, will treat "Comparative Political Party Systems." Volume V, edited by David Apter, of the University of Chicago, will deal with "Political Ideologies in East and West." Correspondence concerning contributions to these volumes should be sent directly to these editors. We welcome ideas for future volumes; they should be communicated to the general editor of the *Yearbook.*

The final editing of this volume, as of its predecessor, was once more facilitated by the Center for Advanced Study in the Behavioral Sciences. I am very grateful to Ralph Tyler, Director, and Preston Cutler, Assistant Director, for their hospitality.

HEINZ EULAU
General Editor

Stanford, California
February, 1960

Contents

Contents

Political Decision-makers

Introduction:

Political Decision-makers
in Contrasting Milieus

by DWAINE MARVICK

Problems in Studying Political Decision-makers

THE MACHIAVELLIAN view of the conduct suitable for a purposeful Prince was given, by Pareto and Mosca, a modern "group" connotation, by linking it to the performance of an "elite" of political decision-makers. Since then, serious scholars have made many diligent and worthwhile efforts to suggest ways in which the backgrounds of those who make public policy shed light on their outlook and performance.[1] Nevertheless, charges of "determinism" and formal "sterility" are not uncommon when elite analysis is presented.

The systematic study of the *cursus honorum* of public men in particular political epochs and under given regimes doubtless has produced some pedestrian work and generated some unwarranted claims. More studies are needed—whether of party-workers, legislators, political leaders, or intellectuals—which improve on the existing pattern. Better conceptual tools are needed; and more effort should be expended in applying familiar research methods in new ways—new uses of interviewing techniques, fresh approaches to historical evidence, novel efforts at participant observation, and innovations in analyzing biographical statistics.

Reinhard Bendix and Seymour Lipset, in a 1957 essay, note that many studies analyze political processes in terms of *who* the leading contenders are, rather than in terms of *what they do*. As a result, the political realm is treated as a mere reflection of the social and economic system from which its personnel are drawn:

> To know who these power wielding individuals are is thought to be sufficient; it is a secondary matter to inquire into how they use their power. That they will do so in their own interest is self-evident, and the nature of that interest is inferred from the status which they occupy. Hence, social and economic status rather than the competing strategies of the political struggles are regarded as the sufficient causes of political decisions."[2]

Bendix and Lipset maintain that in effect, this is to "explain away the very facts of political life,"[3] however inadvertently. Although it is difficult to study the strategies of powerful individuals or groups, focusing on the actions of those in the seats of power is necessary. Moreover, "analysis has the task of explaining the alternatives which were available before the choice was made."[4]

Much of political sociology seeks to trace the impact of social developments on political decision-makers, showing how their discretion is limited by the need to retain support among a self-selective following. Certainly, one important mode by which social and political forces register in policy-making processes would seem to be through the decision-makers themselves and the particular sensitivities and beliefs, skills and interests they bring to the task of *formulating* "the alternatives which were available before the choice was made." Charges against studies of decision-makers which suggest that they "explain away" instead of enlarging our comprehension of political life do not apply to careful inquiry into these aspects any more than others.

Pareto expected all elites to be subject to an inexorable process of deterioration by which they would cease to be "fit to rule"; history, in his phrase, was a graveyard of aristocracies. Pareto felt he could specify how mass manipulation was possible, with details about nonrational mechanisms. Whether elites would be motivated to apply his rules was a quite different question, linked to the historical forces that caused "the circulation of elites" and their gradual loss of nerve and ingenuity. For two thousand years of history, he annotated the cycle of elites rising, growing feeble and inept, and yielding to new elites.[5]

Pareto's elites, whether "lions" or "foxes," were not presented as reflections of their group origins; they were analyzed in terms of their success in setting styles and standards and whether they did what was needed to stay in power, not whether they championed popular causes or represented mass interests. Mosca, in considering that democratic politics had to rely on the merely honest middle-class man, while more aristocratic regimes were staffed by men quick to accept their public duties and having an autonomy safely founded on wealth and status, was appalled at how easily the public man of democratic politics was corrupted in his morals, how vulnerable his personal autonomy was, and how inclined he was to make official decisions on premises of expediency.[6] Michels, noting how any "common cause" was shaped by the organizational requirements of specialization, the routine of work, and the timing of tasks, was led to posit that oligarchy was unavoidable, regardless of the origins of leadership or their early enthusiasm for an ideal program.[7] None of these writers can be said to claim that knowledge of *who* the leaders were, and from whence in society they came, gave a full basis for predicting how they would behave, either as representative men or opportunists. If anything, they tended to slight this set of considerations. Instead, they stressed the extent to which history included accidental developments, men in power made miscalculations, and spontaneous social forces created unexpected problems and imposed forced choices.

Doubtless, the premises of official action do derive in large part from considerations only remotely linked to the backgrounds of decision-makers. The strategy rules of Machiavelli and the elaborate compendium of examples of successful manipulation that Pareto assembled probably have contributed just as much as elite-formation studies to what Aristotle called "practical science." In quite a different way, the same might be said of conventional studies of governmental decision-making; often without any references to the distinctive characteristics of participants, these have shown how institutionalized processes, organizational commitments, and official momentum circumscribe issues and limit choice to a few "appropriate" solutions.[8]

Systematic studies of how the stratification system of a society affects those in the seats of political power have added meaningfully to our understanding of the governmental process.[9] They have clarified probable connections between mutually dependent variables; they have stimulated fresh inquiries into neglected problem complexes; they have permitted recurrent patterns in politics to be viewed from more informed perspectives than before. Still, their instrumental value to those who make public policy is, thus far, rather modest.

Relatively little attention has been given to such matters as the self-image of political leaders, the opinions they hold of one another, their awareness of the processes in which they participate, or their concern with the groups whose life circumstances are affected by their performances. Virtually nothing is known of the differences in commitment to the "rules of the game," which, regardless of the route to power, may be found generally to characterize leaders of middle-class origins or decision-makers reared in a totalitarian political culture. Still less is known of the differences in skill and ability introduced by the selective workings of political-recruitment ladders. Little is available that highlights the process by which political leaders become "professionalized," either in the sense of acquiring a distinctive kind of "know-how" or in the sense of achieving a degree of psychological detachment from the merits of a public policy, seen in terms of public and group interests.

Recent Developmental Studies of Political Decision-makers

Serious empirical research into the socialization and professionalization of those who make political decisions—whether in traditional contexts, pluralist socities, or totalitarian regimes—has substantially increased in volume and quality since World War II. The heaviest emphasis has been on those in formal authority, and on how their social origins and political-mobility channels provide them with distinctive skills and resources, goals and interests, beliefs and styles of action. American political scientists and sociologists in this period have made impressive contributions to the growing literature. There has been important work done on leadership in emergent nations, whether against the background of a folk society or an ancient civilization; the problems of socialization for specialized governmental and political roles have been explored; inquiries into the dynamics of interest-group arenas and organizational alignments have been made; special attention has been given to the study of legislators; including work on their style, interaction patterns, and tendencies toward professionalization. Finally, several able syntheses and attempts at macro-political typologies have been put forward. Regularly in *Administrative Science Quarterly, Conflict Resolution, Behavioral Science,* and *Public Opinion Quarterly,* and intermittently in the more conservative organs of professional associations for political scientists and sociologists, work on political decision-makers which explicitly links empirical data to theoretically generalized problems has appeared.

In Oslo, Heidelberg, Paris, and Florence—to name perhaps the four most important continental centers of inquiry into elite problems—less publicized but stimulating work is carried on. In Norway, Vilhelm Aubert and Ulf Torgersen, at the Institute for Social Research, have established an IBM-card archive of information on "elite personnel" since 1814, and Stein Rokkan and his associates at the Institute have under way various studies of the backgrounds and connections of the politically active candidates at local and national elections, as well as politicians in public office. In Italy, Giovanni Sartori has been studying the careers and performance standards of Italian legislators; his research design focuses on professionalization and elite-circulation phenomena. In Germany, Dolf Sternberger, although his inquiry uses a different typology, is conducting a study of political representation similar to that of Sartori. In France, the work of Mattei Dogan on parliamentary personnel is impressive; it includes not only comparative data for a number of advanced pluralist countries but covers historical periods of fifty to a hundred years, depending on the country, and introduces new refinements in the handling of biographical statistics.

In Great Britain, Derek Scott at Manchester has been conducting an elaborate quantitative analysis of career patterns in the Soviet Union, and Peter Campbell carries forward studies parallel to those of M. Dogan. At Durham, Professor Morris-Jones pursues his inquiries into the recruitment of Indian political leaders. The Nuffield College group has produced a rewarding set of configurative studies of modern electoral campaigns, while interest elsewhere at Oxford is sustained on problems of African development. At the London School of Economics and Political Science, work on contemporary elite circulation is being done by R. T. McKenzie. There, also, W. L. Guttsman continues his detailed and penetrating socio-historical analysis of the British political elites from the early nineteenth century to the present. His articles on the role of the aristocracy in British public life appeared some years ago; in this volume, he turns to the peculiar strains operating on the leadership of the Labour party, which were manifested in the Labour governments of both the interwar and postwar periods.

Since 1952, the various bibliographical publications supported by UNESCO's Committee for Social Science Documentation have greatly facilitated the task of "keeping track" of new contributions to the understanding of elite phenomena. Evaluating these contributions is more difficult. In editing a volume devoted to recent research on political decision-makers, one of the first problems was securing an analytical survey of contemporary work. Harold D. Lasswell agreed to undertake this. He has identified many of those problems of elite research that must have priority if social scientists would fill gaps in existing knowledge, reformulate persistent conceptual difficulties, and clarify recurrent practical choices confronting policy-makers.

Professor Lasswell takes care to show how the premises for political decisions vary with the developmental phase of a political order, i.e., by where a regime stands relative to such developmental constructs as totalitarianism, modernity, and the garrison state. The problems confronting governmental leaders are largely imposed by historical forces; the responses of those leaders are in part understandable only in light of their social origins and routes of ascent to power. The categories that Lasswell uses to summarize recent work provide suggestive new leads, while they also subsume analyses of widely divergent phenomena, variously conceived.

Throughout his essay, Lasswell demonstrates that elite phenomena have meaning only within more comprehensive frames of reference, which need to be clarified in the form of developmental constructs. He notes how persistent has been the intellectual challenge of the Marxist "from where—to what" thesis, in which an integral place is given to a political-elite group. Alternative formulations have been posed, variously stressing the key positions held by intellectuals and professionals, specialists in communications, and specialists in violence. He elaborates his own early contribution—the "garrison state" construct—and discusses recent work that has analyzed empirical trends said to modify its evolvement. In doing so, he poses a dialectical question: is the modern scientific and technological revolution diluting the distinctively "military" outlook that is presumably dominant in the garrison state?

Turning to elite transformations in regimes undergoing modernization, Lasswell notes work on the impact of urbanization, nationalism, and technology. Temporary solutions range from the accommodation elites of the Pueblo Indians to the interlocked leadership formations of the Chinese community in Thailand; more stable solutions are suggested by studies of oriental despotism based on irrigation technology, and by the equilibrium sustained in a feudal order, where elite circulation is not simultaneously a matter of elite transformation.

For studies of totalitarian regimes, Lasswell's discussion of the developmental stages, from "take over" to "totalitarianization," is organized according to the kinds of variables a given study treats as key factors in shaping the road to total regimentation. The utility of his own "interest" typology—

power, wealth, respect, skill, health, and so on—is shown by locating it within a more comprehensive set of rubrics—including culture, class, personality, and crisis—as well as interests, which serve to sort out a growing volume of work.

In examining the tangled problems of elite analysis in industrial and democratic systems, Lasswell stresses the added care required to distinguish actual from nominal decision-makers—a result of the pluralism of advanced societies, necessitating functional terms of analysis rather than conventional conceptual tools. Here, he classifies recent work in terms of the components of "perspective analysis," in order to relate a range of studies examining the outlook of specialized functional elites to a similar diversity of studies focusing on mass belief systems and how they shape public policy. The link between elites and masses is also explored by tracing the histories of political myths and analyzing the characteristics of those who believe them and those who do not.

Specialized elites command different resources, as various studies attest, and this in turn has produced important analyses of elite strategies. In order to integrate these, Lasswell urges that high priority be given to the study of elite and counterelite alignments as pre-outcome stages as well as at conventionally recognized decision points. Furthermore, "sequence studies" need to push beyond formal decision points to trace consequences into the middle distance and to the horizon of policy itself. He pinpoints the available studies touching on these neglected problems of the dynamics of elite analysis; once again, he stresses the intellectual gains in viewing these problems from heuristically posited developmental perspectives.

Throughout his exposition, Lasswell never seeks to "explain away" the realities of politics. Rather, he points to the expanding compass of our common knowledge, gained partly by studies of all those forces and mechanisms that circumscribe choice, as well as by those studies that improve our grasp of the intricate ways in which decision-makers acquire their loyalties and involvement, their skills and resources, and their convictions and standards of performance.

Analyzing Political Decision-makers in Contrasting Milieus

Data-gathering methods are of prime importance in the study of political decision-makers. This volume is organized to reaffirm the value of studies using varied styles of inquiry and quite different kinds of evidence. Professor Shils has worked by methods of sustained field observation and elite interviewing. M. Dogan has developed new methods of coding and handling biographical statistics. Mr. Guttsman has skillfully juxtaposed quantitative trend data with illustrative quotations drawn from letters, memoirs and public records. Dr. Mayntz has maintained an observer's frame of reference while participating for a year in the organizational life of a Christian Democratic party district in West Berlin. By contrast, D. Marvick and C. R. Nixon, studying the electioneering efforts of rival party-workers during the height of a campaign, have used sample-survey techniques to probe the motivations and backgrounds of volunteers in selected Los Angeles localities. Heinz Eulau and his associates have done a rare thing in interviewing projects; taking lengthy standardized interviews with American state legislators in four different political environments, they have encouraged their informants to talk freely and at length, and they have conserved the contextual quality of those comments in the quotations they use.

What Joseph A. Schumpeter called the "paraphernalia" of analysis—the conceptual instruments—are also critically important in analyzing elite phenomena. Because they involve contrasting political cultures or milieus these studies of political decision-makers may seem disparate if looked at from conventional frames of reference. How do studies of intellectuals in "new states," national legislators in France, governmental leaders in Britain, party cadre in Germany and California, and state legislators in America illuminate basic differences in the outlook and interests of political decision-makers?

If looked at in terms of the political culture in which they function, the answer is at least threefold. The perspectives and sensitivities of political decision-makers vary (a) with the modes of legitimacy they adopt or are forced to espouse, (b) with the vocational opportunities by which their skills and resources for political careers are developed or stunted, and (c) with the mechanisms and occasions by which their sensitivity and involvement with politics—their "politicization" level—is evoked, sustained, or muted.

In Max Weber's lecture on "Politics as a Vocation," the careers of those who mainly live *for* politics and those who live *off* politics are contrasted. Convictions and standards that give legitimacy to one's conduct in terms of some public purpose are not necessarily at odds with material rewards from interested sources within the political arena. It is possible to live both for and off politics at the same time.

Those who live for politics are not all alike. The basic variations are the charismatic leader and his followers, the notables and good citizens who feel a sense of civic responsibility, and the ideologues who find meaning in life through programs of social transformation. For each type, political action is based on a different mode of legitimization—articulated in heroic, honorific, or doctrinal terms, respectively.

Nor are those who live off politics led by the same interests. The vocational opportunities include being a government official or party functionary as well as doing work that calls for organizational skill and an administrative commitment. Men trained as advocates or apologists, having communications or legal skills, may find political employment working in behalf of various special interests. We must include also journalists, literary men, teachers, and other intellectuals, whose professions equip them to express their interpretations of society and its problems in readily understood terms. For each type, political activity rests on a different basis for compensation; skills and resources are put at the disposal of organizational, clientele, and public interests, respectively.

Those who live *in* a political orbit, however characterized as to public purpose and vocational opportunity, are not equally constant. The control devices that evoke or mute a voluntary willingness to think and act in terms of political solutions are extraordinarily varied. They include the individual's cultural pattern and style of conduct, his organizational role and status considerations, and those professional interests and codes with which he identifies.

Each of the contributors is concerned with the extent and manner that political decision-makers live *for* a public purpose, although differently conceived; live *off* a political vocation, although variously sponsored; and live *in* a politicized orbit, however differentially evoked or deflected. A brief survey will suggest the complexities characterizing each political milieu; even a partial ordering of the several studies along these suggested dimensions is difficult and should be understood as suggestive only. At one extreme stand the intellectuals of "new states," intensely absorbed in the public purposes that political decision-makers must implement; at the other extreme stand American state legislators, understanding "public service" and only occasionally referring to it. Near the former are the brilliant intellectual debaters of the French Chamber, whose doctrinal pronouncements about party programs serve to obscure the basic class lines of cleavage in the assembly. In the middle, their socialist mission muted by the responsibilities of office and the opportunities for a comfortable career in public life, the modern British Labour leaders are found. In the middle, also, are the campaign militants of rival party groups in Los Angeles, enthusiastic about candidates and issues, but aware also of the social and community contacts to be gained by voluntary campaign work. Nearly as lacking in concern with public policy as American state legislators are the party cadre of a district organization in postwar Berlin. Their energies and interests diverted into strengthening the party organization for electoral victory, they act largely as a "resonating body" for the decisions of higher party leaders.

Charismatic Politics in a New State

In inquiring into the "Dilemmas of Intellectuals in the Political Development of India," Professor Shils considers both accomplishments and urgent needs. Every facet of the unique position occupied by India's intellectuals is traced and evaluated, as he examines the historical circumstances that sustain and transform their role "as the sole modern class in their society."

In India, as in other "new states," intellectuals—those with advanced modern educations and, hence, in contact with Western culture—are not only the articulators of new belief systems. They are, to an extent unparalleled in the West, among the foremost actors on their political stage. They are the creators of nationalist movements and the stabilizers of new constitutional order, the bearers of the administrative machinery and the counselors of those who rule. In these policy-shaping roles, India's intellectuals have often performed with distinction.

But they must play other roles, too. In the public forums of an open society, the intellectuals supply whatever civil and informed criticism is to be found. In India, those forums are too often marked by an uncritical and unfactual negativism, basically because those who stand outside of government have too weak a sense of affinity with those who must make public policy. Professor Shils examines the troublesome ingredients that have led to this development.

Too many Indian intellectuals are habituated to "oppositionalism," engendered during the colonial period, but rooted in deep-seated psychological dilemmas that persist after independence has come. There is pervasive contempt for the "routine politics of the civil order" and for the emerging class of professionalized public men who live off politics. The ideal is cherished of political action taken as a charismatic response to a heroic figure, who champions a cause transcending group interests and who leads a movement needing no organizational machinery. To suggest the sources of their bitterness, disenchantment, and alienation, Professor Shils sketches the sequence of a typical intellectual's life history: leaving school to do errands for the political movement; going perhaps to prison for acts of vandalism; learning there the revolutionary literature of the West; returning to a changed political scene and the uncomfortable duties of school and adulthood.

India's intellectuals, whatever their occupational roles, largely stand outside the circle of active policy-making. Those in the civil service or academic life feel isolated; those in the literary world are constantly lectured at and belittled; those in law, medicine, and other specialized professions not only feel cut off from a forum where common problems are intelligently considered but feel doubts that any public forum of that kind exists. Indian journalism is weak and vulnerable, habituated to a polemical tone, largely unwilling to support incisive analysis of public problems, poorly fed by either academic research or legislative inquiry, and habituated to accepting governmental press releases and to reporting routine parliamentary debates.

In a pluralist society, men must be able to find purpose for their individual lives through careers in a diversity of nonpolitical contexts. But they must also have a sense of their common corporate status. As the problems of modernity are collectively met, Indian democracy will require intellectuals with the qualities of "civility" that can contain and regularize its political life.

Intellectual Politicians in a Class Society

Political decision-makers working in a context of civility found in a western democracy face quite different problems. The motivations, justifications, and opportunities for a political career are more varied and less tension-ridden. Vocational opportunities to live from politics are more numerous and need not be exclusively political. Heroic justification, typical in underdeveloped nations, gives way to doctrinal and honorific explanations, which legitimize not only action but tolerance and delay. Substantive politicization becomes sporadic, even periodic and regular; it blends into the pursuit of organizational interests per se; it is given realism through the development of professionalized attitudes and the cultivation of the "art of the possible."

In a series of earlier publications, Mattei Dogan has systematically explored many of these patterns of western politics. Here a synthesis of his work on France is presented in English. He is able to show how parliamentary life during the Third and Fourth Republics gave a predominant place to intellectuals—those whose former occupations called for scholarly habits and usually an advanced education. Trained as exponents of social interests other than their own and with a social status derived from their special competence and knowledge, they were somewhat aloof from class conflicts. To a former lawyer, with an advocate's detachment from the merits of his client's case, a legislative arena gave new scope to his professional skill. A former academician, schooled in logical exposition and formal analysis, could build a political career in any party by putting his talents to work. Highly politicized, the intellectual deputies rather easily became professional politicians, while their skills gave Chamber debates a distinctive quality. Problems were perhaps posed more abstractly and expounded more ably, but solutions were discussed more unrealistically and debated longer than otherwise might have been the case.

The intellectual façade of French party pronouncements, M. Dogan argues, was created largely by the intellectuals and chiefly benefited their careers. His analysis documents the view that class lines basically define the French party spectrum. The declining weight of intellectuals he links more generally to transformations in the origins and experience of those who make up the main party groupings in the Chamber—transformations uneven in their impact but resulting from the social and political criteria that have come to determine political advancement.

The *cursus honorum* of a French deputy is partly a matter of fortune, friends, and native talent. M. Dogan traces the importance of local elective office, experience in party work, and participation in the activities of non-political organizations, as well as higher education. Three other considerations typically weigh in the balance. Various kinds of journalistic experience has advanced the careers of perhaps one-third of all deputies in the twentieth century. Following a family tradition of active political pursuits adds an honorific note of duty to the sporadic emotional and ideological appeals to political activism; it both mutes and steadies the level of politization. Finally, the history of France has made it possible to acquire, in an heroic context, both the credentials to legitimize public-career aspirations and the skills and resources necessary to earn a political livelihood. Participation in the resistance movements during World War II is the only criterion that evokes the highly charged emotional connotations of the politicized intellectuals in "new states."

Socialist Leaders in a Constitutional Order

Within British parliamentary democracy, the Labour Party came late on the scene. Traditions of party control by front-bench and Cabinet leaders has become familiar in parliamentary practice. The "Changes in British

Labour Leadership," described by W. L. Guttsman, grew out of concepts and early practices developed in the militant and voluntary organizations of a minority-class movement. Its chance to rule in 1924 found it transformed into a national party with a mass following. Labour's elite included many who regarded themselves as delegates committed to socialist action rather than instigators and makers of policy. Furthermore, it had no men experienced in Cabinet life. With its changed political functions, Labour could draw its leaders from outside the working class, at least in part, and hence from men with experience in constitutional rule.

The balance that MacDonald struck between working-class and traditional ruling-class representation in his 1924 Cabinet was nearly fifty-fifty; it was repeated in 1929. With a slight mislodgement of notables in favor of professional career persons, the postwar Labour governments of Attlee struck the same balance. Nevertheless, Mr. Guttsman traces a progressive *embourgeoisement* in Labour governments, linked to the professionalization of political careers. Attlee's middle-class contingent, less illustrious than its earlier counterpart, had been trained inside the Labour Party itself; his working-class associates, from years as members of Parliament, had acquired middle-class standards and the outlook of professional politicians.

In close-ups, Guttsman reveals the transformations of outlook and style undergone by individual personalities. When in power, they fitted rather smoothly into the traditional roles ascribed to ministers, partly because of the criteria used in selecting them, partly through their neglect of wider issues in favor of absorption with administrative results and problems. Parliamentary life itself was an educating and moderating force, lessening antagonisms and muting militancy.

Mr. Guttsman describes the crystallization of a clearly defined party leadership and the development of traditional leader-follower relationships. These were achieved only with acute conflicts. In part, those conflicts were linked to the fortunes of Labour's several factions; in part, social origins and career lines are correlated with clashing political views. But the British Left is increasingly committed to the professionalization of politics and to reliance on a rather small nucleus of leaders who make the vital decisions. "Thus, in the political field the Labour Party seems to be creating or maintaining a static system of stratification, which in the economic and social field it is seeking to destroy."

Party Democracy in a Reconstituted Polity

Reporting from a year of participant observation, Dr. Renate Mayntz provides a systematic commentary on "Oligarchic Problems in a German Party District" in post-Nazi West Berlin. Like voluntary groups everywhere, the lower levels of German party life are characterized by diverse and untidy "housekeeping." Party functionaries give little attention to recruiting new members with leadership potential; rank-and-file interest is slight and desultory when it comes to selecting higher-level party officials; discussion and analysis of policy issues are poor even among the members of district-wide "advisory" committees; when voluntary party-workers talk about strategy and campaign organization, they have somewhat better records of shrewdness and intellectual know-how.

Dr. Mayntz found herself working with several types of party members: opportunists, those with personal or political ambitions; ideological militants; dutiful party affiliates; and the merely gregarious. She identifies various elements—rational and emotional—in the "incumbency argument" used widely in the debates over leadership selection. In raising the question of oligarchic tendencies, she examines the mixed effects of the common practice of "personal union" (i.e., the same person's holding of party offices at different levels) on leadership continuity and member participation in party affairs. She notes that most functionaries are not accountable to the ordinary membership, and she describes the practice of co-optation by unofficial pre-planning of candidate slates.

Michels, too, drew upon his background of participation in German party work. Mayntz's discussion of oligarchy, however, argues that any more catering to ordinary members might well contribute to less responsible and less effective party decisions, so apathetic and inept are many of the rank and file. Moreover, the *de facto* recourse to oligarchic techniques is not, she notes, accompanied by any sustained line of justification for it. Rather, there is a casual and spontaneous growth of legitimizing attitudes about prevailing leadership-selection methods.

What is disturbing is a similar uncritical acceptance of policy decisions from higher-level party officials. "If the lower party level is habitually only a resonating body . . . it will presumably lack the disposition and the organizational instruments to assert control, if, at some future time, these higher leaders should act against the wishes of the membership or act in a way detrimental to the democratic political system." Thus, members are habituated to think of the party's political strength as an end in itself. The very emphasis within party ranks on electoral success reflects this preoccupation, as does the willingness with which activities directly contributing to the political potency of the CDU are accepted and carried out. Even when membership opinions on issues are ventilated at party meetings, the tendency is to evaluate them in terms of their effect on organizational cohesion and support of the party "line."

Political Self-Recruitment in Advanced Pluralist Communities

In "Recruitment Contrasts in Rival Campaign Groups," Dwaine Marvick and Charles R. Nixon explore the manner in which party recruitment is affected by competition, both from the rival party organization and from the diversified nonpolitical life of the locality. They report findings from a study of 300 active party volunteers in selected Los Angeles localities. During the height of the 1956 campaign, long interviews were held, using standardized formats, and the volunteers rated themselves and one another in terms of power, ideology, and reasons for participating.

Necessarily, most inquiries concerning a political-elite structure focus on the institutional scaffolding that houses its organized life, stabilizes its power relationships, and reduces its manpower circulation to functionally intelligible patterns. Instead of concentrating on the intramural processes of each party's organizational apparatus, the design for the Los Angeles study focuses on the common arena of rival campaign groups—the immediate locality in which both sides must recruit their manpower. In an advanced pluralist community, the nonpolitical orbits of life—with family and friends, neighbors and job associates, social organizations and civic associations—compete with politics for the time and talent of the potential volunteer. It is relevant also to ask whether or not different segments in the same localities supply manpower to rival parties with equal favor, and treat them like optional home teams in the same baseball league. What does "the great game of politics" look like to the voluntary campaign worker?

While both parties demonstrably drew their personnel mainly from each community's middle class, each party also had a distinctive appeal in specific areas of the same locality. The Republicans tended to come from the dominant status groups, the Democrats from subordinate strata. It was a conscious sorting-out process, with those who volunteered in the service of each party being ideologically drawn together. Self-styled conservatives went to the Republican camp, liberals to the Democratic banner. To the self-recruited, the rival "home teams" were meaningfully different in substantive political terms.

In urban communities, political parties only sporadically need campaign volunteers. Continuous social and material advantages to a potential party-worker are offered by many nonpolitical groups; primary-group demands on the city dweller also compete for his attention and sense of duty. What factors led those who chose activity in politics to work freely and enthusiastically? Again, ideological convictions and opinions were relevant. The large majority of those studied reported themselves as lacking agreement with their daily associates concerning matters of political ideology. An examination of family backgrounds also disclosed some indications that the "politicized family," in which there is the example of a politically *active* parent, is an important formative condition in prompting people to become active. Blending with these considerations, however, were a substantial set of nonpolitical reasons, frequently acknowledged—fun, social contacts, business advantages, and so forth.

If rival party groups in the same localities are differently composed, reflecting social and economic disparities in the community life, politics is more than just a great game. It is an optional process for resisting or affirming the appropriateness of those disparities. In a stable and diversified urban community, many will ignore that option until the process produces a meaningful election-day choice. Some citizens, however, will have to provide the necessary manpower to make that choice a serious and meaningful one. The Los Angeles study investigates their reasons for entering the campaign arena, and notes the evidence that the choices they helped to pose for the voters were reflections of their own political perspectives and status needs.

Personal Career Plans and the Competitiveness of the Political Arena

In "Career Perspectives of American State Legislators," Heinz Eulau and his associates delineate the vocational outlook of political decision-makers who lack virtually all the attitudes found among the intellectuals in the politics of emergent countries. Instead of a preoccupation with authority as the solution for all pressing public problems, few instances were found wherein men treated governmental solutions as imperative or even necessarily preferable. The job of state legislator is a part-time one. For some, it is simply "something to do"—a fascinating game, the zest for which is "in my blood"; for others, it is vaguely instrumental to some notion of "public service"; for still others, it means specific opportunities to advance parochial projects of reform or innovation. Whether the goals are contributive or exploitative, they lack the pervasive and imperative qualities of charismatic politics.

Professor Eulau and his associates designed their study to permit contrasts in the political-career plans of state legislators in states with substantially different party systems. They explore the ways in which the relevance of social origins and status credentials attenuate as factors determining political advancement; political arrangements and practices are seen as intervening decisively at various points. The competitiveness of a state's politics appears to condition the career perspectives of state legislators in many ways. Heavier stress is placed on professional competence and political skill, and more experience in relevant party and local governmental positions is called for, the more competitive the election process. Where one party largely dominates a state, political careers may be sponsored by interest groups or by associates and friends; where competition prevails, party organizations screen and sponsor their candidates more jealously. Significantly, greater competition is also linked to less talk about performing meaningful acts of public service, group assistance, or local improvement; under more competitive interparty conditions, sensitivity and concern about substantive political issues seemingly wanes, while the interests and difficulties of the party organization per se receive more stress and have more meaning.

Political Decision-makers in Changing Milieus

The criteria for political advancement are constantly being modified. The "circulation of elites," by which younger and more vigorous men learn the trade of politics from those ahead of them, cannot be divorced from the "transformation of elites," which causes new generations of political decision-makers to perform in a different style and to live by different standards of responsible conduct when in office.

Research is needed that will identify the inimitable characteristics of those who rise to the highest rungs of the political ladder, the characteristics that distinguish them from the cadre, whose qualities are more easily imitated. Political leaders of the first order innovate in ways requiring skills and resources not widely available; yet they set styles and impose performance standards which, once demonstrated, can be imitated by others. Accordingly, future decision-makers still at the barrier must find themselves being screened for capacities their elders never had to have, trained to cope with developments only handled experimentally by the incumbent elite, equipped with an awareness and sensitivity to the decision-making problems posed by impending "break-throughs" in science and technology, in genetics and medicine, and in social science.

It seems probable that the world will become progressively a more homogeneous political milieu. The "new states" of today were pressed into their territorial shapes and institutional forms by the matrix of European colonial politics, which is now being lifted. The Fourth Republic in France, wherein a political career meant a legislative career, has given way to the executive politics of the Fifth Republic. The radical program of British Labour was harnessed by adapting its leadership to traditional practices; this was done through professionalization and a broadened recruitment base, but at the cost, perhaps, of dissipating its support in the country. The legacy of the Third Reich's mass regimentation is not easily abandoned; the danger of oligarchic rule is discernible even in the practices of the contemporary Christian Democratic Party, in the complacency of party cadre and the casualness in party circles toward discussion of the problems facing German democracy. The manpower needs of American campaign processes are increasingly met by volunteers. But can those who enter the political arena briefly, then resuming the patterns of their ordinary lives, supply the talent and experience needed to work the cumbersome machinery of free elections? Finally, the reasons for the dominance of American governors in state-level decision-making are not hard to see, when the caliber of emerging leaders among state legislators is assessed in light of Eulau's findings. The more ambitious the politician, the more he was likely to see his chance, rate his assets, and gauge the formidableness of his opponent. Doubtless this greater sensitivity to political complexities will serve, for a time, the private-career interests of such a public figure. But citizens of his state will have to look elsewhere for a political man who seeks to give public meaning to his individual life and whose political vocation most citizens can with profit support. In Max Weber's words, "politics is a strong and slow boring of hard boards. It takes both passion and perspective."

Notes

1. Good surveys include H. D. Lasswell *et al., The Comparative Study of Elites* (Stanford, Calif.: Stanford University Press, 1952), and D. R. Matthews, *The Social Background of Political decision-Makers* (Garden City, N. Y.: Doubleday, 1954).

2. "Political Sociology," *Current So*

ciology, VI No. 3 (Paris: UNESCO, 1957), 85.

3. *Ibid.*

4. *Ibid.*

5. See the comparisons of Pareto and Mosca drawn in H. Stuart Hughes "Gaetano Mosca and the Political Lessons of History," in H. S. Hughes *et al.* (eds.), *Teachers of History* (Ithaca, N. Y.: Cornell University Press, 1954).

6. Gaetano Mosca, *The Ruling Class,* ed. A. Livingston (New York: Mc-Graw-Hill, 1935), pp. 268-70.

7. Robert Michels, *Political Parties* (Glencoe, Ill.: The Free Press, 1958

reprinting), Part VI, "Synthesis: The Oligarchical Tendencies of Organization," pp. 381-409.

8. A useful guide to this body of work is provided by William Gore and Fred S. Silander, "A Bibliographical Essay on Decision-Making," *Administrative Science Quarterly,* IV (June, 1959), pp. 97-121.

9. Much of this material is brought into focus in two recent books: Robert Lane, *Political Life* (Glencoe, Ill.: The Free Press, 1959), and S. M. Lipset, *Political Man* (New York: Doubleday, 1959).

Influence and Withdrawal: The Intellectuals in Indian Political Development

by EDWARD SHILS

Introduction

THE POLITICAL life of the new states of Asia and Africa—its development during the period of colonial rule, the acquisition of power, and the actual exercise of sovereignty in the broadest sense—has been, to an overwhelming extent, the achievement of modern intellectuals. They have not been entirely alone: businessmen have helped with financial support; traditional rulers have added their prestige and sometimes their finances; religious dignitaries have sometimes contributed the authority of their own traditions. As compared with the political life of the more advanced countries, however, the modern intellectuals have occupied a disproportionately preponderant position.

It was the task of the intellectuals to contend for their nations' right to exist, even to the extent of promulgating the very idea of the nation. The erosion of the conscience and self-confidence of the colonial powers was in considerable measure the product of agitational movements led by modern intellectuals. The impregnation of their fellow countrymen with some incipient sense of nationality and national self-esteem was to a large extent the achievement of intellectuals, both secular and religious. The representation of the claims of the nation before their own people, their rulers, and the world, the organization of the movement to gain a share in their own government, and ultimately the establishment of their own sovereignty and its management must all be credited to them. The intellectuals of underdeveloped countries have created the political life of their countries; they have been its instigators, its leaders, and its executants. Until Gandhi's emergence at the end of the First World War, they were its main followers as well, but this changed when the nationalist movement began to arouse the sentiments of the mass of the population.

With the growth of more populistic mass movements with their indispensable organizational machinery and functionaries, the leading political intellectuals underwent a partial transformation. This transformation was accompanied by the coming forth of a new stratum of politicians who were more professional and less intellectual. These changes brought a third development—the disillusioned withdrawal of many intellectuals from active political interest. Thus, the circle has nearly been closed. From opposition and alienation under foreign rule, the intellectuals have returned to opposition and alienation under self-government. Yet, through all these transformations and identities, the fact remains that intellectuals have played, and continue to play, an exceptionally prominent role in the public life of the new states.

The pattern was established in India—the greatest of all imperial territories, the most complex, with the richest indigenous intellectual tradition, and the earliest and most developed modern intellectual class and modern literary and academic culture. The Indian path has been the path of nearly all the colonial countries, qualified by its longer duration, the numerousness and differentiation of its intellectual class, and the nature and responsiveness of its foreign model. These distinguishing features only give to the Indian experience the uniqueness that falls to the eldest and most advanced member of a family, all of whose members face the same fundamental problems with the same fundamental equipment.

1. The Indian Intellectuals as the Creators of the Constitutional Order

Slowly, haltingly, reluctantly, by fits and starts, the British Raj gave way to an Indian constitution. The Government of India Act of 1935 precipitated the framework within which the Constitution of the Republic of India took form. Both were expressions of a long-growing constitutional outlook. It is this outlook, and not just the written constitution of 1950, that orders the life of the Government of India, that makes India the best governed of the new states of Asia and Africa, the most liberal and the most democratic. The competition for this distinction, it is true, is not exacting. However, considering the size of the Indian earth, its immense population, the deep cleavages dividing that population into greatly unequal economic classes and linguistic and caste communities with little sense of affinity with each other, the general poverty and illiteracy, and the strength of both pre- and anti-constitutional traditions, the achievement verges on the grandiose.

Much credit for the achievement must be attributed to the example of British public life and to British policy. It was, however, far from an exclusively British achievement. It is to a great extent an Indian one. It is the achievement of Indian intellectuals—journalists, lawyers, and educators. It is an achievement of the Indian liberals, not just the moderates who came together in the early twenties in the National Liberal Federation of India, but the large body of National Congress leaders who stood in the center of Indian politics until they were displaced by Gandhi.

The Indian liberals have now fallen into obscurity, lost in the shadow of Gandhi's personality and the politics of the Indian National Congress, which he dominated almost from the time of his return to India to his death more than three decades later. Mr. Nehru, in his *Autobiography,* wrote a Congressman's epitaph for Indian Liberalism. The leaders "had long been cut off from effective contact with the outside world," while the "rest of the [Liberal] Party was a vague amorphous lot of people, who wanted occasionally to have the sensation of being connected with political activities. Some of these . . . were undistinguishable from Government officials."[1]

. . . their moderation is really confined to their attitude towards the British government, and they nurse the hope that if they are sufficiently respectful and compromising, perhaps, as a reward for this behavior, they might be listened to. Inevitably they have to accept British viewpoint. Blue books become their passionate study. Erskine May's *Parliamentary Practice* and such like books their constant companions, a new Government Report a matter for excitement and speculation. Liberal leaders returning from England make mysterious statements about the doings of the great ones in Whitehall, for Whitehall is the Valhalla of Liberals. . . . In the old days, it used to be said that good Americans when they died went to Paris and it may be said that the shades of good liberals sometimes haunt the precincts of Whitehall. . . . The liberals . . . have lost touch with both the old and the new. As a group they represent a vanishing species.[2]

Indian independence was primarily the work of Gandhi and the Congress Party. What the liberals and the liberal spirit did was to give form to a constitutional liberal outlook. They agitated for greater Indian representation in the administration, advisory, and legislative councils of the British Raj; and they argued for representative institutions at local, regional, and national levels. When India's British rulers reluctantly and partially brought these institutions into being, the liberals participated in them and tried to make them work—while Congressmen boycotted them and the Swaraj Party tried to break them down by unyielding opposition. By trying to work these institutions, limited though they were in permitting self-government to India, the liberals provided the platform on which present-day Indian representative institutions were built. Participation in them, by liberals and Congressmen, created a body of experience and a set of expectations concerning representative institutions. When the time came for a sovereign India to govern itself, these institutions seemed to be the only significant alternative.

Who were the great Indian liberals? The column of forerunners begins with Raja Ram Mohan Roy, and he is followed by M. G. Ranade. N. G.

Chandavarkar, Sir Pherozshah Mehta, Dadabhai Naoroji, and others—public officials, judges, lawyers, editors, and businessmen by profession; all studious intellectuals, though not necessarily productive scholars, thoughtful about the principles of social improvement and administrative and political action. Ram Mohan Roy was a theological reformer; he could, with Macaulay, be said to be the co-parent of English education in India. He studied Sanskrit, Persian, and Arabic, theology, and law; he translated the Vedas and Upanishads into English and Bengali; he wrote *The Precepts of Jesus: The Guide to Peace and Happiness* (1820) and numerous tracts on theological, social, and educational questions.

M. G. Ranade was a learned judge, a liberal social, economic, and religious reformer, and he wrote voluminously on all of these subjects.[3] Chandavarkar was of the same tendency; his intellectual interests were deep as well as extensive. The scope of his intellectual concerns is shown by his lecture course on Wordsworth's *Prelude,* delivered before the Sunday classes of the Student's Brotherhood in Bombay.[4] Dadabhai Naoroji was a Parsee businessman from Bombay who settled in London and who represented East Finsbury in the House of Commons. He, too, was a man of wide intellectual interests. With Ranade and R. C. Dutt, he is regarded as one of the co-founders of economic study in India. His writings include the classic *Poverty and Un-British Rule in India,*[5] "The European and Asiatic Races,"[6] and much else.

After the forerunners came the Liberals proper: G. K. Gokhale, V. Srinivasa Sastri, H. N. Kunzru, Surendranath Bannerjea, Tej Bahadur Sapru, Telang, M. R. Jayakar, R. P. Paranjpye, C. L. Setalvad, *et al.*—teachers, journalists, lawyers, all of them students of political philosophy and literature.

In the actual drafting of the Constitution of the Republic of India, the central role was played by the late B. D. Ambedkar, a man of powerful mind trained at London and Columbia Universities, from which he held doctorates; and a man who, despite the demands of a lucrative and busy legal practice and Herculean efforts on behalf of the untouchables, always found time to study literature, philosophy, and religion, and to write a good deal.

2. The Indian Intellectual as an Administrator

Indian administration owes no less to the intellectuals than does the constitutional framework of Indian public life. The Indian Civil Service—the "Heaven-born"—was, of course, entirely of British inspiration. It arose from the same utilitarian sources that underlay the Trevelyan-Northcote reforms in Britain itself, and until the seventies it was an exclusively British preserve. A small oligarchy, never larger than thirteen hundred men, it ruled India free of popular or parliamentary control. The first Indians to enter the civil service—both intellectuals of a high order—were Romesh Chandra Dutt and Surendranath Bannerjea; they came in during the early seventies and were the beginning of a trickle which broadened only in the twenties.[7] Both have left intellectual monuments—Dutt in his historical works on Indian economic history and Bannerjea in the Calcutta College which he founded.

Alongside the lofty peaks of the ICS were the lesser peaks of various more specialized services—the Indian Educational Service, the Indian Medical Service, the Indian Forestry Service, etc., and the provincial Civil Service—where educated Indians appeared with increasing frequency as the twentieth century progressed. Below these were the subordinate civil service strata of officials, who, although excluded from the autocratic power of the ICS and the world of the Secretariat, nonetheless carried major responsibilities. These were preponderantly Indian. In their ranks, ever since the British established their ascendancy, were to be found some of the most important figures of Indian intellectual life—Raja Ram Mohan Roy, Bankim Chandra Chatterjee, Professor Sir C. V. Raman, *et al.*

The public services at these levels attracted the best of the modern Indian intellectuals. If we omit the ranks of *pandits* and *sastris*—those custodians of the ancient heritage of Indian learning in religion and philosophy, who became more and more isolated from the main movements of modern Indian life—and concern ourselves solely with those who passed through modern educational institutions, the government service and particularly its highest reaches were the most sought-for goals and the most available channels for India's sharpest minds. Most fathers who could afford the higher education of their sons and wished them to distinguish themselves in life urged them to seek admission into the Indian Civil Service or one of the more specialized corps. (Even those who did not see the ICS as the fitting realization of a promise of true intellectual distinction still wanted their sons to enjoy the prestige and tenure of government service.) There were, indeed, few other channels available to a talented young Indian trying to find an adequate field for intellectual talents and strength of character.

Some distinguished lawyers accumulated large fortunes through their practices, thus enhancing the attractiveness of the legal career. Apart from these, the legal profession was so littered with failures, scarcely eking out a livelihood, that young men without connections ventured into it with great trepidation. Journalism, in the service of Indian-owned papers before independence, was not a professional career but a moral calling, and only those with a political or a proto-political impulse attended to its appeal.

Political life was inevitably rudimentary in an autocratic society, and there were few professional Indian politicians. Science and technology hardly existed as fields of intellectual endeavor, and the best posts were at the disposal of the government in its laboratories, surveys, and colleges. Modern scholarship and university teaching offered few opportunities and little remuneration, while traditional Indian scholarship left its devotees dependent on charity and patronage. Thus, the best brains of pre-independence India were directed toward the public sphere: toward the civil service, the law courts, and a reforming journalism. Of these three, only the civil service offered certainty, prestige, and material rewards on a large scale. As a result, the higher civil service in India, to an even greater extent than in Britain itself, was manned by as educated and cultivated a group of men as have ever ruled a great country.

It is true that the Indian Civil Service has not yet produced scholarly and literary works like those of Matthew Arnold, E. K. Chambers, Humbert Wolfe, Edward Marsh, F. J. E. Raby, C. P. Snow, and others; but the publications of senior civil servants like Romesh Chandra Dutt, V. P. Menon, A. D. Gorwala, Tarlok Singh, and many others are evidence of the high cultivation and studious turn of mind common at the higher levels of the Indian bureaucracy. The government services might not include the most creative members of the Indian intellectual classes, but it involves no stretching of the term to designate them as intellectuals. Despite the very heavy burden of work that a tradition of centralization imposes, made heavier by the socialistic and interventionistic policies of the government, Indian civil servants of the higher levels are impressive in the range and seriousness of their reading, in the alertness and vivacity of their intellectual curiosity, and in the strength and discrimination of their intellectual judgment.[8]

Such were the minds, formed and disciplined by the convergence of Indian and British Brahmanism, that built the tradition of Indian administration. When the British left in 1947, these intellectual civil servants were the force that preserved the country, struggled against great odds to maintain or to re-establish order, integrated the princely states, apportioned the Indian army between the two successor states, and carried on the services necessary for the survival of the larger society. The politicians—Congress and leftist—have disliked them and sought their discomfiture and humiliation. They have not, however, been able to dispense with them.

Today, when the Indian government is struggling to give that society a modern form, the major responsibility is entrusted to the Indian Civil Service and to a lesser but increasing extent to its successor, the Indian Administrative Service. The "socialistic pattern of society" to which the Congress leadership agreed in 1955, depends for its achievement on the labors of the intellectual elite of the civil service.

There are many criticisms of the ICS (and the IAS). There is bitterness among politicians who regard the former as "brown Englishmen," as ex-enemies of Indian independence who now do well from independent India. Among intellectuals, they are often denounced as bureaucrats who have not adapted themselves to a democratic welfare state; but on the whole their intellectual distinction is acknowledged as well as their probity and effectiveness. The disparagement of the IAS by intellectuals outside of the government takes the form of assertions that they lack the "intellectual caliber" of the ICS.

Whatever their reputation—it is shot through with both respect and resentment—there can be no denying the continuing importance, in the national life, of this now-diminishing band of older intellectuals, and of the more-recently ascending younger generation of administrator-intellectuals who are succeeding them.

3. The Indian Intellectual as the Counsellor of Rulers

At the periphery of the Indian Civil (and now Administrative) Service stands a large body of outstanding intellectuals who play a major part, as advisors and consultants, in the formation of policy. Professor P. C. Mahalanobis is perhaps the best known of these. Fellow of the Royal Society and formerly Professor of Physics in the Presidency College of Calcutta, Editor of Sankhya, the Indian Statistical Institute, Chief Advisor to the Planning Commission, a patron and connoisseur of literature and the arts, the guiding spirit of the group of economists who drafted the Plan Frame of the Second Five-Year Plan, Professor Mahalanobis, in an indeterminate way, is one of the "gray eminences" of Indian public life. The Secretary of the Planning Commission is Tarlok Singh, a scholarly graduate of the London School of Economics. Closely associated with the planning process is Professor J. J. Anjaria, formerly of the University of Bombay School of Economics, and now Chief Economic Advisor of the Ministry of Finance. His former Deputy is Dr. I. G. Patel, a gifted and subtle economist trained at Cambridge and Harvard Universities and now Indian representative at the International Monetary Fund. At the Ministry of Commerce and Industry, Mr. K. Ramaswami, an Oxford-trained economist of exceptional intellectual refinement, performs the same function. The Scientific Advisor of the Ministry of Defence is Professor D. S. Kothari of the physics department of the University of Delhi. The head of the Atomic Energy Commission is Professor Homi J. Bhabba, also a Fellow of the Royal Society and Director of the Tata Institute of Fundamental Research; and the Head of the Council of Scientific and Industrial Research is Professor M. S. Thacker, formerly Director of the Indian Institute of Science in Bangalore. (He is the successor of the late Dr. S. S. Bhatnagar, also a Fellow of the Royal Society and one of the great scientific organizers of his generation in any country.)

The numerous commissions of inquiry, patterned from their British predecessors, have offered another set of opportunities for intellectuals to contribute to the formation of policy. The Indian Universities Commission of 1902, the Calcutta University Commission of 1917, the University Education Commission of 1949, the Taxation Commission,[9] the States Reorganization Commission,[10] the Official Languages Commission,[11] the Press Commission,[12] etc., all testify to the strength and continuity of this tradition and to the way in which the intellectuals of India have contributed to the growth of opinion and policy.

Naturally, in the fields of cultural policy, e.g., in the University Grants Committee, and in the numerous Akademis of literature, painting, music, etc., established on the initiative of the Indian government to promote cultural development, intellectuals occupy the leading places.

In the diplomatic field, many senior positions are held by members of the ICS, while some are held by outsiders like the historian, Dr. K. M. Panikkar, or the former Chief Justice of the Bombay High Court, Mr. M. C. Chagla, a man of wide reading and serious reflectiveness. The Indian representative at the United Nations Atomic Energy Establishment in Vienna is Balachandra Rajan, who taught English literature at Cambridge and is a novelist of some interest. The former permanent Indian representative to the United Nations, Anant Lall, is a competent novelist. The newer recruits for the foreign service are outstanding graduates of Indian universities who have had further training at the Indian Administrative School in Delhi and at foreign universities. Some, at least, are scholarly or literary men, and most have lively intellectual interests.

4. The Indian Intellectual as a Politician

Thus far we have considered the role of Indian intellectuals in generating the constitutional tradition of Indian society, and their role in operating the "steel framework," the administrative machinery of Indian society. But what of politics itself, the center of the public sphere?

Indian politics are no longer as pronouncedly intellectual as they were before independence. Still, the fact remains that Indian politics give a greater place to intellectuals than practically any other large society.[13]

At the very center of Indian politics stands Mr. Nehru. No intellectual of comparable quality occupies an equivalent position in any other country. A Cambridge graduate of fastidious intellectual taste, no one could correspond more closely to the stereotype of the leftist upper-class intellectual. During the struggle for independence he was the main bearer in India of the ideas of the European left of the thirties. He was generally regarded as "their man" by the non-Communist intellectuals, the admirers of Harold Laski, the readers of *The New Statesman and Nation,* the adherents to the Left Book Club. It was he who stood up for modern—i.e., socialistic liberal—ideas against the interests of the businessmen and the ideas of the Gandhians within the Congress. He was a friend of intellectuals as well as their standard bearer. He was the President of the Indian National Trade Congress and the creator and patron of the National Planning Commission of the Indian National Congress. He admired the Soviet Union in the cloudy and perplexed way of European intellectuals during the two decades before World War II. He is the author of numerous bulky books, which, in a meandering way, reveal a reflective, cultivated, modern intellectual, full of wistfulness, skepticism, dogmatism, and self-doubt in the presence of his own country. Like most Indian intellectuals, he is oppressed by the material poverty of his countrymen, its industrial backwardness, its thicket of ancient traditions that stir and repel him. At his right hand is his Defence Minister, Mr. V. K. Krishna Menon— again an intellectual of the type so well known in the world's capitals in the twenties and thirties. A student of the London School of Economics, a friend of Harold Laski, one of the first editors of the Pelican books, living from hand to mouth, staying away from his own country as long as possible, yet zealously and aggressively nationalistic, a highly Westernized hater of the West—in some respects, Mr. Krishna Menon is an epitome of the "permanent student" of the species of the Indian abroad.

These two archetypal intellectuals are in an isolated position in a cabinet of veteran Congress politicians, some of whom might well have been intellectuals at one time, but whose intellectual interests the dust of political battle has long since dulled. Humayun Kabir, the Oxford-trained translator of Kant, a poet and former Professor of Philosophy at Calcutta, is perhaps the only other intellectual at this pinnacle of the Indian polity.

Within the *Lok Sabha,* the government draws its support from a parliamentary party in which lawyers make up the largest single group. Support comes also from a large body of "constructive national workers," a specifically Indian form of professional politician-cum-social worker who lives on nearly nothing, and from businessmen, landlords, and farmers.[14] The Gandhian cast prevails in the parliamentary Congress Party. Although there is no strict adherence to Gandhi's practices or teachings, there is a general disposition to distrust the modern intellectual outlook, "the Westernized" secular viewpoint embodied in the Prime Minister, in Mr. V. K. Krishna Menon, and in the life of intellectual circles of the large cities and the Indian Civil Service. At the same time, the peculiar intellectuality of Gandhi leaves its mark on the Congress politicians, so that they are probably more concerned with "principles" and "ideals" than their opposite numbers in the House of Commons, the House of Representatives, the *Chambre des députés,* or the *Bundesrat.*

It is among the opposition parties that intellectuals find a general acceptance, which, in the majority party, only the Prime Minister himself fully enjoys, and which, through his protection and then very unequally, only Mr. Krishna Menon and Professor Kabir share.[15] The Praja Socialist Party is an intellectuals' party par excellence. It was once led by Professor Acharya Narendra Dev, a specialist in Pali, a gentle scholar who ended his career as Vice-Chancellor of Lucknow University. It is now led by Acharya J. P. Kripalani, a Gandhian philosopher, while its leading figure is Mr. Asoka Mehta, who is not only a gifted parliamentarian but an original political theorist and a prolific author of books, pamphlets, and articles, from which his erudition and his theoretical capacities are never absent, however particular and immediate the occasion. Mr. Mehta's intellectual curiosity and energy would be remarkable in a professional scholar; they are unique among politicians. Mr. Jayaprakash Narayan still maintains a strong affectional tie with the Praja Socialist Party; he is, in every aspect of his action, an intellectual in politics—in his dislike of machine politics as well as in his search for ultimate principles. In fact, almost every important figure of Indian Socialism has been an intellectual, e.g., Yusuf Meherally, Achyut Patwardhan, Purshottam Tricumdas, and others. The Communist Party is led in the *Lok Sabha* by Professor Hirendranath Mukerjee, an Oxford graduate, and formerly a distinguished teacher of history at Andhra University, at Surendranath College in Calcutta, and then the University of Calcutta itself. The Secretary of the new Swatantra Party and one of the finest Indian parliamentarians is Mr. Minoo Masani, author of the standard history of *The Communist Party of India* (London, 1954), *Socialism Reconsidered* (Bombay, 1945), and the best-selling *Our India.* Mr. Masani, who was one of the founders of the Congress Socialist Party and of the Socialist Party of India, is now sharply critical of Mr. Nehru's socialistic pattern, and many regard him as too sympathetic with private enterprise. But whatever his course, his intellectual energy continues without diminution. Like Mr. Asoka Mehta, Mr. Masani is an intellectual in politics of the order of Senator Paul Douglas, Mr. Hugh Gaitskell, M. Mendes-France, Herr Carlo Schmid, and Signor Amintore Fanfani. The other major figure of the Swatantra Party is C. Rajaopala-chari, whose intellectual distinction is as outstanding as his political shrewdness.

In its own way, India thus almost appears to be the realm of the philosopher-king. There is perhaps no other country where intellectuals exercise such weighty influence on the public life of their country and where they are entrusted with so many responsibilities, which by and large they execute so ably. Among the new states of Asia and Africa, there is nothing comparable to their proficiency; among the older states of Europe and America, there is nothing comparable to the scale of their public responsibilities. There are, moreover, few countries in which the intellectuals in political life—journalists, professors, and the like—have kept up their intellectual interests and activities as well as they have in India.

5. The Oppositional Intellectual: Life According to an Ideal

This is one side of the picture. The other side is rather different. Despite the exceptional roles that many intellectuals have played in Indian public life, and despite the energy and devotion with which politically influential intellectuals have accepted their responsibilities, the civil life of the modern large-scale state is not to the taste of a major proportion of Indian intellectuals.

For the modern Indian intellectuals of our century, the social and political spheres have come to possess the preponderance which, among traditional intellectuals, is given only to the trans-empirical sphere. Indian political life, like all practical action, continuously confronts the debasing exigencies of all everyday life, and it comes to terms with them. Yet it is also profoundly penetrated by dispositions that are much akin to the tendencies toward withdrawal marking the third and fourth *asramas*—far more so than most Western political life. In this last—and highest—stage of man's life on earth, the deepest of obligations calls for withdrawal from domestic and civil life and consecration of one's remaining years to devotions productive of absorption into Brahma.

The political orientation of intellectuals in most Western countries has, outside of the civil services, a strong bent toward alienation from the routine politics of the civil order. The conflict between the ethics of absolute values *(Gesinnungsethik)* and the ethics of reflective and responsible action *(Verantwortungsethik)* finds intellectuals in our Western societies leaning toward the former. They do so, however, to nothing like the extent found among Indian intellectuals. Nothing moves an Indian intellectual as much as political action that seems to serve not "interests" but ideals or a "cause," the "cause" being itself a movement on behalf of the ideal.

A very large part of the present-day Indian intelligentsia between the ages of thirty-five and sixty were students either at the time of the Civil Disobedience Movements or the "1942 Movement." They responded most eagerly to the call to leave their schools and colleges. Their boycott was partly an adolescent lark, with its usual overtones of revolt against the authority of parents and elders. More seriously, however, it was a revolt against the oppressiveness of everyday life, with its demands for punctuality, diligence, respect for immediate obligations to parents and teachers, etc. It was an adolescent revolt against the adult world—with the symbols of India becoming fused with the aspirations of adolescence, the symbols of British rule becoming fused with the harsh demandingness of the grown-up world. Not at all figuratively and even more fundamentally, the adolescent revolt against parents and teachers and the Indian revolt against British domination coincided with the revolt of the Indian human being against the world of concrete experience, with its demands, responsibilities, and obligations. It was a revolt on behalf of the world of transcendence, where the individual, leaving behind his dust-stained, earthly everyday self, ascends toward absorption into Brahma.

The uncomfortableness of Indian institutions—especially the burdens of family life and of occupational routine, which do not engage and attach the individual's libido—strengthens the Indian intellectual's readiness to soar upward and outward.[16] There are two ways of escape from this institutional burden as it weighs on persons whose individuality is incompletely established. One is to yearn for, and to assimilate as much as possible of, the Western, primarily British, way of life; this is an effort to gratify the rudimentary need for concrete individuality. It is an effort to create a sphere of privacy and personal relationships, to lighten the weight of tradition; and to become an *individual* in one's own right.

The alternative, offered by traditional Indian culture, runs in the opposite direction. It is the transcendence of concrete individuality. In some respects, it is the easier one, more likely to be followed because it is, in a sense, the natural direction of the institutionally burdened human being who is not already anchored by individual, libidinal attachments. The adolescent, whose ego has not yet taken shape, has not yet developed, actually or incipiently, a set of aspirations and images of his adult roles. He does not look forward to his manhood. Tender and touchy, wounded and responsive, the youth is a volcano, ready for eruption, without positive objects, but with much that he would avoid. The call to leave school or college met a passionate response, particularly when a few of the stronger, more aggressive youths took the lead by assailing a teacher or standing before the gate of the college grounds to demonstrate the meaning of civil disobedience. Then, for six months, the youth might have wandered about the country, sleeping anywhere, eating almost nothing, seldom or never writing to his parents, doing the "Jimmy Higgins" work of the national movement. He would distribute handbills, serve as an usher at meetings, do a little agitation himself. There was a vast amount of trivial detail, such as running errands, operating multigraph machines, collecting handbills from the printer, which such boys and young men did. The bolder ones, or those who fell in with bolder ones, might be drawn into the terrorist section of the passive resistance movement. They would be set to cutting telephone wires, destroying a section of railway track, breaking a railway signal box, or burning a post office. At the end of six months or a year, the police would catch up with them. They would be sent to prison, where, being classified in a higher grade, they would be allowed to read books.

Many of the Indian intellectuals now over forty got their best education in prison during the periods of civil disobedience. There they would sometimes read the books they needed for their examinations, but more often they read British and perhaps Marxist political literature.[17] There were long discussions of every topic relating to national independence. Gandhism was confronted by Marxism; revolutionary socialism, by reformist socialism. Indian Marxism had its training establishments in Arthur Road Prison and similar institutions all over India. Laski, Lenin, R. Palme Dutt, Marx and Engels, Ralph Fox and Christopher Cauldwell, G. D. H. Cole, Bertrand Russell, and H. N. Brailsford in politics; Dostoevsky, Chekhov, W. Somerset Maugham, Hemingway, and Gorki in literature were the "set books" of the imprisoned young intellectuals and proto-intellectuals.

When they came out of prison, the movement was usually in a state of suspension. They either went back to live with their families and found the routine deadly, or they tried to maintain themselves by small financial doles or loans from friends or by some uninteresting and irregular work for insignificant wages. Life seemed to have lost its flavor, but they had to struggle on. Their parents, elder brothers, and parents-in-law, if they were married, insisted they do something to settle themselves in life. They had to go back to college for their degrees. They were older than the rest of the students. The principal and teachers were rather timorous in dealing with these "national heroes." Their battle scars were an accusation against their elders, who, by remaining at their posts, had continued to "serve the British." Then too, the police kept their eyes on them. Some could not adapt to ordinary life again, found a rapid succession of miscellaneous jobs, and mourned over the decline in the quality and interestingness of political life.

The 1942 Movement repeated the pattern of the 1931 Civil Disobedience Movement—withdrawal from participation in routine institutions, such as school and family; a quasi-monastic existence, with nothing to live on and no care for the morrow; and possession by the sacred idea of Indian independence. The tension in this case continued up to the actual achievement of independence, although the dissipation of the force of the 1942 Movement a few months after it began brought with it, for a time, the relaxation of disillusionment.

For the officially irresponsible intelligentsia, the real disillusionment with Indian political life came after independence. The days of "sacrifice for a cause" were over. The period of dramatic opposition had come to an end, and the responsibilities and necessities of independence soon began to weigh on the spirit of the intellectuals. There was no more need for abstention from work or study; demonstrations of passive resistance could no longer be as vital as they had been.[18] The younger intellectuals had lived at heroic heights for several years. When victory was won, they found that India was still the backward country of which in their hearts they were ashamed.

Especially heartbroken were those who, in the two decades before independence, lived abroad for long periods, because the police would not allow them to return to India for fear they would become effective agitators, and also because they enjoyed the bohemian and permanent student life in Europe. When they returned after independence, they discovered, like exiles everywhere, that those who stayed at home had either forgotten them or did not want any part of them. Even more distressing, they became aware of how far India really was from being a modern country in its fundamental institutions. The strength of religion, the Hindu populism of the Congress Party, and the shaking of the foundations of Western culture in India made them very unhappy.

More shattering than anything else was the discovery of the identity of the rulers of the new India. The Indian Civil Service—the awful "steel frame," hated and deeply respected because of its distant bureaucratic power, its remoteness, and its identification with Britain—now, without the redeeming feature of being British, continued to rule India under the dominion of the Congress Party. Nor had the Congress Party ever been beloved by Indian intellectuals. They were held to it by the charismatic personality of Mahatma Gandhi and his chosen heir, the leftist, Cambridge-educated, fastidious, ambivalent Brahman intellectual, Jawaharlal Nehru. The death of Gandhi reduced this attraction. In the years between 1948 and the introduction of the ideas of a "socialist pattern of society" at the Awadi Congress session, the Indian intellectuals, particularly those who had participated in the Independence Movement, suffered in a state of embittered disillusionment.

The sources of this disillusionment are easily apparent. The Congress Party, like any party that attempts to cover a whole nation and that aspires to govern the state, requires a machine of party functionaries. Supporters must be rewarded, candidacies for parliamentary seats much be given to those who have a chance to win, i.e., who have or can raise the funds to conduct the campaign and who have the contacts necessary for their promotion and election. Furthermore, parliamentary life is unspectacular. Only a few can rise to oratorical heights, and the vast amount of factual detail relevant to legislation stifles the spirit. As in the political life of all democratic countries, the members of the Indian parliament are more or less average men in their personal, and especially in their intellectual, talents, with a little more vanity, with a bit more talent, with more than average gifts in compromising and arranging. These qualities appeal not at all to the Indian intellectual.

Only a small minority of the intellectuals in teaching, journalism, and literature believe that the parliamentary career is inherently difficult and that Indian parliamentarians are doing as well as can be expected in view of the low level of information and criticism in the country, the lack of parliamentary experience and tradition, and the trying nature of the tasks the country faces. By far the great majority of intellectuals have in recent years been contemptuously hostile toward the present body of Indian parliamentarians. They are often compared unfavorably with British parliamentarians, and, by the generation over forty-five years of age, with the members of the Legislative Councils of the British period. They are often charged with being poor speakers, who scarcely understand or speak English, with being of limited intelligence, and, most important, with not taking their responsibilities seriously.

More basically, the whole business of party politics is assailed as an "essentially dirty game," as "something from which I stay away," as a source of moral "defilement." Sometimes it is said that this is the essential nature of politics; at other times, that this is a special feature of Indian politics today, and that, "as we become more mature," the situation will improve.

When intellectuals were asked a few years ago to name leading politicians whom they respected, the Prime Minister, the then Finance Minister, Mr. C. D. Deshmukh, and Pandit Pant were about the only members of the governing party who came off at all well. It may be noted that the first two are outstanding intellectuals, educated at Cambridge, and Mr. Deshmukh was, until his retirement, a member of the Indian Civil Service. Opposition members, Communists, Socialists, and Jan Sangh leaders were accorded better marks than the members of the Congress Party—except for the three persons mentioned above—even by those who had no sympathy with the opposition parties.

All this boils down to a vote against civil politics and a vote for charismatic politics, for *sadhu* politics. That is the reason why the three greatest living political heroes of the Indian intellectuals today are Pandit Nehru, Vinoba Bhave, and Jayaprakash Narayan. These are regarded as men of integrity, who "care for a cause," "who will make sacrifices," and "who would die for their convictions." Mr. Nehru's popularity is great because, in his commitment to socialism, he has shown his antipathy for the mass of the Congress bureaucrats, place-holders, and the rich men who support the party financially, and his antagonism toward private businessmen and the Indian Civil Service, which he forces to do his bidding while scolding it in public. The occasional darkening of his glory is associated with his compromise with these powers. Vinoba Bhave and Jayaprakash Narayan enjoy their great esteem for other reasons. They lead the life of the *ashram*. They have given up everything and devote themselves exclusively to the redemption of the people. Narayan is especially respected for his decision to renounce party politics to lead the life of a socialist *sadhu*.

This is the true ideal of political life—life on behalf of a cause bound up with an ideal. The ideal must transcend personal interest or even group interest. It must never be sullied by compromise or considerations of success or advantage. There is something repugnant about the exercise of authority by means other than the charisma deriving from a holy mission. This attitude is more characteristic of those who view political life from the periphery than it is of those who, at the center of political life, must cope with the exigencies of every situation.

Thus, there is a tendency among Indian intellectuals who are themselves excluded from power and responsibility to look on politics as a discontinuous activity, as one that should be instigated and undertaken only when a great deal is at stake, or when a great crisis requires action guided by the ideal. This type of politics must be carried out without machinery, without a paid staff, without concessions. Its servants, the followers of the person who embodies or approximates most closely the ideal, should serve not for salary or the expectation of reward, but because of their devotion to the ideal. To do this they ought to renounce their regular obligations and pitch themselves into the movement without regard to consequences for themselves or their kind.

6. The Intellectual in Opposition: Charisma and Collectivism

The intellectuals of the new countries and the politicians who are recruited from intellectual circles are persons who have recently dropped the bonds linking them with their traditional society. They retain the unitary response to charismatic things—regardless of whether they are traditional or newly emergent—which is a feature of traditional societies or enthusiastic cultic associations. The political leaders esteemed by the intellectuals who stand between tradition and modernity are themselves almost always charismatic men in the conventional sociological sense—strikingly vivid personalities and extremely sensitive. In traditional societies, charisma resides in the elders and chiefs who exercise authority over villages and tribes. The charisma resident in the collectivity and inhering in the traditions of the collectivity is intensified in those who rule. When traditional authority disintegrates, the charisma of authority finds new bearers and a new collectivity. The nation becomes the charismatic object, and it is only through their connection with the nation that its charisma flows into individuals. The leaders of a nationalist movement and the rulers of a new country are the most charismatic persons of that country, because they are closest to the source from which charisma radiates.

According to this view, only those who express the charisma of the nation are fit to guide action in society. Those who do not proclaim and manifest their attachment to the ideal are thought to share very little of this charisma. Tribal chieftains, traditional religious leaders, elders of kinship groups, and businessmen all fall outside. The charisma of nationality forms a circle, within which political leaders, agitational journalists, and, to a lesser extent, civil servants find themselves.

Thus, the religious sensitivity common in traditional societies and in the traditional sectors of underdeveloped countries lives on in a transformed way in these societies as they move toward modernity. In its transformation, it penetrates into the life of the apparently "secular" state. There is less discontinuity in this displacement of the locus of charisma from the traditional leadership to the political leaders and higher civil servants, than is generally asserted by those who emphasize the "uprootedness" of the educated elites of the new states.

The prevailing attitudes toward economic policy in the new states disclose intimate continuity with the ancestral sensitivity to charismatic things. The modern leadership of the underdeveloped countries is very largely socialistic in its outlook. Fabian socialists, Marxian democratic socialists, Gandhian socialists, fellow-traveling socialists, Trotskyite communists, Titoist communists, crypto-communist socialists, and outright communists fill most of the political spectrum of these countries. Those who favor a traditionalist, religious state are usually socialists by implication. There are very few liberals in the economic sense, few who expect or wish to see their country make its economic progress through the "private sector." Although wealthy merchants have political influence, there is little moral sympathy with their activities or outlook—such influence is indeed one of the reasons for the intellectuals' disenchantment with the day-to-day politics of the new states.

It is usual to attribute the socialistic orientation of the Indian intellectuals to the atmosphere, in the twenties and thirties, of the London School of Economics, where so many of them studied, and to the personal and literary influence of the late Professor Harold Laski. There is some truth in this assertion. Even as a description of the Western determinants of Indian collectivism, it is an excessively narrow caricature, but it points toward one important exogenous factor. What it neglects are the profound endogenous forces of ethnic solidarity, religious disparagement of chrematistic activity, and respect for collective authority. The acknowledgment of these forces by no means denies the effective influence of Western European socialist teaching on the Indian intellectual.

The political orientation deriving from the deeper trend of Indian life and its immanent transformations and that which came from an admiring contact with certain features of British intellectual life are much more in harmony than in conflict. Both move in the same direction. Both are indifferent to, and even repelled by, everyday life, and above all by an economic life directed toward private gain. Both are impatient with the humdrum of traditional life, with its inertness and compromise. Both wish to see life lived in accordance with an ideal emanating from some creative source, from a genius, from a hero, from a lofty and inspiring authority.

Against this background, one may see why Indian intellectuals should incline toward any doctrine containing a derogatory attitude toward routine economic life and the man who devotes himself entirely to it. Thus, the businessman is a *bête noire* of the Indian intellectuals. The Brahman ideal of selfless devotion to the ideal, to the cultivation of the utterly unattached state of mind, contrasts sharply with the implicit businessman's goal of amassing money in large quantities. This attitude derives in part from the Brahmanical contempt for economic life, but it is also influenced by what the Indian intellectuals learned from Britain itself and from the strata of

British life in India that they really respected. The influence emanating from Britain was far wider and deeper than that which came from Harold Laski's lectures, books, and from his personal charm and kindness toward his Indian students.

More important was the general attraction of the Indian intellectuals to those elements in British life itself that looked down upon the businessman from the point of view of aristocracy and gentry. The whole post-Victorian movement in English literature, from Wells, Shaw, and Galsworthy through D. H. Lawrence and Aldous Huxley, to W. H. Auden and the left-wing poets of the thirties, has had a tremendous impact on the imagination of the Indian intellectual. It criticized bourgeois, mercantile Britain while being British. It fitted in with the Brahmanical attitude toward economic life, and it found there an agreeable foothold. The foothold was enlarged by the delight in British journalistic and social science literature of the twenties and thirties, when Houghton Street epitomized British intellectual socialism, and before Professors Hayek, Robbins, and Plant became ascendant in the school. Laski and Hugh Dalton, within the school, John Strachey, and the Left Book Club under Laski, Strachey, and Gollancz had impressive influence in Great Britain at this time. Their influence on Indian students in Britain was at least equalled by their influence in India on the young college and university teachers and their more politically alert students who never went to Britain. Their influence was brought weekly to India through *The New Statesman and Nation,* which, while no longer so popular as it was twenty-five years ago, is still the most widely read foreign intellectual publication in India.

The quarter of a century between 1920 and 1945 was the heroic period of the Indian intellectual. It paralleled the exhilarating times of the Civil Disobedience Movement, imprisonment, and the growth of National Socialism in Europe. It is still looked back on by many as a time when life had meaning and direction. It was a time when intellectuals *counted* in the political life of their country.

7. *The Intellectual in Opposition: Outside the Pale*

For those who had the heroic experience of the Independence Movement, immediately or vicariously, and who did not go on to the actual responsibilities of governing the country or important institutions within it, the years since Independence have been sad. How they contrast with the earlier times! The ICS men who once ruled the country, while they now stand practically at the pinnacle, are now under the even less endearing authority of politicians, less well educated than they and hostile to them for their Western ways and tastes. The university intellectuals feel left out of things. They feel not only isolated from the people, but despised and scorned by the politicians who rule from the center and from the capitals of the states. In the colleges and universities, they feel particularly the harsh hand and

unsympathetic view of the politician who interferes with university administration and who talks to professors as if they were his servants. The professional literary man, whether a free-lance writer or a teacher, feels that he
cultivates a literature that the world has forgotten or never known; however much he loves it—outside of Bengal—he deems it a small literature
without grandeur or fame. If he is an Indian-language journalist, his standard
of living and his professional life are poor—transcribing and adapting
releases of the government press officers or news articles from the bigger
English-language newspapers. If he is a painter, he has to depend to a large
extent for the sale of his pictures on the interests of Western businessmen,
diplomats, and tourists.

He is lectured at by everyone. Government leaders tell him he must
serve the economic development of the country, that he must learn Hindi,
Sanskrit, engineering, and technology. If he is a scientist, he is told by the
Prime Minister that he must not make atomic bombs (as if any Indian scientist
could, without the permission and support of the very person who scoldingly
tells him he must not do so). He is told that he pursues false gods and that
his language puts him out of touch with the people. If he is religious, he is
told that his superstitions are holding the country back; if he is a non-believer,
he is told that he has sacrificed the heritage of his country. If he goes abroad
to study, he is told that when he returns he must not expect to live or work
under the conditions that prevailed abroad; when he returns, he is left to
cool his heels for a long time before he finds any employment for his skills,
acquired with much expense and difficulty.

In almost every one of his occupations, the Indian intellectual leads a
poor life. In the intellectual occupations he is very ill-paid and works under
unremittingly harsh conditions. He is treated with contempt by those in
authority, within his own institutions and outside them. In a relatively idyllic
place like Poona, some of the Brahman intellectuals say that intellectuals
are respected and that their high esteem is inherited from the Brahman's
traditional status, but this experience is by no means usual. Even in Poona
it is not so widespread as those who assert it believe, and in other places
the situation is worse. The middle classes which once looked up to the
educated man, and especially to the college teacher, now look upon him as if
he were an insignificant clerk.

The fact is that more than half of the Bombay University teaching staff
had been, at one time or another, approached by students or their friends and
kinsmen seeking special favors in examinations in return for payment.[19] This
shows how little respect intellectual life and the standards on which it rests
enjoy in the Indian middle classes.[20] The assertion, by an important politician
of Uttar Pradesh, that the universities should be staffed by dispossessed
Maharajahs and Zamindars, is only one more instance of this. The most
common derogation of the college and university takes the form of comparing a member of the teaching staff with the traditional *guru* who taught without remuneration. Indeed, the very fact of the full-time intellectual's under-
payment is held against him.

Those intellectuals who do other than intellectual work—physicians, law-

yers, higher civil servants (the Indian Civil Service and the Indian Administrative Service), sundry appointed officials, and politicians—do not suffer the
disrespect encountered by the full-time intellectual. Nevertheless, in both parts
of the intellectual class, intellectual activities are necessarily conducted
without a sense that there is, somewhere in India, an invisible forum,
nationwide as well as local, where their thoughts or writings could be expressed, listened to, and appreciated.

There are undoubtedly many gratifying occupational activities in India.
High officials enjoy the challenge of their work and the feeling of contributing to the country's welfare and progress; engineers have a sense
of getting a job done; businessmen enjoy the combat and the victory; a
small number of political leaders, chief ministers and cabinet officials, enjoy
their labors—the exercise of authority, the deference, and the participation
in important decisions. In each of these occupations, there are a few intellectuals who either address the wider public or who consume with relish the
products of the intellectual activities of others. A small number of the better
scientists and university vice-chancellors and high administrators, several
editors, and the tiny handful of successful, self-sustaining free-lance writers
also feel that they count for something in the world.

The vast mass of intellectuals, however, are not in such a fortunate
situation. The Indian intellectual suffers bitterly from the neglect consequent
on the absence of an intellectual public, as much as he does from the
contempt of the powerful and his own misgivings about his "Indianism"
and the value of his work.

The Indian intellectual might justly and sympathetically be described
as "the insulted and the injured." Is it, therefore, any wonder that he
dreams of a vaguely socialist India, like the Britain of his student years,
of an India with the enthusiasm of the years in which the struggle for
national independence was at its height, or of an India where the whole
country is mobilized behind a grandiose undertaking of self-improvement,
such as he thinks is being done in the Soviet Union or China? In these
situations, the Indian intellectual sees himself either treated with respect
and consideration as a dignified person with individual merit, or he sees
himself rising above himself, fused with some higher state of being—the
people or the nation—fused with a secular equivalent of Brahma. In both
of these alternatives, he dreams of finding a solution to the wearying existence
that prevents him from attaining either individual liberty or spiritual liberation, and that condemns him to a dreary round of affectionless, unrewarding,
and unrewarded activity in institutions that he cannot care about.

These are some of the reasons why the Indian intellectual is so often
a "leftist." From the deeper traditions of his own Indian culture, from the
modern intellectual traditions in which he has been educated, and from
his depressed status in India today, he yearns for a better society where
men will be free to express themselves, where greed and selfishness will be
absent, and where all will move forward toward an ideal in which Indian
tradition and modernity will be in harmonious fusion, and in which the
Indian intellectual will come into his own.

8. The Intellectual as the Bearer of Public Opinion: Civil Criticism and Uncritical Negativism

The depressed and antipolitical attitudes of the Indian intellectuals outside the government deprive public life in India of some of the most important contributions intellectuals can make to their country. Because of their general feeling of alienation and rejection, as well as because of numerous institutional and economic factors, Indian public discussion exhibits neither the diversity nor the factuality necessary for an informed and effective public opinion.

Denunciation in rhetorical grandeur and perpetual complaint about all manner of iniquities were characteristic of Indian political journalism before Independence; they were poor preparation for the discriminating appraisal and matter-of-fact criticism required for liberal self-government. Journalism in India before Independence was the service of a higher cause, not a profession or a business. The idealistic alienation of a large part of the present-day Indian intellectual class fosters the persistence of the unfactual and the vague, which were characteristics of that journalism. When the entire regime is at fault, what is the good of scrutinizing it in detail? The political negativism of much of the Indian intelligentsia is by no means, however, the sole cause of the undifferentiated and unrealistic state of public discussion.

The tendency of the Government of India and its satellites to employ so many of the best young men leaves relatively few for the press and for those phases of university study that continuously interact with public opinion. It is not that there are no excellent young correspondents, editors, etc.; but they are very few and they work in an inhospitable milieu. Neither the professional circles in which they move nor the intellectual audiences for which they write give them the stimulation and response that keeps wits sharp and minds well stored. The governmental pre-emption of so many of the best minds, which could contribute to vital public discussion in newspapers, periodicals, and learned publications, is a considerable handicap to Indian public discussion.

Some of the other handicaps are more obvious—for example, the high illiteracy rates and the poverty of the mass of the population, which restrict the circulation of newspapers and therewith the income from sales and advertising by private business. Newspapers, as a result, exist usually on a very narrow margin and come to depend on government advertisements or announcements for a larger share of their advertising revenue than in the West. One instance of withdrawal of advertising by a provincial government from a single critical newspaper goes a long way. Most other newspapers become extremely cautious about criticizing the government on sensitive points. It also makes for circumspection in inquiring closely into such subjects. Even the economically strongest newspapers in India have been cautious in opening their columns to well-informed critics, however responsible and cogent, when they wish above all not to have trouble with the government.

The poverty of the press also means that, for the vast majority of journalists, salaries are poor. The press consequently finds it difficult to attract and retain high-grade young men. Staffs have to be small, with the result that there cannot be sufficient specialization to develop the *expertise* necessary for useful evaluation and criticism of governmental policies. Even the larger, more prosperous papers, with more specialized and well-educated staffs, do not go in for independent inquiry, for the persistent pursuit of a "story." The tough-minded critical accumulation and assessment of facts are not widely practiced skills in Indian journalism, even at the heights.

Indian editors do not, on the whole, expect their reporters to dig for facts; they could not easily find reporters in India who could dig for facts even if they wanted them to do so. Indian reporters do not think that they are called upon to unearth facts as part of their job; they feel their explorations are over when they have been given a briefing or a "handout" by a government press officer. As a result, the press tends to be stuffed with the reported speeches of cabinet ministers and members of parliament, and with the substances of official releases. Leaders and turnover articles are seldom based on ample study of the details of governmental or private economic policy and activity. They tend to be very general, either affirmative or denunciatory, without differentiated argument. Even significant reports, very factual in character, by parliamentary inquiry committees, find little response in the press, because they are not in harmony with its professional tradition.

This unfactual disposition of Indian journalism is reinforced by journalistic traditions inherited from the struggle for national independence. Aside from the British-owned and British-edited newspapers and periodicals, which avoided criticism and detailed inquiry into the activities of the Raj, the main style of the Indian press during the time of foreign rule was hortatory and polemical. The meticulous search for details and matter-of-fact analysis were not regarded as necessary or appropriate, except among a restricted band of liberal nationalists, whose patrician liberalism was swept away with the rest of the Victorian inheritance by the more populistic nationalism which Gandhi brought to the fore in the second quarter of the present century. But even they did not have the resources—financial or personal—to acquire and print facts.

The machinery of the Government of India for making detailed information available is not always very helpful in overcoming this reluctance of Indian reporters. The reports of parliamentary proceedings take a very long time to appear in print. Reports of government departments and public corporations appear only after much delay and are hard to obtain. The Government of India and even more the governments of the states seem sometimes as if they do not want their actions to be critically analyzed, thus continuing the practices of India's foreign rulers, British and Mogul, and of the Maharajahs for whom all government actions were *arcana imperium.*

There are other obstacles to the emergence and effectiveness of responsible criticisms of governmental policies in India. Even if the full supply of facts were accessible, and there were a corps of well-qualified evaluators in journalism and the universities, sympathizers with the aspirations and the difficulties of the government are reluctant to criticize it in public. The most secure as well as the most unstable of the new states are feeling their way amidst great difficulties. In India, at least where national sentiment is more stable, some of the more circumspect intellectuals appreciate their national independence too much to wish to give the appearance—above all to foreigners, but also their own public—of "letting the side down" by public criticism. They are aware that their new state rests on weak foundations, which are recurrently shaken by traditionalistic and communal loyalties, and on an impoverished and depressed peasantry, and that the dangers of internal subversion are not entirely absent. They wish to avoid anything that would enfeeble the authority of the government or hamper its efforts to create a vigorous consensus in support of its steps to improve the country's economic life.

This reserve on the part of some of the very best-informed and most intelligent journalist-intellectuals in India is supported also by the hierarchical traditions of Indian society, which endow those in authority with charisma, thus inhibiting flexible and rational criticism. (This same traditional attitude, which heightens sensitivity to the charismatic component of authority, is also responsible in a great many cases for much irrational, unfactual criticism, since a large part of the structure of politics and government is bureaucratic and untraditional, and therefore lacking in the charismatic quality which calls forth supine assent.)

In the Indian press, as in the press of other states, there is no dearth of abusive criticism. Some comes from sensation-mongers, some from those who wish ill to the government, some from disappointed idealists whose struggle for national independence was motivated by deep ethical feelings and an ideal of a dignified national existence that has not yet been realized. Very little of this criticism is matter-of-fact or well informed about the dreadfully difficult problems of trying to govern a disunited, traditionalist population by methods appropriate to modern unified countries. The hostile critics, even those who share the general aims of the government, lack both the factual sense and the facts themselves on which realistic assessment could be made and constructive suggestions offered to government and the politically interested public.

Frequent and considerable though its shortcomings might be, Indian parliamentary debate could contribute valuably to the formation of public opinion. It could do so, however, only through a continuing scrutiny and criticism of government, a consequent pressure on government to justify its actions in a reasoned manner, and reasonably adequate reports in the press. There are Indian parliamentarians who speak on the basis of careful study and wide experience. In India, the parliamentary reporting function is rather well performed in the daily press. *The Hindu, The Times of India, The Statesman,* and the other leading English-language dailies are outstanding in their coverage of debates in the *Lok Sabha.*

The reporting of, and comment on, the ensuing debate in the press and the due notice of it in the more literate sections of the political public could then enter the obscure channels through which public opinion is formed. On the whole, however, this adequate reporting passes unappreciated by Indian intellectuals. There is very little interest in the parliamentary proceedings. The general disrespect for party politicians attaches also to their activities in Parliament.

It is generally felt among Indian intellectuals that the members of the *Lok Sabha,* particularly those elected on the Congress ticket, are there because they have demonstrated their (now suspected) heroism and sacrifice in the campaign for national independence, rather than their merits in particular professions and occupations requiring solid knowledge and responsibility in taking risks and running complex economic organizations. There is some truth in this judgment. Even where their original educational attainments were high, years of political agitation, imprisonment, and the rough and tumble of oppositional journalism and politics have left many Indian politicians standing where they were in their early twenties. Their equally gifted contemporaries who went into administration gained the advantage of elaborate knowledge and political experience. In the conflict that occurs in all governments between the civil servants and the legislators who would control them, and that is aggravated under conditions of underdevelopment and large-scale governmental economic operations, the Indian legislators are at a disadvantage. They need all the help they can get from intellectuals in journalism and in the universities. Unfortunately, the Indian intellectuals are neither inclined by sympathy nor able by their skill to provide such help.

In some respects, the back-bench legislator of the ruling and the opposition parties—the party politician—is as disesteemed by the intellectuals of the underdeveloped countries as the businessman. In any conflict between, on the one side, the few outstandingly charismatic political figures who led the national struggle and the civil service and, on the other side, the ordinary legislator who is only a local or second-rank figure, the sympathies of the intellectual outside the government are with the former—in so far as they are with either. The press and university intellectuals do little to aid the ordinary legislator. The poorly qualified parliamentarian who reads little and meets few persons, and who could raise his intellectual level, thus renders himself more worthy of the intellectuals' scorn.

An effectively critical and independent evaluation of economic policies and practices could, in any case, never be carried out solely by the newspaper and periodical press. Much of the work of the press in this regard depends on more basic inquiries, such as could be conducted, and in some countries are conducted, by the staffs of independent universities, colleges, and research institutes. The views of scholars, in the form of journal articles, monographs, books, lectures and seminars, and newspaper and periodical articles, can contribute greatly to the guidance and critical understanding of government action. Formal convocation of university intellectuals as consultants and advisors on governmental economic activities is no substitute for these other forms of expression of opinion, however desirable and important in itself. Such occasional drawing-in of the better university economists and anthropologists can provide, under favorable conditions, a more detached and broader perspective, which the planners and administrators cannot get themselves. Fruitful consultation is possible, however, only where the consultants can draw upon a rich stock of knowledge that they have accumulated through their own and other scholars' research. Such research is useful to public life when its results enter, however generally, into parliamentary and public debate. It is also useful in so far as it sets a standard of detachment and seriousness in the analysis of public issues.

Unlike the situation in the West, the academic life of India has no real tradition of detached factual research on issues of importance to the public good. The work of the Oxford Institute of Statistics; the Cambridge Department of Applied Economics; the National Bureau of Economic Research, so closely connected with Columbia University; the continuous stream of individual studies, by qualified university economists, sociologists, and political scientists, of the problems, policies, and activities of concern to the government; and the research publications of para-academic institutions like the National Institute of Economic and Social Research in London, the Acton Society of London, the Brookings Institution in Washington—these have no equivalents in the new countries. The small Gokhale Institute of Economics and Political Science in Poona is almost unique in underdeveloped countries for its intellectual independence from government and for its empirical bent. The National Council of Applied Economic Research in New Delhi has not yet had time to demonstrate its capacities in this sphere. The inquiries sponsored by the Committee on Research Programmes of the Planning Commission seem, on the whole, to be fairly useless and lifeless compilations, of value to neither the government nor the enrichment of the social sciences.

In the countries that have undergone a slower and more decentralized development than India is contemplating, parliament and press and the independent intelligentsia were joined by a mass of voluntary associations seeking to prevent abuses and to further their own aims. India is somewhat better off in this regard than most underdeveloped societies. The modernization of Indian society before Independence was only partial and not very autonomous. The Civil Service and the universities, which were the chief elements of modernity, were created and controlled by the foreign ruler; the only autochthonous modern institutions of public life were some colleges, the opposition press, agitational political movements, and bodies like the Servants of India Society, the Deccan Educational Society, the Ramakrishna Mission, the Arya Samaj, the British Indian Association, and a number of businessmen's and landowners' associations. Social work and national revival through religious thought and political agitation preoccupied much of the rather limited range of Indian voluntary association. The seedbed of modern civic life was scarcely prepared under colonial conditions, although what there was, was impressive in its intellectuality and its selflessness. Since Independence, the educational and social service elements of Indian civic associations have certainly not shared the same fate as Indian intellectual politics. They do not, it is true, engage the interest of the most eminent intellectuals as they did fifty years ago when social service, education, and national regeneration formed a single relatively undifferentiated program. They have fallen into the hands of a lesser intelligentsia—less cosmopolitan less cultivated than the great forerunners—but the activities still go on. Their range of interest tends to be local and particular and to be non-political as well.

Where modern interest organizations do exist, as in the case of manu-facturers' or merchants' associations, they find it difficult to put their case before the public. The atmosphere is unfavorable to their representations, and intellectuals are generally reluctant to enter their employ because they think that the service of business is a betrayal of the ideal. India does have pressure groups and they are active. However, partly because of their own na-ture and partly because of the nature of the intellectuals, the procedures that they follow in order to influence governmental policy do not improve the quality of public opinion and, in any case, seldom have the support or sym-pathy of intellectuals.

The intellectual infra-structure of political life thus seems to be feebler in India than it was before Independence. Religious and social reform move-ments in those days attracted intellectuals of a high order, and they created an atmosphere conducive to the characteristic political outlook of their time. This is no longer so. The withdrawal of affirmation of the intellectuals, their disillusioned apathy, has gone too far.

9. The Transcendence of Alienation

The immense gap separating traditional from modern society in India must be filled by intellectuals if it is to be filled at all. Intellectuals in India, as in the other new states of Asia and Africa, must provide the administra-tive leadership and the administrative *expertise* which the traditions and situations of their countries and their own preconceptions demand of them. This, in large measure, they are already doing. They must also create the public opinion and furnish the experts' criticism and judgment without which the plans of their governments will go astray.

This, however, can be done only if some of the intellectuals who are first-class in their native abilities and attainments are not drawn into govern-ment or even into politics. It can be done only if, outside of the circles of governmental authority, there are strong circles of able intellectuals—well endowed by nature, training, and experience to understand, appreciate, and criticize the undertakings of their governments within the framework of a fundamental sense of affinity.

The more distinguished intellectuals who enter governmental administra-tion acquire practical experience and sharpened judgment. To their excellent endowment, they add the sobering and toughening knowledge that comes with responsibility for the day-to-day management of affairs. A tiny handful in private business, and a number not much larger in journalism and the universities, possess equal capacities and attainments. But the great majority of intellectuals in India are alienated from the centers of public life.

They are disillusioned and unhappy about the course of events. They feel that great ideals have been deserted for the sake of trivial advances. In part, their disillusionment is a response to the real difficulties of independent national existence; in part it is a product of the confrontation of the vague and heroic idealism of opposition by the obduracy of reality.

The civil problem of the Indian intellectual, therefore, is the development of a capacity to avoid an alienated and uncritical negativism when he stands —as most persons, intellectuals included, must stand, even in a democratic society—outside the circle of the active exercise of authority. There are many obstacles to solving this problem. The poverty of so many of the intellectuals, and the widespread incidence of unemployment and malemployment, which falls especially heavily on the younger generation and which leaves scars that endure long after employment is found, represent only one factor in this alienation. The deeper traditions of the Indian intellectual —endogenous and exogenous, Hindu, Indian and Western—likewise render it difficult for him to maintain a sense of affinity with authoritative institutions in which he plays only a peripheral part. The very pattern of modernization that the leadership of India has chosen, and that even the alienated intellectual who has no central place in the machinery of development thinks is in general the only feasible pattern of development, will not make it any easier.

Still, everything changes in the course of time, and even the deepest traditions possess potentialities of innovation. For a century, American intellectuals were alienated from the American political order, and at the end of that century they seemed to stand further from it than ever before. Yet they, too, have made their peace with it, and by their own changing attitude, brought about modifications in that order which made reconciliation no unreasonable or undignified action. The same possibility is certainly available to the Indian intellectual.

Notes

1. Jawaharlal Nehru, *An Autobiography* (London, 1936), p. 409.

2. *Ibid.*, p. 413.

3. *Essays on Indian Economics* (Bombay, n.d.); *Miscellaneous Writings* (Bombay, 1915); and *Religious and Social Reform* (Bombay, n.d.).

4. Reprinted in summary in Narayan G. Chandavarkar, *The Speeches and Writings*, ed. V. Kaikini (Bombay, 1911), pp. 425-523.

5. London, 1901.

6. Read before the Ethnological Society in London in 1886; reprinted in Dadabhai Naoroji, *Speeches and Writings* (2d ed.; Madras, 1917), pp. 535-572.

7. In 1929, there were 249 Indians out of a total of 1,122. In 1939, 540 Indians out of 1,299. Cf. Phillip Woodruff, *The Guardians (The Men Who Ruled India,* Vol. II [London, 1955]), pp. 363 ff.

8. It is, of course, easier for them to maintain their intellectual interests than it is for most Indian intellectuals. Their high incomes, the spacious quarters that they enjoy by virtue of their appointments, the superiority of the libraries of the Ministries, the continuing recruitment of some of the intellectually best-endowed graduates of Indian universities and of those who have studied abroad, as well as the challenge of high policy and great responsibility, keep a sharp

edge on naturally first-class intelligences.

9. Among the members of this Commission were Prof. V. K. R. V. Rao, then Dean of the Delhi School of Economics, and later Vice-Chancellor of Delhi University, a graduate of Cambridge and pioneer in the study of Indian national income. The chairman was the late Dr. John Mathai, a graduate of the London School of Economics, a member of the Tariff Commission, and for a long time a teacher of economics, also at one time Vice-Chancellor of Bombay University.

10. The chairman of this commission was Dr. K. M. Panikkar, the author of *Asia and Western Dominance,* the *Citizen and the State,* and many other historical and theoretical treatises, as well as numerous novels in Malayalam.

11. This commission included nine academic men, the most famous of whom was Prof. S. K. Chatterjee, the eminent Calcutta University linguist.

12. This commission included many well-known scholars, such as Acharya Narendra Deva, the late Vice-Chancellor of Lucknow University; Prof. V. K. R. V. Rao; Dr. Zakir Husain; and several scholarly newspapermen, Mr. J. Natarajan, and Mr. Chalapati Rao.

13. The powers of the Vice-President of the Republic of India are indeterminate, but there can be no doubt of his eminence as an intellectual. Dr. Sarvepali Radhakrishnan is a graduate of Oxford. He was Professor of Philosophy at Madras, George V Professor of Philosophy at Calcutta, and Spalding Professor of Eastern Religions and Ethics at Oxford. He is a Fellow of the British Academy—the only Indian member— and is a Fellow of All Souls. In 1949, he became Indian Ambassador to the Soviet Union and, in 1952, Vice-President of the Indian Republic. As chairman of the University Education Commission, he has left a permanent stamp on the development of the Indian university. As a scholar, his historical works and his learned editions of the Bhagavad-Gita and the Upanishads make him one of the most distinguished living authorities on Indian thought. In no other country does a scholar of such continuing and solid achievement hold such an exalted position.

14. Lawyers make up 25 per cent;

"public workers," 17 per cent; "land," 19 per cent; and business, 10 per cent. "Press" and "education" together comprise 15 per cent. Cf. W. H. Morris-Jones, *Parliament in India* (London, 1957), p. 119.

15. In the state legislatures the Congress Party has usually a smaller intellectual representation. The cultural level is definitely lower than in the *Lok Sabha* (cf. Morris-Jones, *op. cit.,* p. 120). But there are striking exceptions: for example, in West Bengal, the Chairman of the Legislative Council is Professor Suniti Kumar Chatterjee, the linguist; in Uttar Pradesh, the Chief Minister has long been Dr. Sampurnanand, a scholarly politician who has written, among other works, *The Individual and the State: A Study in Political Theory* (Allahabad, 1944), and who, amidst the heavy burdens of office manager, finds time to continue his studies. In the governorships of the states, there are such eminent intellectuals as Dr. Zakir Husain, formerly Vice-Chancellor of Jamia Milia, now Governor of Bihar; and Mr. Harekrushna Mahtab, novelist, historian, and journalist as well as politician, now Governor of Uttar Pradesh.

16. A clever person has said that communism is an alternative to juvenile delinquency. About India it could be said that Anglophilia, truancy, the Independence Movement, and the life of the *sannyasin* are interchangeable, in the sense that they are all efforts to transcend the demands of routine tasks and obligations.

17. Those who practiced Gandhist exercises in prison—spinning, praying, and reading sacred texts—tended to become the workers in the party machine; ultimately, many of them became members of the Union and State Governments and parliaments. The tension between the intellectuals and the politicians, so strong at present, received some of its impulsion from those prison encounters of the more Westernizing radical intellectuals and the Gandhian intellectuals who were often at least as Westernized in their education. However, the tension has sources older than either of these two factors.

Gandhi himself felt that the Indian spirit had been enfeebled and corrupted by British power and English culture and sought to free his countrymen from them. He distrusted the modern intellectuals for their acknowledgment of the authority of the British in culture, politics, and administration. He brought a wholly new spirit into the Independence Movement. Before Gandhi, the movement was, on the one side, in the hands of liberal constitutionalists who, highly educated themselves, envisaged a regime ruled by the highly educated; on the other side were the people who sought to exclude the liberal constitutionalists. Gandhi changed all of this by combining the peacefulness of the liberal constitutionalists and the populism of the terrorists. As a result, although intellectuals continued to play an important role, both among adults and among students, they were condemned by the Gandhians, particularly the Westernized ones, and many were led to divest themselves of their Western culture and paraphernalia.

18. Wise heads in the middle and older generations attribute some of the student indiscipline of the past decade to the establishment of a tradition of "demonstrative politics" during the struggle for independence. There is a certain resemblance here between Indian student behavior and that of the younger members of the German *Freikorps* after World War I. Many of the youths in these military formations were just too young to have been called up for service at the front. Their adolescent imaginations had been stirred, and the Armistice deprived them of the chance to turn their phantasies of heroism into action. They were "warriors without a war." The Indian students are "rebels without a cause."

19. N. J. Wadia, Vice-Chancellor of Bombay University, in his introduction to the *Report of the Enquiry on the Problems of Teachers* (including standards of education) in the University of Bombay, conducted under the auspices of the University of Bombay Teachers Association (Bombay, 1954.), p. vi.

20. Further professional opinions about the low esteem in which college and university teachers are held and the teachers' reaction to it are to be found in Poona University Teachers Association, *Papers Read at the Second Conference of the College Teachers of the Poona University Area* (Poona, 1955), pp. 25-46. It is noteworthy that these observations emanate from Poona, which is one of the places in India where intellectual activities have traditionally been most esteemed and where there is a long history of distinguished educational and intellectual accomplishment.

ii

Political Ascent in a Class Society: French Deputies 1870-1958*

by MATTEI DOGAN

The Length and Insecurity of Legislative Careers

IN WESTERN European parliamentary democracies, especially France, few men have in the past been able to make a true political career outside of the national legislature. It was not enough to be elected a deputy. It was necessary also to remain one.

Certainly, the length of a legislative career is not a sufficient criterion for distinguishing important political men from unimportant ones. Some persons of first importance have, for various reasons, been seated in parliament only for a short time. Nevertheless, there is a very significant relationship between the duration of the *mandat parlementaire* and the importance of the political roles performed. Normally, access to prime political functions is gained only after a very rich legislative experience. There are few major exceptions to this rule, and those only at certain historical turning points. Most of the time in France, men who play important political roles are men with long legislative careers. Among these, one finds the most interesting types of professional political figures. Thus, analyzing the duration of legislative careers is an appropriate means for considering—as objectively as possible—the importance of various political men and for developing a typology of political elites.

---

*Translated by Elizabeth Wirth Marvick and Dwaine Marvick.

One of the essential characteristics of a legislative career is its insecurity. No sooner is the candidate elected than he becomes a candidate once again. The desire for re-election is very often a fundamental motivation of political deportment. The degree and causes of the insecurity of a legislative career may be clarified by examining the margin of votes which carried the candidate to parliament and the circumstances which ended the candidate's period of office.

DURATION OF LEGISLATIVE CAREERS

During the 70 years of the Third Republic, 4,892 deputies were seated; in the Fourth Republic, 1,112 deputies were elected from metropolitan France.

Of the 4,892 deputies in the Third Republic, 2,271 or 46 per cent were only elected once; 1,032 or 21 per cent were elected twice, and 1,589 or 33 per cent were seated in at least three legislatures. Of the seventeen legislatures of the Third Republic, fourteen lasted four years; two, five years; and one legislature, only one year. Thus, more than two-thirds of the deputies had relatively brief legislative careers, usually only a few years, at most eight.

The 2,271 deputies elected only once collectively had about 9,000 years of service. On the other hand, 496 deputies who had been in five to twelve legislatures collectively had some twelve thousand years of experience. Measured in years of Chamber service, more than half of the Third Republic deputies were needed to equal these 496 deputies. Although amounting only to 10 per cent of the legislative roster, these 496 had held their seats a very long time; each one twenty years at the least, often a quarter or third of a century, or even more (Table 1).

We should also note that most of the deputies first elected in 1936 had no opportunity to be elected a second time; nor were those first elected in 1932 and re-elected in 1936 able to serve in a third legislature. The events of June, 1940, even put an end to the legislative careers of some deputies first elected before World War I. Similarly, the Assembly of 1871 was elected under very unusual circumstances, and that of 1876 lasted only a single year. For the Third Republic then, if we eliminate the two first and the two last legislatures, limiting our analysis to the thirteen "normal" legislatures of the period 1877-1932, we may establish a "standardized duration" of parliamentary careers, with abstract values, but with a sociological significance like that of certain demographic calculations. Thus, during the "normal" phase of the Third Republic, a few more than a third of the deputies held office for only one term; fewer than a quarter succeeded in being elected twice; and two-fifths won between three and ten times.

According to this standardized measure, 3 per cent of the deputies were in at least seven legislatures and typically kept their seats about a third of a century. Nevertheless, these privileged few accumulated 12 per cent of all the years of legislative service—that is to say, nearly as many as the 36 per cent of deputies seated only once.

The continual renewal of the Chamber's personnel may be compared to the movement of sand dunes. It is the sand on the surface that is moved by the wind. In the same way, at each general election those deputies tend to be swept aside who have been seated for relatively short times, especially those with only one mandate. Certain deputies seated for a very long time constitute a "cemented sand," which electoral turbulence does not dislodge.

Actually, the older legislators have even further opportunities to entrench themselves. There is a direct correlation between length of time in office and re-election on a first ballot. In the elections of 1936, for instance, seven-tenths of those elected for the fifth time, and three-quarters of those elected for the sixth to ninth times, were re-elected on the first ballot. Two-fifths of those

Table 1

Continuity and Length of Service in the French Chamber of Deputies: 1870-1940

| | NUMBER OF TIMES ELECTED AS DEPUTY | | | | | | | |
	1	2	3	4	5	6	7 or more	TOTAL
Deputies with Continuous Service	2,271	870	525	314	171	95	91	4,337
Deputies with Discontinuous Service	—	162	142	112	62	42	35	555
Total:	2,271	1,032	667	426	233	137	126	4,892
Percentage distribution:	46	21	14	9	5	3	2:	100
Duration of Terms (in years)	4	8	12	16	20	24	28-50	
Total Years of Service	9,000	8,250	8,000	6,800	4,650	3,300	4,000	44,000
Percentage distribution:	21	18	18	15	10	8	10:	100

Table 2

Length of "Parliamentary Mandates" in the Fourth Republic (Deputies Elected in Metropolitan France: 1945-58)

| PERCENTAGE DISTRIBUTION: | NUMBER OF TIMES ELECTED DEPUTY | | | | | | TOTAL | NUMBER OF DEPUTIES |
	1	2	3	4	5			
Communists	30	13	20	14	23	:	100%	(246)
Socialists	33	20	14	11	22	:	100	(198)
Radicals, RGR	49	18	11	16	6	:	100	(124)
MRP	32	16	21	12	19	:	100	(216)
Moderates, PRL Independents	51	17	13	11	8	:	100	(152)
RPF Rep. Soc. "Gaullists"	58	29	6	4	3	:	100	(91)
Extreme Right, "Poujadists"	100	—	—	—	—	:	100	(44)
Unclassifiable "Transfuges"	—	25	25	25	25	:	100	(41)
Total, Fourth Republic:	40	17	16	12	15	:	100%	(1,112)

coming up a third or fourth time also obtained majorities on the first round. Conversely, only a third of those who had only been seated in the Chamber for one term, and 13 per cent of the new candidates, escaped a run-off. This tendency also holds for other elections, notably those of 1910, 1914, 1928, and 1932.

For the problem which here concerns us, it is of only slight interest to establish the average duration of the mandate. Such an average conceals the essential distinction between those deputies seated only a few years and usually forgotten quickly, and those who retained their mandates for twenty-five to thirty-five years, inscribing their names on parliamentary history. Nevertheless, we may note that the average duration of the mandate was nine and one-half years under the Third Republic. In the British House of Commons, the average was nine years between the two world wars. In the French Chamber (leaving out the initial period of the Third Republic, to which the question does not apply), the average length of service of the deputies varied little by legislature; while in the House of Commons, by reason of the unequal terms of legislative sessions, it varied greatly—ten years on the eve of the 1922 elections, six years when the 1923 elections occurred.

The disuse of the right of dissolution, the multiple membership of deputies before the "crystallization" of legislative blocs in 1910, the existence since that date of a large number of unstable blocs and parties with indefinite boundaries under the Third Republic—these are reasons enough for us to study as an aggregate all actual legislators without distinction as to party.

Certain deputies were seated, without interruption, from their first election to the end of their last mandate. Others, after having received mandates a few times, either did not present themselves again or suffered an electoral defeat and returned to the Chamber only after an absence of some time. Of the 2,621 deputies who belonged to at least two legislatures, 2,066 or fourth-fifths were seated without interruption, while 555 served nonconsecutive terms. Nevertheless, when we think of deputies with discontinuous mandates we must not regard as typical those legislators who were seated for one legislature, retired for another, and returned for a third only to be upset for the fourth. During the greater part of their legislative careers, these deputies with discontinuous mandate remained continuously in office: 89 per cent did not interrupt their terms more than once; 10 per cent, no more than twice, one per cent, three times; only one person, four times. Moreover, half of those who interrupted their terms more than once started out in parliamentary life between 1871 and 1877—that is to say, at the moment when, from the electoral point of view, the Third Republic was still in a state of gestation.

Almost all of those deputies who came up for re-election sought it in the same *département* where they had been previously elected. Of 4,892 deputies in the Third Republic, only 110 changed *départements* during their careers as deputies; 17 others also changed when transferring from the Chamber to the Senate. Out of these 127 deputies—2.5 per cent of the total—93 changed their *département* once; 22 changed twice; and 12, three times; often by returning to a *département* which they had previously represented.

The continuity in time and fixity of locale of the great majority of parliamentary personnel are intimately linked. The relationship is operative in two senses: (1) electoral success keeps the deputy in his district; (2) remaining in the same district is a principal factor in the stability of his tenure.

Under the Fourth Republic, of the total of 1,112 deputies elected from metropolitan France, 446, or 40 per cent, were elected only once; 190 more, or 17 per cent, were elected twice; and finally, 476 deputies, or 43 per cent, were elected three to five times. The duration of mandates was very much shorter under the Fourth Republic; the Assembly elected in October, 1945, lasted only eight months, that elected in June, 1945, only five months, and that of 1956 did not finish its last term. Under the Third Republic, all the legislatures except one lasted four or five years.

If the duration of the parliamentary career is one criterion to be used in defining professional political men, the candidate's age at his first election must be taken into consideration. Around a third of the deputies were under forty when first elected; another third, between forty and fifty; and the final third, more than fifty years old. Contrary to expectation, the tenure of legislators did not vary much with age when first elected. In the French political system, deputies elected when they were already quite old were hardly likely to be professional political men. They might have become interested in politics and given a great deal of time to it, but except for those who were exceedingly well off, they must have pursued an occupation and identified essentially with social activities other than political. As for the deputies elected while still young, most of them remained in parliament a very short time and must, therefore, be classified as nonprofessionals. Only those young deputies who became old deputies may be considered as professional political men of the legislative type. To this category belong between three hundred and four hundred deputies from Gambetta to Clemenceau, from Poincaré to Auriol. Four or five hundred other deputies may be considered semiprofessional political men.

THE INSECURITY OF THE PARLIAMENTARY CAREER

What factors account for the turnover of personnel in the Chamber? Two are of particular sociological interest: electoral defeat and changes in candidacy. If very extensive, this indicates rejuvenation; and if slight, an oligarchical structure (in the etymological sense). To separate these two factors we must proceed by elimination. Let us first exclude the 600 deputies of the last legislature of the Third Republic. Let us also exclude 650 deputies who died in office. Mortality is a natural turnover factor which plays the same role whether members are elected or named for life; it is a function of the average age of legislators, which for the Chamber was about 50 years (at the start of a session). This average age depends in turn on the age when starting legislative life and especially on the duration of legislative terms. Indeed, mortality was much higher among deputies seated a long time in the Chamber (those who were older) than among the beginners, who on the average were younger. As a result, it was higher also among deputies attached to very old parties on the legislative scene than among members of recently created parties.

Had there been no Senate, the personnel changes in the Chamber would have been slower, because 548 deputies would not have left to enter the Senate, and some of the 93 permanent senators appointed from the Chamber would have remained there. Moreover, 200 deputies became senators after having been defeated in Chamber elections; and 100 deputies, notably in 1876 and 1919, declined to seek re-election by universal suffrage because they preferred to win approval before the Senatorial College. In total, 938 deputies became senators. On the other hand, 100 deputies resigned their seats for various reasons: to accept nominations as ambassadors, colonial governors, or to international bodies, or for reasons of health.

After eliminating these, 2,600 deputies remain—more than half of the actual total for the period—whose careers ended by not being re-elected. Around 800 did not run again for election to the Chamber. We may conjecture that perhaps half of these retired voluntarily, while the others dropped out because they knew they had no serious chances. They may not have succeeded in obtaining the wished-for nomination or the necessary support for an electoral campaign, or their electoral situation may have been compromised in other ways. Finally, 1,800 deputies sought re-election and failed.

To these 1,800 deputies actually defeated, one must add the 200 who became senators after losing Chamber elections and the 400 deputies virtually defeated—those who retired from the electoral battle to avoid very probable, if not certain, defeat. To sum up, 2,400 deputies out of 4,300 (setting aside 600 incumbent deputies in 1940), or 55 per cent, finished their legislative careers in electoral defeats (either effective or virtual).

Why were more than half of the changes in Chamber personnel due to electoral defeats, when voting alignments in the French electorate changed so little? It is because these defeats were only partly due to general shifts in public opinion. The shift of a very small fraction of voters from Right to Left or vice versa, so as to reverse the pluralities between them, could result, through abstentions when the run-off elections took place, in replacing an old deputy by a new one as well as losing the constituency for his party. Given geographic stability of candidacies, a lost constituency for a party, nine times out of ten, would mean a vanquished deputy; a retained constituency would mean the deputy's re-election; a constituency gained would mean a new deputy. If, for example, a party lost half of its old constituencies but gained as many others, the number of seats would remain unchanged: half of the incumbent deputies would be defeated, and their places taken by new ones. Thus, a party would have replaced half of its legislators, even though practically all its *candidates* were the same—each in his own constituency.

Under a system of proportional representation, a change in opinion by a very small part of the electorate produces an equivalent change in parliamentary representation. By contrast, under a system of single-member districts with a run-off election, such as that used in the Third Republic, there is a discrepancy between realignments in the electorate and the turnover of parliamentary personnel. A change in the opinion of 10 per cent of the voters may—if these voters are randomly distributed among all districts—result in the replacement of a third of the actual Assembly members, thanks to changes of districts among the parties. In a single-member district system with only one election, such as that of Great Britain, effects are amplified still more. In that country, a relationship has been established between the total number of votes won by each party in all districts and the number of seats divided among them, a relationship that is reflected in the turnover of parliamentary personnel. This is what British specialists call "the law of the cube." Under a system of uninominal election with two rounds, because of the multiplicity of parties and the withdrawal of some candidates, such a relationship does not exist. Instead, a bonus number of seats is awarded to the stronger parties and the weaker ones are at a disadvantage, except for regional parties.

But, whatever the electoral system, whether proportional representation as under the Fourth Republic, or a single-member system with run-off elections as under the Third Republic, or a single-member district system with only one election as in Great Britain, or proportional representation with a preferential vote as in Italy, the re-election of deputies often depends on a small number of votes. An analysis of the French elections from 1889 to 1919 shows that about one third of the deputies were elected with a margin of less than 10 per cent of the votes cast (and quite often with a margin of less than 5 per cent of the votes). Only four or five hundred voters of the district need change their minds at the next election to prevent the re-election of these deputies. In Great Britain, in the elections of 1955, more than one hundred deputies were victorious over their opponents with a margin of less than 6 per cent of the votes. In Italy, the preferential vote can have at best a marginal value.

The fact that re-election is uncertain is reflected in the psychology of legislators. In France, even those deputies seated in parliament for a long time were forced to risk, every four or five years, losing their seats. This remark is not contradicted by the fact (previously emphasized) that deputies had a greater chance of being re-elected the longer they had been in the Chamber. The risk, moreover, was usually substantial. It was not easy for a defeated deputy to take up the threads of his original profession, once defeated. Eviction from parliament very often meant a loss of social status—whether to a provincial doctor, a middle-level bureaucrat, a modest businessman, a high school professor, or a farmer. Even for the professional political man, it was a blow.

The Preponderance of Intellectuals in Parliament

Parliament may reflect the interests, aspirations, and opinions of the electorate—divided though it be—without being, from the point of view of socio-economic composition, a miniature of the nation. It may be perfectly representative, if that means that it includes champions of the interests of all social categories; nonetheless, its members may come from certain social strata which are not at all a sampling of the electorate. Knowing in what measure legislative personnel are recruited proportionally from the various classes of society is a secondary matter. It is more significant to inquire into the social origin of legislators in terms of their vertical social mobility and in terms of their socio-political ascent.

Diverse sources were used to classify deputies socially and by occupation. This has permitted us to establish discrepancies between the self-declared vocations of the deputies themselves—when they were running as candidates—and their principal occupations. Certain vocations have for campaign purposes more resonance than others. It is not a question of false declarations; the deputies simply did not always indicate the occupation which constituted the principal source of their income, mentioning instead a secondary occupation or a more "salable" title when before the electorate. Thus, a certain industrialist with a degree from a technical college insisted upon his title of engineer rather than that of entrepreneur. A certain business executive preferred to indicate on the electoral list that he was a journalist, by-passing the names of the companies which he directed. The director-general of a bank presented himself before the electorate as a member of the board of trustees of a famous school. A high official, possessing a title of nobility, called himself an "agricultural developer." A lawyer considered himself a farmer, and so on. In such cases, we have classified by the real vocation or principal occupation.

Vocation usually means, of course, *former* vocation. Deputies cease, generally, to pursue effectively their original occupation during a legislative session. A man who makes a career of politics abandons his vocational career. Once elected deputy, he attaches more importance to the first than to the second. A doctor, for example, does not become a political man in order to defend the interests of the medical body. From the moment he obtains a parliamentary seat, he is no longer a doctor; he is henceforth in everything a deputy. His preoccupations will be political; socio-economic problems will present themselves in electoral terms. Originally a doctor, he may nevertheless support to a certain degree, a hospital-reform program opposed by doctors. He may support the demands of farmers, if the latter are numerous in his district and if he has need of their votes. He may vote for a law protecting tenants, even if he is a real estate owner, because he may attach more importance to his re-election than to the revenue from his real property. In such a case, he will have become entirely a political man.

Many deputies had abandoned their original occupations even before their first election. A lawyer who was mayor of the chief city of a departement was, even then, looking less for new clients than for voting support in the coming legislative elections. A teacher who was executive secretary of his political party's departmental federation was concerned less with the education of children than with enlisting militant supporters, voters, and so on. Furthermore, many deputies had only pursued their original occupations a very short time, whether because they were elected when very young or because they were engaged in active politics when still young. Entry into parliamentary life at a young age reduces the influence of the original vocation upon political attitudes.

GENERAL CHARACTERISTICS OF INTELLECTUAL PARLIAMENTARIANS

We may classify deputies into two large categories: intellectuals and nonintellectuals. The first category is by far the most important. In it, we include writers, teachers, lawyers, journalists, magistrates, doctors, engineers, architects, and schoolmasters—vocations normally demanding a certain scholarly bent, and, in most cases, possession of a degree. More than half of the 6,000 French deputies elected between 1871 and 1958 may be considered intellectuals in this broad sense.

Thanks to research in electoral sociology, to historical studies, to regional monographs about the political attitudes of various categories of voters, and to information possessed about various types of political formations, we know something of the social origins of voters, partisans, militants, and managers of various parties. A basic finding emerges.

The proportion of intellectuals, negligible in the mass of voters and even among ordinary partisans, increases progressively—crowding out other occupational categories—among militants, delegates to annual conventions, members of local and regional committees, municipal and departmental councilmen, directors of parapolitical organizations and of national associations. There are variations, of course, according to the times, the parties, and the regions. If parliament is not, from the socio-political point of view, the image of society, it is above all because, like a magnifying glass, or even more like a distorting mirror, it enlarges out of proportion the silhouette of the intellectual, in all the colors of the political horizon.

Intellectuals are today, as yesterday, a very small part of the electorate, constituting at the beginning of the Third Republic about 2 per cent of the labor force and 4 per cent in the 1950's. They are neither owners of the means of production, nor wage-earners, in the Marxist sense of these concepts. They cannot be considered, in terms of the division of labor in society, as exploiters nor as exploited. They remain outside of the antagonisms generated by the social interaction involved in production. They do not constitute a class from the economic point of view; they do not manifest specific characteristics sociologically speaking—that is, they do not display a consciousness of being a social class distinct from others. As political men, they speak for social interests not their own. Even if rich, their knowledge and competence constitute the only capital they can bring to bear in the exercise of their vocation or office. They can adapt themselves, except for the lawyers, to any kind of social system—from classic liberalism to socialism—without their incomes or their social status being profoundly modified. Whatever the degree of socialization of the economy, they exercise the same functions, and they retain the same positions in the social hierarchy. They escape the conflicts between classes.

From 1871 to 1898, about two-thirds of the deputies were intellectuals (in the sense that we have just given this concept), with very slight variations from one legislature to another. From 1898 to 1919, the proportion of intellectuals stood at an average of 60 per cent. It was 54 per cent for the period between the two world wars, and 48 per cent among deputies elected in metropolitan France during the Fourth Republic.

These averages, however, conceal important party differences. From the start of the twentieth century until 1919, more than two-thirds of the radical deputies were intellectuals while this was so for little more than one-third of the conservative deputies (those of the Right) and two-fifths of the socialist deputies. Between the two world wars, intellectuals constituted nearly 70 per cent of the radical grouping in parliament, as against 17 per cent of the Communist bloc, 53 per cent of the socialist contingent, and less than half of the conservative element. Under the Fourth Republic, 70 per cent of the radical deputies could be classed in the various categories of intellectuals, as against 23 per cent of the Communist deputies, 18 per cent of the Poujadists on the extreme Right, and fewer than half of the moderate deputies, Gaullist or Popular Republicans. On the other hand, the proportion of intellectuals among the socialist deputies became, in the aftermath of the World War II, as high as among their radical colleagues (69 per cent).

At the start of the Third Republic, most of the intellectual deputies were men of the Left or Left-Center. Toward the end of the Third Republic, most of their successors were sitting in the Center or Right-Center of the semicircle at the Palais Bourbon.

Of course, the notions of Left, Center, and Right are used here in a "geometric" sense, because the "Republican" of 1930 was very different from that of 1876. His etiquette had not changed; but the social, political, and economic problems had greatly changed, so much so that his position on the parliamentary arc had shifted in this time from Left to Right. The seats of the extreme Left had been occupied successively by Radicals, Socialists, and Communists. These last—the Communist bloc of the Fourth Republic—included very few intellectual deputies, in contrast with the radical group of the end of the preceding century. The extreme Left of the 1950's was a social and economic grouping, that of the 1870's was more of a political bloc. During the last thirty or forty years, the proportion of intellectuals has been small, not only at the extreme Right of the parliamentary semicircle, but also at the extreme Left.

Despite this, the category of intellectual deputies seems multi-faceted from the political point of view. The wide range, however, can be reduced by distinguishing different types of intellectuals and by taking into account their social origins, socio-economic status, and the socio-political climate of their electoral districts. One can then establish significant variations between political-party affiliation and these criteria.

Intellectuals, in general, are heterogeneous from the political point of view, not only because they include diverse occupations (although all may be considered intellectual ones), but above all because of their different social origins. Moreover, there exists within each subcategory of intellectuals, a professional hierarchy, such that one's rank may cause one's social perspective to vary. Rank determines from which social level one's clientele are drawn. On account of this, the country doctor had every chance of being a Socialist or Radical and the great chief of a Paris hospital of being a conservative. Most men seeking a political career, furthermore, adapt themselves to the political climate of their districts. For this reason, too, the intellectual could easily be conservative, Catholic, or moderate, in the West of France; Radical or Socialist, in the Midi.

Schumpeter, in examining the role of intellectuals in political life, noted

Table 3

Original Occupation of Deputies in the Fourth Republic: 1945-58

	COMMUNISTS	SOCIALISTS	MRP	RADICALS RGR	MODERATES PRL INDPTS.	RPF REP. SOC. "GAULLISTS"	EXTREME RIGHT "POUJADIST"	UNCLASSIFIABLES, "TRANSFUGES"	TOTAL	Percentage Distribution
Workers	99	11	21	—	1	1	—	—	133	
White-Collar Employees	37	16	19	2	—	—	—	1	71	21
Subordinate Government Workers	7	15	5	3	1	—	—	—	31	
Farmers	29	10	29	11	40	12	—	5	136	12
School Masters	29	32	1	2	—	—	1	1	66	
Professors	12	35	21	13	7	7	—	4	99	
Journalists	5	19	17	12	6	2	1	2	64	
Medical Doctors and Pharmacists	3	13	15	13	8	10	3	—	65	
Lawyers	2	28	25	28	38	11	2	8	142	
High Government Officials	3	4	9	8	6	7	1	4	42	48
Engineers and Architects	4	5	11	8	9	8	—	9	54	
Cadres	3	9	14	4	7	2	1	3	43	
Merchants	1	2	15	5	6	6	29	—	64	16
Industrialists, Directors of Societies	—	2	9	14	16	18	6	3	68	
Army Officers and Ecclesiastics	1	—	3	1	6	6	—	1	18	
										3
Women without Professions	11	1	2	—	1	1	—	—	16	
Total for Deputies of metropolitan France:	246	198	216	124	152	91	44	41	1112	100%
Percentage Distribution:	22	18	20	11	14	8	4	3	100%	

that "their minds are similarly furnished" and that this fact "facilitates their mutual understanding and forms a link between them." In France, at least, it was the intellectuals who most impassioned political debates in the Assembly under the Fourth Republic, as under the Third. They were very often the most intransigent ideologues. Their "minds were similarly furnished" in the sense that they were apt to pose problems abstractly, with more or less sincerity, and often to expound them with ability. But this aptitude meant that they often proposed unrealistic solutions; and that they fixed upon subtleties and neglected essentials, thus uselessly complicating and prolonging parliamentary debates by inventing false problems and disagreeing among themselves. Examination of participation in major debates shows that, among the intellectual deputies, there was the least "mutual understanding." It is among them that most of the "availables" are found, who sought to give to their personal rivalries a political significance, this being particularly true of moderates who "did not have to submit themselves to the discipline of any party."

The psycho-political consequences arising from the presence of so many intellectuals in the French Assembly can scarcely be exaggerated.

The proportion of intellectuals in a legislative assembly does not reflect closely the economic substructure of a country; rather, it is a function of each nation's social-psychological stratification system and political superstructure. A comparison of France, Great Britain, the United States, Germany, Italy, Sweden, and Holland is sufficient to convince us of this. To the extent that political parties do not form their own cadres, they chiefly recruit their representatives and their leaders from the social elite, that is, from universities, higher administration, union federations, the army, churches, the bar, the press, the medical profession, the engineers, the landed aristocracy, the rural squirearchy, financial circles, and large-scale industry. In doing so, they take into account, whether consciously or not, the importance of numerous factors, such as the various social and occupational levels among the voters, party followers, and militants; the acceptance of the traditional social hierarchy or a part of it; the party ideology; the influence of parapolitical organizations, such as unions; the sources of income for the election campaign; the social status and prestige of various subgroups in the social elite; the procedures adopted for nominating candidates; the social composition of nominating committees, and so on.

Thus, if there are scarcely any persons of working-class origin in Congress in Washington, it is partly because there is not in the United States an important working-class party. Such a party does not exist because men who, according to objective criteria, belong to the working class identify themselves as middle-class. There are many reasons for this self-identification: the absence of traditions of subordination, substantial horizontal and vertical mobility for the working class, the historical presence of many immigrants at the base of the social pyramid, and so on. By reference to such psycho-social factors we also try to understand why businessmen are prominent in the House of Representatives and in the Senate, while, in each, intellectuals form only a minority, although an important one.

If, in the British House of Commons, one important group derives from the labor-union elite and another very influential one from the aristocracy, the cause is found in a whole series of factors, ranging from the regional concentration of the working-class population, especially the miners, to the old nobility's adaptation to new conditions of economic life while maintaining its prestige. Nevertheless, 40 per cent of the members of the House of Commons elected in 1951 and a few more who were among those elected between 1955 and 1959 may be considered intellectuals (in our sense); one may add perhaps 5 per cent of the notables and other men who, before their election, pursued no vocation but engaged in advanced studies.

Intellectuals are inevitable and indispensable in any civilized society. They form an important part of the political elite at all levels. That which varies from one country to another, from one social system to another, and in the same country from one epoch to the next, is the social origins of intellectuals and the upward social mobility linked to education. Whatever the routes of upward social mobility, however low the social levels at which they begin, whatever the volume and rhythm of social ascent that uses education as a springboard, one must admit that in every country political elites derive in great part from intellectual elites. This is true even in the USSR, where the intelligentsia, the higher administrative ranks, and the upper technical cadres of industry furnished more than two-fifths of the 1954 members of the Supreme Soviet. In the so-called underdeveloped countries or those economically backward, intellectuals very often predominate in legislative assemblies, in certain cases holding as many as 80 per cent of the seats. Intellectuals who embark on political careers may "come from the people" or belong to the "oligarchy"; the important fact is that they are numerous in practically all parliaments, particularly in France and Italy.

One may distinguish among French legislators several types of intellectuals, two of which seem particularly important: jurists and teachers.

THE MEN OF LAW

The number of lawyers, notaries, barristers, and magistrates among legislators has always been very high in the French parliament, even in the revolutionary assemblies at the end of the eighteenth century. People like Danton and Robespierre were lawyers. There were 237 men of law in the Assembly elected in 1871; 192 in 1876; 202 in 1877; 193 in 1881; 186 in 1885; 174 in 1889; and 175 in 1893. One finds a progressive diminution beginning during World War I. In 1928, jurists were no more than 140; in 1936, 122; in 1945, 73; and in 1956 in the last elections of the Fourth Republic, 69 lawyers were elected.

In the first legislatures of the Third Republic, two deputies out of five were lawyers. Lawyers represented 29 per cent of the actual legislators of the period 1898 to 1914; 24 per cent of those elected between the two world wars; and only 13 per cent of the deputies of the Fourth Republic. However, even in the years after World War II, lawyers were the most numerous occupational group in parliament.

The proportion of jurists was even higher in the Italian Parliament. In the constituent assembly of 1946, 35 per cent of the deputies came from legal work, and as many in the Chamber elected in 1948. Among Senators elected in that same year, 56 per cent were jurists, mostly lawyers. The loss of seats suffered by the Christian Democratic Party in the elections of 1953 brought a diminution of men of law both among the deputies (27 per cent) and senators (35 per cent).

In Britain, of 630 deputies elected to the House of Commons in 1951, there were 120 barristers and solicitors, or 19 per cent of the parliamentary body. This proportion was not changed by the elections of 1955.

On the other hand, in the German Reichstag and, later, in the Bundestag, jurists were not one of the most important groups. In the elections of 1919, 8 per cent of those elected were lawyers; 4 per cent were lawyers in the elections of 1924 and 1928. In the legislatures of 1949 and 1953, 7 per cent of the deputies were jurists.

The lawyer is one of the most familiar figures in the legislative milieu, because juridical vocations seem to predispose men to a political career. The important role that lawyers play in political life, a phenomenon not unique to France, is largely explained by the fact that they possess many of the qualities required by political men: the habit of speaking in public, oratorical talent, knowledge of legal questions, and so on. Knowledge of legal techniques is a great advantage for those engaged in politics, where each action is translated into a legislative text. One pleads in a legislature as one pleads before a court: it is a question of convincing. It little matters to the lawyer whether his client is right or wrong. If the latter is a criminal or if he is innocent, he must equally be defended. His role is not to make "justice" prevail, but to defend his client's cause.

Successful lawyers are those who know the techniques and legal procedures and who make use of them with talent, not those who seek only clients whose causes are just. Lawyers comport themselves the same way in political life. Most of them adhere to a party without much preoccupation with ideological problems. Very often, the lawyer who is a deputy can, better than a deputy who was once a businessman, defend the interests of businessmen on the legislative stage, in the same way that, before a court, he can better defend an accused person than could the accused himself.

In many regions, French peasants long preferred to vote for lawyer candidates instead of one of their own, for they needed an effective defender. Lawyers, more than all the rest, go into politics not because they have fixed interests of their own to defend, but because they know how to defend any economic or social interest, sometimes with much sincerity. At the beginning of their political careers they are polyvalent. As a result, they are easily adaptable.

By contrast, men of other socio-economic categories adhere at first to a political ideology. It is only later that they acquire a command, through long experience, of legalistic parliamentary techniques. Workers, for example, are men who, by reason of their social position, adopt certain opinions and only afterwards, as party militants or cadre members, learn the political profession. Businessmen know well what it is they have to defend long before they know how to do it. For this reason, sometimes, they act through persons interposed between them in the political arena; they appeal notably to lawyers, whose political candidacies they often support.

The large number of lawyers among legislators is also explained because the legal profession may be temporarily abandoned and taken up again in case of electoral defeat. There is no incompatibility between the legislative function and the vocation of law, as there is for many other professions. On the contrary, political success improves the lawyer's reputation at the bar. His political fame is embellished by his fame as a lawyer and vice versa. In fact, according to many witnesses, certain young men chose the legal profession with the intention of thus preparing themselves for a political career.

Many of the most important political men of the Third Republic and of the Fourth were originally lawyers: Gambetta, Thiers, Jules Ferry, Viviani, Waldeck-Rousseau, Grévy, Floquet, Flandin, Millerand, Méline, Steeg, Fallières, Doumergue, Ribot, Sarrien, Loubet, Leygues, Laval, Lamoreaux, Goblet, Sembat, De Monzie, Monis, Paul-Boncour, and Paul Reynaud, as well as Auriol, Coty, Schumann, Mendès-France, Ramadier, André Marie, Edgar Faure, Gouin, Pflimlin, le Troquer, and Monnerville.

THE EDUCATORS

In Thibaudet's *The Republic of Teachers,* one of his chapters is entitled "Heirs and Scholars." He states here that "teaching is the only career recruited practically exclusively from among scholars, the sons of impecunious good families. . . . The French University in its three orders is one corporation of scholars." Most teachers were and are men with a Leftist tendency stemming from their social origin. Since they are the local elite in provincial towns, and since the exercise of their profession leaves them some leisure, many of them engage in active political life.

At the start of the twentieth century, instructors in the public schools were divided between the Radical and the Socialist parties; in the middle of the twentieth century, between the Socialist and Communist parties. They remained "geometrically" on the Left, doubtless because of their modest social origins. This is not peculiar to France. Everywhere in Europe, the teacher and the priest are intellectuals of the villages or small towns. They "come from" the people in both cases and they remain there. But for nonsocial reasons, they orient themselves differently on the political stage, and the influence they exert is not of the same nature. In certain regions of France, the priest exercises an indirect influence on political life, through the religious sentiments of the faithful. However, he rarely engages in political activity of a militant kind. Since 1900, no Assembly has included more than three or four ecclesiastics. By contrast, a very large proportion of teachers could be found in the ranks of the Communist Party and above all in the Socialist Party. One may estimate that about a quarter of those on the federal executive commissions of the Socialist Party during the Fourth Republic were teachers, many of whom were schoolmasters. Political activity is, moreover, one of the few ways that remain for them to enlarge their horizons. It is also a means of upward social mobility. While the son of a schoolmaster may hope to rise to a better social status than that of his father, the schoolmaster himself cannot improve his fate. He may not change his vocation because he has no capital. But if he has vision, political activity opens new doors, and he can engage in it at a very young age.

During the last 40 years of the Third Republic, 63 schoolmasters were seated in the Chamber for a greater or shorter length of time. During the 15 years of the Fourth Republic, 66 schoolmasters were elected deputies. Only rarely did they play political roles of the first order on the national level. More often, the former schoolmaster was the perfect example of a middle-rank deputy. However, even if he is not a deputy, a district or municipal councilman—or even a candidate for these posts—the schoolmaster exercises an indirect influence on political life because, just as Thibaudet noted, he shapes the "overseers of political elites," that is, the voters. Thibaudet aptly comments, in his *Republic of Teachers,* "in the provinces the teacher holds the first place and, in the village, leaving aside the priest, there remains only the schoolmaster."

For the period 1898 to 1940, out of a total of 2,786 deputies, there were 177 who had formerly been engaged in either secondary or university instruction; for the Fourth Republic, 99 teachers out of 1,112 deputies were elected from metropolitan France. At the start of the century, most of these teachers were radicals of various hues, while very few were socialists or moderates. Between the two wars, teachers were more numerous in the socialist ranks; still, almost half of them belonged either to the radical element or that of the radical Left, while a fifth belonged to the conservative bloc. Under the Fourth Republic, the majority of the deputies who had taught in high schools were of a socialist or Communist tendency, while the majority of university teachers were attached to the MRP, the radical group, or to the moderates. A third of the Socialist deputies of the Fourth Republic were teachers (professors or schoolmasters). Before the war, the Radical Party was two-headed: its two leaders, Herriot and Daladier, were both teachers. Under the Fourth Republic, Guy Mollet, the Secretary General of the Socialist Party, was also a teacher. So also were Bidault, Teitgen, and deMenthon, the leaders of the MRP, and Cachin, one of the four secretaries of the Communist Party. The role of teachers in legislative debates is only equalled by that of lawyers. In no other western country can one find so great a penetration of the national legislature by educational personnel.

In France, the ranks of primary and secondary instruction have been for a long time one of the bastions of the Left Laïque (Socialists, Communists, and Radicals), especially in little towns. In Italy, by comparison, where the relationships between school, church, and state are different, instructors are in many regions more favorable to the Christian Democratic Party. Moreover, the political advancement of instructors is much less important in Italy than in France, while that of university professors is very important today as it was before the Fascist regime. In the political history of France and Italy, there are many examples of statesmen, party chiefs, and formulators of doctrines who were originally professors.

Social Classes and Political Elites

Changes occurring from one generation to the next in the social recruitment of legislators cannot be seen clearly unless one takes into account not only the occupation of the deputies but also the social origins of their family. Two men, one born in a bourgeois family, the other in a modest family, are likely to espouse different political views—if not diametrically opposed ones—even if they follow the same profession and attain a similar rank in it. This is especially true for those deputies whom we have called intellectuals. To classify a deputy according to the social origin of his family, we need to control the occupation, social position, wealth, the social status of his father, and, where possible, of his paternal and maternal grandfather. The data at our disposal for these purposes have gaps—notably for the period 1900 to 1919. These gaps frustrate analysis but they do not prohibit it.

We may distinguish five classes: working class, lower-middle class, middle class, upper-middle class, and nobility. For the working class, the nobility,

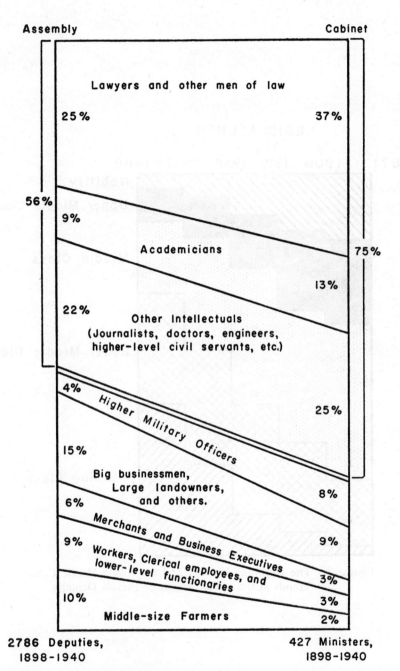

Assembly   Cabinet

Lawyers and other men of law

25%   37%

56%

9%

Academicians   75%

13%

22%   Other Intellectuals
           (Journalists, doctors, engineers,
           higher-level civil servants, etc.)

4%   25%
     Higher Military Officers

15%

     Big businessmen,
     Large landowners,
6%   and others.   8%

     Merchants and Business Executives
9%   9%
     Workers, Clerical employees, and
     lower-level functionaries   3%

10%   3%
           Middle-size Farmers   2%

2786 Deputies,   **427 Ministers,**
1898-1940   **1898-1940**

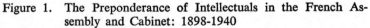

Figure 1.   The Preponderance of Intellectuals in the French As-
            sembly and Cabinet: 1898-1940

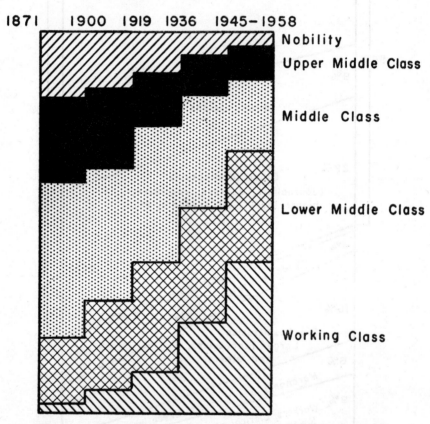

Figure 2.   The Declining Nobility and the Rising Middle Class:
Trends in the Social Origins of French Deputies

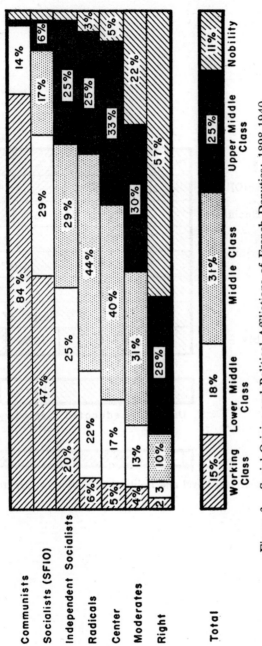

Figure 3. Social Origins and Political Affiliations of French Deputies: 1898-1940

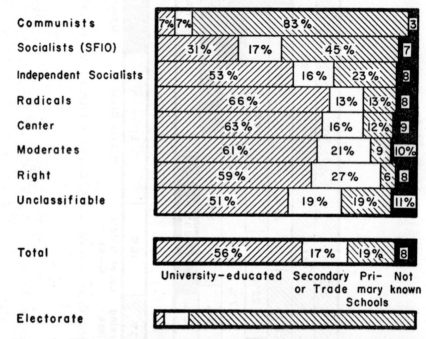

Figure 4. Educational Level and Political Affiliation of Deputies: 1898-1940

and the upper-middle class, no insurmountable difficulty is presented, but the distinction between lower-middle class and middle class is not always clear. To explain why this particular distinction is difficult, we would have to go into the entire morphology of French society and its evolution. Let us merely say that the distinction between lower-middle class and middle class may be considered as approximate.

In this classification, a lawyer who is the son of a small businessman is categorized as lower-middle class; a lawyer who is the son of an industrialist is classed in the upper-middle class; and a lawyer who comes from family bestowed with a title of nobility is given the grade which is his in the social hierarchy. A teacher who is the son of a butcher, and his colleague who is the son of an important doctor in a Paris hospital, are distinguished according to the social positions of their fathers, and so on. Thus, lawyers, journalists, or teachers often become Socialists or conservatives, Catholics or Radical anticlericals in the cradle.

FROM THE REPUBLIC OF DUKES TO THE REIGN OF THE
MIDDLE CLASS AND LOWER-MIDDLE CLASS

In the first elections of the Third Republic in 1871, 226 candidates were elected who came from families holding titles of nobility, as well as many other candidates allied by marriage with noble families. One deputy out of three had blue blood. Representatives of the old nobility were less numerous in subsequent assemblies, but up to the end of the century they constituted a very important element in the Right wing of the parliamentary semicircle. In the period from 1898 to 1919, 11 per cent of the deputies came from the nobility or aristocracy; between the two world wars, 9 per cent; under the Fourth Republic, 3 per cent.

About 40 per cent of the deputies in the early legislatures of the Third Republic came from the upper-middle class; 35 per cent, in the period 1898 to 1919; 21 per cent, between the two world wars; and 18 per cent in the Fourth Republic. During this time, the economic circumstances and the social position of the upper-middle class were appreciably modified; in consequence, so were its influence and political power.

The representatives of the upper-middle class quickly took the best places following the invitations of Gambetta: "You have it in your power to take an immense role in this Republic, a privileged role, because you have the leisure of fortune, the education, and social influence. Go along with us. We can assure you rank, honor, and a power which will permit you to exercise your aptitudes for the benefit of all."

Up to the end of the nineteenth century, very few deputies emerged from the working class—either rural or urban. In 1900, one could find only 30 deputies of very modest social origin, and these had mounted the social ladder either by study or union activities. Opposite them, were 175 deputies who came from the nobility and between 130 and 140 deputies born into upper-middle class families. At the end of the Third Republic, parliament presented a different social complexion: scarcely 40 nobles and patricians, against whom were ranged 110 deputies of proletarian origin and 120 deputies who came from the lower-middle class. In forty years a profound revolution had occurred in parliamentary representation.

A new transformation was produced after World War II: half of the 1,112 deputies elected in metropolitan France under the Fourth Republic originated in the middle class, and one-fifth in the lower-middle class. However, the proportion of deputies of proletarian origin did not grow under the Fourth Republic as it did in the period between the two wars.

The proportion of deputies that one may classify in the middle or lower-middle class changed from about a third for the period 1898 to 1919, to about half for the period 1919 to 1940, and to about 70 per cent for the Fourth Republic. The political ascent of the middle and lower-middle class was achieved to the detriment of the upper-middle class and the nobility. After the Republic of Dukes, after the Republic of Notables, after the Republic of the Upper-Middle Class there came, with the Fourth Republic, the reign of the Middle and Lower-Middle Class.

SOCIAL ORIGINS AND POLITICAL AFFILIATIONS

The correlation between the vocations of deputies and their political affiliations has only a limited meaning because of the numerical importance of legislators who could be considered intellectuals. On the other hand, the link between the social origins of deputies and their political leanings is clear, as Figure 4 demonstrates for the period 1898 to 1940. This figure is not rigorously precise. Not only are there difficulties in assigning deputies by the social origins of their paternal family, but also there are difficulties concerning their classification according to political tendencies. Before 1910, deputies could belong simultaneously to two or three legislative blocs; after this date, certain deputies often left one group in order to join another. The French parliament has always been characterized by a multiplicity of groups and by their instability. Besides, deputies seated for 15 or 20 years in the Chamber, without having abandoned their original political affiliation, were "pushed" toward the Right in the semicircle by the creation of new groups on the Left or by their own increased strength. In certain cases we have had to proceed arbitrarily. Nevertheless, the data which have been used to elaborate this graph were carefully established and the possible margin of error is believed to be slight.

It can be shown that the social origin of a deputy's family, with all its social-psychological implications, more often than his vocation, determined his political affiliation and orientation as a legislator. Socio-political cleavages had deep roots. In terms of social origin, there were fairly important differences between the deputies of the Right and Center-Right; similarly there were major differences between the deputies of the Left-Center and the moderates. While more than half the deputies of the Right were born into old noble or patrician families, this was true for less than a quarter of the moderate deputies and one-tenth of the deputies of the Left-Center. The proportion of deputies born into working-class families was almost twice as large among the Communists as among the Socialists and four times as great as among the Independent Socialists. The proletariat and old nobility were very rarely represented among the Radicals; two-thirds of the Radical deputies originated in the middle or lower-middle class.

For the Fourth Republic, a contrast by parties between legislators of working-class origin and the deputies coming from the old nobility or the upper-middle class is less striking than for the period 1898 to 1940, because of the importance in practically all parties of men originating in the middle or lower-middle class. Nevertheless, two-thirds of the 246 Communist deputies of the period 1945 to 1958 were sons of workers, while almost half of the deputies elected in 1951 as candidates of the Gaullists (RPF) came from upper-middle class families. More than half the deputies of other parties (Socialists, MRP, Radicals, Moderates, Poujadists) originated in middle- or lower-middle class strata.

Of 198 Socialist deputies in the Fourth Republic, only a few were sons of the proletariat, while 10 had family attachments in the upper-middle class; 90 per cent were born into families of the middle or lower-middle class. The social origins of Socialist deputies were, thus, greatly modified from one generation to the next. In the period 1900 to 1919, the socialist parliamentary group was not large, but two-thirds of its members came from working-class strata. Between the two wars, the Socialists gained many legislative seats, but only 45 per cent of their 249 representatives in this period were of working-class origin. Under the Fourth Republic, the *embourgeoisement* of the Socialists occurred. Progressively, the Socialist Party lost its working-class basis to the Communist Party, not only in its cadres and its legislative bloc, but also among the voters.

In the ranks of the MRP, a party of Catholic inspiration, there are more men of working-class origin than in the Socialist Party. We must emphasize that for the working class the roots of socio-political mobility changed, during the Fourth Republic, to the Communist Party; while the British parallel of the Socialist Party, the Labour Party, favored the political promotion of unionized workers, as did the German Social Democrats before 1932.

To sum up, the correlations between social origin and political affiliation do have significance on the French legislative scene. If the significance is not greater, one must seek the explanation in the fact that the link is no longer as strong among voters, either. The factors determining the political choices of voters include two that seem particularly important in the selection and stratification of political elites.

Political attitudes are not only a function of socio-economic factors, but also of religious sentiment. It is because of socio-economic status and religion that the MRP became, under the Fourth Republic, the party which was socially most heterogeneous among the voters and consequently among the elected candidates as well. More than any other party, men of proletarian origin were to be found in the ranks of the MRP side by side with men of middle-class origin, by virtue of their common religious beliefs. At the legislative level, with only few exceptions, notably in the Socialist Party, such men did not meet each other except in the ranks of the MRP.

French parties, with the exception of the Communist Party, seek to represent several social strata. As many authors have noticed—Seignobos, Siegfried, Goguel, Labasse, and Lavau, among others—parties do not clearly specify their social identity. Their titles are equivocal. Political etiquette has required neutralization. But this has not been a camouflage to conceal parties which corresponded definitely to social classes. It has been simply an abstraction, a mystification, the origin of which is to be found in the history of the Third Republic's beginnings. Intellectuals were largely responsible for this abstract character of political life in France. They also were the beneficiaries in the distribution of legislative seats.

For these reasons and others, in France as in most European countries, political divisions did not coincide exactly with socio-economic divisions. However, at least for the Fourth Republic, socio-political cleavages can be shown which were significant at all levels of political activity. Comparing the social composition of the electorate, the party cadres, and the legislative representatives of each political tendency, certain similarities are observable. Where workers predominate in the electoral clientele, they also predominate among militants and among legislative representatives. Where farmers are numerous among the voters, they are also numerous among party actives and among elected members. The political inclinations most welcome among the urban bourgeoisie are represented in the national assembly by many men who come from the upper-middle class. If the electoral base of a party is very heterogeneous socially, the legislative group which represents it is also heterogeneous. The degree of heterogeneity at the base is reproduced also at the summit of each political organization.

The Sequence of the Cursus Honorum

Before being elected a deputy, one must first be a candidate. In studies of political elites, how candidates are nominated is, in one sense, more important than how the electorate comes to ratify these nominations. In a legislative election, a candidacy is not improvised. A long preparation is required, either knowingly or as a result of chance events. In most cases the deputy gets to parliament only after the age of forty, but he forges the first political weapons well before this age. Where and how may he begin in political life? Which roads may he take? What hurdles must he surmount to obtain a legislative seat?

There are many roads leading to parliament, and the importance of each varies with the social milieu, the parties, and the historical periods. They may be rectilinear, or in zig-zag lines. The stages may be more or less numerous. The cursus honorum may be slow or fast. Any typology of political careers necessarily carries with it some arbitrariness. Nevertheless, one may distinguish certain sequences and ascending steps of a socio-political nature, always understanding that these distinctions simply reflect the necessities of analysis; in reality, many factors intervene simultaneously or successively in the career of the same political man.

Let us examine briefly seven considerations in the selection of legislative personnel, those which seem to us most important, at least, in France: a university education, experience in either departmental or municipal administration, journalistic affiliations, participation in party activity, work in a union or occupational organization, and accepting politics as a hereditary vocation. A special consideration should also be mentioned: participation in the resistance to the Nazis during World War II (for the Fourth Republic), or participation in the opposition before 1870 (for the first phase of the Third Republic).

Of course, other factors in the selection of legislative personnel also apply. Fortune certainly is important. Except in working-class parties, men without fortune have been handicapped. For higher officials, having been attached to a ministerial post, as a close collaborator of a political personality, was a good point of departure for a seat in parliament; several dozen higher officials followed this route. Again, having the sponsorship of a political leader was a help; many young deputies profited from it. Such leaders as Gambetta and Clémenceau were able to "name" many deputies by having them invested officially as party candidates. After 1900, for a while, Masonic lodges played a certain role in the choice of Radical candidates. Conversely, a good number of legislators were "named" and "launched" by Catholic organizations—in the 1880's as in the 1950's. One might add to the long list of factors which favor a political career: the youthful oratorical talent which leads to becoming secretary of the bar association, the skills of a pressure group's professional director, the social prestige of a nobleman, or having transformed a provincial medical practice into an electoral clientele. We set out, however, to emphasize only a few key aspects of socio-political advancement.

THE SCHOOL AND SOCIO-POLITICAL ASCENT

In France, as in all of old Europe, it is via the school that one mounts the social ladder and accedes to functions of responsibility in society. In the first decades of the Third Republic, the political elite was essentially recruited from among the graduates of the university. During this period, fewer than 1 per cent of French youth benefited from higher education; however, about three-quarters of the deputies had taken some advanced instruction before undertaking their political careers.

The university has been, for a long time, the most important nursery of political men. The proportion of deputies, however, who went through the university before engaging in politics has progressively diminished: 70 per cent for the period 1871 to 1898; nearly two-thirds between 1898 and 1919; more than 55 per cent under the Third Republic between 1919 and 1940; half under the Fourth Republic. One might enter parliament without formal education. But the university graduate has generally been better armed for a political career and has had more chances of success than the self-educated.

Since the Restoration and the Second Republic, politics has always appealed to people in university areas, from the Latin Quarter to the University of Toulouse. Biographies and memoirs of political men yield much significant evidence in this respect. Many statesmen began their political apprenticeships

Table 4

Scholastic Training of French Deputies: 1898-1940

POLITICAL TENDENCIES LEVEL AND NATURE OF STUDIES	Communists	Socialists	Ind'pt Left	Radicals	Center	Moderates	Right	Unclassified	TOTAL	NUMBER OF DEPUTIES
Law[1]	2%	15%	32%	36%	40%	39%	39%	30%	33%	(924)
Letters[2]	3	6	4	7	3	2	3	1	3	(108)
Medicine[3]	2	8	9	17	13	9	4	10	11	(304)
Science[4]	—	2	8	6	8	11	14	11	8	(211)
Training Colleges	5	11	2	3	1	1	—	—	3	(70)
Secondary and Trade Schools	2	7	14	10	15	20	27	19	15	(409)
Primary Schools	83	45	24	13	12	9	6	19	19	(523)
Not Ascertainable	3	6	7	8	8	9	7	10	8	(237)
Totals:	100	100	100	100	100	100	100	100	100	(2786)
Number of Deputies:	97	370	169	580	584	747	165	74	2786	

1. Of these 924 deputies who had been students of law, 122 had pursued studies also in the Faculty of Letters or the School of Political Science.
2. Studies offered by the Faculty of Letters: philosophy, history, geography, literature, etc.
3. Including students of pharmacy.
4. Including these major schools: Polytechnique, Centrale, Mines, Arts et Métiers, Saint-Cyr, Navale.
5. Most of the "not ascertainable" category probably did not have university educations.

while they were students. Certain famous schools were, at various times, very "politicized": L'Ecole Normale Superieure, for example, sheltered Painleve, Poincare, Thomas, Herriot, Soustelle, and many others. In his book, *From Jaurès to Léon Blum—L'Ecole Normale and Politics* (1938), Hubert Bourgin comments humorously that it had become a "political seminary." But the principal "laboratory" for training political men was the Faculty of Law, out of which came, between 1876 and 1885, nearly half of the deputies; 40 per cent between 1889 and 1893; 38 per cent from the period 1898 to 1919; 32 per cent between the two world wars; and 23 per cent of the deputies elected from metropolitan France under the Fourth Republic.

In preparing and selecting legislative personnel, the school has not played an identical role for all parties or for all periods. Most of the Socialist deputies elected before World War I ended their studies after only elementary instruction, at about the age of twelve or thirteen; some, after a few years of vocational studies at the middle level. These deputies largely entered politics through working-class unions. In contrast, only 10 per cent of the Socialist deputies of the Fourth Republic abandoned their studies before adolescence, and the majority had university training and a university style in political life.

One may establish the opposite tendency for conservative and moderate deputies. At the end of the nineteenth century, most of these had university backgrounds, while nearly half of their successors under the Fourth Republic benefited only from primary or middle-level instruction. The latter, in most cases, entered politics through agricultural unions.

These data show that the routes of political ascent vary, not only from one party to another, but also within the same political persuasion from one epoch to the next.

LOCAL OFFICES

The offices of mayor and municipal or departmental council members have been, since the start of the Third Republic, legally compatible with a seat in parliament. In a country like France, heavily centralized administratively, this was very often politically useful. At the departmental level, the prefects embodied the power of the central government, while the deputies represented the citizens. The important fact is that for many legislators the first step in their *cursus honorum* was the holding of a local elective office. The majority of candidates in legislative elections were chosen from among municipal mayors, councilmen, and departmental councilmen. This observation holds for the twentieth century as well as for the end of the nineteenth.

More than two-thirds of the deputies in the period 1900 to 1940 were elected to a local office before becoming "representatives of the nation." For the Fourth Republic, a lower proportion of deputies followed this path; after the liberation, many deputies were recruited from the Resistance cadres, secretly formed against the German occupation forces—an aspect of the *cursus honorum* which will be examined later. Still, perhaps two-fifths of the Fourth Republic deputies started out in municipal or departmental assemblies.

This sequence was the classic one for certain socio-economic categories, notably doctors, small and middle-sized farmers, hereditary proprietors of the old nobility, industrialists, and businessmen. Other occupational categories could more easily skip the local step. Deputies who did not have local political attachments were mostly higher administrative officials, university professors, Parisian journalists, higher-level executives, or big businessmen.

The importance of this sequence has varied also according to political tendencies. Many Socialists, Communists, Radicals and Popular Republicans were party militants before being candidates in legislative or senatorial elections. Other political groups more often recruited their local cadres from among men who had already exercised the functions of municipal or departmental councilmen or mayor. Local office holders were already known by the voters of the constituency; they had resources in the form of "connections"; they enjoyed a certain popularity. Moreover, the Parisian leaders of moderate political groups were interested in recruiting them and in giving them official party endorsements. To put it another way, the conservative deputy of the Third Republic normally began as an independent candidate in local elections. The patronage which he later obtained was a confirmation of his initial political successes on the local level.

In this regard, there are important national differences. In Great Britain, it is above all the working-class deputies who have had experience in local administration, while the majority of Conservative deputies go directly to Westminster. In Italy, since 1946, deputies have only rarely been recruited from among municipal or provincial councilmen, and the legislators who take local offices are comparatively few in number. Italian parties have relatively numerous incumbents for which offices must be found—therefore, personal accumulation of offices is avoided as much as possible. Moreover, Italian law prevents holding a legislative office and that of mayor in cities of more than 30,000.

When they run as candidates for election to the French Chamber, local office-holders do not fail to make a point of their services rendered to the *commune or département*: "I solicit your votes because I have a long experience in municipal and district administration"; or, "I have been president of your departmental assembly for twelve years and I know the problems of our constituency"; or "Thousands of good men have spoken to me in the hearings which I have regularly held in the town hall"; and so on. A content analysis of electoral propaganda, notably the "declarations of belief," which would-be deputies have addressed to voters since 1881, throws light on the importance of experience in local affairs before "climbing" to Paris.

Fewer men followed this path in reverse, and they were usually seeking local offices to consolidate their legislative positions.

Under the Third Republic, departmental councilmen normally obtained in legislative elections more votes in their own *cantons* than they did in other *cantons* of the constituency. Under the Fourth Republic (which adopted *scrutin de liste),* the candidate at the head of the list preferred to choose as his running mates councilmen from other *cantons*.

JOURNALISM

To be elected it is first necessary to be known; one must disseminate a program and propagandize. For the candidate, the press is a means of making himself known to the voters of a constituency. For the deputy, the press is a means of maintaining contact with his voters with a view to re-election.

Under the Third Republic, the embryonic organization of many political groups or coalitions of groups was the editorial board of a newspaper. In the absence of organized parties with many members, the editorial boards of certain large newspapers sometimes played roles as executive committees for political groups.

The French press has long been very decentralized; the circulation of the provincial press—made up of a very large number of small local or regional newspapers—has on certain occasions been larger than that of the Parisian press. The man who sought a legislative seat had to assure himself of a newspaper's support, or found a new periodical. Often, running a newspaper was a point of departure for parliament.

One may distinguish three types of parliamentary journalists. The first is the authentic journalist who came to politics through journalism, the man whose principal political weapon is his newspaper. The second is the legislator who is not a professional journalist, much less a first-class one, but a person for whom a newspaper is nevertheless one of the means of action and attack. He has not come to politics through journalism—rather, political activity has led him to an interest in journalism. First he was a political militant, then a political journalist, finally a deputy. The third is the amateur journalist—the occasional journalist who is neither publisher, nor editor, nor regular contributor to a newspaper. He simply collaborates with various newspapers in his constituency. This kind of legislator, for whom the press has not really been a political device, is very common, so much so that it is scarcely an exaggeration to say that every legislator is a part-time journalist. In his book, *The Parliamentary Profession* (1937), Andre Tardieu remarks, "all members of the parliamentary profession need journals, but not all in the same way. Parliamentarians of the first rank need journals with a large circulation . . . and parliamentarians of the middle rank small local journals. . . . No provincial journal is without a parliamentary representative, and reciprocally, no parliamentarian is without a journal."

It is difficult to establish precisely the numerical importance of each of these three types of parliamentary journalists and to measure how political careers have been advanced by journalism. However, for the period 1898 to 1940, out of a total of 2,786 deputies, at least 900—that is, one-third— found in journalism a route for rising, to some degree at least, in the political hierarchy. Among these, about one hundred fifty were professional journalists, and two hundred fifty to three hundred started in a different occupation but became regular journalistic contributors before reaching the legislature.

The link between political advancement and journalism has not been the same in all sectors of public opinion represented in the legislature. Under the Third Republic, it diminished—going from Left to Right. During the Fourth Republic, other routes were used more often to accede to the Palais-Bourbon, so that journalism sometimes became superfluous; about a sixth of the deputies of the Fourth Republic, compared with a third of their predecessors, had their *cursus honorum* in politics marked by journalistic activity. This leaves out those deputies named to head party newspapers because they enjoyed parliamentary immunity; it is not easy to apply legal sanctions to the responsible head of a publication while he is a member of the national legislature.

Max Weber observed, after World War I, that in a greater and greater measure, politics was being carried on publicly with spoken or written words; for this reason, the political publicist and particularly the journalist had become the most important representative of "the parliamentary species." However, in France, in contrast with Germany, the silhouette of the journalist in the parliamentary milieu is the more prominent, the further back in time. History retains the names of Louis Blanc, Brisson, Thiers, Jules Ferry, Raspail, Paul Bert, Deschanel, Pelletan, De Rémusat, Laboulaye, and many others. History has already forgotten the names of most of the journalist-legislators who functioned toward the end of the Third Republic. Nevertheless, at any time in legislative history, among the most influential people are those whose political advancement was, at the start, made through journalism—such as Jules Guesde, De Jouvenel, Yvon Delbos, or Francisque Gay. Many of the heads of parties in the Fourth Republic began their careers as journalists: Bidault, the leader of the MRP; Daniel Mayer, Secretary

General of the Socialist Party; Martinaud-Deplat, Secretary General of the Radical Party; Cachin, one of the secretaries of the Communist Party, and so on, as well as many men who exercised governmental functions.

PARTY ACTIVITY

Those deputies who belonged to well-organized parties with many militants and many followers—notably the Communists, Socialists, Radicals in certain regions, and Popular Republicans—were, in most cases, workers in the regional or departmental organizations of their party before they were named as official party candidates for the Chamber or the Senate. It is apparently necessary to gain credentials in the party organization before being able to reap the honor of carrying the party flag and representing it in elections. Certain parties, notably the Socialists, require of their candidates many years as a party militant. Even when such a requirement is not formally imposed, a man who has not been active for many years is usually not known by the party's departmental sections. Isolated, he has few chances of obtaining the nomination.

Militant activity in a party favors political promotion in two ways: by the apprenticeship which it provides and by the relationships which it establishes. It is necessary to learn the techniques and rules of the game; it is necessary to present evidence of one's capacities and loyalty. The militant must make a name for himself, exercise greater and greater responsibilities, and show himself to be patient (up until the moment when the deputy resigns or dies), before his hour approaches.

Normally, Communist or Socialist candidates were, when nominated, responsible to local party units, as departmental committee members if not secretaries of departmental organizations. In the Socialist Party, combining legislative office with the office of departmental committee head was very common. The Communist Party practiced a division of labor: when a board secretary became deputy, another militant was placed at the local organization's head. The Radical Party kept alive the hope of dividing honors in order to manipulate the susceptibilities of certain local personalities; in fact, most of the Radical deputies did not preside over their constituency committees, although in practice they often dominated them.

A political career in a party and by a party is only possible if there are parties. Under the Third Republic, there were none that represented the moderate sectors of opinion. In the Fourth Republic, there were two parties not of the Left which were relatively well organized: the MRP (Catholic) and the RPF (Gaullists). The former was established immediately after the liberation, but many of its deputies came from the ranks of Catholic organizations; the latter, founded in 1947, had a very short existence, and most of its deputies came from the resistance hierarchy. Political careers formed through the route of the party have been much more common in Great Britain, Weimar Germany, the Scandinavian countries, or republican Italy than in France.

UNION WORK

For industrial workers and salaried employees, the political ladder more often begins in the union. Typically, men of these modest social origins were militant unionists before becoming militant politicians, union leaders on the regional or national level before becoming deputies. They prepared for their political activities by union activity. A miner, a metalworker, a railway employee, or white-collar worker has, in practice, scarcely any possibility of a political career if he is not known and appreciated by his fellow workers, and if he is not influential in his union. Union organization and promotion indirectly facilitates rising in the party's municipal, departmental, or regional hierarchy. For workers, salaried persons, and petty officers, the party hierarchy is the only source of municipal, cantonal, or departmental offices; and, in turn, it is generally necessary to hold one of these offices before seeking a legislative seat.

This *cursus honorum* is typical, but the number of deputies who were originally workers or salaried persons has never been great in the French parliament. French unionism has remained outside of parliamentary life for a long time. An apolitical constitution adopted by the Union Congress of 1906 has had its consequences for the advancement of workers in parliament. Union leaders from Pelloutier to Jouhaux have rarely been members of parliament. Unionism has only very lately become a means of access to parliament. In 1936, at the time of the Popular Front, one-quarter of the Socialist deputies were union members. At that time, too, most of the Communist deputies came from union organizations, but the Communist group was not large—one of the reasons for underrepresentation of the Communist vote being the electoral system. Twenty years later, in 1956, one Communist deputy out of two, one Socialist deputy out of five, one MRP deputy out of ten was a union member.

In contrast with the British Labour Party and the German Social Democratic Party, the Socialist Party did not owe its life and its power to the union movement. Furthermore, the importance of the union route in the selection of deputies is tending to decrease in many other countries. In Great Britain before 1940, more than half of the Labour deputies came from unions, compared with a third since 1945. In the Bonn Republic, as compared with the Weimar Republic, German deputies who have made their careers in and through the Social Democratic party, that is to say the party officers, are more numerous than are the unionists. In Italy, only a quarter of the Socialist and Communist deputies from 1946 to 1958 followed the union route. One might establish a sociological rule for most European countries which holds for the first half of the twentieth century: as the number of Socialist and Communist deputies increases, the proportion of unionists among the deputies in these blocs tends to decrease.

HEREDITARY POLITICAL VOCATIONS

Access to parliament by a hereditary path has been more frequent than is generally imagined. In this regard, we may distinguish three categories of deputies.

First, there are sons of the great political families of the Monarchy or of the Empire. One finds them in rather large numbers in the early assemblies of the Third Republic: De Broglie, De la Rochefoucauld, Bonaparte, Colbert, De Breteuil, De Chabaud-Latour, De Choiseul-Praslin, Decazes, Duvergier, De Hauranne, De Girardin, D'Harcourt, De Juigné, De Rohan-Chabot, and one hundred others. Certain of these families were represented in parliament under the Third Republic by two or three deputies or senators, sometimes by four or five.

The second type of deputy following a hereditary path is one who, by virtue of being a nobleman, a squire, or a great landed proprietor, possesses a very good electoral situation: the electoral constituency has been in effect a familial fief. When a father dies, one of his sons succeeds him in parliament. The seat as deputy has been transmitted from father to son or uncle to nephew in the same way as the family fortune. The phenomenon of political inheritance may be seen in all French areas, but most particularly in north-western and southwestern France and in Corsica. We may estimate that more than three hundred deputies of the Third Republic inherited from an ancestor their electoral support and parliamentary seats—and sometimes also their particular political ideology. These hereditary deputies were seated, with rare exceptions, among the ranks of conservatives. They grew up, in the heart of their families, in a political atmosphere; but one might say, in Max Weber's terms, that most of them neither lived from politics nor for politics. They derived their income from other sources. In contrast with their British counterparts, they adapted themselves rather poorly to the economic evolution of their country. Few of them gave up their land in order to invest capital in industry. Their conservatism was landed conservatism. Generally, a political career was not for them a means of enrichment. At the time of their election they already belonged to the social elite. They represented traditional forces—economically, morally, and politically. Very few of them were illustrious in the political life of the nation, but they were well known and popular in their local electoral constituencies.

The third type of deputy following a hereditary political vocation is the product of universal suffrage. He can be distinguished clearly enough from the two other types. He came from the upper and middle bourgeoisie and not from the old nobility. His political affiliations were generally Republican and often oriented to the Left. What he inherited, above all, was an interest in politics, if not a political passion. Sometimes he was the son, grandson, great-grandson, or even the nephew of a legislator of the First, Second, or Third Republic, or perhaps of a liberal legislator during the Monarchy or the Empire. However, he did not secure his parliamentary seat as an inheritance or as family property; he had to gain it himself. Again, he might be a son, grandson, or nephew of a journalist or political writer, of a prefect or other higher officer, of a mayor or a departmental or municipal councilman, and so forth. Admittedly, this family background might better prepare him for a political career, since his name would be known by the voters, and he might more easily obtain his party's nomination or the support of para-political organizations, thanks to the connections of his family. It was not a question, however, of inheriting the parliamentary seat itself. The inheritance was, rather, of a social-psychological nature: an inclination for politics. This third type of political inheritance was found among at least six hundred deputies under the Third Republic and about one hundred fifty deputies in the Fourth Republic. More than half of them were relatives of members of parliament.

One may estimate that, altogether, about a thousand deputies of the Third Republic received a political inheritance in one form or another. However, the importance of each of these three types of deputies benefiting from political inheritance varies considerably over time. The first type was common during the first twenty years of the Third Republic. The second was significant throughout the Third Republic but has declined progressively since 1900. The third type is renewed with each generation.

THE RESISTANCE

The routes just indicated were followed, in France, by most deputies in "normal" times. But the deputies elected at the start of the Third Republic and at the start of the Fourth Republic must be given special attention. It is necessary to keep in mind a new aspect of the *cursus honorum:* opposition to the defunct regime. The changes of regime in 1870 and 1945 were ac-companied by changes in political personnel. The adversaries become the rulers.

Many deputies elected during the first phase of the Third Republic had begun their political careers before 1870 by creating an intransigent opposi-tion to the government of the Second Empire. Almost a quarter of the deputies elected in 1871 were known for their resistance to the imperial regime. The great majority of these former opponents were Republicans, and most Re-publican deputies had been intransigents.

The elections of 1871 were a success for the monarchists becaus? they had foreseen the peace with Germany. The Assembly elected in 1876 in-cluded a larger proportion of Republican deputies and former opponents of the Empire. In fact, out of the total of 526 deputies elected in 1876, there were 171 who had opposed the Empire. Nor did their numbers diminish in the Assembly elected in 1877. In the years that followed, there was a progressive diminution in the number of Empire opponents, but this fact may be explained by the aging of the generation which was politically mature under the Second Empire. Still, out of 577 deputies elected in 1885, 102 forged their first political weapons in resistance against Napoleon III and his regime. In 1893, a quarter of a century after the fall of the Empire, one still finds in the Chamber a group of 70 deputies who had fought for the Republic under the Empire.

As for the resistance to the Vichy regime and the German occupation, we may say that the network of the Resistance flowed into the political arena. Passive resistance to the occupation was a fact for the large majority of the French population. But the Resistance network did not include, most likely, more than 1 to 2 per cent of the adult population. By active resisters, we mean the organizers, directors, members of secret movements, members of the Free French movement, those condemned to death, political deportees, interned persons, the *maquisards* and the "escapees." From this very small

Table 5

Selection of Legislators in the Fourth Republic From the Ranks of the Resistance

	Communists	Socialists	Radicals	MRP	Moderates	Gaullists	Poujadists	Unclassified	TOTAL
1) Deportees, condemned to death, arrested by Gestapo, interned, anti-Pétain deputies in 1940:	24	27	13	10	14	11	—	2	101
2) Resistance from abroad— London, Algiers, etc.; followers of Gen. de Gaulle:	7	5	17	11	7	16	3	8	74
3) Founders and heads of the Resistance; leaders of Free French, of secret unions, of political organizations:	42	27	5	21	5	13	1	6	120
4) Cadre and actives in the Resistance and in other secret groups:	161	87	14	65	6	13	1	8	355
5) "Compagnons de la liberation" and holders of the "Medaille de la Ressistance," not classified under the preceding rubrics:	—	24	7	15	3	7	—	3	59
6) Holders of Croix de Guerre or other military honors (1939-45):	—	4	16	8	10	10	4	1	53
7) Prisoners of war not otherwise classified:	—	2	3	2	3	3	5	1	19
Not Active in the Resistance									
Under 21 in 1943:	12	—	1	2	3	—	3	—	21
Over 21 in 1943:		15	32	43	69	7	19	5	190
No accurate information	—	7	13	39	22	11	5	6	103
Collaborators and retainers of official posts during the Vichy regime	—	—	3	—	10	—	3	1	17
Total deputies elected in metropolitan France:	246	198	124	216	152	91	44	41	1,112

NOTE: This table is additive, but certain deputies could have been classed under several rubrics. Those classified under a given rubric are **not** here classified under other rubrics. Some classifications are necessarily arbitrary, and it is probable that lacunae exist in the documentation available. It is estimated, however, that most deputies classed under the heading "No accurate information" were **not** active participants in the Resistance.

minority of active resisters, came 80 per cent of the deputies elected after
the liberation in 1945 or 1946. Two-thirds of the deputies elected in 1951
and 1956 were also former members of the Resistance. The proportion would
be ever higher if one left aside those new deputies who were not adults
during the war years. The number of resisters was high in practically all
parties, notably among the Communists, Socialists, Gaullists, and Popular
Republicans. But among the moderate bloc and the Poujadists, resisters did
not constitute the majority.

The important fact here is not that the voters chose candidates who
could claim the title of "member of the Resistance." Rather, parties chose
their candidates from among the resistance movement—more especially, the
cadres of the Resistance became the party cadres. Immediately following the
liberation, parties were disorganized. They emerged from secrecy. Some
were reconstituted by the leaders of the Resistance. Other resisters created
new groups. Communists and nationalists, Catholics and laymen, socialists and
conservatists had met side by side in the ranks of the Resistance. Thereafter
they were separated, but they had been in all cases best placed for political
promotion. Activity in the Resistance is the principal aspect of the *cursus
honorum* of parliamentarians in the Fourth Republic, and this is not only
true from the numerical point of view.

The role of the Resistance in the selection of the political elite is shown
also in the choice of many leaders from among men who exercised functions
of great responsibility in the Resistance. Leaders of parties were, for the
most part, chiefs of resistance movements. Most ministers were chosen from
among famous members of the Resistance. Many political men of the first
rank had been Resistance figures of the first rank: General de Gaulle, Presidents Auriol, Queuille, Pléven, Mendès-France, René Mayer, Edgar Faure,
Gouin, Jules Moch, Le Troquer. Presidents Blum, Paul Reynaud, Robert
Schumann and Marie had been deported, as well as fifteen ministers of the
Fourth Republic. About twenty other ministers had been imprisoned under
the occupation. Presidents Bidault and Laniel directed the National Council
of the Resistance, and approximately thirty ministers directed secret movements—Combat, Franc-Tireur, Libération-Nord, Ceux de la Resistance,
Cahors-Asturies, Alsace-Lorraine, Béarn, and so on.

In other countries, too, former members of the Resistance and former
prisoners became political men; participation in the Resistance as a stage in
the *cursus honorum* was common in Italy, as well as in Holland, Norway,
and Denmark.

Conclusions

Whatever may have been their original occupation, once elected, deputies
ceased to pursue it, with rare exceptions. They had to give nearly all their
time to political activity. Parliamentary activity was all absorbing. Sessions
normally lasted from eight months to a year, although attendance at all
chamber sittings was not obligatory. During the session, provincial deputies

came into Paris almost every week, and most of them remained in the capital four or five days a week. Committee work and conferences of parliamentary groups, transacting legislative correspondence (certain deputies received hundreds of letters each month, to which they replied), the political discussions, intervening for constituents with the central bureaucracy, preparing for debate, drafting legislative proposals, and thousands of other tasks left them scarcely any time to pursue other occupations.

When he returned to his constituency for a week end, the typical deputy was visited by many voters who sought his help in their personal affairs, requesting his intervention with the prefecture, the mayoralty, or some other level of bureaucracy. He also tried to make his constituency rounds, since his re-election depended on maintaining contact with his voters. Deputies who were responsible for the preparation of reports on proposed legislation, deputies who presided over legislative committees, and deputies who were the leaders of parties or other political groups had still greater demands made on their time.

Although deputies were fully occupied, and although since 1910 they received a salary that assured them of financial resources sufficient to meet their needs and provide for their families, still it is difficult to conclude that the majority of them were professional political men.

As we have noticed, few deputies had long legislative careers. Both before their first election and after their last term, the majority were engaged in an occupation, from which most of their income derived. Moreover, nearly half the deputies in the Third Republic began their legislative careers after the age of forty-five. Although a third of the deputies did start before the age of forty, most of these did not retain their seats for more than four or eight years.

In France, apart from a legislative career, men who lived by politics were few in number. The political parties had few permanent salaried workers, and local elective posts, such as that of mayor, paid poorly—except in certain larger cities. Only since 1930 have certain men been able to engage in stable and salaried political activity, in unions or professional associations.

If we eliminate those who had only brief legislative careers, the deputies during the period 1870 to 1940 who might then be considered as professional men constitute approximately one-fifth of the total number: about a thousand out of a total of 4,892 deputies.

Of course, the idea of a professional political man can be given a larger meaning to include the man who enters politics very early, well before his election to the legislature, and who becomes intensely active politically while continuing his occupation, using it for political purposes. This type would include the higher-level bureaucrats who had long been ministerial assistants, political journalists, teachers who often gave as much time to politics as to teaching, lawyers who took political cases, and so forth. In this sense of the term, the number of professional political men may be considered twice as large. No special preparation was necessary to enter upon a legislative career, and, quite naturally, a large part of the legislative personnel was recruited from occupations or activities close to politics:

journalism, the higher civil service, the bar, unions, and so forth. The parapolitical profession leads to politics. But it tends to produce semiprofessional political men.

During the last half century, political problems have become increasingly technical. The versatile politician has progressively yielded to the political specialist; the dilettante, to the expert; the wealthy notable, to the economic specialist. Certain types of professional political men were increasingly replaced by others less broadly cultured, but whose competence in a limited field was greater.

Having noted this trend, one may still distinguish among legislators, and particularly among professional political men, several types: the doctrinaire and the tactician, the idealist and the realist, the man who persuades and the man who commands, the propagandist and the organizer, he who circulates in official circles and he who works in committees, the national personality and the local celebrity, the squire and the literati, the government official and the temperamental oppositionalist, the sincere man and the hypocrite, the intriguer and the conciliator, the calm man and the passionate man, the conservative and the revolutionary. Parliamentary fauna present great diversity indeed, in "the Republic of Dukes" and "the Republic of Committees," described by Daniel Halévy, as well as in "the Republic in Congress" (R. de Jouvenel), "the provincial Republic" (J. Fourçade), "the Republic of Parties" or the "Republic of Deputies" (R. Priouret).

In spite of diversity, legislators of all epochs and all political persuasions had one thing in common, evidenced from numerous autobiographies, confessions, and memoirs: the *will* to make a political career. One does not involuntarily become a political man. In order to be a legislator, a man must first wish to be one, even if, out of modesty, he does not acknowledge it. To enter into public affairs, he must take the initiative; he will not be solicited unless he draws attention to himself. A simple calculation enables us to say that during the 90 years of the Third Republic and of the Fourth, nearly 40,000 men were candidates in assembly elections. Many tried three or four times without success; only 6,000 were ever elected.

If, in identifying a political elite, it is necessary to consider success as important a factor as intelligence, power, influence, and so forth, then these 6,000 deputies were an elite, for they were chosen from among many actual candidates, who in turn were selected from a still larger number of virtual candidates. But of these 6,000 deputies, how many played a truly important role in political life? How many have left a name in French political history?

One may assume that the alphabetical indexes of the twenty or thirty principal works of political and social history on the Third and Fourth Republics would largely include the names of the most important political men from 1870 to 1958. Providing these works are chosen carefully and obvious gaps are filled in, one may find here the names of those who were most influential in the political arena. This technique for identifying political personalities of the first order is subject to some errors. Nevertheless, it is one of the most serviceable and objective when examining the distant political past.

Out of 2,000 names thus listed, only 1,500 are those of legislators. In other words, many of the great political personalities never sat in parliament. Very often, they were not even political men in the strict sense of the term. They included high military officers, talented journalists, diplomats, higher civil servants, church dignitaries, and writers. On the other hand, many of the parliamentarians whose names *do* figure in the alphabetical indexes of these historical works were ministers, or leaders in parties, unions, or para-political groups who had published works of political doctrine, held important posts in the higher civil service, or had been captains of industry. It is largely because of their activity *outside* the legislature that they are mentioned in political history.

Nevertheless, during the Third and Fourth Republics in France, in contrast to most other Western democracies of that period, the center of political gravity was the legislature—except during World War I. Under the Fifth Republic, it centers in the presidency. But for how long? In Great Britain, the Government has long held the reigns of State. Under the Weimar Republic, with its well-organized political parties, political initiative came from party headquarters. Elsewhere, it was the court circle, the higher administration, or the army that provided the main political machinery. The ministerial instability that France experienced for ninety years was the result of the total power of a divided legislature, which, in Gambetta's phrase, gave the appearance of a "broken mirror." It was a legislature lacking organized parties and often cut off from the real country. In it, to use Schumpeter's formula, "the political profession developed autonomous interests." Personal rivalries were given free reign; the rhetoricians, the lecturers, and the doctrinaires participated in a sterile game.

The idea of legislative representation has two meanings: an image in miniature of the electoral body or a selection of the best ruling class. The French legislature, like all legislatures, did not reflect by its composition the social structure of the country. Nor does it seem arbitrary to say that among the deputies of the Third and Fourth Republics were relatively few of the best men in France. Electoral contests kept many men of great worth out of parliament—unfortunate candidates beaten by experts at garnering electoral support, by men with a parochial viewpoint who knew how to meet the voters on their own level.

In each legislative assembly, there were several personalities of great worth, not all of whom were professional political men. But the majority were men of average or even mediocre ability, and this fact, together with the rules of the parliamentary game, limited considerably the influence of vigorous personalities. The votes of deputies are counted, they are not weighted. For this reason, ordinary deputies, deputies without vision, although they are unnoticeable during the legislative debates or in the work of committees, although they are, as *individuals,* inconspicuous figures, nevertheless possess collectively a political role of great importance. In this sense, it is more important for political sociology to study the typical deputy than to gather evidence about the atypical personalities.

iii

Changes in British Labour Leadership*

by W. L. GUTTSMAN

Introduction

THIS ACCOUNT of the development, structure, and function of the leadership of the British Labour Party has been conceived primarily as a socio-historical study. The history of the Labour Party has, so far, been written largely in terms of its policy and of the spread and working of its organization. By concentrating on the leading strata of the party I hope to fill some gaps in existing accounts and, further, to add to our understanding of elite-formation and of attitudes toward political leadership in working-class mass organizations.

Insofar as this is a historical study it should be made clear from the outset that it is based almost entirely on printed and published sources. No interviews with Labour politicians were conducted, nor were manuscripts or archival sources used to any significant extent.[1] The value of this type of analysis must lie in the approach and interpretation, not in the discovery of entirely new facts.

A sociological analysis of the leadership of a political party, such as is

---

*This paper was completed in the summer of 1959. It does not, therefore, take into account the deep conflict inside the Labour Party and its leadership which followed its defeat in the General Election of October 1959.

attempted in this paper, must seek to study definite groups over a definite period of time. Labour parliamentarians and Cabinet Ministers are suitable groups for such an investigation because they are clearly delimited and institutionalized groups of manageable size. The period chosen was from 1906—when a sizeable group of Labour M.P.'s entered Parliament for the first time—to 1955.[2] Members of Parliament and Cabinet Ministers are responsible for political decisions on the executive and the legislative plane, and they undoubtedly occupy leadership positions. Are they, however, *the* Labour leaders, or are there significant elements in the national leadership of the Labour Party who do not enter the House of Commons? Furthermore, do those who emerge as leading personalities inside the Parliamentary Labour Party tend to be selected for Cabinet office if and when opportunity presents itself? I think that with the growth of Labour's parliamentary representation and with the decline of sectional organizations within the party the national leadership has become increasingly synonymous with the group of Labour M.P.'s.[3] Those who reached prominent positions in the labour movement have drifted sooner or later into Parliament, and, in the struggle to achieve national renown, membership in Parliament is a considerable asset.

The representativeness of the group which reaches the Cabinet is more difficult to assess. The conventions governing the selection of men for membership in the Cabinet and the administration in general mean that we are concerned with a selection process in a homogeneous milieu. However, while the Prime Minister must choose parliamentarians—largely, members of the House of Commons—for his Cabinet, he will nevertheless take into account other factors than the individual's position in the party in making his choice. He will no doubt think twice before neglecting the representatives of important minority groups, but he can, on the other hand, influence the composition of the top-most party leadership by his choice. To a considerable extent, Cabinet membership determines present-day and future leadership position.[3a] These problems will be discussed later.

The only men who are influential in the Labour Party and who are not included in the above groups are those trade union leaders who participate to a significant extent in the *political* activities of the labour movement without occupying formal political or parliamentary positions. Their influence is based solely on their position in the industrial movement. To have included this group would, however, have presented considerable problems of definition and selection. By studying the men who occupy the trade union seats on the National Executives of the Labour Party, we would have missed many of the really influential trade union leaders. Even if a representative group could have been found, the paucity of biographical material would have presented serious obstacles to evaluating their role and contribution. I therefore decided to omit this group except for those trade union leaders who were in Parliament.[4]

The occupational and educational backgrounds of Labour leaders have been analyzed, as these two factors are the most telling indicators of class and social status. In order to pinpoint changes, I have contrasted both groups at different periods of time. The sociological analysis may help us to understand other divisions within the wider political elite. Labour movements, especially those exercising governmental power or aiming to do so, are customarily rent by a conflict between a "left" and a "right" wing—between conservative "go-slowers" and radical "whole-hoggers." To throw light on this phenomenon, the social antecedents of those members of the Parliamentary Labour Party (PLP) who have shown determined opposition to certain aspects of Labour policy are examined. While this "left-wing" is not a socially homogeneous subgroup of the elite, there are indications that, even *within* the labour movement, social background and career lines are correlated with political attitudes.

A merely formal analysis of the leadership of the Labour Party would, however, be of limited interest. The British labour movement has a strongly democratic tradition and greatly developed local loyalties. From a loose federation of trade unions and socialist societies composed almost entirely of working-class men and women, it grew into a nation-wide organization, centrally directed and with a significant portion of members belonging to the middle class. Professional people and white-collar workers are especially noticeable among the group of active party workers and in local management committees, who, among other things, select the party's parliamentary candidates.[5]

The Labour Party elite must be seen against this background, and I have sought to take account of the ideological factor and of the changing and conflicting concepts of the role of political leadership held by Labour leaders. To understand the early antagonism between the Labour leadership and the serried ranks of aristocratic and bourgeois politicians whom they encountered in the House of Commons, we must consider not only the social gulf which existed originally between the two groups but also the existence in Labour's ranks of an antitraditional attitude toward political power. In the course of its evolution, Labour leadership grew gradually into the existing pattern of the British political elite without, however, losing its own identity. Its personnel has been increasingly recruited from the ranks of the middle class. Its concepts of leadership have widely assimilated the attitudes that had been customarily held by men of the older political parties. This process was, no doubt, facilitated by changes in the character of political representation as such; it must be seen against the background of a changing society, which has opened and widened avenues of social mobility. All of this affects the political-selection process and the character and composition of a socialist party. The *embourgeoisement* of the Labour Party is nevertheless a surprising phenomenon. I believe it is of general significance for our understanding of the social movements of the West European social-democratic type, as well as of the relationship between the working class and its elite.

In investigating the backgrounds and careers of Labour politicians, I had to rely in most cases on a variety of biographical reference works. Entries in these are admittedly brief and sometimes inadequate. They are also subject to falsification—deliberate and involuntary. By using a number of different sources and by cross-checking data, an attempt was made to make these as reliable as possible.[6] For the group of Cabinet Ministers and for a number of other Labour politicians who achieved renown much fuller sources were often available. The biographies, autobiographies, and other memoir literature which record their lives have been used here for the social analysis of Cabinet membership as well as for the more general discussion of leadership inside the Labour Party. In addition, the reports of party conferences, contemporary pamphlet literature, and to some extent the socialist periodical press were used to bring out the salient points of the discussion on Labour leadership and to illustrate the ideological dimensions.

The use of this latter kind of material poses no special problems. The views of individuals taken from their own speeches and writings at the time can be accepted as evidence of current opinion, provided a fair selection is made. This is not so with the biographical, autobiographical, and memoir literature. The reporter or the biographer is obviously not an objective observer: he writes after the event—often with a delay of years, perhaps decades—and even if he is not writing an "apologia" or presenting a case, he is selective in his narrative. May we really use isolated references to behaviour and attitudes, lifted in turn from selective and retrospectively written accounts, as the basis of sociological generalizations? The problems raised are akin to those with which the methodology of historiography continues to battle, but only specific points relevant to this study can be discussed here.

We are mainly concerned with three types of evidence: statements made by individuals about their own attitudes and actions; factual evidence about the actions of others; and evaluations of the actions of others and inter-pretation of their attitudes. Of these, it is the last type which seems most liable to be distorted. To give a concrete example of this, Beatrice Webb is quoted repeatedly as a witness of the social climbing and social distance inside the labour movement and its ruling group. But we know that her slightly priggish and moralizing defiance of "Society" may have colored her judgment of the motives of others in this respect. If we do utilize her diaries, it is because they constitute one of the few contemporary accounts of the labour movement available so far and also because, as a highly intelligent observer, she sees beyond outward appearances. In any case, the quotations used in these as in other instances should be regarded as being more in the nature of illustrations of general propositions advanced than of their proof. An analysis of this kind must start with certain hypotheses about the kind of tensions likely to develop inside the Labour Party elite. Such hypotheses derive in part from the formal social analysis of its personnel and the study of Labour ideology on the subject of leadership, and also from the general impression created by the study of Labour Party history.

In the discussion of ministerial experience, biographical and memoir literature will generally form the bulk of the actual raw material, and the comparatively small volume of this kind of literature means that there will be less scope for generalizations. The evidence which emerges from an individual's life history can, however, often be tested by relating it to what we know otherwise about his actions and their contemporary assessment. Sidney Webb's undue deference to the views of his advisers, general cautiousness, and a certain lack of political touch emerge already from Beatrice's diary. It is pinpointed in the contemporary discussion, and we find confirmation of it in later assessments.[7]

In general, we must conclude that the evidence which is available is unlikely ever to permit a kind of quantifying analysis. The most we can hope for is to be able to describe and classify the kinds of attitudes that may be observed and to diagnose typical and deviant behaviour.

The Emergence of a Parliamentary Party

The party which in 1906 astounded itself and the British public by returning twenty-nine members of the House of Commons would hardly have imagined that after ten years some of its members would occupy the front bench. Only its more far-sighted and politically conscious leaders would have thought that within less than a generation a party which was at least formally committed to carry out a socialist policy would exercise governmental power—but not parliamentary control—in Great Britain.

The men who were elected in 1906 were a mixed lot. Professed socialists like Keir Hardie and MacDonald, and Snowden mixed with independently thinking trade union leaders—Clynes, Crooks, and Hodge—as well as with those who were really Liberals at heart—Shackleton, Bowerman, or Roberts. The majority of them owed their success at the polls to electoral agreements with the Liberals, or at best, they were returned on minority votes in three-cornered contests.[8]

The very basis of the Labour Representation Committee's success, therefore, implies that there were severe limitations to the political freedom to maneuver which the newly constituted Labour Party enjoyed. Many felt warmly toward Liberals and most of them were electorally tied to the Liberal Party. Individual members of the PLP frequently defied the party whip, either by abstaining from a vote or by opposing their colleagues in the division lobby. For example, M.P.'s representing strong interests in shipbuilding or naval activities tended to vote with the government in support of the naval estimates.[9]

After 1910, a vote against the government could, under certain circumstances, entail its defeat and bring on a general election, where the success of those who might face Liberal opposition instead of co-operation would be in the balance. This situation brought about the first sustained discussion as to the role and purpose of Labour leadership.

From the very start, however, Labour's role had been circumscribed by the limited objectives which the Labour Representation Committee (LRC) had set itself. During the first decade of its existence, in putting itself forward as the spokesman of "Labour," it thought in terms of the specific interests of an economic group and did not conceive itself to be the spokesman of the general community's interests. The 1906 election manifesto of the LRC, endorsed by each candidate, spoke of the House of Commons which "is supposed to be the people's house and yet the people are not there. Landlords, employers, lawyers, brewers and financiers are there in force, why not Labour? The Trade Unions ask the same liberty as capital yet they are refused. . . ." This allusion to the encroachment on trade union liberty by judicial decisions (such as the Taff-Vale case) precedes reference to a small list of specific reforms and, finally, in a general way, the need for the social amelioration of the condition of the very poor.

Without exception, the twenty-nine men who were elected under LRC auspices were men of working-class background. Labour leaders of middle-class origin who came predominantly from the ranks of the Fabian Society, the Social Democratic Federation, and to a lesser extent the ILP, either did not seek election, or if they did, were unsuccessful like J. B. Glasier. The picture is in no way different if we add to this group the twenty-odd Lib-Lab M.P.'s (i.e., those trade unionists, mostly miners, who sat on the Liberal benches until 1906 when the majority joined the Labour group). Labour and Lib-Lab M.P.'s alike were born mostly in the 1850's and 1860's and, thus, did not benefit from the Education Act of 1870. Although the majority had received some formal schooling, it rarely extended into their teens. Their subsequent self-education must be seen against this background. From their own accounts of their early reading and of the books which influenced them most, an interesting picture emerges.[10] We find that specific socialist literature is referred to only by a minority, and even the English utopian thinkers and philosophical radicals are, with the exception of John Stuart Mill, rarely mentioned. Of later reformers, Henry George's name is frequently given. There is some influence of the Fabians and two lone voices mentioned Marx. In general, we find that the most influential social thinkers are Carlyle and Ruskin, but it is significant how often religious writings —the Bible and sermons—are mentioned, and also how many of these working-class politicians referred to the influence of poetry.

Some Labour leaders had, in the course of their political careers, moved upward; either through marriage or their own efforts, they had entered the lower strata of the middle class. This was true of men like MacDonald or Snowden. For the majority, however, political activity, before the introduction of salaries for M.P.'s, meant continued material hardship. Their hardship, moreover, is the more significant as it must be seen against the background of well-to-do, if not opulent, living, which was the rule among M.P.'s and the higher social order to which most of them belonged. Jowett was later to write that "Labour members who entered Parliament after state salaries were paid had little idea of what it meant to be an ILP M.P. during the first four years of my Parliamentary life."[11] M.P.'s who belonged to the ILP were allowed 200 pounds annually out of the parliamentary fund created by the Labour Party. This sum had to pay not only for their expenses at Westminster but also for the needs of their families. It proved hardly sufficient, and men like Jowett and Snowden tended to supplement their salaries by outside activities—mainly journalism. M.P.'s whose candidature had been sponsored by trade unions were generally better off. If they were officials of the unions they continued to draw their salaries—or at least a part of them.

In many cases, they received a special allowance to permit them to carry out their parliamentary work.

As a group, the PLP lacked discipline. The men who formed it were united only in their class background. Their political views, extent of parliamentary activity, and attitude toward other parties varied with character, intellectual activity, and integrity. In the first five years, the PLP Chairman alternated between four individuals: Hardie, Shackleton, and during Hardie's illness, Henderson and Barnes. In 1911, MacDonald took over.

The changes in the leadership were partly due to the currently held view of the role of the chairman. He was regarded more as a spokesman and representative than as an initiator of policies and a leader of men. It also reflected the uneasy alliance between the socialist and the trade union elements in the PLP. Keir Hardie found the burden of his chairmanship irksome and the effects stifling. "The strongest reason to get out of the Chair," he wrote to Snowden, "is that I may be able to speak out occasionally. In the last session the party has practically dropped out of public notice. The comic papers and the cartoonists are ignoring us, a fatal sign. . . . By another session those of us who believe in fighting will have to get together occasionally on our own account and if we cannot drag the party with us we will 'gang oor ain gait.' "[12] Shackleton, on the other hand, who would have been Hardie's natural successor (having already exercised the chairmanship during the latter's illness) refused nomination in 1908 because he thought that he could not be sure of the support of the socialist Labour M.P.'s. Henderson was elected instead, but he succeeded no better than Keir Hardie to impress the stamp of his personality on the PLP. The party continued to be an uneasy alliance between trade union representatives and socialist politicians. The bulk of the work in the House of Commons was carried out by a small number of active and devoted members, and it is hardly surprising that this group was almost synonymous with the convinced socialists on the Labour benches. The ILP members were, in any case, the only ones who were quite free to devote the whole of their time to affairs at Westminster. For the trade union leaders and officials who were in Parliament, politics had mostly to be combined with union activity, and few of them had undergone the kind of apprenticeship to parliamentary activity that is to be found on the platform or in journalism. Even when at Westminster, Snowden tells us, they tended to "spend their time in the smoking room or on the terrace."[13] The more humdrum the work, the less the attendance. On the Standing Committee on the Housing Bill, in 1908, Labour M.P.'s had recorded only half the possible attendances.

Barnes, as Chairman of the PLP, put his finger on a tender spot when, in 1911, he complained about "the irregularities of attendance on the part of some of the members. The main cause [of which] is no doubt the fact that the unions have not sufficiently released their members from trade union work." He went on to say that "it was a matter for serious consideration . . . whether [the party] should prolong indefinitely a system of dual service which operates so as to prevent efficient work being done in Parliament."[14]

The loyalties and sense of cohesion among Labour M.P.'s were put further to the test by the events following the 1910 elections. The decline in the Liberal Government's majority meant that the Labour Party occupied a strategically important position at Westminster. A move against the government could—if the Conservatives decided to support it—result in the defeat of the government and a general election. If that were to occur, the position of the Labour Party, it was argued, would be precarious. With depleted funds, it would have to meet with Liberal opposition where there had been none so far. The discussion about the role and purpose of Labour leadership which developed in that situation is examined further below. Here we must note that in the following years the PLP tended to refrain from too-violent criticism and opposition of Liberal policy and measures.[15]

MacDonald, who had just succeeded to the leadership of the PLP—and who clearly meant to keep it—was the chief advocate of a policy of limited objectives and tactical advances, which he defended with great force at the 1911 Labour Party Conference. "The foundations of the new Jerusalem" he averred "could not be laid by simply quoting meaningless sentences."[16] The trouble with his policy was perhaps not that he was mistaken but that, as Snowden later put it, he failed to combine a policy of co-operation with reasonable aggressiveness and thus conveyed the impression that he was willing to sacrifice the independence of the party to political expediency.[17] In any case, the following years saw a growing estrangement between the parliamentary leadership of the party and sections of its rank-and-file supporters in the country, especially within the ILP. The conflict over policy and parliamentary tactics showed itself also in the PLP, but the most decisive break occurred over the attitude toward the war. While the majority of the PLP supported the government, five of the seven ILP members opposed it and desired an early peace.[18] The proposals for military conscription, however, aroused considerable bitterness in the ranks of Labour, and opposition to it lasted a long time. Yet in the end, after the bill had been so amended as to meet some Labour objections, only ten Labour M.P.'s voted against it.[19]

With the advent of the coalition in May, 1915, Labour entered the government. Of the thirty-odd Labour M.P.'s who supported the war, nine found their way onto the Treasury Bench. Three served under Asquith, and later, under Lloyd George, Labour had six places in the government. Three men reached Cabinet rank, and the rest served mainly as junior ministers or as whips. The Labour Ministers were mostly in their 50's and 60's; they had been in Parliament for about ten years. With a few exceptions, they had neither opportunity nor outstanding ability to make their mark as administrators or to contribute to the war policy in general, except as defenders of governmental policy in the Trade Union movement. It seems significant for the character of this first group of Labour leaders that only a minority continued to play a leading part in Labour Party politics after the war. Only Clynes, Henderson, and Walsh held office in the first Labour Government. Indeed, four Labour Ministers defied the decision of their party to withdraw from the coalition after the end of the war. However, after the general election of 1922 even the last of these disappeared from the political scene.

The Changing Social Structure of Labour Leadership

The character of the parliamentary representation of the LP which emerged from the 1918 general election did not differ materially from that of the old PLP. The party went to the polls as a declared socialist organization and put 357 candidates into the field; it polled about 2,500,000 votes. But the few candidates who were successful came almost entirely from the ranks of the trade unions. The defeat of most of the ILP candidates —including MacDonald, Snowden and Jowett—concentrated even more the narrow sectional character of Labour representation. Forty-nine M.P.'s had been sponsored by trade unions; eight had been elected under the auspices of the newly founded constituency Labour parties. Four M.P.'s, although elected as independents, joined the Labour forces shortly afterward. One of these, Brigadier General Sir Owen Thomas, whose career in the Labour Party was short-lived, was the only Labour M.P. who neither by origin, upbringing, or occupation belonged to the working class.

From then onward, however, the character of Labour representation changes and widens. It becomes a national party, contesting a growing number of seats, no longer exclusively active in constituencies predominantly working-class in character, working through local party organizations open to individual members of all classes of the community. Accordingly, it begins to draw its parliamentary candidates from outside the working class. While "safe seats" still tend to be held by trade union candidates, and while their chances of success are thus great, the expansion in the numbers of Labour M.P.'s is largely accounted for by candidates with other backgrounds. The total number of seats fought for by trade union-sponsored candidates fluctuated within comparatively narrow limits throughout the period from 1918 to 1955. In years when many non-trade union candidates won at the polls, the strength of the trade union component within the party was relatively reduced. In general, the trade union bloc found its strength within the PLP almost inversely related to the over-all size of the Labour Party's victory. The figures in Table 1 tell the story of Labour's changing structure of representation only in the barest outline. Not all trade union-sponsored candidates were actually officials of the unions concerned; some were rank-and-file members only; others have been active members at one time but wandered off into other occupational fields, keeping the union membership. In another sense too, the occupations covered by unions changed during this span of years. The advent of white-collar unionism and the organization of scientific and supervisory workers further complicated the picture. It is nonetheless justifiable to conclude that the trade union-sponsored M.P.'s tended to be men of working-class origin, although some had moved away from the working class, occupationally and possibly socially, even before they entered the House of Commons.

The bourgeois element in the PLP was to be found among those who did not even formally enter politics via the trade union route. It was a political army which waxed and waned with the strength of Labour's parliamentary representation. A breakdown into its social components shows clearly how the Labour Party absorbed into its leading strata the representatives of older radical groups (mostly of upper-middle-class origin, rentiers, or

Table 1

Distribution of Labour M.P.'s According to Sponsorship by Trade Unions

ELECTION	LABOUR M.P.'s ELECTED WITH TRADE UNION SPONSORSHIP (Per Cent)	LABOUR M.P.'S ELECTED (Number)	LABOUR CANDIDATES (Number)
1918	80	61	357
1922	60	143	414
1923	53	191	427
1924	59	152	514
1929	40	288	561
1931	69	49	491
1935	51	154	552
1945	31	393	604
1950	35	315	612
1951	36	295	614
1955	35	277	620

professional men) who had lost their political footing with the decline of the Liberal Party (Table 1).

This breakdown also shows how the Labour Party attracted sections of the intelligentsia and the new middle class, including men who had themselves risen from the working class. The analysis (Table 2) of occupations followed by the non-trade union section of the PLP during these years, as well as their educational background (Table 3) makes this clear. It shows that only about one-third of this group still belonged to the traditional class of Labour M.P.'s; that is, only a third had spent their preparliamentary careers in factories or mines, followed possibly by a spell of office in a trade union or other working-class organization. If we consider the over-all percentage of Labour M.P.'s who had originally followed working-class occupations, whether or not they were trade union-sponsored M.P.'s, we see that the proportion was at an all-time high of 92 per cent in the 1918 period. It dropped to 70 per cent for the years 1922-24; it fell further to 60 per cent in 1929, rose to 75 per cent two years later, and fell again to 64 per cent in the 1935 period.

That a substantial proportion of those who followed middle-class occupations had themselves risen from the working class indicates broadly the degree of intergenerational social mobility. Adequate data about parental occupations is not available, but some inferences can be drawn from an analysis of the educational background of these non-trade union-sponsored Labour M.P.'s (Table 3). In 1918, this component of the PLP had been at a disadvantage insofar as educational opportunities were concerned—fully ten out of the eleven for whom educational data are available had completed elementary school and no more. The size of this group (i.e., those who completed only elementary school) declined considerably in the years that followed. It dropped to slightly less than 50 per cent during the twenties, and dropped further in 1929 and 1931 to a figure that accounts for roughly two out of every five non-trade union-sponsored M.P.'s. In 1935, however, it rose again to 53 per cent. At the opposite end of the spectrum, throughout the twenties and thirties, only one in six of this group could be said to have experienced a conventional ruling-class education—public school with possibly Oxford or Cambridge thereafter.

Table 2
Occupations Followed by Non-Trade Union Sponsored Labour M.P.'s*

	1918	1922	1923	1924	1929	1931	1935
Percentage Distribution							
Working Class	64	28	38	34	33	20	32
Professional Class	18	46	42	47	44	67	49
Middle Class and Upper Class	18	26	20	19	23	13	18
	100	100	100	100	100	100	100
CASES:	(11)	(57)	(89)	(62)	(168)	(15)	(71)
Numerical Distribution							
Working Class:							
Manual and Clerical Workers and Shop Assistants	1	8	20	12	25	2	11
Officials of Trade Unions and other Working-Class Organizations	6	8	14	9	31	1	12
Professional Class							
Journalists	2	6	9	5	20	1	3
School Teachers	—	8	10	7	19	2	6
University Teachers	—	4	3	5	7	2	5
Doctors	—	2	3	3	9	2	2
Lawyers	—	4	8	5	13	3	11
Clergymen and Others	—	2	4	4	6	—	8
Middle and Upper Class							
Managerial and Administrative, including Government Service and Forces	—	3	4	3	9	1	2
Estate Agents, Builders, Farmers, etc.	2	4	4	2	9	—	2
Entrepreneurs	—	5	6	5	11	1	9
Rentiers	—	3	4	2	9	—	—
Total ascertained:	11	57	89	62	168	15	71
Not ascertained:	1	—	1	1	5	—	4

*Refers to last occupation followed before entering Commons.

It is against this background that the first two Labour administrations must be viewed. Looking back on their personnel and policies after a quarter of a century, it is difficult, if not impossible, to understand the fear and apprehension caused in 1924 by the prospect of a Labour government.

Table 3

Educational Backgrounds of Non-Trade Union Sponsored Labour M.P.'s

	1918	1922	1923	1924	1929	1931	1935	Total
Percentage Distribution								
Elementary Schooling	91	47	49	47	44	36	53	46
Limited Schooling	—	11	14	11	16	21	10	16
Adequate Schooling	9	26	23	26	27	29	21	24
Prestigeful Schooling	—	16	14	16	13	14	16	14
	100	100	100	100	100	100	100	100
CASES:	(11)	(55)	(86)	(62)	(158)	(14)	(68)	(215)
Numerical Distribution								
Elementary School Only	10	26	42	29	69	5	36	98
Grammar School Only	—	6	10	6	24	3	6	32
Boarding School Only	—	—	2	1	1	—	1	3
Elementary School and University	—	1	3	2	5	1	3	5
Grammar School and University	1	10	12	10	26	2	10	33
University, earlier Schooling unknown	—	3	5	4	13	1	1	14
Public School Only	—	2	4	3	6	1	3	10
Public School and University	—	7	8	7	14	1	8	20
Total ascertained:	11	55	86	62	158	14	68	215
Not ascertained:	1	2	4	1	15	1	7	22

Asquith told Parliament that his post bag had been heavy with letters from people of all political persuasions, imploring him to save the country from the impending catastrophe by agreeing to a coalition. While he regarded these fears as exaggerated, he nevertheless felt it incumbent upon him, on another occasion, to reassure his hearers that "if a Labour government was to be tried . . . it could hardly be under safer conditions."

In preparing the distribution of portfolios for his first government, Mac-Donald is said to have expressed to some of his colleagues his disgust at the poor material at his disposal. Even allowing for the disdain felt by the leader of the LP for his intellectually and socially less well-endowed colleagues—a disdain that seems to have bordered at times on the pathological—there was substance in his plaint. A British Cabinet tends to be based on the personnel and tradition of its predecessor Cabinets. MacDonald could not fall back on any experience of office-holding among his colleagues: only Clynes, Henderson, and Shaw of the Labour members in the House of Commons had even been in the coalition government. Moreover, MacDonald was not bent on making an impression of daring innovations. Contrary to those who thought that Labour's task in office should be the formulation of a bold socialist program, he desired to show the public that his government was composed of competent and level-headed administrators. He felt that, on the one hand, he had to satisfy the desire for office among his senior colleagues and give representation to the trade union movement; on the other hand, he desired to secure for his Cabinet at all costs some of the cachet connected with persons of accepted social position and political renown.[20] Only five days after the election, in December, 1923, MacDonald met Haldane by arrangement, and offered him anything he should choose; according to Haldane, this included "the leadership of the House of Lords, the Chancellorship, Defense, Education, and the carrying out of my plans [probably concerning defense and reorganization of the administration of justice]."[21] Parmoor too was approached before Christmas and persuaded to accept the office of Lord President of the Council. Noel Buxton, J. C. Wedgewood, C. P. Trevelyan, and Lord Chelmsford completed this group of former Liberal or Conservative politicians who had come to support the Labour Party.[22] We can add to this group Lord Thomson, who had joined the Labour Party after a distinguished military career. He had fought the 1922 election as a Labour candidate and was a special friend of MacDonald.

This group of men, belonging to the traditional ruling class of Great Britain, of aristocratic and upper-middle-class origin, is nearly as large as that of the men who had entered politics via a professional career in trade unions or political organizations. Only a mere handful of Labour Cabinet members reached leadership and office by different routes. Table 4 presents a breakdown of the 1924 and 1929 Labour Governments on the one hand and the two post-World War II Governments on the other. Using a combination of class-background and occupational-career lines to establish the types discussed above, it demonstrates clearly the bare majority given to working-class representatives in the Labour Governments of both the earlier and the later period. On the other hand, it shows that the representation from the aristocratic and upper-middle class declined slightly between the two periods, and gave way to professional career persons coming from the middle and lower-middle class.[23]

From this evidence, it would seem that the social composition and character of Labour Cabinets remains substantially unchanged from the time of the first Labour Government. The balance struck by MacDonald in 1924 between working class and traditional ruling class did not only affect the kind of Cabinet which he formed again in 1929,[24] it equally expressed itself in Mr. Attlee's choice. Yet the third Labour Government, of 1945, was separated from the first two by more than just a gulf of 15 years, which in itself meant that only a minority of its members had seen Cabinet office in 1929.[25] There have been general changes of great magnitude in the social structure of Britain and all the more so in the Labour Party, as a factor in the political system, and in Parliament itself. This basic historical fact influenced in diverse ways the character of Labour leadership in the postwar years.

The 1945 election continued the changes which had begun in the interwar years. A record poll had resulted in an overwhelming Labour majority at Westminster. The Labour poll of nearly twelve million contained approximately three million middle-class votes and the PLP showed a larger proportion of middle-class members than ever before.[26] The fact that about one-third of

Table 4

Career Patterns of Members of Labour Cabinets: 1924-50*

	1924	1929	1945	1950
1) Aristocratic or upper-middle-class background, with a professional, entreprenuerial, or rentier career:	7	5	4	3
2) Middle- or lower-middle-class background, with a professional career:	2	2	4	5
3) Middle- or lower-middle-class background, with a business career:	—	—	—	—
4) Working-class background, with a professional career leading to middle-class status:	—	2	1	1
5) Working-class background, with a business career leading to middle-class status:	1	1	—	—
6) Working-class background, with a career as an official of a trade union or other working-class organization:	9	9	10	9
7) Working-class background, with a career occupationally confined to the working class:	1	—	1	—
Totals:	20	19	20	18

*In terms of class background and occupational routes.

the Labour M.P.'s entered Parliament directly from the armed services makes accurate occupational analysis difficult. But there were at least as many members of the professions (more than one-third) as of manual workers or trade union officials. The teachers had ousted the miners as the strongest occupational group on the Labour benches. The educational backgrounds of Labour M.P.'s had further changed in favor of those who had received a higher education. Probably not more than one-third had ended their scholastic career in elementary schools. About one-third had been to a university, and one in eight had gone either to Oxford or Cambridge.[27]

To be able to compare Attlee's postwar team with the group of Labour Ministers in the interwar years, we must study the occupational- and political-career data of Labour ministers more closely. All but two of the members of MacDonald's Cabinet who did not belong to the working class had started their political careers in the older parties. Some could say with C. P. Trevelyan:

> I was born a Liberal for I had behind me two generations of eminent service given through that Party to their country, by Lord Macauley and Sir George Trevelyan. I was, however, much more than a Liberal by inheritance. I remained a Liberal by deliberate choice, though many influences compelled me to seek a more advanced party.... The war has brought a wholesale transference of the working class vote from Liberalism to Labour and with that has come, in my view, the end of the supremely valuable part played in our history by the Liberal Party.[28]

Others felt moved to join the Labour Party because that party embodied among its aims particular reforms dear to their hearts. Haldane was propelled toward the party by his interest in education, especially adult education. Parmoor and Ponsonby had, during the war, become pacifists and fervent advocates of the League of Nations.

The trade union leaders and party officials who, in MacDonald's day, formed the bulk of the working-class party leadership differed in career patterns from their successors who achieved office twenty years later. Not only was their own early experience often formed under liberalism and their first step in local politics often taken under the Liberal banner, but the formative influence on most of them was that of the industrial struggle and the work needed to put the union organization on its feet. From experience as back benchers in a small isolated party, they moved almost at once directly into Cabinet office. Only four of them entered the House of Commons before reaching the age of thirty; their Cabinet experience covered their fifties and sixties. John Hodge, General Secretary of the Steel Smelters and one of the first Labour Ministers (he became Minister of Labour in 1916 and later sat in the War Cabinet), equated socialism with municipalism. He thought that "while the ideals of Socialism may be theoretically correct, at the moment they are unobtainable. In Glasgow you have practical Socialism in her water supplies, her markets, her gas and other undertakings." In his parliamentary campaigns, he was anxious to stress that he did not stand against the Liberals.[29]

Mr. Attlee's middle-class colleagues in the Cabinet received their political training mainly inside the Labour Party. Their occupational careers followed more clearly a definite pattern: public school education, university training, a professional career—predominantly in law or in teaching. Those who stepped into politics from officialdom in trade unions or in other working-class organizations did so earlier in life than their predecessors of a generation before. Their experience in office before they entered the Cabinet had been varied. Morover, they had, through their activities as Members of Parliament, acquired middle-class standards and the outlook of professional politicians.

In Table 5, a number of comparisons are made between the groups of Cabinet Ministers for the two periods under discussion, showing the contrast in backgrounds and training which has been discussed. The development of Labour leadership, as shown in this profile, highlights the changing character of a cadre of politicians in a highly complex democratic society. It illustrates quite clearly the trend, observed first by Max Weber (and, incidentally, when he was speaking of British politics), away from politicians who live *for* politics to those who live *from* politics.[30] The number of politicians for whom politics is not only a way of life but a livelihood has steadily increased in Labour's ranks. As the Labour Party was growing toward political maturity in the time when this process was going on, it has probably shared in this development to a greater extent than the Conservative party. Its basis is, of course, the existence of stable political organizations on the one hand and the payment of Members of Parliament on the other. The former makes it more certain that a political career, especially a parliamentary career, once seriously embarked upon, will be guaranteed a fair degree of continuity. Both parties are by now firmly entrenched in a large number of seats, and an electoral disaster such as overtook the LP in 1931 is not likely to recur. The payment of members—although far from lavish and even meager compared with other legislatures—is now recognized as payment for services performed. Its real value is today probably twice that of the income of the average wage earner, yet few M.P.'s, even on the Labour benches, are entirely dependent on it.

Table 5

Labour Cabinet Ministers Contrasted: 1916-35 and 1935-55

	PERIOD WHEN IN OFFICE	
	1916-35	1935-55
I. Age of Entry into Politics		
Under 30	2	1
From 31 to 35	3	6
From 36 to 40	8	11
From 41 to 45	5	10
From 46 to 50	7	3
From 51 to 60	3	3
Sixty-one and over	4	—
	32	34
II. Class Background		
Aristocracy	1	1
Neither aristocracy nor working class	12	14
Working class	19	19
	32	34
III. Occupation		
Landowning	1	—
Rentier	2	1
Profession	9	15
Commerce and Industry	2	2
Trade union officials, etc.	14	15
Other	4	1
	32	34
IV. School Education		
Elementary	16	18
Grammar	9	5
Public	4	11
Other	3	—
	32	34
V. University Education		
None	20	17
Oxford	4	6
Cambridge	1	5
Other Universities	7	6
	32	34
VI. Ministerial Career		
Stepped straight into Cabinet office	23	3
Held only an office as departmental head or equivalent before entering the Cabinet	1	4
Held only a junior office before entering the Cabinet	8	18
Held both junior office and departmental headship before entering the Cabinet	—	9
	32	34

Despite increased public and parliamentary duties, which are the lot of all conscientious M.P.'s, there seem to be increasing opportunities for outside earnings, even for those who do not undertake part-time professional work. Opportunities arise from journalistic writings, lecturing, broadcasting, and paid forms of public relations work. While the parliamentary salary is today probably worth no more than when it was first introduced, it is yet, thanks to taxation and general shifts in income, nearer to middle-class standards than it was in 1912, when parliamentary salaries were first introduced. In addition, there is a vastly greater number of perquisites and privileges falling to the lot of even the unknown back-bencher than ever before. Government and business dispense a much greater degree of hospitality than before the war, let alone before 1914. Places on foreign missions and delegations are within the reach of M.P.'s who will bestir themselves; they in turn widen the opportunities for extra-parliamentary activity and earnings. Being an M.P. has become a marketable commodity—even without such dubious forms of activity as guinea-pig directorships.

Finally, the Government has today an increasingly large number of offices at its disposal with which to reward its followers. This is not only through jobs in the administration itself, although even those have increased in significance (in a fairly evenly divided House of Commons today, one member in five of the party in power may hold office), but also through posts in the nationalized industries, other government agencies, or foreign representations. With such avenues of advancement at its disposal, a major party can promise its followers a fair degree of security in their political pursuits.

As politics becomes more like a profession, it also becomes more middle-class. As the only party whose political representation was not already entirely middle- or upper-class in character, the Labour Party leadership is clearly influenced by this process. Indeed, the PLP and its leadership are perhaps even more middle-class in character than these tables and figures suggest; at the same time, this professionalization of politics probably has increased the cohesion within the PLP and in its leading strata. The effects of professionalization on the relationships between leaders and led will be examined later.

Labour Leaders and the Ruling Class

Until the advent of the first Labour administration, British governments had formed an integral part of the country's ruling class. Its very strength and adaptability greatly derived from the fact that its members mixed and moved easily with those who, whether in the civil service or in the armed forces, were their formal subordinates. This very subordination of the heads of bureaucracy and of the army and navy, whose ability often exceeded that of their masters, and who were nearly always greater experts at the job in hand than the men they served, was made easier by the fact that both groups shared the same ethos of rule and acknowledged the same rule of conduct. The tradition of the great "gentlemen class" embraced them all; it even extended far into the ranks of those who owned and directed the enterprises of industry and commerce.[31] It is true that since the middle of the last century "new men" had increasingly penetrated into government, but their influence and position was marginal, and they tended to be absorbed into the traditions of the ruling class. This is proved by the facility with which newcomers were assimilated after a fashion (and not without the support of the "victims") by "Society"—the London "salon" and the country house. By tracing the relationship between Labour politicians and society, we can show more clearly the place of Labour leadership in the social structure.

In this connection, it is important to distinguish between the occasional M.P. of working-class origin who had entered the House of Commons during the last quarter of the nineteenth century and the representative of a working-class organization seeking to represent the aspirations of his class in Parliament within the framework of a distinctive Labour Party. Those earlier public figures regarded themselves as bound up socially and politically with the Liberal Party; their parliamentary careers more often than not were steps in a general process of upward social mobility. Keir Hardie observed that "the working man's representative [in Parliament] thinks more of his own reputation in the eyes of the House than of the interests of his suffering brethren in mill and mine. He desires to be reckoned a gentleman, fit to take his place as a member of the 'finest club in the world.' "[32] On the other hand, the early Labour Party M.P.'s were quite clearly condemned both by their politics and by their poverty to stay outside the circle. Hardie's cloth cap and grey woolen suit (although meant as an act of defiance) were yet a symbol of distinctiveness which even top hat and frock coat could not have surmounted.

The European War caused some breaking down of social barriers between Labour M.P.'s and the members of the ruling class and of the two major parties. The coalition brought Labour leaders into social as well as political contact with the bourgeois parties, a process which was helped by the innumerable governmental and departmental committees and missions which flourished as a result of increased governmental activity. The situation was eased further by the fact that from 1916 onwards the Prime Minister was a man of lower-class background. Lloyd George was himself an ideal intermediary between the different social groups. Finally, we must ascribe at least part of this coming together to the slight blurring of the lines of social division which came about under the impact of war.

The situation during hostilities was, however, in some ways unique. The first Labour Government presents a better picture of the position of Labour leadership in and with regard to "Society."

Since its inception, the Labour movement in Great Britain had criticized the British upper class and poured scorn and invective on the extravagances and economic wastefulness of the lives of the rich. Its spokesmen had agitated against the snobbishness of Britain's antiquated class structure and against the *accoutrements* of upper-class life, which helped to perpetuate the pattern. Court ceremonials formed an important part of this. On taking power, Labour leaders were faced with this aspect of the problem as one calling for personal decision. How much of the decorative part of the British Constitution were they to observe? The first and most obvious case arose in connection with the wearing of court dress. George V, as we now know, was a stickler for etiquette and deeply concerned with preserving the traditions of the Court, of which dress seemed to him of paramount importance. Even before Labour came to power, the King had expressed his concern about the party's position with regard to dress: before inviting MacDonald to the Palace in 1922, he inquired through Lord Stamfordham whether the Leader of the Opposition would come in court dress when invited to Buckingham Palace.[33] MacDonald replied in the affirmative, which we can now readily understand: "He liked pomp and ceremony; he had an intense and abiding sense of the picturesque and a deep love of the ordered and ancient and the hierarchical."[34]

The problem arose again on a wider scale when it came to the presentation of the Cabinet. With the exception of Jowett and Wheatley, the whole Cabinet appeared in court dress when kissing hands. This was no doubt partly due to MacDonald's influence, but it also showed the rather unquestioned acceptance of tradition on the part of the majority of the Labour Cabinet.[35] Social recognition by the Court was regarded by many Labour leaders, and especially by their wives, as a desirable thing in itself rather than as an irksome duty. Mrs. Clynes wrote to the papers suggesting that the daughters of Labour leaders should be presented at Buckingham Palace.

A minority sought consciously to prevent this involvement with "Society." Beatrice Webb, who throughout the periods of the two Labour Governments tried to avoid being roped into the circle of Court and other social functions, sought to create for the Labour leadership something equivalent to a "society" life without being "Society" in the traditional sense. Her vehicle for doing so was the "Parliamentary Labour Club," which she helped to found and which, she hoped, would bring the various strata of the party leadership, especially their wives, together for friendly social intercourse. She did not want "the PLP to become the plaything of London Society and the despised of the more serious elements in the Labour movement. . . . the personal conduct of the Labour members and their wives will be just as important as the political policy of the Labour Cabinet, perhaps even more so, as [the latter] must be qualified by the fact that the Party is in a minority and personal conduct can be settled with a single eye as to what is desirable from the standpoint of the future society."[36] It is significant, however, that the club, set up with thoughtful care, proved to be a comparative failure. The various social sets among Labour Ministers kept apart. Those who could, sought entry into real society. And "Society," always eager to absorb the *arriviste,* extended a helping hand. The Snowdens, Beatrice Webb noted in her diary in September 1929, "had spent yesterday with the Connoughts and the day before with the Balfours at Fisher's Hill."[37] Barnes, Snowden, Thomas, and Henderson could be found at Clivedon on weekends, although no doubt rarely.[38] MacDonald's own liking for "Society" is well known. "He went out of his way to tell me," Beatrice Webb relates, "that he was going to stay with

Mrs. Biddulph—the Honorable Mrs. Biddulph, he added—and then described her as a patron of good English craftsmanship in furniture. Then I am going to stay at————with the Princess Hartsfelt. She was a Cunningham, you know, do you know her? A remarkable woman."[39] Such conduct embittered sections of the Labour movement and contributed to the antagonism increasingly felt by the left wing for the leadership of the party; it was bound to weaken the opposition to the economic system which formed one of the bases of Labour's political appeal.

In addition to "High Society," there was the political society formed by Labour itself—or rather by the progressively minded counterelite, of which the intellectual wing of the Labour movement formed a significant part. With the increase in the Labour Party's "respectability," this group formation increased in size and significance. Its scope is difficult to define. Its economic basis was a middle-class salary (and possibly a small private income), weekend cottage, motor car, and not much spare cash but a fair amount of spare time. The ties connecting these circles were intellectual interests rather than social pursuits, common concern with social and cultural endeavor rather than family connection. The men and women who belonged to these circles were writers and journalists, lawyers, university teachers, and artists, left-wing professional politicians, and younger administrators. They met in central London flats or in smaller houses in the inner suburbs on weekends and at holiday parties. The Webbs themselves attempted throughout their lives to be a center of such society, although Beatrice's unself-conscious self-importance and her "sense of mission" probably permitted little genuinely spontaneous social intercourse to develop. She writes of one such weekend in her diary:

A really useful weekend with Lion Philimore who left me to select the party. The Alexanders, Greenwoods, Colonel Williams and ourselves went down to Kendal on Saturday. Patrick Hastings and his wife motored down for lunch and tea on Sunday, the Bernard Shaws came over in the afternoon, and the Oswald Mosleys motored down to lunch. The conversation was exclusively political—I doubt whether during these 40 hours there was a single allusion to women, wine, horses, sports, scandal or money-making. . . . Undiluted public affairs and the philosophy upon which these are based was the order of the day.[40]

The effectiveness of such gatherings is difficult to assess; their impact on politics in the short run may have been small. In the long run, the mental climate which they created is important. In such circles—as on a more institutionalized level in Fabian summer schools—newcomers are introduced into the political scene, they see the ropes which support the props, they get a feel for the political stage and possibly they meet some of the chief actors.

"Left-wing" society served, and probably still serves in its own way, as much as a center for political advancement of those who aspire to a "political" (not necessarily parliamentary) career in the Labour Party as real "Society" did—and does—for the "bright young thing" on the Right. Lord Pakenham, who held ministerial office between 1948 and 1957, relates how, when defeated at Oxford in 1945, his friends, especially Evan Durbin, insisted that he "must nevertheless be got into Parliament and at once." The whole episode, as related in his diary, is instructive:

He swept aside my dubieties. Action had to be taken and was taken forthwith. By Sunday, Hugh Dalton was Chancellor of the Exchequer; he was staying with Bill and Mary Piercy at Burford and [we] were motoring over to tea, hoping for something though I know not what. [Dalton] visualized my position with alacrity, insisted that I must at all costs be associated with the great social experiment that was about to be conducted, and that evening found time to write letters to half a dozen leading members of the Government, commending me to their attention.[41]

Like all "societies," British left-wing society is exclusive. It is true that breeding or wealth are not prerequisites for entrance. But intellectual ability, middle-class cultural tastes, a university background—these probably are. The trade union leaders of the middle ranks, energetic and able local councillors of working-class origin, are unlikely to find their way into it. As a social network, this society is also strongly London-centric, favoring men with connections in the metropolis. Other centers are, of course, in the universities, especially Oxford. There the circle around G. D. H. Cole was, by all accounts, a breeding ground for future Labour politicians.[42]

Beatrice Webb described in her diary a visit of a women's organizer of the Labour Party for Northeast England and her husband. She was a graduate, he a scientific worker, probably also university-trained. The diary provides a candid picture:

[They were] distinguished people, intellectually and morally, but possessing no social status . . . we took them to see the Snowdens and also the Ponsonbys, both being among Mrs. Fenn's forty MP's for whose women's section she is responsible. But by the Snowdens she was treated just as a salaried subordinate to whom they were distantly civil. Arthur Ponsonby was more forthcoming but in neither case was there the remotest recognition that this man and woman were among the elite.[43]

The Job of Politics

Over 40 per cent of all Labour Cabinet Ministers (26 out of 63) advanced straight from a position as a private Member of Parliament into Cabinet office, without in most cases even the indirect experience of government which the Conservative or Liberal back-bencher tended to receive by contact with colleagues when his party was in office. The experience of departmental administration, enjoyed by many others, was likewise limited, due to the short duration of the earlier Labour administration. Only during the life of the third and fourth Labour Governments do we find anything resembling the usual *cursus honorum* inside the administration.[44]

Labour politicians who had sprung from the working class were especially liable to be pitchforked straight into Cabinet office.[45] They reached the governmental front bench without the preparation for political office which family background and education tended to give to members of the other two parties. Their training ground for politics had not been the debating society of one of the older universities, or the officers' mess, the board room, or the landed estate, but the platform, the office desk, or the negotiating table. Their entrance into politics was that of men representing their union or their movement and not of men seeking to embark on a public career or gain office. MacDonald and Snowden, a colleague thought, were "aloof from sectional interest, always seemed to have a wider outlook on political affairs than the men who came into politics through industrial channels."[46] Smillie, who had been offered the post of Food Controller during the first war, had declined because "he felt that [his] life's work was with the miners [and that he] had no special qualifications for such a post."[47]

The Webbs had poured scorn on the narrow-minded and slow-thinking trade union officials who formed the bulk of the PLP between 1918 and 1922. Yet after the formation of the Government, Beatrice Webb was forced to report that the civil service was pleased with their new masters, that they eagerly devoted themselves to business, were anxious to learn and lacked any "side" in the exercise of their duties. "Whether its policy is right or wrong, Labour will prove itself emphatically fit for *administration* and that is what the Service likes." [48]

On the other hand, it is interesting that, almost from the first, expertise did play a part in the allocation of office by Labour Prime Ministers. In 1924, Snowden was *the* financial expert of the party and his appointment as Chancellor of the Exchequer was natural. His second-in-command, Willie Graham, was equally a specialist. Lord Parmoor, the Lord President of the Council, had been active in League of Nations matters and accepted office on the express understanding that he would be given an opportunity to concern himself with League affairs. Brigadier General Thomson fitted into the Air Ministry while at the Board of Trade. Sidney Webb was a man who had devoted the previous thirty years to the study of industrial and social questions.

It is especially in the economic field that posts have tended to go to "experts." Beginning with Dalton in 1945, successive postwar Labour Chancellors have been economists or, like Cripps, men with long experience as administrators in the economic field. The second post in that sphere, the presidency of the Board of Trade, has likewise been held by men with professional qualifications; indeed, the presidency became under Attlee almost a stepping-stone for the chancellorship. Attlee was inclined to fill ministerial vacancies from the ranks of parliamentary secretaries or other subordinate ministers who had served in the department and could be expected to know the ropes. This was so, not only when he formed his administration after the war, but also when filling vacancies between 1945 and 1951. The typical Labour minister was much more than his opposite number of the Conservative side an administrator on a comparatively narrow front.

The appointment of the "second-in-command" to the top position is, of course, widespread throughout bureaucratic structures. It has become almost the rule in the succession to the general secretaryship in British trade unions.

It may be the natural consequence of the aforementioned professionalization of the political career. In a sense, this tendency agrees with the complex and technically intricate task of departmental administration; whether it also serves the need for dynamic leadership on the part of a government seeking to effect fundamental changes through administrative measures is, of course, another matter.

To be a learner in the exercise of government or an expert directing a large department can lead one to neglect wider issues. Absorption in administrative action by which positive results can be achieved comparatively quickly may make men more ready to accept existing conditions. Sir Almeric Fitzroy (then Clerk of the Privy Council) reports a conversation with Clynes, then Deputy Food Controller:

> Whose period of office has clearly been of great educational value. . . . Clynes has profited greatly by contact with the larger outlook of Lord Rhondda of whom he spoke with sincere praise. It was significant to hear from him that Labour at large had ceased to take any strong interest in the reform of the House of Lords and gave as his principal reason the sturdy defense of individual rights for which members of that assembly had made themselves conspicuous.[49]

When he held office again seven years later, he apparently still felt himself a learner in the art of government. His civil servants were always at his side, "advising, coaching, checking and, in short time, I gained a measure of knowledge necessary in matters where perhaps national safety and the spending of millions was concerned."[50]

There is, of course, nothing peculiar in this situation. Every Cabinet Minister is invariably dependent on his permanent officials for advice and guidance. In the context of this paper it is only interesting to observe how Labour leaders conceived their own role in the exercise of power. MacDonald expressed probably not only his own views when, on the advent of the first Labour Government, he said to a vast gathering in the Albert Hall in London:

> We shall take office . . . in order to try and settle the manifold and pressing difficulties that beset our nation, Europe and the whole world at the present moment. My task and my colleagues' task is going to be to mobilise all men and women of goodwill and sane judgment. . . . I want a Labour government so that the life of the nation can be carried on. 1924 is not the last year in God's programme of creation. We shall be dead and gone and still the journey will be going on, still the search for the Holy Grail will be made by knights like Keir Hardie.[51]

Even allowing for the fact that the scope of action of the first two Labour Governments was severely limited, there is little evidence that newer lines of policy, aiming at far reaching changes, even of a noncontroversial character, were attempted by any of the departments. Beatrice Webb refers to her husband's work in the 1924 Government in the following terms:

> Sidney does his level best for his country and his party; he works up to the limits of his strength during the working months. But in his heart of hearts he remains essentially a detached observer without any keenness for one way or another or as to his own continued participation in the exercise of power.[52]

This absence of personal involvement in the general issues of political power is confirmed by a study of Sidney Webb's correspondence. We can observe it during 1924 and to an even greater extent during the period of the second Labour Government, when Sidney, then Lord Passfield and aged 70, was continuously longing for the day when he would be released from office. His frequent letters to his wife show great absorption in his administrative tasks and little mention of the general issues with which the government was confronted. "I am snowed under with papers and problems which leaves me little time for anything else," he wrote to her in 1930 when he was Secretary of State for the Colonies and the Dominions.[53] It is pathetic to find how little the authors of the 1909 report on the "Prevention of Destitution" wrote and apparently thought about the vast misery in their midst. (Beatrice's diaries for 1929-31 are equally silent about the unemployment problem).

Compared with others and with the pressure of work during and after the war, the duties of the Colonial Secretary of 1929-31 could not have been too onerous. His working day was usually over in the early hours of the evening and there were still long weekends spent at Passfield Corner where private social life continued. One of his successors in the postwar Labour administration worked at quite a different pitch. It was rare, P. C. Gordon-Walker reports, for him to get to bed before 2:00 A.M. and there was practically no time for nonofficial activities.[54] The scope of governmental activity under Attlee was, of course, more far reaching than under MacDonald. More Cabinet meetings, and, above all, more Cabinet committees, all no doubt with heavier agendas, were demanding the attention of Ministers. Yet Ministers are still primarily heads of departments, and this sets limits to the amount of planning that can be done collectively. "Ministers conceive a deep distaste for embarking upon projects that will entail more and larger meetings with their colleagues. This means that even Socialist Ministers are selective about the sector of the national life that they can attempt to plan."[55]

The problems arising at the intersection of administrative exigencies with those of personal relationship go to the very heart of governmental planning. The number of issues affecting more than one department are always too large—and often also too technical—to be decided on by the Cabinet. Neither the Labour Government, nor for that matter any other Government of recent years, appears to have found easy solutions to this. Labour administrations have tended to seek co-ordination through a system of committees, preferably under the chairmanship of a Minister without departmental duties. The effectiveness of such ministers charged with "functional tasks," and with it largely that of the system, will depend on their personality and the pressure which they can apply on their subordinate colleagues.[56] In 1924, Webb was chairman of a committee composed of the Ministers of Health and Labour, and some other more junior members, to deal with housing and unemployment. However, the committee split immediately into subcommittees on each of the two subjects under the chairmanship of their respective departmental heads who, he said, "ran away with their respective subjects" and "could neither be helped, usefully criticized or controlled."[57] J. H. Thomas, who as Lord Privy Seal was charged with the direction of unemployment policy in 1929, was equally unsuccessful in, and probably also incapable of, devising any remedies. Arthur Greenwood, who held the same office between 1945 and 1947, was given general supervisory duties in the field of reconstruction without having any apparent success. It seems that mere co-ordination without clearly defined powers and concrete tasks is a difficult and dangerous undertaking. Lord Inman, Greenwood's successor, was pitch-forked into politics and into the Cabinet at the same time. High but vague hopes were aroused by the appointment of this successful businessman. As he himself candidly admitted, he felt himself quite unequal to being a general without an army, and he left the Government as suddenly as he had entered it, expressing his regret that he had not been allotted specific departmental duties.[58]

General political decisions taken by Labour Cabinets, committees, or individual ministers have to be transferred into administrative action through the civil service. In the discussion on Labour's administrative tasks, especially before the experiment was made, there were many voices which foretold a conflict between Labour Ministers bent on radical changes, and their depart-mental advisers seeking to preserve the ways of the department and possibly so bitterly hostile to Labour's aims as to stultify them by lack of co-operation. Those who have written of their experience as Labour administrators are in agreement with Herbert Morrison, who found that "the British Civil Service is loyal to the government of the day" and who adduces his own experience to support this.[59]

Yet Labour Ministers have also sometimes sought to counteract possible opposition from their departments by bringing with them a few advisors from outside the department. When Henderson took over the Foreign Office in 1929, he not only presented his senior officials with copies of the Labour Party program ("Labour the Nation") but he brought Lord Cecil in as his advisor and appointed, as his Parliamentary private secretary, Philip Noel-Baker, one of the party's experts on international affairs. The policies pursued by the first two Labour Governments were, however, on the whole sufficiently traditional not to engender the opposition of the officials. We do not as yet know enough about the position under Attlee to say with cer-tainty that conflict never occurred.

When we look at the activities of private Labour members in the House of Commons, we can likewise observe the influence of long-established political and parliamentary traditions on their behavior and opinions. Labor M.P.'s, with few exceptions, submit to the traditions of the place and succumb to the *genus loci*. Parliamentary life itself becomes an educating and moderating influence. The mores of the House lessen antagonism. The great formal egalitarianism of the rules of the House, the privileges which the Member of Parliament enjoys, and the deference shown to him by officials and servants of the House strengthen the individual's self-esteem, and no doubt combat feelings of separateness. New loyalties are created. It would take a very strongly developed feeling of loyalty to one's own group together with a set of clear-cut differentiating factors for a section of M.P.'s to keep entirely apart from the main stream. The Irish Nationalists, who had both these characteristics, achieved such distinctiveness. The Labour Party was not so favored by external circumstances. Observers used to the rigid social divisions of continental parliaments marvel at the degree of intermixture in the British House of Commons. "A division of tables in the dining room of the 'House of Commons' in the same manner as in the restaurant of the Reichstag would be unthinkable in England," writes a German journalist in 1929.[60]

The only attempt at complete parliamentary and social isolation by Labour M.P.'s came from the group who were elected for Glasgow and neighboring constituencies in 1922 (the so-called "Clydesiders"). Representing constituencies with traditions of militant unionism and elated by the unexpected size of their electoral victory (all but two of the eleven Glasgow constituencies returned Labour candidates), they came nearest to expressing sentiments of class war on the Labour benches. During the period of the first Labour Government, they resolutely fought to stay away from all social functions that might be regarded as corrupting or compromising. Yet with that quixotic combination of extreme radical views and strong national pride which we find in the British labour movement, David Kirkwood, one of their leaders, could not disguise some admiration for his opponents. He relates that he was rebuked for abusing his opponents and was told that such behavior was pointless, that "these people have a code! They will listen to argument but abuse does not interest them." This he found true: "the 'conventions' of the House of Commons are strong to bind. At first I thought they were nothing more than surface politics. They are not, they are the foundations of the parliamentary system."[61] Kirkwood himself was to embrace parliamentary conventionality to the full; he accepted a peerage from Mr. Attlee and, without explicitly accepting the contemporary social system, he thought that those who directed it were able and, within their lights, disinterested men.[62] Robert Smillie, who as a politician was admittedly never in the front ranks, expressed similar sentiments:

> In my young and callow days I was probably a little prejudiced in favor of my class and hot with resentment against those whom I regarded as their oppressors. But experience teaches and I now know that a gentleman is a gentleman whatever his rank in life may be and always will be trusted as such.[63]

The violation of accepted rules of parliamentary conduct and the "offices" against the decorum of the House—which occurred occasionally, mostly by members from the Clyde—were abhorred by many. Snowden regarded the speeches of the Clydesiders as soapbox stuff delivered for consumption at home. MacDonald was very apologetic to the King about the singing of "The Red Flag" when the latter charged him with permitting it. He begged the King to remember "the very difficult position he was in, vis-a-vis his own extremists . . . his followers had got into the way of singing this song and it will be by degrees that he hopes to break down this habit."[64]

The singing of "The Red Flag" was repeated after the victory in 1945, but, despite Labour's great parliamentary majority and the much more radical character of its policy, there was less class and party antagonism between 1945 and 1951 than in the prewar parliaments. The wartime coalition and the large middle-class contingent on the Labour benches weakened the feeling of antagonism and helped the party to add social to political recognition. During the 1920's, a Labour M.P. with a solid middle-class background and upbringing might experience a cooling off of social relationships with friends and relatives; this was less likely to happen after 1945.[65] With the party in power, Labour politics could provide a career for the ambitious professional man or even the entrepreneur.

This was obviously less so during the 1920's and 1930's, when the political fortunes of the party were at a much lower level. What caused men of the middle class to link their fortune with that of the Labour Party and to act contrary to what could then, much more than now, be legitimately described as the interests of their class?

The motivation of political activity and partisanship is usually based on a variety of factors. For the Labour M.P. from the professions or from business, economic factors could not have been of great importance during the interwar years. Indeed, there is evidence that, for many, activity in Parliament entailed financial sacrifices. Some probably entered the House of Commons with the hope of attaining office. C. Aitchison, a Scottish barrister, had unsuccessfully contested a seat in Scotland in 1924 as a Liberal—and strongly anti-Labour—candidate. He soon afterwards joined the Labour Party, fought a Glasgow constituency in 1929, and, despite defeat, was appointed a Law Officer for Scotland (Lord Advocate).[66] A seat was found for him in Kilmarnock. He stayed Lord Advocate throughout the period of office of the second Labour Government and followed MacDonald into the National Government.

Some men whose professions brought them into direct contact with working-class life were propelled into politics by the deprivation and poverty which they saw. The life of Alfred Salter, who, following his experiences in the Bermondsey slums, gave up an apparently brilliant career in medical research to become first a general practitioner in that district of London and later a member of the ILP, an immensely active local politician and Member of Parliament, is an example of this kind of approach to politics.[67]

Another way into Labour politics stems from a concern with particular issues and reforms for which the Labour Party was just the right political instrument. A number of Liberal M.P.'s came into the party via the Union of Democratic Control, which they had joined mostly during World War I as a result of opposition to the conduct of the war and the war aims and where they met pacifist and independently thinking Labour men. Two of this group, E. D. Morel and Norman Angell, were attracted to the Labour Party through the latter's foreign-policy program. Angell had been "enraged by the mass stupidity of [Conservative] policy" and attracted by Labour's internationalistic outlook. He joined the party and became a parliamentary candidate. When seeking election in 1922, he was supported by men of all shades of opinion. He did not get into the House of Commons until 1929, but then his reputation brought him immediate rewards. He was elected to the Consultative Committee of the PLP, the body representing the Labour back-benchers. His position in politics can be judged by his attitude toward MacDonald's National Government. He refused to support it, despite pressure from the Prime Minister, not because he objected to its formation but because he "shrank from facing the censure of old friends," an action which he later regretted.

Charles Roden Buxton was another Liberal whose motives for joining the Labour Party derived largely from his views in the field of foreign policy and from general religious precepts. "It was axiomatic with him," wrote his sister in her biography, "that politics could and should be informed by the Christian spirit. Considerations of Party were not negligible but they did not interest him for their own sake. In his last years he collaborated over foreign affairs more with former political opponents than with members of the party to which he belonged."[68]

We are touching here on the general problem of the intellectual in politics. The Labour Party, which had arisen out of an act of protest against existing conditions, naturally attracted various kinds of social critics. Some intellectuals were clearly attracted by the more fundamentalist approach to politics which the party offered. At the same time we can observe how the original rebelliousness which caused their identification with a socialist policy was applied to the party and to its policies. The intellectual has in consequence frequently been distrusted by other sections of the labour movement as one who is disinclined to adhere loyally to the party line. Many individual examples of this could be given. The relationship of intellectuals to deviations and opposition inside the party is discussed further below.

Labour's Concept of Leadership

By the time Labour representation came to Westminster, the British party system had reached a definite stage in its development. The two major parties were clearly divided, without that blurring at the edges which still characterized the party system in the 1850's and 1860's. Conservatives and Liberals were mass parties with "pseudo" democratic organizations in the country. Neither the National Liberal Federation nor the Conservative National Union had any decisive influence over the leadership of its party. The management of elections and the conduct of parliamentary policy were firmly vested in leaders who, by virtue of their personal qualities and, more often, their former office as Prime Minister or appointed successors of such, ruled over their parliamentary bloc without more than an occasional challenge in the exercise of their authority. Lowell has shown how the degree of independent voting in parliamentary divisions declined steadily throughout th second half of the nineteenth century, and that party discipline was finally established by the beginning of the twentieth century.[69]

The Labour Party did not originate in the tradition of the two patrician parties, which had gradually broadened their bases and had grudgingly given way to pressure from their "popular" organizations below. Its constituent bodies—trade unions, socialist societies, and the ILP—were imbued with a spirit of democratic organization and sentiment. Members and leaders were social equals acting in a fairly close cameraderie, which facilitated the discussion of policy issues at all levels and permitted a vigorous criticism of aims and policies. The organization of the PLP after 1906, as we have seen, was loose. The office of chairman was what its name implied; the incumbent's task was conceived more as that of the formal head and organizer than that of "leader." Hardie apparently thought that the position ought not to be held continuously by one person.

Frequently individual M.P.'s would refuse to follow the party whip, when to do so would have been likely to offend important interests in their constituencies or in the bodies which they represented. There was nearly a break in party ranks over the attitude toward women's suffrage. Attendance of M.P.'s in the House of Commons was often lax; we saw that in 1911 Barnes, then chairman of the PLP, criticized absentees in his report to the Annual Conference of the LP. In the following year, MacDonald used the same platform to criticize the open expression of divergencies of opinion among Labour M.P.'s.

In some respects, this nonconformist tradition lingered on and permitted the coexistence of different strands of the labour movement and considerable ideological diversity within the Labour Party. It enabled the party to be divided over the issue of World War I without bursting the bounds of unity in the labour movement. It is reflected also in the conscience clause of successive standing orders of the PLP, which permitted M.P.'s to abstain from voting where matters of conscience were involved.[70] The scope of the individual M.P.'s freedom, as defined by the standing orders of the parliamentary party, has not changed perceptibly since they were first introduced. The sanctions invoked, however, for a breach of party discipline have become more clearly defined in later standing orders. What is more to the point, they have been more frequently applied lately.

MacDonald, who became *de facto* leader of the party in 1911, when he was elected to the chairmanship, saw clearly the need for a unified and disciplined party. Leadership for him was more than an administrative task. When his name was mentioned as a possible successor to Hardie in 1908, he wrote to Bruce Glasier that "to take the job for a period of two years at the maximum is a bit discouraging."[71] He saw the Labour leader as both pacemaker and disciplinarian. It might be left to the movement to set the sights on the far horizon, but the leader was to determine the road and tempo of advance:

> The responsibility of leaders to the mass must be secured but democracy which gives leaders no power will soon discover that it can do nothing. The problem of democracy is how to retain leadership with authority, and yet to limit the authority so that it is not dictatorship.[72]

He regarded the political, i.e., legislative and administrative function as an essentially specialized one, which only a minority could undertake. This minority ought to be small, certainly smaller than the House of Commons as it was (and still is).[73] He recognized that governmental office and political leadership in general demand a man's full-time attention and that the job of politics is a professional activity like any other. "The art and science of government is one of the most difficult of all arts and care should be taken to enable it to command the most skilled intelligence.[74] The Labour Party, he thought, had not so far adapted its method of selecting candidates to the need of the House of Commons; it still chose men because of their "status in local bodies or in organizations whose method of work and training are not those of the House of Commons."[75]

Against this view of a political leader as expert and professional, deciding himself and unfettered on the line of policy to be pursued, other leaders of the ILP, especially Fred Jowett, advocated a different theory of leadership. For them, the politician remained in close contact with his followers and carried out, in Parliament, the policies on which the party had agreed. MacDonald saw political tactics determined by the parliamentary situation, regarded a group of Labour M.P.'s as good in itself, and in consequence, was loath to weaken the power of the Liberal Party and possibly cause a general election which might weaken Labour's position. Jowett, on the other hand, believed that Labour M.P.'s should pursue a vigorous socialist policy. To vote on issues according to their merit, to carry one's convictions into the division lobby, was not only a matter of intellectual honesty but essential to gain mass support. Jowett further believed that such a policy would have beneficial effects on the whole system of parliamentary government. "I believe that the Party which sets itself to establish the authority of the elected representatives of the people against the successive juntas of which governments are composed will do a great service to the country and increase the respect of the public for parliamentary government." This he declared in a speech as chairman of the 1910 conference of the ILP. He went on to join the issue:

The ordinary wayfaring man cannot understand why Members of Parliament should not vote for the things he had advocated merely because such a vote would be considered as a vote of censure on the government of the day. All this jiggery pokery of party government, played like a game for ascendancy and power, is not for us.[76]

Jowett's point was taken up in a publication emanating from some of his Bradford friends. Known as the "Green Manifesto," it reverberated throughout the labour movement. The authors condemned the opportunist tactics of the majority of the Labour Party leaders, claiming that individual M.P.'s were more concerned to keep their seats than to pursue definite policies. If the Labour-Socialist alliance, which formed the basis of the Labour Party, was so ineffective, it might not be worth while to continue with parliamentary activity. Alternatively, the authors thought that it might become necessary for "our movement [to] assert its democratic claims by definite mandate."[77]

This was one of the few concrete proposals made for a reform of the relationship between leadership and mass movement. Another was that of the committee system, which Jowett sought to apply to governmental policy-making. Each department of the administration, Jowett thought, should be assisted in its work by a committee of M.P.'s, which would discuss all proposed measures and have access to all relevant information before the matter was brought to the whole House of Commons.[78] This was clearly more than a procedural device; it aimed at making Parliament more directly democratic and the Cabinet less omnipotent.

MacDonald, on the other hand, regarded the concentration of power in the Cabinet as the logical outcome of social development. Parallels to it could be found in all large organizations. To combine the committee system with responsible government, he thought, the committees would have to be party committees, but this would only further enlarge the power of the government vis-a-vis the House of Commons. MacDonald clearly envisaged a socialist party that would be like other parties and would work the parliamentary system in the same way as those had done in the past. All other views he regarded as retrograde and utopian at the same time. Socialism could be achieved only through a "socialistic" party, i.e., one which would be victorious when, as one of the major parties, its principles and policies had been naturally accepted by a majority of the population; a "party which accepts the socialist point of view and approaches the industrial problems of society with socialist assumptions in mind." Men who instead seek to establish a "socialist" party with its own methods, rather than those hitherto used in the British parliamentary system, would fail, "because its methods would be contrary to those by which society evolves."[79] MacDonald praised the fact that the British electoral system compels a party to attain a majority representation, because it forced a socialistic party to be active in local politics and serve an apprenticeship in municipal affairs, so that the party "is entrusted with legislative responsibility only after it has proved itself in administrative work."[80] Thus, for McDonald, the Labour Party was set firmly on the path already trod by the other two parties.

The way in which the first Labour Government was formed is proof both of MacDonald's ascendancy and of the status of the leader. When, after the general election of December, 1923, the question of a Labour Government was first mooted, discussions took place at various levels of Labour Party leadership. The NEC of the party, the TUC, and a group of leading Labour M.P.'s met to discuss the problem. All declared themselves in favor of taking office, and at each of these meetings Sidney Webb was at pains to "emphasize the enormous difficulties at all times, and in all parties, of constructing a Cabinet. . . ."

It was realized that the only conceivable way of doing the job was to leave it entirely to the one person who might be charged to do it, namely MacDonald; and I got the meeting to acquiesce in a self-denying ordinance that no one of us would seek to interfere for himself or otherwise. I had very vividly in mind the possibility of an attempt to get all appointments made by vote of the party meetings and I was delighted to find that this was not proposed or even mentioned by anyone. Nor was it ever suggested when the party meeting came to be held on the assembly of Parliament. The responsibility of so sudden and unexpected an assumption of office gave the party a shock which sobered even the wildest shouters.[81]

In the end, some pressure was brought to bear upon JRM, mainly through Henderson, both with regard to his own post and with regard to the composition of the Cabinet, although not about the distribution of offices.

It was MacDonald's view, not Jowett's, which determined the structure of the Labour Party and of Labour leadership. The defeated view erupted from time to time, however, and the controversy has been renewed, but whatever the intellectual strength of the argument of those who have sought to widen the extent of direct democracy inside the Labour Party, it has received little support from those in key positions. The Webbs were firmly convinced of the importance of strong Cabinet rule and the assertion of strong leadership. Their criticism was directed at the *type* of men who hitherto tended to emerge in this process. MacDonald's veneration for the established institutions of leadership was not shared by Sidney and Beatrice Webb. Instead of the existing governing class, they desired "an elite of unassuming experts who would appear to be no different in status from common men."[82]

The 1918 Constitution of the Labour Party, which laid the basis for a mass party, at the same time strengthened the hand of the big battalions, i.e., the power of the large unions which, in effect, meant the power of their leadership. The NEC no longer consisted only of representatives of trade unions and of ILP and socialist societies, elected by their delegates. Instead, the representatives of all sections of the movement were now to be elected by the Conference as a whole.[83]

The concentration of power inside the national party was matched by that inside the PLP. In 1922, with a quarter of the membership of the House of Commons and with general recognition as the official Opposition, the parliamentary leaders of the party felt they had arrived politically. They were revered and deferred to by new entrants into the House of Commons. They were the men who had raised the banner of the party in the dark days, had struggled against great odds, and had been hounded for their convictions (like MacDonald and Snowden). On them rested the patina of tradition; theirs was the glory of the head which had turned gray in the service of the movement. Uncritical followership was matched by demands for unquestioned trust. In 1924, large groups in the Labour Party and many of the "experts" on foreign affairs sought to bring pressure to bear on MacDonald, to persuade him to conclude a treaty of alliance with France. These attempts to force his hand angered the Prime Minister. "What we want," he told Norman Angell, who had sought to intervene, "is for the *New Leader* to carry on socialist propaganda and I want the ILP to carry on socialist propaganda, instead of which everybody wants to be a Cabinet Minister, or, if they do not want to be a Cabinet Minister, they want to make a Cabinet of their own."[84]

With a labour movement which, in its lower echelons, was still essentially democratic and egalitarian in organization, there was bound to be a reaction.

It came with force when the events of 1931 had turned the party's attitude toward MacDonald from admiration to bitter hatred. His character was reassessed; his conduct of Labour policy was questioned. Moreover, the party sought to guard itself against a repetition of the experience of 1931 by restricting the power of the leader of the party, especially in his role as actual or potential Prime Minister. In 1932, C. P. Trevelyan, an early critic of MacDonald (he had resigned from the Government in 1931 because of its failure to advocate a socialist policy), expressed the view that "we are a more democratic party now than ever, and new times require new systems —not necessarily by great breaking changes, but by great evolutionary developments in the direction of giving the mass of the movement a chance of saying how it shall be ruled."[85] Eventually, the NEC (which had consulted other sections of the labour movement), produced a report which it submitted at the 1933 Annual Conference. It advocated therein that, in the event of Labour again forming a government, the Prime Minister should consult with a committee of three members of the PLP and the Secretary of the Labour Party about the formation of his Cabinet. It also proposed that the Prime Minister should be subject to majority decisions of the Cabinet, and that he should ask for the approval of the Cabinet and of the PLP before deciding on a dissolution. The hedge around the powers of a Labour Prime Minister which these proposals erected was hardly made of thorns, and it was only natural that a more rigorous policy should have been advocated. However, a resolution to vest the selection of the Government in the hands of a committee composed of members of the National Joint Council of the Labour Party and of the Co-operative Party was defeated by a majority of three to one. In any case, even the mild proposals advocated and adopted in 1933 were forgotten in 1945. "The passage of time and further experience had led to these proposals being tacitly dropped," Attlee has told us in his autobiography.[86]

Cohesion and Conflict inside the PLP

From the very first the ties which bound the Party together were of the loosest possible kind. It has steadily, and, in my opinion, wisely, always declined to be bound by any programme, to subscribe to any dogma or to lay down any creed. . . . on the contrary, its strength has been its catholicity, its tolerance, its welcoming of all shades of political and even revolutionary thought, providing its chief object—the unifying of the workers' political power—was not damaged.[87]

The words in which G. J. Wardle, as chairman, characterized the Labour Party at its annual conference in 1917, could hardly describe the reality of relationship inside the party today, at its lowest, and even less at its highest, levels; although many of its members—from the humble and starry-eyed party officer of a local constituency organization, to one of the party's leaders speaking on the level of lofty platitudes, might subscribe to this description.

The crystallization of a clearly defined party leadership and the development of traditional leader-follower relationships have been described. The emphasis on internal party discipline and the insistence on a party program, however lax in execution, followed the evolution of the party from minority to majority status. At the same time it is idle to pretend that the insistence on formal unity could abolish conflict at any level. No amount of disciplinary action against local party members or parliamentarians could prevent the expression of conflicting opinions and the occasional revolt of minority groups.

In the early days of the Labour Party, the conflict of opinion was most obvious in the movement at large. The parliamentary party was, as we have seen, a comparatively loose alliance of representatives of the trade unions and of the ILP and other socialist organizations. With the emergence of a large leadership group, both inside the House of Commons and in the country as a whole, controversies centered increasingly on these groups; indeed, they may well be regarded as the initiators of controversies. The movement as a whole, certainly local party organizations, largely reverberate with the issues thus posed.[88]

A fairly formal analysis and description of some phases of the opposition inside the parliamentary party will, of course, not fully account for the emergence of conflict or the strength of rival factions. However, it may give some indication of the bases of certain lines of division among the Labour M.P.'s. The divergencies of opinion and the extent of the factions are best observed when the party is in office. Political opinion is put to the test of departmental policies and day-to-day administrative decisions. At the same time, loyalty and unfailing support in the division lobbies is expected of every Labour member. To oppose one's own Government by vote, even on comparatively minor issues, incurs the opprobrium of fellow M.P.'s and even more of the party leadership; we must take its expression generally as a sign of fundamental conflict.

During the first Labour Government, the back-bencher M.P.'s of the party, although restive, never failed to support the Government. The center of criticism was the ILP group in the PLP. It could claim that 129 M.P.'s (of 191) were ILP members; it counted 45 whose candidature had been endorsed by the party. They probably formed the bulk of the "regular ILP meeting [where] the business of the week is discussed, not with a view to developing points of difference but mutually helping one another in giving more efficient service. On some matters there are differences of opinion but they are never allowed to impair the splendid unity which is characteristic both of the ILP group and the wider parliamentary party to which it is proud to belong."[89] There was criticism of the Government's foreign policy and still more of its ability to tackle the unemployment problem by other means than those of orthodox public finance, but none of this led to any tangible repercussions inside the PLP. Only the Clydesiders, as we have seen, engaged in a silent opposition to the Government by boycotting its social functions.[90]

Scottish ILP members were to be prominent among the small knot of M.P.'s whose opposition to the policies of the second Labour Government carried them into the division lobbies, but only a minority of that group followed this line. It was altogether a rump of ILP members who pursued an independent line of opposition to the Labour Government. Nearly half the M.P.'s elected in 1929 were members of the ILP, and 37 of them had been ILP sponsored candidates. Those who were prepared to turn against their front bench were a much smaller number. This group, which acted definitely as "a party within the party," deciding regularly on its parliamentary action, numbered only 14 to 16. It originated in a resolution of the 1930 conference of the ILP, which declared that the ILP was an independent socialist organization with "a distinctive position within the party," and that it was "unreasonable to ask members of the Party to accept without question all the proposals of the government when these proposals are not themselves subject to the decisions of the Parliamentary Party . . . and often do not agree with the Party programmes as defined by the Party Conference."[91]

M.P.'s who belonged to the ILP were informed of this declaration and were asked to support the ILP aims in the House and vote against the Government if its proposal went contrary to declared ILP policy.

The ILP M.P.'s who followed conference decisions believed that they were carrying out the wishes of the movement in the country. Criticism of their action, J. Kinley, M.P., said at the ILP Conference in 1931, should be countered by the reflection that those who were Labour M.P.'s were not the Labour Party. The Labour Party was in the country. The movement sent the members to the House. Their main task should therefore be to put the program of the party into legislative form. "If the government would do so, there would be no need for a 'left wing' group."[92]

Within the general framework of discipline which the leadership of the ILP sought to impose on its Members of Parliament, there was yet to be as much latitude as possible on issues where no party-line policy existed. Thus, even within the small group of ILP Members of Parliament, there was division over the treatment of denominational schools in connection with the Government's education bill.[93] In other respects, too, the ILP leadership sought to preserve the independence of their M.P.'s against the demands of the movement. At the 1931 conference, ILP M.P.'s were criticized for not using the private-bill procedure to bring in measures advocating the principles and aims of the party. In reply, Campbell Stephen, one of the leading M.P.'s of the Labour Party, said that "bills were drawn up by Members with special knowledge . . . [and that] Members were interested in particular subjects not definitely ILP policy, matters of local interest for example, and those Members might introduce a Bill on these matters."[94]

The opposition to one or another aspect of Government policy was, of course, not restricted to the ILP faithfuls; others took part now and then: indeed, a total of 119 Labour M.P.'s voted against the Government in 17 different divisions between August, 1929, and January, 1931.[95] The ILP faithful, however, formed the nucleus of most of the opposition moves. The bulk of this opposition arose over the treatment of the unemployed or other financial measures seeking to restrict the numbers of those entitled to certain kinds of financial assistance, such as educational grants. When the "left wing" attempted to express more general disquiet at the policy of the government, as in the amendment to the vote on the King's speech at the beginning of the session in 1930-31, the vote was a complete failure. Only 13 MP's expressed their regret that the speech contained no proposals for "a socialist reorganization of industry, agriculture and banking . . . and for a fairer distribution of the National Income."[96]

Even at the end of the Labour Government's term of office, therefore, its support had not perceptibly decreased. The introduction of yet another bill to regulate unemployment benefits was the signal for renewed ILP attacks. During the various stages of the bill, the Government was challenged on seven different occasions by some of its supporters. But neither amendments to the bill nor general opposition resulted in more than 25 Labour M.P.'s voting against the Labour Government. Only 4 of these were trade union M.P.'s; only 8 had originally followed working class occupations, and the same number had finished their education in the elementary school. Those who subjectively identified themselves most strongly with working-class demands were occupationally much less working-class than the PLP as a whole. The bulk of the working-class M.P.'s remained loyal to the party leadership and so, of course, did the majority of middle-class M.P.'s. How then did the faithful and the rebels regard each other?

The prophets of "socialism in our time" saw the faithful whipped to dance around the golden calf of the leadership. So Jennie Lee thought; she "was totally unprepared for the solid rows of decent, well-intentioned, unpretentious Labour back-benchers [who] in the long run . . . did the most deadly damage. Again and again an effort was made to rouse them from their inertia. On every occasion they reacted like a load of damp cement. They would see nothing, do nothing, listen to nothing that had not first been given the seal of MacDonald's approval."[97]

For the middle-of-the-road Labour M.P.—earnest, hard-working, unambitious, and unimaginative—the opposition was just a group of cranks. The then chairman of the PLP described the viewpoint of the middle-of-the-road group:

> The sincerity of these difficult members . . . was never questioned . . . but they were in essence . . . political individualists as insofar as they considered their own convenience before the needs of the Party, they were bad colleagues. They believed themselves to be moved by principles, whereas they were really the victims of pride . . . what for the sake of the Labour Party others had to endure they would not have. The immaculate purity of their Socialist conscience was not to be fouled by such base contacts and compromises as others had to make . . . as players in the Party they would do everything except pass the ball.[98]

The opposition inside Labour's ranks in Parliament during the period of the postwar Labour Governments and the years following them permits a more detailed knowledge of what, by and large, constitutes Labour's "left wing." Opposition during these more recent years has been more widespread, involving both larger numbers of people and a wider range of issues. In addition, the size of Labour's majority in the first postwar Parliament and the suspension of the standing orders of the PLP during most of these years, have combined to facilitate the expression of opposition to the Government.

Pressure from the whips and the strong feelings of loyalty no doubt dissuaded some critics of the Government from expressing their views in the division lobbies; but, by and large, deed seems to have followed thought. This view is borne out by the fact that the distribution of voting in opposition to the party whip or the party line does not follow a purely random spread. During the period 1945-54, the Government (or after 1951 the party leadership) found itself opposed by its own tail on twelve important occasions.[99] These involved a total of 540 individual acts of opposition and 213 M.P.'s—just under half of the total number of those who sat on the Labour benches during these years.

Among those who opposed, four groups can be distinguished:

a) Pacifists, i.e., all those who rejected outright the Government's conscription bill—39 members.

b) Those of the non-Pacifists who voted only once or on one issue against the Government—97 members.

c) Those who opposed the Government twice or more often—77 members.

d) Among this latter group are 24 members whose opposition was persistent, extending to four, five, or even seven different occasions.

Pure pacifism inside the PLP was very much an issue which moved older and more seasoned politicians. A large number of them had passed through the ILP; over one-third had sat in the House of Commons before 1945—mostly as early as the twenties. The character of this group is similar to that of the opposition during the second Labour Government; indeed, we can find many direct links between the two groups. Originating largely in working-class or lower-middle-class homes, many had risen through the educational ladder and had become members of the professions; only 15 were still following working-class occupations or worked for working-class organizations by the time they entered Parliament.

When we look at the general, not specifically pacifist, opposition, and compare this group with the PLP as a whole, an interesting picture emerges. The more frequent the opposition, the less representative of the Labour benches as a whole is its character. Thus, one-third of all Labour M.P.'s in the 1945 House of Commons had been in Parliament before that election; among those who opposed the Government on only one issue, the corresponding percentage is below 25; among the 24 "persistent offenders," all but two had entered the House in 1945 or later. Nor did the opposition tend to come from trade union-sponsored candidates: trade union M.P.'s constituted only 33 per cent of all of the three post-1945 Parliaments. For the group of M.P.'s who opposed the party leadership on only one issue, the percentage was 25; for the persistent offenders, 12 per cent. By comparing the social character of (a) all those who opposed the leadership two or three times and (b) those who did so four times or more, further light is shed on the character of this intraparty opposition (Table 6).

It is significant that the opposition to the actions of Mr. Attlee's Government and to his later leadership arose largely over foreign and defense policies. It is here that policy decisions came into conflict with traditional socialist sentiment and the declared aims of the party. In the field of economic and social security, on the other hand, the Labour Government proceeded to carry out its declared policies, and consequently aroused less antagonism. But these issues were clearly not those which the labour movement and the mass of Labour's followers regarded as vital. It is probably for that reason more than any other that the opposition lacked, at least in its beginning, *organized* support outside Parliament. Unlike the opposition during the period of the second Labour Government, it lacked an organizational, and, in part at least, an ideological basis. A comparison of individual divisions shows that each attracts a slightly differently constituted opposition. Bearing in mind the fact that we are concerned with small numbers in any case, the divisions show the representativeness of different opposition views. Thus, the revolt against "18-months conscription" attracted a most widely scattered support; the attack on Mr. Bevin's Palestine policy, on the other hand, seems the most narrowly based of oppositions (Table 7).

Yet it would be completely wrong to regard each issue as unique and independent; the series of votes which we have considered show a much greater degree of interconnection than would have resulted from complete randomness. Through its different configurations, there persists a general "oppositionalism"; it has links with acts of defiance toward the party line in the period before 1945, and we can pursue its continuance after 1954,

Table 6

Composition of Voting Blocs within the Labour Party in the 1945 House of Commons*

| | PARLIAMENTARY LABOUR PARTY VOTING BLOCS | | | |
	Occasional Defectors (53)	Persistent Offenders (24)	TOTALS IN 1945 (394)	TOTALS IN 1951 (295)
Education:				
Elementary school only	13	5	—	74
University (other than Oxford or Cambridge)	18	7	c. 101-136	122
Oxford or Cambridge	11	6	c. 46- 59	57
Occupation:				
Professional	28	16	c. 130-165	133
Lawyers	(5)	(4)		
Teachers, Lecturers	(4)	(3)		
Journalists, Authors	(13)	(4)		
Other professions	(6)	(5)		
Entrepreneurs, Managers	5	2	c. 23- 31	17
Manual workers, clerks, and working-class group officials	16	5	c. 125-155	108
Others	4	1	c. 20- 38	37
Unknown	—	—	c. 23- 78	37

N.B. "Occasional defectors" opposed the leadership twice or three times; while "persistent offenders" did so at least four times.
*The figures for the composition of the PLP in 1945 are taken from Ross, **op. cit.**, and from McCallum and Readman, **The British General Election of 1945.** Neither figures are complete nor entirely reliable. The 1951 figures are derived from D. Butler, **The British General Election of 1951.**

Table 7

Composition of the "Revolt inside Labour's Ranks" in Post-War Years

PERCENTAGE BREAKING WITH LEADERSHIP	Conscription (1947)	Palestine (1948)	Defense (1952)	Hydrogen Bomb (1954)
Trade-union sponsored M.P.'s	19	3	18	18
Elementary school only	48	4	27	25
University education	32	75	56	46
Manual workers, party or Trade Union officials	36	—	26	26
Professionals	36	76	62	56
(Numbers involved)	(73)	(30)	(57)	(61)

despite the fact that the PLP reimposed its standing orders and the "big split" appears to have been healed.[100]

Conclusions: A Growing Elite in a Changing Society

The advance of the Labour Party, from a small organization led by a group of parliamentarians of varying views and sometimes conflicting loyalties to a mass party which eventually became the sole bearer of governmental power, is a unique social and political phenomenon; among parties of the Left in western Europe, only the Norwegian Socialist party knows a parallel. The Labour Party's history has been repeatedly described and various aspects of it (e.g., foreign policy) have been investigated. In this paper, an attempt has been made to analyze the development of its leadership cadre and the attitudes and problems of its elite.

The party in its *status nascendi* did, of course, not lack leadership; on the contrary, it was served fairly devotedly by three groups of functionaries. Each fulfilled an essential task at that particular juncture. It had a group of local leaders, who sought to organize the supporters of socialist policies mainly in the industrial areas of Scotland and northern England, Lancashire, and the Midlands. Secondly, there were the officials of sympathizing trade unions—regional or national—who were active in municipal politics and in the House of Commons. Finally, there was a small bunch of socialist propagandists—publicists and intellectuals in general—who gave a considerable part of their spare time; and, in a few cases, men and women of independent means who gave their whole time, to further the cause of Labour. The qualities required of the early generation of Labour leaders were more those of character, coupled with the ability to put oneself across, facility in writing and speaking, oratorical gifts, and physical endurance, rather than intellect or expertise.[101]

Since then, political leadership in the Labour Party has become institutionalized; it follows a career pattern of full-time activity not dissimilar to that of other professions. Parliamentary activity or trade union leadership has become increasingly *the* road to political eminence. The NEC of the Labour Party is today composed either of second-ranking trade union leaders (the really important ones prefer to go on the TUC rather than on the executive committee of the Labour Party) or of leading parliamentarians, especially ministers or ex-Ministers. Harold Laski was the last member of the Labour party executive who was not either an M.P. or an ex-M.P. (the women's section apart). This has meant also that the leadership is increasingly centered in London, where, apart from the Labour Party and the TUC itself, all the major trade unions and other semipolitical working-class organizations have their headquarters.[104]

The constitution of the ILP provided for the representation of all the regions on the party's governing body. On the NEC we could still, in the first twenty years or so, find men whose political reputation was largely made in the provinces. Whatever regional activity, as distinct from local, exists today inside the Labour Party is entirely directed toward organization and education; the regional conference of the ILP, where policy was discussed, has no present-day equivalent. Today, political reputation is increasingly made in Parliament itself or in junior office, and the selection occurs largely through the existing leadership. It is only when a vociferous and able oppositional group in the PLP succeeds in gaining first the ear and then the votes of an active minority in local party organizations, as was the case with the Bevanite "rebels," that a change in the composition of the party leadership can take place.

It is perhaps in consequence of this that the influence and importance of the charismatic leader has declined in the Labour Party. Moreover, while a strong personality is probably essential, and while the ability to achieve transference, as well as attractiveness of voice and mien, are no doubt helpful, we must not forget that modern means of mass communication can do much even with mediocre talents.[102] It is also clear, as Max Weber pointed out forty-odd years ago, that the very act of a democratic election invests leaders with a charismatic authority.[103] Professor Laski's suggestion to Mr. Attlee, apparently made in a conversation between the two men, that Attlee should hand over the leadership to someone who had "more of the essential gifts" seems based on a misconception of what is required, however justified it may have been on other grounds. Attlee's reply that, as Laski had pointed out, he had "neither the personality nor the distinctiveness to tempt [him] to think that [he] should have any value apart from the party which he served," is on the other hand, a typical Attleean understatement. It is the very identification of leader and party which makes for the strength of his position.

The leadership is also helped in maintaining its position of power by the party bureaucracy. The growth of the Labour Party headquarters and, in this connection, especially its research and publicity departments, has put at the leadership's disposal a civil service which is invaluable during the period when the party is in opposition and which gives the leaders a great advantage over party members in the lower ranks, including probably the majority of Members of Parliament.

This largely self-recruiting leadership becomes increasingly distant from the rank and file of the party membership. Indeed, it might be accurate to speak of a series of concentric and increasingly narrower circles into which the Labour Party is divided, each fairly self-contained and with recruitment proceeding generally only from one parallel to the next. The ideal-type *cursus honorum* inside the Labour Party is still that which starts from local party membership and proceeds via officership in local organizations or trade unions to municipal elected office, and then via the House of Commons to the Treasury Bench. In this, the British Labour Party is distinct from the Conservative Party. Of late, however, other and extraordinary ladders of advancement have increasingly been used. Cripps, to give but one example, was recruited for the Labour Party largely through the endeavors of Herbert Morrison. He was hardly expected to start his activity in the local party organization. The question of finding a seat for him was apparently discussed at the highest level, as his father could write to him after a visit to the Webbs, that "the question of a proper London constituency for you arose . . . they [the party leaders] have a very sympathetic attitude *to your claim.*"[104]

In an increasingly mobile society it seems only natural that a growing proportion of Labour M.P.'s should belong occupationally to the middle class. Although many of them will have risen from the working class, their attitudes must be colored by their own social position. In addition, we have seen that the very atmosphere of the House of Commons, of which the Labour Party now forms an integral part, conditions its members. All this need not necessarily mollify them or weaken their socialism—we have seen how just the left-wing opposition reckoned a large number of middle-class M.P.'s among its supporters—but it hampers communication between leaders and followers. Thus, in the political field, the Labour Party seems to be creating or maintaining a static system of stratification which it is seeking to destroy in the economic and social field.

Up till now, the influx of men and women from the ranks of wage-earners or their representatives into the House of Commons has been maintained largely through the "proprietary boroughs" which are in the hands of the trade unions. This pre-emption of a third or a quarter of all Labour seats by trade union nominees is, however, only a custom, although one hallowed by tradition and also apparently supported by party headquarters.[105] It need not necessarily continue on that scale; recent shows of unrest in local Labour Parties suggest that it will not do so. We have even less reason to assume that the composition of future Labour Cabinets will follow the tradition of shared representation between the middle-class and the working-class element in the PLP. Beatrice Webb thought, in 1930, that

every succeeding Labour Prime Minister in the construction of a Cabinet, will be confronted with the necessity of including . . . the representatives of the great organized industries [i.e., the principal Trade Union leaders] . . . just as the PM 200 years ago had to have the Duke of Newcastle or of some equivalent nobleman in his Cabinet, so the Labour PM in the 20th century will find it necessary to include in his administration the General Secretary or other official of the miners, cotton operatives (etc.) together with the representatives of the Consumers' Cooperative Movement. This firm anchorage of the Labour Party in the working class organization may be deemed a guarantee that Labour administrations will continue to represent adequately four-fifths of the population.[106]

Mr. Attlee's Government remains somewhat in this tradition. But with the exception of Mr. Bevin, the ministers who had entered politics via the trade union movement hardly belonged to the top ranks of trade union leaders, nor perhaps even to the second drawer.[107] Since then, there has been still less evidence that leading trade union officials are eager to exchange the real power which they hold in the industrial field for the vague and possibly wholly illusory power which might be theirs as members of the House of Commons or even as Junior Ministers.[108]

Beginning with MacDonald, the British Left has increasingly held that the professionalization of political activity and the existence of a comparatively small nucleus of leaders who make the vital decisions—subject to referendum-like approval through general elections or party congresses— are necessary developments in the modern state exercising wide economic and social controls. It is clear that this development increases the social stratification inside the field of politics, either directly through power as a dimension of social differentiation, or indirectly through the socio-economic standards imported from the world outside into Labour politics. There is little evidence that "successive Labour administrations [have] maintained by precept and example, the modest personal expenditure and unpretentious ways of social intercourse implied by the ideal of equality between man and man."[109]

This is not the place to consider whether they should have done so, nor to ask whether the above-mentioned trend has been inevitable. One thing seems clear: the development has led to tensions inside the wider labour movement, tensions which have been created through the ideological precepts of a primitive (i.e., original) egalitarianism and the belief in direct democracy which have been inherent in the British Labour tradition.

Notes

1. I had access to the Lansbury Papers and the Passfield (Webb) Papers, both of which are deposited in the Library of the London School of Economics. I am grateful to the Passfield Trustees for permission to consult the latter and to quote from them.

A bibliography of the general literature on the history and structure of the Labour Party can not be given here. For a treatment of the social structure of Labour Cabinet Ministers see Jean Bonner, "The Four Labour Cabinets," *Sociological Review*, VI (July, 1958), 37-48, and also a forthcoming book (in

Polish) by Professor Baumann of Warsaw University.

2. This paper was substantially completed before the British general election of October, 1959.

3. The most significant development in this direction has been the disaffiliation of the Independent Labour Party from the Labour Party in 1932 and its subsequent sharp decline as a force in Parliament and in the country.

3a. Cf. Herbert Morrison, *Government and Parliament* (London: Oxford University Press, 1954), p. 29.

4. There has been a marked tendency

for the principal trade union leaders (general secretaries, etc.) to refrain from seeking a parliamentary career.

5. Detailed investigations of the membership of Labour party constituency organizations and of their activities are unfortunately rare. See, however, J. Gould, "Riverside: A Labour Constituency," *Fabian Journal,* November, 1954; W. Fienburgh a. o., "Put Policy on the Agenda: A Study of Labour Party Organization," *Fabian Journal,* February, 1952; and A. H. Birch, *Small Town Politics* (London: Oxford University Press, 1959), chap. v.

6. The relevant reference works are: *Who's Who; Who Was Who; Dod's Parliamentary Companion; The Times House of Commons* (for each general election); *The Labour Who's Who* (1st ed., 1927; 2d ed., 1927). The latter work contains nearly 2,000 entries.

7. Cf. T. Drummond Shiels, "Sidney Webb as an Administrator," in M. Cole (ed.), *The Webbs and their Work* (London: F. Muller, 1949).

8. Of the 29 M.P.'s elected under the auspices of the LRC in 1906, 24 were elected without Liberal opposition or with implied Liberal tolerance. They had either a straight fight in a one-member constituency or they were running tacitly in harness with a Liberal against Conservative opposition in double-member constituencies. Cf. F. Bealey, and H. Pelling, *The Labour Party in British Politics, 1900-1906* (New York: St. Martin's Press, 1958), pp. 298-99.

9. Cf. W. P. Maddox, *Foreign Relations in British Labour Politics* (Cambridge: Harvard University Press, 1934), p. 209.

10. Cf. "The Labour Party and the Books that Helped to Make It," *Review of Reviews,* XXXIII (1909), pp. 568-82. This article gives the responses of 45 (out of 51) Labour and Lib-Lab M.P.'s to questions on early reading and intellectual influences.

11. Fenner Brockway, *Socialism over 60 Years: The Life of Jowett of Bradford 1864-1944* (London: Allen and Unwin, 1946), p. 70. Yet even the position of salaried Labour M.P.'s was not an easy one, certainly not in the period of high prices immediately after World War I. With a parliamentary salary of $400 and a grant from his trade union,

Shinwell found, in 1922, that he had just over £5 a week to spend in London. Of this, he paid 15/s for a small room in an unfashionable district. "Meals in the House were quite beyond the means of most Scottish members and we used to walk miles to discover cheap and clean food." E. Shinwell, *Conflict without Malice* (London: Odhams Press, 1955), p. 82.

12. P. Snowden, *An Autobiography* (London: I. Nicholson and Watson, 1934), I, 174.

13. *Ibid.,* p. 216.

14. *Report of the Labour Party Conference of 1911,* p. 31 (from the report on the work of the PLP).

15. Only 31 (of 42) Labour M.P.'s voted in favor of "Right to Work" resolution in 1908, and only 17 supported Hardie's motion denouncing the use of police and soldiers to break up a strike in a colliery. On the other hand, a minority on the Left, mainly ILPer's decided to vote on issues according to their merit and in this frequently defied the decisions of the group. Thus, Jowett, Lansbury, Snowden, O'Grady, and Thorne voted against the National Insurance Bill, as they objected to the contributory element in its financial structure. P. Snowden, *op. cit.,* p. 228.

16. Report of 1911, *op. cit.,* I, 218.

17. *Ibid., passim.*

18. I.e., Hardie, MacDonald, Snowden, Jowett, Richardson, and, on the other hand, Clynes and James Parker.

19. Cf. Reid, *op. cit.,* p. 217.

20. Beatrice Webb wrote, in January, 1924, that "Sidney came away feeling that the Cabinet would err on the side of respectability—too many outsiders, too many peers. J[ames] R[amsay] M[acDonald] oddly enough does not like the plebeian element and chooses as his intimate associates not the workmen but the lawyer or big administrator with the manner and attitude of the ruling and thoroughly comfortable class." *Diaries, 1912-1924,* ed. M. Cole (London: Longmans, Green, 1952), p. 263.

21. Sir Frederick Maurice, *Haldane* (London: Faber and Faber, 1937-39), II, 137.

22. Lord Chelmsford was not even a member of the Labour Party. In the 1924 edition of *Dod's Parliamentary Compa-*

nion, he is still described as a "Conservative." His entry in 1925 carries no party label. In 1929, he is described as "Labour." The 1932 edition says "Socialist."

23. Beatrice Webb analyzed the 1929 Labour Government along similar lines and came to the following division of the Government, including the Under-Secretaries:

Manual Workers	17
Lower-Middle Class	9
Old Governing Class	10
Aristocrats	4
	40

Diaries, 1924-1932, p. 210. See also *Political Quarterly,* 1930, p. 104-9.

24. Sixteen of the nineteen members of the second Labour Government had served in the previous administration, 12 in the Cabinet.

25. Of Attlee's 20 Cabinet Ministers, only 4 had sat in the second Labour Cabinet.

26. Bonham, in *The Middle Class Vote* (London: Faber and Faber, 1954), estimated that one-third of the middle-class vote went to Labour in 1945, and less than one-fourth in 1951. The middle-class vote accounted for about 18.5 per cent of total Labour Votes in 1945.

27. Cf. J. S. F. Ross, *Parliamentary Representation* (2d ed.; London: Eyre and Spottiswoode, 1948), and R. B. MacCallum and A. Readman, *The British General Election of 1945* (London: Oxford University Press, 1947), *passim.* This trend has continued in all postwar elections. The breakdown for the 1951 PLP is given in Table 6.

28. C. Trevelyan, *From Liberalism to Labour* (London: Allen and Unwin, 1921), p. 29.

29. J. Hodge, *Workman's Cottage to Windsor Castle* (London: Sampson Low, 1931), p. 138.

30. Cf. Max Weber, "Politik als Beruf," in *Gesammelte Politische Schriften* (Munich: Drei Masken Verlag, 1921).

31. I am, of course, thinking in this connection of those occupying the top positions in the civil service and the armed forces.

32. In *The Miner,* 1887.

33. Dalton, *Call Back Yesterday* (London: Muller, 1953), I, 145.

34. A. M. Hamilton, *Remembering My Good Friends* (London: Cape, 1944), p. 128.

35. In the case of the second Labour Government, MacDonald sent out a circular requesting the wearing of court dress for the swearing-in ceremony. Attlee did away with this custom in 1945 (in agreement with the Palace).

36. *Diaries, 1924-1932,* p. 5.

37. *Ibid,* p. 220.

38. Thomas Jones, *A Diary with Letters* (London: Oxford University Press), 1954, p. xxxv.

39. Beatrice Webb, *op. cit.,* p. 117.

40. *Ibid.,* p. 16-17.

41. F. A. Pakenham, *Born to Believe* (London: Cape, 1953), p. 132. Cf. Hugh Gaitskell: "At Oxford in the Twenties" in A. Briggs and J. Saville (eds.) *Essays in Labour History in Memory of G. D. H. Cole* (New York: St. Martin's Press, 1960).

42. There were, of course, also non-bourgeois social nuclei which became influential in the labour movement. They are, by the nature of things, even more difficult to trace. For an account of one such, see T. Brennan, "The White House," *Cambridge Journal,* January, 1954.

43. *Op. Cit.,* p. 83.

44. Labour's share in the wartime coalition helped in this.

45. The specialization of political offices, especially junior ministerial appointments, and the stress on expertise in the selection for office have tended to reduce the proportion of politicians who step right into Cabinet office.

46. D. Kirkwood, *My Life of Revolt* (London: G. G. Harrap & Co., 1935), p. 217.

47. R. Smillie, *Life for Labour* (London: Mills & Boom, 1924), p. 176.

48. *Op. cit.,* p. 4.

49. Sir A. Fitzroy, *Memoirs* (New York: Doran, 1925), II, 45.

50. J. R. Clynes, *Memoirs* (London: Hutchison & Co., 1937), II, 45.

51. *Diaries, 1924-1932,* p. 42.

52. Quoted in M. A. Hamilton, *J. R. MacDonald, 1923-1925,* p. 29.

53. Letter of March 13, 1930, in Passfield Papers.

54. P. C. Gordon-Walker "On Being a Cabinet-Minister," *Encounter,* April,

1956. Morrison has given a similar picture of the burden of a Cabinet Minister in charge of a major department. *Op cit.*, pp. 62-63.

55. Gordon-Walker, *op. cit.* p. 22.

56. There has been little thinking by Labour politicians about the problems of cabinet government. The division between departmental ministers and those in charge with specific functions was —very briefly—discussed by Attlee in "The Labour Party in Perspective" (pp. 128-30 of 1949 ed.).

57. Passfield Papers, IV, 18, f. 25.

58. Inman, *No Going Back* (London: Williams and Nortgate, 1952),

59. Morrison, *op. cit.* p. 335. See also E. Shinwell, *op. cit.*, chap. xix and xxi *passim.*

60. E. F. Wertheimer, *Portrait of the Labour Party* (London: G. P. Putnam's Sons, 1929).

61. D. Kirkwood, *op. cit.*, p. 202-5.

62. See especially the last two chapters of his autobiography.

63. *My Life for Labour* (London, 1924), p. 133. See also G. N. Barnes, *From Workshop to War Cabinet* (London: Jenkins, 1923), pp. 70-75.

64. H. Nicolson, *King George the Fifth* (London: Constable & Sons, 1952), p. 386. (From Lord Stamfordham's Memorandum to the King on the formation of the first Labour Government.)

65. Cf. Sir P. Hastings, *Autobiography* (London: Heineman, 1948).

66. The absence of suitably qualified lawyers on the Labour benches made it particularly easy for a man like him to gain office.

67. Cf. F. Brockway, *Bermondsey Story: The Life of Alfred Salter* (London: Allen and Unwin, 1949).

68. V. de Bunsen, *Charles Roden Buxton, A Memoir* (London: Allen and Unwin, 1948), p. 13.

69. A. L. Lowell, *The Government of England* (New York: MacMillan, 1916), Vol. II, chap. xxxv.

70. This was generally held to apply to issues involving pacifism. However, absolute pacifism has declined inside the Labour party, and the clause has been invoked on a variety of issues and by non-pacifists.

71. G. Elton, *The Life of James Ramsey MacDonald* (London: Collins, 1939), p. 161.

72. J. R. MacDonald, *Socialism* (Indianapolis: Bobbs-Merrill Co., 1924), p. 230.

73. *Socialism and Government* (London: Independent Labour Party, 1909), I, 107-26.

74. *Ibid.*, I, 124.

75. *Parliament and Revolution* (Manchester: National Labour Press), p. 61.

76. Quoted in Brockway, *op. cit.*, p. 104.

77. L. Hall, a.o. *Let Us Reform the Labour Party* (Manchester: Privately printed), p. 14.

78. Cf. Jowett's article in *Clarion*, July 24, 1908.

79. *Socialism and Government*, II, 12.

80. *Ibid.* I, 137.

81. Passfield Papers, IV, 18, f. 4.

82. Beatrice Webb, *Diaries, 1924-1932*, p. 171, in reference to Haldane's death and their difference of opinion on the subject of the ruling class.

83. In 1937, the party reverted, however, to its old practice. The representatives of the various sections are now elected by the sections (*trade unions, constituency parties, and socialist societies*). Only the 5 women members of the Executive are elected by the conference as a whole.

84. Norman Angell, *After All* (London: Hamilton, 1951), p. 243. Some sections of the ILP took a very similar view to that of MacDonald of their task. See Clifford Allen's speech as chairman of the ILP conference in 1924.

85. *Report of the Annual Conference of the Labour Party*, 1933.

86. Attlee, *As It Happened* (London: W. Heinemann, 1954), p. 156, quoted in R. T. McKenzie, *British Political Parties* (London: W. Heinemann, 1955), p. 332. I have drawn frequently on McKenzie in describing the post-1931 development.

87. *Report of the Annual Conference of the Labour Party*, 1917, p. 82, quoted in McKenzie, *op. cit.*, p. 473.

88. The problem of the relationship between the different levels of Labour Party opinion formation and policy-making and that of the ultimate locus of power inside the Labour Party has not yet been fully clarified. See the contro-

versy between S. Rose, R. T. McKenzie, and R. Miliband in *Political Studies,* between June, 1956 through June, 1958.

89. Report of the NAC of the ILP to the 1924 party conference *(Conference Report,* p. 45).

90. Cf. Letter of Sidney Webb, to his wife, of February 12, 1924.

91. Quoted in G. D. H. Cole, *A History of the Labour Party from 1914* (London: Rutledge and Kegan Paul, 1948), p. 246.

92. *Report of the 1931 Conference of the Independent Labour Party,* p. 34. See also Jowett's defense of his part in the opposition, in the *Bradford Pioneer* (Brockway, *op. cit.,* p. 289).

93. The amendment proposed that the bill to raise the school-leaving age to 15 should not come into operation until provisions had been made for the extra burden thrown on the denominational schools. Thirty-seven Labour M.P.'s voted with the Conservatives on this issue. In thus voicing the demands of strong minorities in their constituencies they defied a party direction, given at the time of the election campaign, which warned candidates against giving pledges on this issue.

94. *Report of Independent Labour Party Annual Conference,* 1931, p. 39.

95. Cf. F. Brockway in the *New Leader,* January 23, 1931.

96. Hansard (5th series), Vol. CCXLIV, col. 307 *et seq.*

97. Jenny Lee, *Tomorrow Is a New Day* (London; Cresset Press, 1939), p. 145.

98. H. Snell (Lord Snell) *Men, Movements, and Myself* (London: J. M. Dent, 1938), II. Snell was at that time chairman of the PLP.

99. The following "acts of opposition" were analyzed:

1. Amendment opposing the appointment of part-time directors moved in the committee stage of the Civil Aviation Bill; August, 1946 (21).

2. Amendment on foreign policy tabled during the debate on the address but not voted on when called; November, 1946 (43).

3. Amendment on conscription during the same debate (46).

4. Second reading of National Service Bill opposed; March, 1947 (73).

5. Third reading of the same bill opposed; May, 1947 (39).

6. Signatories to the "Nenni" telegram, congratulating Nenni on his electoral victory, despite the fact that Nenni's party opposed the Saragat Socialists with whom the Labour Party had ties as fellow members of the Socialist International.

7. Motion opposing Government policy on the employment of civil servants who were Communists or Fascists. Supported by only five signatories when forced to a division; March, 1948 (41).

8. Second reading of Palestine Bill opposed; March, 1948 (30).

9. Critical amendments to Government of Ireland Bill; April-May, 1949 (58).

10. Conservative Government's statement on defense opposed in division, contrary to party policy of abstention; March, 1957 (57).

11. Motion to approve order in council to extend National Service Act from 1954 to 1959 opposed; November, 1953 (40).

12. Amendment to Atomic Energy Bill, aiming at the banning of the hydrogen bomb; April, 1954 (61).

100. For example, the debate on defense in March, 1955. The Labour party had put forward a mildly critical amendment. A section of the PLP desired an equivocal banning renunciation of nuclear weapons and abstained in the vote on the amendment. Of the 62 who did so, 32 had been concerned in the original Bevanite revolt on defense in 1952.

101. Cf. Some of the biographies and autobiographies of early Labour leaders, e.g., Stewart's *Life of Keir Hardie,* Brockway's *Life of Jowett,* and Snowden's *Autobiography.* See also John Paton's *Left Turn* and, for a slightly later period, Shinwell's *Autobiography.*

102. Shinwell, *Conflict without Malice* (London: Odhams, 1955).

103. See M. Weber on the inversion (Umdeutung) of charisma, in *Wirtschaft und Gesellschaft* (Tuebingen: Mohr, 1921), chap. ii, para. 14.

104. E. Estorick, *Stafford Cripps* (London: Heineman, 1949), p. 79 (my

italics). Pethwick-Lawrence's entry into Labour politics proceeded in a similar fashion.

105. Recent happenings in connection with nominations to traditional trade union seats suggest the use of this ancient term. It seems that custom inside the Labour Party—though not the law of the Land—gives the trade unions an option to fill a seat once held by trade unionists, with another similarly sponsored candidate.

106. Beatrice Webb "The Disappearance of the Governing Class," *Political Quarterly*, (1930), pp. 104-9.

107. Bevin's entry into Parliament actually followed on his appointment as Minister of Labour and probably would not have happened otherwise.

108. In 1955, only four minor trade unions were represented in Parliament by their general secretaries. Cf. B. C. Roberts, *Trade Union Government and Administration* (London: Bell, 1959), p. 387.

109. Beatrice Webb. *op. cit.*, p. 109.

Oligarchic Problems
in a German Party District

by RENATE MAYNTZ

The Setting of the Problem

RECENT history confronts the western democracies with a serious challenge to evaluate the efficiency of their political systems. Within this context the results of my case study about leadership selection in a democratic political party in postwar Berlin have significance.

Political democracy at the time of the Weimar Republic was plagued by conflicts and shortcomings, which contributed to its brusque end in 1933. After World War II, only West Germany had the chance to make a new start. The threatening proximity of totalitarianism—in the Soviet Zone and the Soviet satellites—and the memory of the defeat from within that German democracy had once before suffered, make vital the questions of how well genuine democratization has taken root and how it is effectively shaping present-day political life in free Germany.

Postwar research in Germany has mainly emphasized political organizations and processes at higher levels, such as the Laender or the Federal Republic.[1] To estimate the extent of substantive democracy, knowledge is also needed about the internal processes of party activity at lower organizational levels. Otherwise it is difficult, if not impossible, to say how far the political parties of Germany have become effective means for political expression and participation, rather than simply agencies for oligarchic control.

To investigate leadership-selection processes and related activities of a German party organization involves analyzing the functional processes found wherever political democracy exists. Although this study is distinctively concerned with postwar German politics, its findings should be relevant beyond the local situation.

An analyst of any democratic political system has in mind a number of functions which political parties should perform if that system is to work effectively and approximate democratic ideals. One of these party functions is to present suitable candidates to the electorate, which, in turn, is to make the final choice. Where party organizations have a virtual monopoly over nominations, even a well-informed and interested citizenry cannot elect representatives of ability and political consequence unless it is presented with appropriate choices by the parties. Here the intraparty processes of candidate selection are decisive.

In analyzing these selection processes two criteria can be applied. The first refers to the democratic character of the process. Capable and willing citizens should be able to rise to positions of political leadership; selection should be characterized by democratic "open-ness." The second refers to the practical outcome of the process, that is, to the quality—in the widest sense—of candidates. Clearly, a given process might satisfy only one criterion, or neither.

Linked with their function of sponsoring candidates, parties must present to the electorate meaningful choices on relevant policy issues. In voting for a given candidate, citizens are said also to subscribe to a particular stand on policy issues.[2] In order to evaluate how a party performs this function, we must first answer three major questions. First, does a party's platform adequately express an alternative view on the crucial policy issues which the government (at all political levels) is called upon to handle? Second, are the views championed by a party the result of an opinion-formation process which not only gives party members at the lowest level a chance to participate, but which also considers the opinions and wishes of the party's relevant public? Third, what are the qualifications and claims to democratic legitimation of those party leaders? In a given party, these criteria may be met in whole, in part, or not at all.

Competition between rival parties is essential to a democratic political system. This competition is expected not only to stimulate political interest and a large election turn-out (something which a single party in a totalitarian country can also do), but it is also expected to stimulate citizens to make politically responsible choices. To be a serious rival force, able to compete successfully, every party must seek to be an effective organization. To this end, processes such as recruiting members, training officers, allocating tasks, and activities serving organizational maintenance must be sustained at significant levels.

This brief discussion of some functions which a society committed to political democracy can expect from its political parties has remained on a normative level. Democratic parties themselves accept these values as limiting conditions, if not as factors determining their activities. However, how far a specific political party accepts, as its proper and perhaps noblest goals, the functions attributed to it by an observer is an empirical question. From the party viewpoint, the primary organizational goal is to achieve power in order to realize certain intentions—possibly stated as an ideologically based program—through participation in governmental decision-making.[3] Perceiving power as an instrumental value, rather than an end in itself, is more appropriate for ideologically based parties, such as one finds in Germany, than for platform parties, like those found in the United States. However, even in parties which, in order to legitimize their striving for power, stress the superiority of their political outlook, there is a tendency in day-to-day political action for power to be seen as an end in itself. This is particularly true for organizational subunits, which have no part in any governmental implementation of the party's program.

For the party, various secondary goals stand in a means-end relation to the primary organizational goal of maintaining and increasing its power. Achievement of these secondary goals can be evaluated in terms of efficiency, a standard common to all formal organization and relative to their goals. Any set of party activities, particularly those important in creating the basis for successful competition, can be evaluated against this standard.

Several of the activities required if parties are to fulfill their functions within a democratic political system would be seen by a party as means to achieve its organizational goal of power. With reference to democracy, selecting able candidates is important because the electorate must be presented with significant choices. For the individual party, nominating attractive candidates is a means to win votes. The candidate most attractive to the party is not necessarily the best. Societal functions and organizational goals do not coincide entirely; here is a possible source of strain. Again, party organizational strength is essential for effective political competition, while organizational strength increases the individual party's chances for success in the power struggle. The limiting condition here lies in the possibility that an individual party may seek continued dominance, i.e. the virtual elimination of competition.

Where conflicts occur between preferences for the democratic model and demands for organizational effectiveness, strong discrepancies between party behavior and the normative expectations of them arise. The ideal model of a functioning democratic system stipulates not only certain outcomes—e.g., selection of *qualified* candidates, statement of *salient* issues—but also certain modes for achieving these outcomes—e.g., not by arbitrary decisions of an oligarchic ruling group, but through democratic processes involving the whole membership. The democratic model is partially institutionalized in a nation's constitution and election laws, thus setting legal boundaries to the actions of parties. Moreover, democratic norms are embodied in party constitutions, and are reflected also in their organizational structure. The democratic model's demands concerning intraparty processes are particularly stringent regarding elections and the distribution of decision-making authority. Constitutional limitations and party acceptance of democratic values, however, do not guarantee realization of the norms, if demands of organizational effectiveness conflict with demands for democratic behavior. The observer, given several different standards of evaluation, faces an intellectual dilemma; the participant is subject to conflicts arising not only from the nature of the political order but from the structural constraints of his party organization as well.

The Contribution of this Case Study

A case study of party-leadership selection in one district organization of the Christian Democratic Union (CDU) in West Berlin can only make a very modest contribution. It seemed an appropriate way to investigate the functioning of lower party levels.[4] To gain full insight into the political processes of a local party organization, extensive participant observation was called for. This required choosing a manageable unit. Limiting the study to one particular party seemed necessary when it was realized that free access to the organization's activities and documents would only be granted to a researcher who confined participation to a single party, thereby achieving a minimum level of apparent identification, and thus alleviating the caution and suspicion of those being studied.

A number of controls were introduced in choosing a particular party for study. Ideologically, the CDU stands between the parties of the Right and of the Left; its structure is neither as loosely joined nor as tightly centralized as that of other German parties. Care was taken to select a district organization that occupied a middle position in size, relative strength, and representativeness of social composition. In none of these respects, then, did the unit studied represent an unusual or extreme case.

In spite of these controls, the results permit only very limited generalization. The organizational structure investigated was distinctive; in its constitutional and actual arrangements, in its program, and in the social composition of its membership, it reflected a party different from other German parties. It was located in a metropolitan community, and it belonged to a CDU Land organization with a distinct history and traditions.[5] These features suggest the main limitations on generalization.

One may ask whether the relevance of the results for comparable party units in other localities is restricted because the study took place in West Berlin. The unusual political situation of West Berlin certainly impressed its mark on the Land organizations of all political parties. But at the time of the study, this had little discernible influence at the lower levels of party organization; nothing was observed that seemed to invalidate the choice. On the other hand, there were advantages: in West Berlin, three levels of party organization—local, district, and Land—were present within the same community.

West Berlin, which has the status of a city-state or Land, contains twelve administrative units—the boroughs *(Bezirke)*. They have their own assemblies and enjoy a small measure of self-government. The existence of these governmental subdivisions is reflected in the organizational structure of political parties. Thus, the CDU in West Berlin has twelve district organizations *(Kreisverbaende)*, officially named after the corresponding boroughs. Each district in turn includes a number of locals *(Ortsgruppen)*, the party's lowest organizational units. The formal organization of the district is graphically represented in Figure 1.

Membership in the CDU is formal. A prospective member applies in writing, and his application form is routinely processed and approved. Members pay monthly dues and carry membership cards.

In 1957, when the field work took place, the district party organization studied (hereafter called the District) had slightly over 1,000 members, nearly two-thirds male. The District's corresponding borough had a population of 200,000. The age structure of the party membership, with 44 per cent born before 1900, and only 14 per cent later than 1920, reflects a problem which plagues practically all parties. Among the District members, workers were markedly underrepresented compared with the borough population. Similarly, Catholics were overrepresented, accounting for one-third of the members, but only one-eighth of the borough population. The direction of these differences is characteristic of the CDU membership throughout the Federal Republic.[6] The District is located between the suburban area and the downtown center of West Berlin. It is neither a clearly working-class section nor one of the "better" bourgeois sections of the city.

The History of the District

The selection of leaders in an on-going organization follows formalized and habitual procedures. It is quite different from the way leaders emerge in an unstructured situation, such as the founding of a new party organization. How do the first nuclei form? What changes result from institutionalizing the selection procedures? Do the founding fathers maintain their positions during this process? These are important research questions. This case study throws some light on them, since the CDU was founded in 1945,[7] and District records date back to that time.

The organization of anti-fascist parties was authorized by the Russian Commander on June 6, 1945. On June 26, the founding proclamation of the CDU was issued by a small group that had been politically active in the Weimar Republic and/or the resistance movement. Since this was to be a new party, building on diverse political traditions, no reservoir of former members existed to rally around their old leaders. Nor was it possible, as with the Social Democratic Party (SPD) and the Communist Party (KPD), simply to re-establish an organization by activating latent patterns and behavior routines.

From the beginning, the leadership group at the central office had an organizational blue-print in mind for the emerging party. The hierarchy of locals, districts, and Land organizations was not the result of differentiation *after* the organization grew, but was rationally planned even before all Berlin boroughs had locals and district organizations. Members were recruited to fill the empty niches in the organizational plan. Early in August, 1945, the city office issued a precursor of the later party constitution, seeking to regulate uniformly the payment of dues, record-keeping, reporting, and other bureaucratic matters. These rules had been worked out without much participation by groups at the district level. Realization of these organizational demands was only gradually achieved, but the early attempts contributed significantly to the emergence of a unitary party structure.

The CDU party organization's growth in Berlin proceeded in two ways. First, those who were active at the Land level were sent out to organize projected districts. Second, the small informal groups of politically interested persons that had emerged in the different boroughs of Berlin about this same time were absorbed. These small groups had formed spontaneously and independently and had little mutual contact. They included persons who had been politically active before the Nazis came to power and had only waited for the end of the war to resume their activity. Others were motivated by anti-Fascist attitudes, the experience of the complete breakdown, and a desire to help in rebuilding a democratic order. The Soviet occupation authorities had themselves taken some initiative in bringing politically interested anti-Fascists together, following a program to further the organization of anti-Fascist parties of the bourgeois middle.[8]

After some persons had thus met, they were usually active in recruiting others, especially persons of presumably superior ability, and educational and professional standing. While members of these groups clearly intended to become politically active, their intentions were not implemented, and the exact political direction to be followed was still undecided, by June, 1945. By contrast, this indecisiveness was not usually found where former Social Democrats or Communists came together. When the CDU founding proclamation appeared, some of the groups decided to join and made contact with the city office. Occasionally, this was because a member was personally acquainted with someone in the CDU founding group at the city level.

Those who set up the CDU Land organizations apparently realized that, while guiding party growth toward consolidation in a unitary form was important for subsequent smooth functioning, other needs were initially better served by maintaining a rather open and loose structure and, thus, organizational elasticity. Particular importance was attached to recruiting as many persons with leadership ability as possible, and making the best use of them by giving them responsibilities at once. Therefore, formalized democratic election procedures were not yet instituted. The city office advised groups forming in the boroughs to set up action committees by informal agreement, and to designate persons as leaders of future locals. In general, the aim was to bring every capable new member willing to assume responsibility into the leading group. To achieve a responsible position was at that time largely a matter of wanting to lead and winning the confidence of those in the first informal nuclei. Regular intraparty elections took place only in the spring of 1946.

To constitute a borough-wide district, it was often necessary for independently formed groups to merge. In view of the disorganization and destruction resulting from the battle over Berlin and the defeat, it is not surprising that the political groups in the boroughs, whether independently formed or initiated by the city office, were often not aware of each other's existence. The small degree of consolidation already achieved by the various informal groups before the establishment of a bureau-wide organization helped to minimize the rivalry and reluctance which might easily have impeded the mergings. There was some competition for the leading positions when groups were asked to merge, but the sense of growth and manifold opportunities for action mitigated even such rivalries.

The foundation of the District corresponded to the pattern outlined here. Four informal groups in the borough became the nucleus of the CDU District. Only one had been initiated by the city office, the other three later decided to join the CDU. At first, they merged two by two and constituted separate district organizations in the two temporarily established administrative parts of the borough. Later, after a short struggle for supremacy, the two party units merged into one District, in the late fall of 1945.

Before their inclusion in the CDU, the informal groups left room for a greater diversity of political aims and orientations. In two of the groups, a number of members rather favored joining the Catholic Center Party (Zentrumspartei), whose revival they expected. Others, although interested in democratic reconstruction, never intended to become regular party members. Of the fifty known members of the four initial groups, nearly half either failed to join the CDU or relinquished membership shortly after doing so. Others became and remained CDU members for some time, but had died or moved away by 1957. At that time, less than one-quarter of the original fifty were still members in the District, half of them active in some party office; the others, simply as rank-and-file members. The founding fathers of the District had not retained their leading position as a group.

This first phase in the District's history was characterized by a rapid aggregating of persons strongly motivated to become active and by a subsequent sifting process in which the less or differently committed left the emerging organization. This phase was also characterized by strong enthusiasms and self-denying devotion to party work, and by considerable informality and a provisional quality in the patterns of interaction and activity. More than ten years later, the District presented a substantially different picture.

The Collection of the Data

The field work for this study was done in 1957, when this author—as the only person engaged in this research—spent eight months of intensive participant observation in the District. During these months, I became a regular and accepted fixture at local, board, committee, District board, and *Fraktion* meetings, as well as at larger political functions and at the plenary sessions of the borough assembly. At the same time, intensive interviews were conducted with all occupants of party offices above the local boards, and including local chairmen. Key informants were interviewed repeatedly, and meetings always offered opportunities for additional informal contact and supplementary questions. One particular difficulty was in avoiding being identified with any particular section, organ, or, above all, contending faction or antagonistic group within the District, and yet to maintain an attitude of sympathetic understanding toward every one of these groups. While my acceptance soon became obvious from the uninhibited scheming, planning, criticizing, and discussion of rather delicate personnel problems that went on in my presence, the majority probably never realized the nature of my interest nor the fact that I was not a member of the organization.

In addition to observation and intensive interviewing, a questionnaire was given to all members of the largest District local. The District's written records were all evaluated, thus affording, among other things, retrospective information. The year 1957 was an off-election year, so that only the annual intra-party elections could be observed directly. However, written and oral information was collected concerning the selection of candidates for the most recent city-wide elections, those of 1954.

The offices involved in the District's intraparty elections were mainly at the two lowest party levels. With few exceptions, they were voluntary or honorary positions; the only paid party functionary was the District secretary. Several categories of honorary offices were filled annually: the local boards and their chairmen, the chairmen of committees at the District level, the delegates these committees sent to their counterparts at the Land level, and positions on the District board. Every four years, candidates for the borough assembly and for the Berlin House of Representatives were elected; they received a fixed remuneration, necessary because of the time and effort required. The only full-time, paid, elective offices at the District level were those of city councillors *(Stadtraete),* who were the top officials in the borough administration. At the Land level, the equivalents were the senators *(Senatoren),* who constituted the cabinet of the Land, i.e., West Berlin, government.

The case study was guided by a set of open questions, rather than by a limited number of specific hypotheses. The first group of questions refers to a process preparatory to leader-selection within the organization, namely, the recruitment of members and, among them, of potential leaders. Specifically, we will ask: Is there any deliberate effort to recruit potential leaders, or do such persons seek party membership on their own initiative? Who does the recruiting, and what qualitative criteria are used?

The second group of questions refers to the nature of the selective process within the organization. What are the constitutional provisions for a democratic selection process, and how well are they observed? Are elections manipulated from above, by competing factions, or by a minority intent on oligarchical rule? What selection criteria operate in the decision for or against a given candidate?

The manner of election being determined, we turn to factors that influence the subsequent performance of leaders. Are the office-holders trained for their tasks, and if so, what does the training emphasize? How clearly are the leadership roles formally defined, and what are the shared expectations of the members as to leadership behavior? How much initiative and discretion do office-holders have in fulfilling their tasks? What pressures to conform are brought to bear upon them, and what sanctions can be and are applied in case of deviance? Do situational pressures cause leaders to neglect certain functions?

The last group of questions refers to certain characteristics of the elected leaders, which result from selective processes and self-selective tendencies. Therefore, we must further ask: What motives cause leaders to run for office? Are different types of persons attracted to different offices? What roads of advancement lead to a given type of office? How do office-holders differ from the rank and file in terms of socio-economic status, religion, political interest and tradition, and general social participation? How high are turnover and continuity in the leadership group? What are the decisive factors determining these rates?

The presentation of results will follow this sequence of questions. In the field work itself, answers to the four sets of questions were of course sought simultaneously. The field analysis did not work its way up from the local to the district level; rather, observation started at all levels and for all party organs at about the same time. Each set of questions will be applied to the leaders in the different types of offices before discussion proceeds to the next set of questions. While the reporting procedure tends to separate analytically what was in fact observed as one complex functioning whole, it has been adopted deliberately. It facilitates certain comparisons; furthermore, it permits the reader to see, at each stage, the whole of the District organization.[9]

The Recruitment of Party Members

The occupants of all offices in the CDU District organization are elected by, and selected from, the party members. The constitution provides that nobody can assume an office before he has been a party member for at least one year.[10] Moreover, none of the District offices can be filled by co-optation, a procedure permitted only for certain offices at the Land level. In an unusual degree, then, the quality of the leadership depends on the quality of members recruited into the party, and a study of leader-selection must include an analysis of membership recruitment.

New members in the District were recruited with hardly any conscious or deliberate effort to obtain potential leaders. Most of the reasons for this can be easily specified. First, there was no perceived shortage of aspirants for the more important offices, including the chairmanship of local boards. Second, rank-and-file members felt and sometimes spontaneously urged that leaders should emerge from within the group, and not be brought in from outside. For public office and for high echelons of the party organization, members felt that a period of service in a lowly position was almost a necessary preparation. Of course, those who held party office were less likely to express these views; officers did sometimes try to recruit persons whom they had mentally earmarked as valuable future aspirants for office.

Recruitment is a task, however, which the constitution vests in the locals as units. The main reason for the lack of qualifying standards for new recruits is the way in which the various locals performed this task.

Locals were motivated to recruit because more members meant more money,[11] more delegates to the district delegate assembly, and a better reputation as a successful and effective local. Indeed, growth per se was one criterion by which the success and effectiveness of a local party unit were judged.

This led to an emphasis upon quantity rather than quality in recruiting. At the local level, there was little appreciation that selective recruitment might be more important than the total number enlisted. For the CDU as a whole, the dues and votes of new members are of relatively minor importance. The biggest expense items, such as campaign costs, are met by contributions, rather than by that portion of the dues to which the Land organization is entitled.[12] Nor is there any clear evidence in the Federal Republic that a party's election success is, in some direct sense, a function of its formal membership size.

In short, the party as a whole does not need members primarily as dues-payers and voters. Still, like any political organization, the CDU as a whole always needs more active helpers, and a reservoir of talent from which attractive candidates and efficient functionaries can be developed as articulate and influential propagandists of the party views. This should lead to recruiting efforts which focus on specific types of people. But, in fact, there has been no successful attempt to develop standards based upon these needs and thus to define recruitment for the locals. Consequently, little has counteracted the tendency for locals to focus on their own goals.

Locals did not generally instruct their members how to recruit. Most local chairmen did not even emphasize this task, beyond occasional remarks at monthly meetings and public praise of those who had brought new members. Over one period of 18 months, ending in July, 1957, the District membership increased from 840 to 1,008 persons. This 20 per cent *net* increase was a balance between the old workers lost (about 16 per cent) and the new members gained (some 36 per cent).

An evaluation of the records showed that members were lost, with equal frequency, for two main reasons: because they voluntarily left the group or because they moved away from the District. About 10 per cent of the new recruits were transfers who had come from other districts, where they had already established CDU membership. Most new members, however, were directly recruited into the District organization from the area's population.

Among the thirteen District locals, in this eighteen-month period, only one showed a net increase significantly above average. In this local, which nearly doubled in size, the board chairman had constantly and strongly emphasized the importance of recruitment. Some years before, another local had shown similarly impressive growth. Both of these examples, however, also indicate that the mere drive to recruit, without equal emphasis upon qualitative standards, results too often in a notable lack of discrimination. Many members were brought into both locals who were party liabilities rather than assets. In both cases, recruitment methods occasionally were so aggressive that they amounted to luring or bringing pressure to bear on prospective members to join. The dubious value of such recruits was indicated by the resulting series of unpleasant incidents. In one case, many members had to be struck from the list simply because, after having signed up, they did not even pay their dues.

In general, only a small minority in each local did any recruiting at all, and most of that was among their acquaintances, as opportunities arose. CDU members seem plagued, probably more than SPD members would be, by a bourgeois bashfulness, being reticent to show themselves as dedicated partisans when not among known party sympathizers. Members are also up against a popular attitude: widespread unwillingness to join any political party. CDU District members perceived this realistically, and it further dampened their recruiting efforts. Party members seldom made sustained and forceful efforts to proselytize or convert; more often, recruitment seems to have been a "trigger event," which consisted of bringing someone into the party who was already a sympathizer.

In spite of these limitations, the personal contacts of party members are of singular importance in the recruitment process. By 1957, new members almost never came on their own initiative, merely appearing at a party headquarters and seeking admission.[13] Immediately after the founding of the CDU, in 1945, the situation had been substantially different.

Generally, the recruitment standards in use, as these could be understood by listening to party workers describing and recommending new recruits, were rather modest: it was enough for the new member to be reputed as an average decent person, a life record without strong visible blemishes, and a willingness to pay dues. If the new member was also willing to participate actively and possessed some claims to expertise or revealed some leadership qualities, this was of course welcomed. But only a few recruiters, themselves mostly office-holders, consciously sought to enlist persons with these qualities into the party. On the other hand, there were a few very ambitious recruiters who neglected even some of the minimum rquirements. If membership participation in most locals, however measured, fell quite short of the desirable levels, this was in part a result of the recruitment standards maintained.[14]

New members have to be formally admitted to the party by the District board, which passes judgment on an application sent to it after endorsement by the local where the recruit seeks admission. In reality, however, the District board did not function as a selective filter in this process. Its judgment was a mere formality. The real decision rested with the local board, which in turn relied upon the recruiter's recommendation. Since there is no period of waiting or apprenticeship, the actual responsibility of the recruiter is considerably larger than the constitutional provisions concerning membership would indicate.

The recruitment efforts of various locals were typically considered unsuccessful by many party leaders. Nor was it simply a question of quantitative insufficiency. Since only a minority of the CDU members—themselves a tiny minority of the population—recruited at all, not all "approachable" persons in the community were asked to join. The Land office, at certain intervals, therefore launched large-scale recruiting campaigns by sending out a large number of written invitations to join. Special propaganda material usually accompanied these letters. The locals were also requested to help; for instance, by sending members to "follow up," visiting those who, having received an invitation, had expressed interest.

Insufficient recruiting activity by the locals thus led occasionally to the initiation of recruitment drives at higher organizational levels. This same process may be observed for other tasks which the rank and file perform inadequately; probably a general organizational principle is involved. However, in the District, even these shifts in the level at which recruitment campaigns were executed could not make up for the lack in selective recruitment. As far as a conscious search for potential leaders was concerned, recruitment was almost at random.

How Members are Attracted to the Party Organization

Since joining is voluntary, the party—like any other such organization—must offer some inducements to prospective members. It would be unrealistic to assume that more than a small minority deliberately joined as a means to reach a desired power position. Joining the party also provided limited opportunities for social and business contacts that could be of personal advantage. Beyond such inducements, the fund of more explicit "payments" was limited by the relatively scarce opportunities for patronage.

A further inducement may be a sense of moral satisfaction in taking part in public life. However, party membership is not commonly considered to be an essential element in an adult's social role—whether that of citizen, community member, or member of any occupational class.[15] Only a comparatively small part of the Federal Republic's electorate are members of any political party (3.6 per cent),[16] and, judging from the results of a 1954 public-opinion survey, only an added 6 per cent were willing (even conditionally) to join a party.[17]

The fact that being a party member is not a typical adult role, coupled with the negative attitude in Germany toward joining political parties, helps to explain why recruitment is sporadic. Thus, the motives of those who do join have greater significance. An organization, like an institution or profession (e.g., the police force or the priesthood), may unintentionally attract a particular type of person; subsequently, this type of person in turn may leave a distinctive mark upon the organization. Should this psychological selectivity in joining a political party tend to attract, say, corruptible persons bent upon achieving and wielding power for its own sake, the harm that could be done to the body politic served by that party would be great indeed.

During the interviews with District office-holders, they were asked their reasons for joining the CDU. From various observed and incidental documentary evidence, the motives of rank-and-file members may also be inferred. Although the data of this study are not sufficient to make quantitative statements about the proportions of different membership types or the relative importance of various motives for joining, a number of types of party members were found in the District. Stable patterns in their behavior served to differentiate them, and these in turn were readily related to particular reasons for joining party groups.

Three types of members were found to be characterized by different "instrumental motives," to use Parsons' terminology. First, is the opportunist and seeker of petty advantages. In fact, the party cannot give much help to those who are seeking jobs, housing accommodations, contracts, or free vacations for their children, and so forth. However, in the District, what little the party was believed to offer did attract some members. The opportunists's motive rarely led to very active participation, particularly not in any party office demanding much time or effort. This cost was apparently too great to be worthwhile, in light of the relatively small material gratifications offered or hoped for in party work.

A second type was motivated by a drive for power; political ambition led some members to participate actively and to strive for influential office. A third type seemed motivated by personal ambition; politics was a means of making a living, either directly by getting a paid party office or elective office on a higher level, or indirectly by furthering a career in the Berlin administration. Political and personal ambitions converge, but there are important distinctions: the personally ambitious often seems quite professionally oriented, little interested in wielding influence for its own sake, not attracted by political machinations, and often less ideological in his partisanship than the "politician."

A fourth observed type was normatively committed, motivated by genuine political interests and ideological identification with the party program. Frequently, one specific program was of greater importance than others to such ideologues. Most members of this type were willing to assume office, many quite desirous of doing so. Often, they had joined the CDU very soon after its foundation or their own return from captivity. The older usually had records of political activity dating back to the Weimar Republic. Among the younger, anti-communism and anti-marxism were strong motivating factors. Moreover, the normative commitment easily went hand in hand with a desire to link one's professional career with party activity. This subtype might be called the most valuable one found among CDU office-holders.

Normative or ideological commitment does not necessarily lead to active participation. This was shown by a fifth, quite frequent type: the person who joined the CDU to prove his faith in the *Weltanschauung,* or ideological basis of the CDU. Members like this were usually very partisan in their views, loyal in voting and continuing their membership, and regular in paying their dues. Otherwise, they were often inactive to the point of not even attending the monthly meetings of their locals.

A pure embodiment of any one of these types was, of course, rarely if ever found. This is even more true for the sixth and last type to be mentioned, the "joiner," who is apparently motivated by gregariousness and a desire to belong. He must have at least one other motive to make him join a political party instead of some social club or voluntary association, which might satisfy purely social needs even better. In the District, the joining motive in itself was not conducive to seeking higher office or the responsibility of leadership. But it did bring the member to his local unit's monthly meetings.

Nonparticipating members, participating rank and file, and office holders may be expected to reveal characteristically different motivational patterns.[18] At this point, let us consider a few data about participation. The holders of the highest District offices—the chairmen of committees, District board members, and borough assemblymen—comprise only 4 per cent of the total membership; if lesser functionaries are included—such as local board members, regularly attending committee members, or delegates—office-holders account for roughly one-fifth of the total membership. Analysis of attendance at meetings of the District's largest local for a period of eighteen months revealed that about half the members came to only one-tenth of all meetings, i.e., came barely once a year. These we shall call "inactive members." Only a quarter of this local's membership attended an average of eight out of ten meetings; this included most office-holders. The meeting of a typical local at the time of the study and during the preceding years usually found from one-quarter to one-half of the members present. The average was about one-third. Even local chairmen who urged attendance strongly, by letter or in person, could not raise it above half the paper membership.

Selecting Leaders

The routine recruitment methods observed in the District in no way assured that party members were qualitatively select citizens. Perhaps it is generally the more active and politically responsible citizen who lets himself be inducted into a party. But our brief consideration of motives for joining suggests that this hope is only partly justified. It is, then, of crucial importance whether intraparty processes of leadership-selection tended to promote the best-qualified members.

The CDU party constitution provides for a selection process that moves in steps from the lowest to higher levels of office. Only offices at the local level are to be filled directly by the vote of the whole membership; at higher levels, delegates do the voting.

The election rules laid down in the constitution were, in general, closely adhered to in the District. Rare cases of slight deviation were observed. These were due mostly to negligence plus a desire for simplification, or to idiosyncratic interpretations of unclear rules; seldom were deviations the results of deliberate attempts at manipulation. Observing constitutional rules was a norm of primary importance; practically every member was strongly committed to do it. Indeed, on many occasions the constitution was quoted to decide controversies on procedural issues. Those whose views were not supported in the rules gave immediate, if disappointed, acquiescence.

Even full adherence to the letter of democratic rules does not guarantee, however, that their spirit will animate the selection process. Thus, formal constitutional provisions stipulate who elects the party officials at various organizational levels. These provisions had the probably quite unintended effect of producing markedly different interest in the elections for different offices. Local members were most interested in elections where they could vote directly. At the District level, delegates voted according to their own opinions, instead of expressing the wishes of those to whom they owed their mandates. Similarly, the practice of preplanning, observed in local elections, while it violated no formal rule, clearly ran counter to the meaning of intra-party democracy.

Selection processes were observably different for various offices. The number and quality of aspirants for a given office proved important factors. Certain kinds of positions, because of the opportunities they gave, attracted members with particular motives. Committee chairmanships or elective administrative offices thus tended to attract members with professional interest in the subject matter. The latter kind of office also attracted persons interested in political careers. Again, the offices in the upper party hierarchy that carried organizational authority, that gave the incumbent greater access to the public, and that enhanced his prestige, were the goals of those ambitious for deference and those striving for the inherent satisfactions of power.

Later, we will discuss the observed measure of correspondence between the type of office and the motivation and characteristics of office-holders. There was, for members highly motivated to assume office in the first place, an attraction toward higher party levels. This produced a dearth of better-qualified aspirants for lower-level offices; furthermore, the lower-level the office, the fewer its aspirants. These statements and their consequences for the selection process will be borne out as we turn now to the elections for various bodies.

1. LOCAL ELECTIONS

Once a year, the members of a local elect their board (of eight to fifteen members), including its chairman and some delegates to the District Delegate Assembly. The interest of members in these elections proved to be very slight—evidenced by particularly low attendance on such occasions—unless a speaker or some other attraction had been scheduled for the same evening. Among those with no intention of seeking office, and with weak organizational identification (as distinguished from ideological orientation), the problems of city or federal politics generally evoked more interest.

Another important feature of local elections has been the shortage of aspirants, especially evident in the smaller locals. Aside from the chairmanship, local offices were not very attractive: the costs, in terms of time and effort, were relatively high; and the rewards, in terms of prestige, power, participation in policy-making, and material or job advantages, were rather low. For some, just beginning their political careers, service on a local board has been a stepping stone and pre-condition to higher offices. Once their goal has been achieved, they often withdraw their services from the local. Others, with support from higher party officers or with noteworthy qualifications as an expert of some kind, can forego this step. No other party offices were filled as often as those on the local board by members who did not desire to hold office, but who consented to be elected out of a sense of party obligation.

The shortage of candidates necessarily lowered the qualitative selection standards. Only where several contestants aspired to an office could their respective abilities be compared before casting one's vote. Members who had to be urged to take office were probably less motivated to perform well in office than those who competed for a post. Many shortcomings in the locals were the result of these conditions.

Because of the shortage of candidates, the common practice of partially preplanning local-election choices seemed to contribute directly and effectively to the selection of a new board. This preplanning was usually done by the chairman and his board members, who got together before the election, discussed possible candidates, and agreed among themselves who would best fill at least the major offices of the board. Sometimes the preplanning group included only a part of the old board, or a clique within it. Preplanning was seldom applied to the party-assembly delegates, but it was more or less customary for newly elected board members to be named also to these delegate posts.

The agreed-upon nominations of such preplanning groups were subsequently made at the election meeting. Although the practice was not exactly constitutional, members did not ordinarily object if they saw that they themselves could not make better nominations. In fact, many were probably not aware of the planned origin of the nominations. Of course, the members at the meeting could advance counternominations. However, when they came to an election meeting, most of them had no specific plans in mind except for the office of chairman. They were quite satisfied if someone else made the nominations on which they were to vote.

Preplanning, as observed, was a local process into which the higher party officials hardly ever intruded. Of course, the opinion of a local member who held office on a higher party level would be considered, even if he had no offiicial position in his local. A member of the District board or its chairman also occasionally was interested in who would be the next chairman of a local other than their own, particularly if there was reason to fear that a person considered unsuitable or even harmful to the party would be elected. But the most that could be, or was, done even in such a case was to give advice to an influential and personally known member of the local in question.

Constitutionally, locals possess considerable autonomy; this structural characteristic of the CDU is anchored in its ideology. The locals guard their autonomy firmly. Any visible attempt to exert pressure from outside would meet with fierce resistance and might well boomerang unpleasantly upon its initiators. This is substantiated by reports about incidents involving inter-ference in previous years.

The dangers inherent in preplanning are easily noted: a tendency to perpetuate those already in office and to hold down new aspirants, particularly if their views are not congenial to the preplanning group. These dangers, however, only become real if there are more candidates than offices to be filled, which is practically never the case in local elections.

If nominations were made spontaneously by the rank-and-file members attending the election meeting, they would still focus largely around previous office-holders, because of their greater visibility and familiarity. The rank and file of a local, even that minority which regularly attended the monthly meetings, could hardly develop in the course of a single year adequate or extensive personal knowledge as a basis for an accurate judgment of po-tential candidates. Perhaps the situation would be different if the members of a local had frequent contact with each other outside of the party meetings, but in the District this was not often the case.[19] The territorial boundaries of a local did not correspond to anything like a neighborhood in the socio-logical sense. Besides, sometimes up to half of a local's members lived outside of its territorial boundaries, in spite of the fact that this was deemed undesirable by constitutional provision. As a result, the chairman and his board members regularly had the most extensive personal knowledge of potential candidates and could judge best the abilities and possible willingness to serve of individual members.

Aside from incumbents, spontaneous nomination might be made of easily visible members, such as someone who stood out in the discussions at monthly meetings, or a person of high social status. In any case, only those present at an election meeting would thus be considered. Nonattendance was often an easy way out for members who were able but unwilling to assume the responsibilities of party office. Those in the preplanning groups, on the other hand, contacted the members they thought capable before the election and persuaded them to stand for an office. It was much more difficult to refuse such a direct request than merely to withdraw after being nominated spon-taneously. Thus, the practice of preplanning actually activated members to serve the party. It was also observed that, rather than leave even a single willing party member without office, the chairman would often suggest, and the members vote to create, a new post on the board. Even in the 1957 election of the largest and particularly active local where some offices had several contestants, nobody nominated was left without an office, even if not the office originally desired. The reservoir of willing candidates was completely used up.

The local elections were thus largely rank-and-file acclamations of deci-sions made beforehand, at least as far as the more important party posts were concerned. Under such conditions, the election itself assumed the char-acter of a ceremonial ritual which had the form but not the content of on-the-spot decision-making. The rank-and-file members seemed to delegate a good part of their elective functions to an active minority. Yet they did retain full opportunity for control, and figuratively stood ready to resume control should they become dissatisfied with the active minority's preplanning, or as soon as they had definite alternative preferences of their own. The preplanning minority was fully aware of this potential control, which kept them from openly acting contrary to the wishes and opinions of the rank-and-file members.[20]

What appeared to be a mere ceremony at times suddenly sprang to life and became a process of decisive importance when conflict arose within a local and opposing candidates or factions fought for power. Such cases were very rare. In most years the elections in all thirteen District locals followed the pattern outlined above.

If conflict did arise, it was more often caused by individual ambition and personal animosity than by ideological issues. The rivals did, however, activate latent differences within the membership in their effort to secure a sizeable following, so that in the end the younger and older, Catholic and Protestant, left-wing and right-wing factions seemed to rally around opposing spokesmen. The fact that such divisions formed rarely, disappeared quickly, and hardly ever involved the whole membership of a local, is due to the relatively easy access to board offices which ambitious individuals have and to a general lack of pronounced tensions among the rank and file, whose limited interest and rather low organizational identifications made for considerable tolerance.

2. ELECTION OF THE DISTRICT BOARD

In marked contrast to the informal co-optation patterns that characterized local elections, the annual process by which the District board and its chairman were elected was both more competitive and more formalized.

First, there has been no scarcity of aspirants for District board offices. These posts carry more prestige, greater authority, constitute important stepping-stones for a political career, and permit participation in more important decision-making than occurs at the local level. At the same time, most of them require less time and effort than is called for from a local chairman or treasurer.

The election of District board members is performed by the District assembly. All local chairmen are *ex officio* members of the assembly; in addition, each local sends one elected delegate for every twenty-five members. In 1957, 80 per cent of these elected delegates were members of their local boards, and the rest were either past or present holders of other local offices.

Although the delegates who had the right to vote for District board members were typically interested and in full attendance at such elections, they did not feel accountable in any meaningful degree to the locals from which they came. Their votes were cast according to their own opinions and previous deliberations, although the local chairman has a particularly strong if not often decisive influence over others from his local. The members of their locals were not even asked for their opinions before District elections. Nor did the rank and file show much spontaneous interest. They lacked, even more than in local elections, the personal knowledge and insight necessary to form judgments concerning the suitability of alternative candidates, particularly candidates from other locals.

The members of a local had only sporadic opportunities to observe even incumbent District board members in action. Thus, they have little basis for evaluating their performance in considering their re-election. Of the rarely attending half of the membership of the largest local, 50 per cent reported in 1957 that they did not know the District chairman even by sight, although he had been in office several years. Fully 83 per cent reported they did not know any District board member except possibly the chairman. On the other hand, for the most regularly attending quarter of the same local's membership, which includes most of its office-holders, the corresponding figures were 7 per cent and 41 per cent.

Locals compete with each other for District board positions; this competition inhibits preplanning like that found in local elections. It is conceivable that a large clique within a District board could make an election plan. But this could only be successful if a full slate were agreed upon, and if the election strategy of the various locals could also be decisively influenced. Informants told of situations in other districts where clique control existed, but it definitely did not in the District studied, where no such unity existed in the board or in any large clique on it. Board members were more effective in influencing their locals to vote *against* certain incumbents seeking re-election or the favorites of rivals already on the Board. In 1957, the participant observer could watch as many local delegations made independent plans, some in opposition to each other, some forming coalitions and making agreements of mutual aid for election night.

Each year, prior to the District board election, a special committee with one representative from each of the thirteen locals met to draw up a nominations list. Usually such a list named only one candidate—the candidate getting the most committee votes—for each office. Since the delegates came with rather firm intentions, however, the committee's recommendation often did not affect their preconsidered course, taken either as a delegation or coalition. If necessary, they nominated their own candidate during the assembly meeting and voted for him.

The stimulus of committee nomination brings votes to a nominee only in a situation of pronounced fluidity of opinion and indecision among the voters. The main function of the nominations committee seemed to be that, while it met, each local (through its representative) gained an impression of how strong the backing for different candidates was likely to be. Sometimes a particular local was induced to change its plans. When strong and even open conflict existed, a local sometimes had its representative vote in the nominating committee so as to conceal its real plan. In 1957, the committee changed procedure and presented several nominations for each office. In this case, of course, the nomination list provided even less guidance.

These remarks do not mean that delegates never decided how to vote during the assembly elections after they got there. Delegations from particular locals did not always make plans for every office. The discussion of individual candidates at the assembly meeting itself sometimes drew attention to facts that changed some delegates' opinions; occasionally a favored candidate was unexpectedly rejected. The "counter measures" launched by his supporters called for a change in plans. Again, a new candidate might suddenly be thought of, nominated, and elected without much previous deliberation. In the 1957 District elections, examples of each of these possibilities were observed.

In general, each local delegation voted unanimously for or against particular candidates. There were some cases, however, where the voting alignment cut directly across delegations. Voting in 1957 was practically always by secret ballot, a procedure that a single assembly member may demand. Only when unanimity prevailed was voting done by raising of hands.

While attending numerous discussions where delegates tried to decide whether to vote for or against a particular candidate, this observer noted the use of a number of selection criteria. First, in deliberating about a candidate, his probable performance in office played a large part. A second factor was representativeness, considered in a variety of senses—political, geographic, and social. These rational criteria were sometimes applied in an emotional sense, when they became mere loyalty or attraction for a person possessing certain characteristics.

There is, prior to the discussion of a candidate's qualifications, a basic prerequisite of success which he must generally meet: he must be known to a majority of delegates. This could be achieved in a number of ways. Previous office-holders of district-wide renown had a distinct advantage. High professional prestige or being known as a former high official in a nearby district were among the other ways by which this basic requirement was met.

Although the constitution did not forbid it, it was practically unheard of for anyone not at least a delegate and thus present in the assembly at election time to be nominated to the District board. This effectively limited the number of possible candidates in yet another unwritten way.

Given some familiarity with a candidate, delegates were often preoccupied with his credentials and the quality of performance to be expected from him. A candidate was expected to have a record of active participation and familiarity with District and party politics. Beyond this, different qualifications were stressed depending on the office in question. There was, however, little agreement concerning what were a given office's most important requirements. In 1957, for instance, delegates debated whether, for the treasurer, occupational experience with bookkeeping was more important than personal connections with potential contributors. On that same occasion, there were delegates who felt that a District chairman should have a conciliatory and diplomatic attitude, while other delegates felt that a District chairman should be a man primarily known for the firmness of his views and the strength of his fighting spirit. On still another office, the problem was posed whether a person with an impressive record of party work and commitment to the District was to be preferred to a person with high party prestige as a member of the West Berlin government.

One explanation for the lack of agreement concerning desirable qualities is the lack of conciseness in defining many official roles. Moreover, those tasks which the constitution and the unwritten party tradition do assign to particular roles are diverse; sometimes they call for rather opposite kinds of skills, character traits, and social assets. Agreement among the delegates about the selective standards—which of course need not lead to unanimous voting for particular candidates—presupposes not only a clear image of an office's requirements but also agreement upon the relative weight given to different and not necessarily complimentary qualities. In the absence of both, fitting a candidate to an office is difficult. Lack of clarity concerning what should be expected from an office-holder also makes it difficult, after a person has achieved office, to judge his performance and thus his merits for re-election.

Another major selection criterion is related to the representativeness of a District board candidate. Whether representativeness referred to political subunits or to social and geographic groupings, applying it as a criterion could of course present serious conflicts with the application of probable-performance standards. However, often the District board itself was seen as a co-ordinating and integrating center of party activity; in this sense, the representativeness of its composition was directly and functionally relevant.

Apart from constitutional provisions governing the District board's composition,[21] the delegates openly or covertly consider the appropriate representation of major occupational and religious groupings. In 1957, propaganda for particular candidates as being labor representatives, self-employed artisans, or spokesmen for independent businessmen was made openly during assembly debate. On the other hand, a candidate's religion, while definitely of importance in the private deliberations, was never mentioned openly in discussing his merits. The CDU is strongly motivated to play down religious differences in its ranks and to prevent religious factions from developing. This is widely feared as a potential source of party disunity. As soon as strong rivalries develop on any other count, however, the campaign tends to activate any latent religious factionalism by bringing religion into the private deliberations.

Even among delegates who did consider the candidate's religion, there existed no agreement about the "right" board ratio of Protestants to Catholics. When the members of one religion felt that a proportionate representation norm would restrict the number of offices they could otherwise occupy, they denounced such quotas as unjust. When they saw such norms, on the other hand, as desirable barriers to the overproportionate success of the rival religious faction, they advocated them as reasonable.

In 1957, some Protestant delegates argued for a District chairman who was a Protestant, on the grounds that he represented the party's religious majority. Some Catholic delegates argued that this was not valid; they favored a rival candidate, a Catholic, on grounds of his ability and past level of activity.

In general, although religion was a criterion, it was only one among many aspects of "representativeness." The support for a candidate showed no obvious correspondence to his religion. A criterion of greater strength was the locality from which he came. Every local party unit preferred a candidate from its own ranks. This preference was sometimes observed to override considerations of probable poor performance. Although this kind of local partisanship may sometimes lead to a mediocrity's election, it does stir strong interest among a local's rank and file.

Geographically proportionate representation was clearly expected by most delegates. Thus, one relatively large local party unit covertly criticized a smaller one which had succeeded in filling more District board offices than it had. Every year since the foundation of the Districts, between seven and ten of the thirteen locals have had at least one member on the District board; only the smallest local has never had a representative.

Clearly, geographic representation operates as a criterion, but other kinds of representativeness and questions of the probable quality of performance have, in many cases, overridden the fact that a particular local already has its quota. Members of outstanding quality or ambition could reasonably hope to be elected.

One test of the probable performance from a candidate was his past performance. Those officers who had fulfilled their tasks adequately or had at least not shown serious deficiencies had rational arguments in their favor and also could claim a certain loyalty. For an incumbent seeking re-election to be supplanted by a newcomer was regarded as a personal rebuke and a vote of distrust. An incumbent is known, and in this minimum sense he has a good chance of being-relected. His experience can be looked upon as a relatively safe indicator of his future performance. Indeed, this may be so, where the job's requirements are little known, or varied and complex. In contrast, there is inevitably a risk involved in electing a new person, whose qualifications have had no empirical test.

This particular set of rational and emotional appeals prevents more incisive consideration of the qualifications needed for insuring high job performance. The very effectiveness of the "incumbency argument" strengthens a tendency toward oligarchy, the perpetuation of the current leading group in office. Thus, the argument is dysfunctional to selection of board members on grounds that relate to their qualifications and merit, and, at the same time, it is dysfunctional to rank-and-file control through intra-organizational democratic processes. Against these points, one must balance the fact that the effectiveness of the "incumbency argument" helps to preserve continuity in the party's leadership group and to inhibit the disruptive rivalries which develop when many people develop personal ambitions for more power.

A candidate's election to the District board is the result of a complicated process, involving both rational deliberation over his merits for the office and his "group representativeness" in a variety of appropriate senses, and also involving more emotional appeals to loyalty—to a member of one's own religion, to a member of one's own local party unit, and to an incumbent if there is one. In a later section, we will consider the effects of this selection process on the District board's composition.

3. SELECTION OF COMMITTEE CHAIRMEN

At the District level, the party apparatus involves a rather elaborate committee structure. The constitution establishes seven committees whose official functions may roughly be termed advisory; in addition, three "work-group" committees have constitutional status. Each annually elects its own chairman and other appropriate officers. Two of the three "work groups" *(Arbeitsgemeinschaften)*—those for women and work-place groups—in composition and actual functioning are very similar to the advisory committees.[22]

The seven advisory committees are concerned with specific subject matters, as for instance "economic policy" or "cultural and school affairs." In 1957, these committees averaged about thirty-five members, most of whom were representatives from local party units while the rest were *ex officio* members. Actually, these committees did not give advice to other party groups at the District level and they participated only very occasionally in policy formation on higher levels. Mainly they served to inform their own members about a policy field and to get them to understand and agree to CDU policy in a specific area. Moreover, they provided safety valves for the expression of doubt, opinion, or criticism, and thus provided a measure of organizational hygiene.

For the nine District-level committees thus in question, the processes by which leaders were selected showed a number of common characteristics. First, the interest of committee members in the annual election was rather low. The committees had little group cohesion, due to infrequent meetings, annual changes in membership, and low attendance. Partly because committee work was informative but gave little real opportunity to participate in policy-formation, members were only limitedly involved. Second, there was little competition for committee offices and a strong tendency, reinforced by the members' inertia, to re-elect incumbents. Here, loyalty and the other elements of the "incumbency argument" operated strongly. Demands for geographic representation were largely irrelevant in these elections, as is true also for notions that certain categories of members should be represented by quota. Except in very rare cases of dissent and rivalry, elections of committee officers were not preplanned, though their outcome was predictable in most cases. Finally, the most important selection criteria proved to be expertise. This criterion was, understandably, most specific in committees with a clearly defined and narrowly circumscribed area of interest, as for instance, cultural and school affairs. It became progressively more difficult to apply when the subject matter of a committee could only be characterized as "women's interests and problems" or "questions of general politics" *(allgemeine Politik)*.

4. NOMINATION OF CANDIDATES FOR GENERAL ELECTIONS

Every four years, when city-wide elections approach, the District assembly nominates candidates for the borough assembly. Their number is determined by how many seats the party expects to win (15 to 20 in past years), plus a sufficient number of substitutes. At the same time, the District assembly nominates for each precinct within its territory a candidate for the Berlin

House of Representatives. (Until 1957, precinct and local boundaries did not coincide.) From the retrospective information available, the selection processes in determining these candidates were very similar to those involved in electing District board members, except for the relative importance of some selection criteria.

Thus, rivalry among the locals, especially concerning borough assembly nominations, appears to have been at least as great as in District board elections. Pronounced interest in these nominations existed even at the level of the local boards, although not among the majority of the rank-and-file members. Prior to the decisive assembly meeting, each local board decided upon the list of candidates it would like to see nominated. Typically, without seeking the views of the local party members, this list went to the District office. There, a master list of nominations was compiled and used as a guide during assembly voting.

Local patriotism was justified as a valid selection basis by the argument that borough assembly nominations should be based on territorial representation, i.e., that each local should have at least one member in the borough self-governing body. In 1954, only one very small local in the District had not achieved this aim.

Another criterion which weighs more heavily in borough assembly nominations than in filling District board positions is group representation. There were always more aspirants than nominations to be made. In making up the list of nominees, care was consciously taken to represent young members, women, major occupational categories, and special groupings such as refugees. Catholics and Protestants were deliberately nominated in the ratio corresponding to membership composition. Use of these criteria was justified by the argument that all important categories of the electorate deserved to have someone with whom they could identify or whom they would see as their representative or spokesman.

Whenever a means-end relationship was clearly perceived between a specific selection criterion and the shared goal of achieving election success, the District assembly showed remarkable agreement about its acceptance and the priority to be given to such a criterion. The desire to appeal to the electorate effectively thus lay at the base of efforts to nominate persons of high public prestige; this gave an advantage to ex-members of the borough administrative council. The related desire to avoid reinforcing unfavorable CDU stereotypes helps explain why the party conscientiously refrained from nominating religious figures.

Standards that have to do with the probable quality of a nominee's performance were difficult to apply in making nominations for the borough assembly. Performance standards and the credentials sought in nominees could not be very high, since the majority of the aspirants had little expert knowledge or experience in borough administration.

The position of borough assembly member per se was not very attractive: it involved much time and effort without substantial remuneration or significant increase in prestige for anyone beyond the lower social strata. Those who viewed borough assembly services as a steppingstone in a political or administrative career normally refused renomination once they had achieved their higher goal. A significant number of qualified aspirants was probably eliminated by the rule that no one employed in the borough administration could be a borough assembly member, although the rule did not apply to someone employed by the city-wide administration.

For these reasons, although qualifications for office were considered important, they were neither very strictly defined nor very rigorously applied. District officials frequently commented that while there was no lack of candidates for borough assembly seats, there was a serious shortage of well-qualified aspirants. The majority of those elected to this office for the first time were, in fact, ill-equipped to fulfill their duties. After several years of incumbency, considerable improvement in skills and knowledge occurred. Functionally, renomination of incumbents was thus definitely advantageous.

In the past, the Land level of the party took little interest in the candidates nominated for borough assemblies in West Berlin. In accordance with the party constitution, this was every district's own affair. The situation was different when nominations were being considered for the Berlin House of Representatives.[23] In this case, the constitution provides the Land board with a certain measure of influence over district nominations, and the actual influence was probably greater than the constitution visualized. Not only were the district nominations discussed beforehand with the Land board, but the higher body also used its rights to propose one candidate of its own for each district. In 1954, the District agreed to nominate a second candidate whom the Land board wanted. In this instance, both candidates backed by the Land board belonged to districts other than that which officially nominated them.

Berlin parliamentary candidates, in short, were thought of as drawn from city-wide rather than district bases, although the districts displayed considerable interest in having their own members nominated. Local patriotism was, however, largely irrelevant in view of the small number of such nominations made by each district—less than ten in the District investigated—and in view of the type of office involved. Criteria concerning the qualifications for performance were high and could be more freely and fully applied in these cases than for borough assembly nominations.

District level officials, including delegates also active on the Land and city levels of party work, showed especially strong interest in, and influence over, these nominations to the Berlin legislature. Among other reasons, this was because district-level officials had more insight into, were more familiar with, and were more involved in higher-level party politics and in city-wide politics generally.

According to the constitution, each district also selects city councilors who are to represent the CDU in the borough's administrative council. Nominations are formally made by the borough assembly *Fraktion,* and the whole borough assembly votes on such nominations. In selecting these candidates in previous elections, District officials had to take into account special considerations. First, they were sometimes hampered by coalition agreements made on a city-wide basis between the major political parties. For example, a coalition agreement once specified which political party was to have the position of borough mayor for each borough. Second, the opinion of the other political parties in the borough had to be taken into account, since a minimum level of good will and mutual acceptance of each other's councilors was considered necessary to secure continuing co-operation in borough administration. While the Land board has interfered only occasionally—and extraconstitutionally—in the selection of city councillors, the District has taken care not to nominate any one in disgrace with the Land board. The District chairman, as an *ex officio* member of the higher body, is usually the liaison figure in the informal consultations.

Candidates for city-councilor posts are also drawn from a city-wide rather than a district base. Two of the District's three city councilors, at the time of the study, had come from other districts when first nominated; one still retained his membership and even an office in another district. An extensive knowledge of persons is required for any district official who wants a decisive voice in these nominating deliberations.

The District also has a role in the annual election of a Land executive board. This board is elected by the Land assembly. In 1957, shortly before the election, its candidates were discussed in the District board. For this occasion, those delegates who were not *co ipso* District board members had been invited. The discussions were guided by candidate listings provided by a Land nominating committee. It was evident that board members without party offices taking them outside the District lacked the insight and knowledge necessary to form an independent judgment or to offer alternative candidates for these higher offices. Accordingly, they relied largely on the opinions of those who did have such credentials. Local boards and the District assembly were not asked for their views and did not participate in the deliberations on the Land executive board selections.

Depending on its stake in a Land board election, a district delegation (present in the Land assembly for the voting) may vote according to a predetermined strategy. However, delegates in the Land assembly tend sometimes to be identified strongly with a special party grouping within the CDU, which cross-cuts district boundaries (such as the youth union), and accordingly cast their votes independently of, and even contrary to, the advice of their own district board.

It is not surprising to find a sharp increase in competition where these high party offices are involved. At the same time, however, the more exacting standards exclude aspirants with insufficient qualifications from being seriously considered as candidates. The field of possible candidates is further limited because no district delegation can afford to offer as its contender anyone who is unknown to other delegations. These conditions tend to strengthen oligarchic tendencies, which depend also on the widespread disinterest among the CDU rank-and-file membership.

Comparison of these different leadership-selection processes permits some summary statements. First, the amount of competition for a given type of office and the extent of interest displayed by those eligible to vote are positively correlated. Both interest and competition were higher for District board offices and for legislative nominations than for local board offices and committee chairs. The amount of competition itself, which depends largely on the attractiveness of an office, seems to stimulate interest among the voters. In addition, it is probable that District board offices and seats in the borough and city legislature are considered to be of greater consequence by the electors; therefore, the question of who will win them arouses more interest.

In local elections, where the reservoir of willing party-workers is in general fully utilized, the demands made of candidates in terms of skill are the lowest. The decisive factor is willingness to assume office, so that, in spite of the practice of preplanning, hopeful candidates easily find a post. Qualitative considerations begin to be made where voters can choose from among several candidates. But since qualitative standards are rather vague, and competing selection criteria enter the picture, there is no guarantee that the candidate most suited to an office is the one selected.

Role definitions and performance expectations play only a small part in party-leader selections. When the electorate is not guided by a clear qualitative frame of reference, other selection criteria gain more influence. Accordingly, a certain disjunction develops between selection and performance: performance comes to be determined largely by factors that operate after the winner assumes office. Analysis of leader performance bears this out fully, as will be seen; formal norms, informal expectations, subjective role perceptions, and elements inherent in an office's organizational situation are key factors that largely determine performance.

Finally, the leaders in higher offices were elected without any significant participation by lower party levels. In electing the District board, the assembly delegates (who were mostly local board officers) deliberated among themselves, without considering the opinions of local members. Correspondingly, Land assembly delegates (most of them District board officers) elected the Land executive board without deference to the opinions of other District officers (District delegates, for instance), or to the rank-and-file party membership. A potential danger exists in the degree of insulation against control from lower levels which this situation affords to higher party officers. Of course, the lower levels are by no means forcibly excluded from the deliberations; they do not rise up and demand to be heard. Moreover, the practice seems quite reasonable in view of the lack of insight and familiarity with potential candidates—the prerequisites for sensible judgment—among members not immediately involved in an election. In this situation of restricted democratic control in selecting leaders, democratic control via processes of opinion-formation and participation in policy-formation assumes increased importance as a possible alternative. Some evidence will next be presented about the actual extent of such control.

The Performance of Party Leaders

1. FORMAL ROLE DEFINITIONS

In any organization, the behavior of members newly assigned to positions is largely determined by the definition of their organizational roles. The extent to which the expected role behavior for certain tasks is spelled out clearly may be regarded as an index of organizational formalization. When organizational behavior is extensively determined by role prescriptions, it is less likely to depend on the personal characteristics of role incumbents.

Formalization can have negative as well as positive consequences. Generality, and even looseness, in behavioral prescriptions leads to greater adaptability to unpredictable situations. It preserves organizational elasticity. But if role prescriptions are vague, inherent tendencies toward goal displacement are likely to work themselves out more easily and, idiosyncratic role perceptions might influence the organization's functioning in undesirable directions.

In the District, the constitution is the formal source of role definitions. Its prescriptions for different areas of party life vary considerably in their specificity. Set forth in great detail are election procedures and the organization form and composition of the various party organs. Defined in more general terms are the hierarchical relations between local, district, and Land levels of party organization. Each level's sphere of autonomy is indicated, and, where applicable, its authority is noted over the levels below it. Even less specific are provisions about the interrelations between different party organs on the same organizational level.

In prescribing the tasks of different party organs or the duties of occupants of particular offices, the constitution is most specific on organizational maintenance tasks, e.g., admission and registration of members, dues collection, distribution of funds, reporting, sending invitations to meetings, and so forth. Other tasks are typically mentioned only summarily, without specifying how they are to be fulfilled. Thus, facilitating opinion-formation among party members is spoken of as a local party unit task, without indicating how it should be performed or giving any standard for evaluating good or insufficient performance. Similarly, the District assembly's major task is described as that of deciding "about the political work and the intraparty activity of the district." In an equally vague way, each district board is charged with "directing the political and intraparty work of the district." Again, the various district-level committees have their function defined merely as "advisory." Some, especially the work groups, have elaborate working rules; even so, their task definitions lack specificity.

In any large-scale formal organization, the long-term objectives, often highly general and abstract, must be translated into specific subgoals and tasks standing in means-end relationships to the former. The defined subgoals are differentially allocated to subunits and different organizational levels. They include service, maintenance, and co-ordinating functions. In CDU districts, these functions are both clearly defined and allocated, but not infrequently their relationship to the higher organizational objectives lacks clarity.

One good example has been provided by the recruitment procedures, which also illustrate how goal displacement may result from insufficiently gearing subgoal activities to higher organizational goals. Similar goal displacement tendencies are to be expected when, for example, constitutional provisions spell out the tasks of maintenance processes but neglect to specify other functions. The limited amount of time and energy available in any subunit for routine party work was used primarily to accomplish the clearly defined duties. Quality of performance on these points could, understandably, be evaluated rather easily. There was but one paid functionary in the District studied, so the charge of overbureaucratization might seem at first inappropriate. Still, local boards and the District board spent their efforts mostly on routine tasks that kept the organization going, and executed special tasks assigned to them from time to time by higher party levels. Otherwise, the District's performance of non-institutionalized functions has been haphazard, discontinuous, and decidedly insufficient.[24]

Functions insufficiently fulfilled at lower party levels tend to be shifted to the Land or even the federal level of organization, if their fulfillment is regarded as necessary at higher levels. We have already noted this in the matter of recruiting party members. It was also the case for political propaganda activities, designed to influence and activate the general public and to explain the party's governmental policies. Policy-formation likewise tended to shift to higher levels, where it probably received a far warmer welcome than did the burdens of conducting recruitment drives. It would, however, be a gross exaggeration and a dangerous simplification to say that party leaders consciously intended to monopolize decision-making and policy-formation and to maintain an oligarchical power position. Within the CDU, this charge was sometimes made. However, a larger part of the rank and file (nearly half in the largest local) were, in their own words, "quite satisfied" with the influence they had. Those who were not often desired only the chance to express their views and criticisms to some higher party official, not a greater actual opportunity to participate in policy-formation processes.

To institutionalize policy-formation in ways that would insure participation by lower-level officials and ordinary party members was usually described as very difficult by party leaders, particularly those on higher levels. First, where quick decisions were called for, an institutionalized process would be too slow. Second, greater political insight, factual knowledge, and interest in policy would be demanded from lower-level personnel than they actually possessed. Third, higher-level officials would have to formulate highly complicated questions in terms of easily understandable alternatives which rank-and-file members could understand and choose between.[25]

So far as day-to-day politics and much legislative policy-making are concerned, the arguments concerning delay and the question of competence have a certain validity. The party apparatus is not meant to be an instrument for continuously conducting referenda among those interested enough to become members. Elected leaders do have delegated authority for making decisions.

The need for speed and competency seems much less important when it comes to major questions of the party line on certain issues or long-term policy positions. Even here, it is true that higher party leaders went to little trouble to solicit opinions from lower levels, although they might feel bound to defer to unsolicited wishes if these were clearly expressed. In general, higher party officials tended to emphasize developing lower-level consensus for decisions already made. But there was no conscious or deliberate attempt to keep lower units oriented toward maintenance subgoals, in order to prevent their developing strong opinions on public-policy questions that might interfere with the processes by which higher officials decided these matters. The District board, the District-level committees, and the borough-assembly group were happy about every resolution received from a local party unit; they were certain to pass it on to higher authority if they could not act on it themselves. Nor was there evidence that higher organs either suppressed or disregarded proposals coming in this way from the local units or from a district-level unit. Of course, since the process was not institutionalized and the necessary preconditions of information, insight, desire, and time hardly existed, the upward flow of advice and opinion was only a trickle. Some proposals were so ill-advised or so vague as not to be taken seriously.

One major organizational objective was directly reflected in party activities. Consciousness of power as a basic aim was pervasive, down to the lowest level. It was never forgotten, even by the comparatively inactive rank-and-file members. A wide variety of behavior was judged in terms of whether it increased the party's power position relative to that of other rival parties. As might be expected, power came to be seen as an end in itself, because the District level of party organization was so largely disassociated from the formation of governmental and legislative policy positions espoused by the CDU.

2. TRAINING PARTY OFFICERS

Training party officers is particularly important where formal task specifications are insufficient and where, partly because of this ambiguity, the selection process does not insure a fit between person and position. But neither in the District nor at the Land level of the CDU was there any institution which would systematically train future officials by imparting to them the necessary knowledge, techniques, and practical application.[26] The monthly meetings of the local party units served mainly to pass on general information, and usually featured a speaker on some political topic. The same was true for the "educational service" lecture *(Bildungswerk),* a special series at the District level, attended by a comparatively small group of volunteers, and for the lecture meetings of the District-level committees. In several, the topics and discussions did center on one particular area of interest and policy. But meetings were far too infrequent and attendance was too irregular for committee members to acquire any real expertise. On the Land level, various units occasionally organized daily or weekend meetings to discuss selected topics including parliamentary procedure, propaganda techniques, and similar matters. Infrequent meetings reaching only a fraction of the members, these could hardly be called training sessions, in the above sense.

The other main opportunities to learn how to do party work came through observing officials carry out their duties, filling a minor office as preparation for a higher one, or acquiring specialized knowledge outside the party in certain occupations or group-membership roles. For instance, lawyers, civil servants, and administration employees had a differential advantage in seeking political careers.

Training arrangements are generally absent in voluntary organizations. Typically, the offices are honorary posts except for a few paid functionaries. In party work, this has serious consequences, considering the central importance of parties in democratic political orders. Since no aspirant to an office can show a "diploma" certifying his ability to perform official tasks adequately, selection in terms of qualifications for the post is largely a trial-and-error affair, which strengthens the tendency toward re-election of incumbents, and decreases the chances for aspirants who possess no extra-organizational claim to status or expertise. Furthermore, lack of special training facilities for party officials does lower the quality of performance, at least temporarily, whenever a new incumbent is needed. This is especially disadvantageous when the gradual expansion of governmental activities and the increased complexity of legislation demands professionalized politicians in elective public offices, parliamentary positions, and at party organizational levels that influence policy.

The party cannot, however, simply be accused of neglecting its function. The problem of political training raises a conflict between functional requirements and democratic values. On the one hand, it may seem necessary to create careers for professional politicians that will attract qualified personnel. To achieve this, continuity in employment and material security are required with opportunity for regular advancement based on performance rather than electoral accidents. Regular training for such careers cannot be institutionalized unless real opportunities exist for pursuing them. On the other hand, these career opportunities will not exist, given the probable "turnover" when politicians are elected through democratic processes.[27] In addition, there is some fear that if the political parties were to train politicians, doctrinaire partisans would be created, and party strife and conflict would increase, while the chances for political compromise would diminish. The ideal still lingers on—increasingly utopian in modern society—of the politician, especially a parliamentary representative or elective official, as a person who serves the commonweal unbiased by complete identification with any strict party line.

The training of his successor by an incumbent raises similar problems. An elected official cannot be expected to train his momentarily successful rival. Considering the margin of uncertainty in democratic elections, the effort could well be pointless.

The lack of institutionalized training within the CDU is linked to the deficiencies in role definition. Preparation for a given role is only possible if its tasks are specified. If training for certain offices were started, this by itself would probably result in pressure for clearer task definitions.

3. OTHER DETERMINANTS OF LEADER PERFORMANCE: INFORMAL EXPECTATIONS AND SUBJECTIVE ROLE PERCEPTIONS

The constitution, the primary source of formal role expectations, is not equally specific concerning the tasks of different office-holders. It is not clear, moreover, how fully known are those formal norms that do exist, or how fully accepted they are, either by the office-holders themselves or by the members.

Where the constitution is specific, the provisions were generally known and accepted by the office-holders to whom they applied. Rank-and-file members, while summarily accepting the constitution's authority, were usually only superficially aware of its provisions. Thus, of the rarely attending half of the largest local's membership, 48 per cent were not familiar with the Land constitution, and 72 per cent were not familiar with the District constitution, by their own admissions. Only 8 per cent and 3 per cent respectively said that they knew the constitutional provisions at the two levels "well." Only for the frequently attending minority in this local were these figures significantly better.

Apart from constitutional rules, two types of norms can be distinguished which guide the behavior of leaders. First, the specific expectations of authorized party superiors regarding the behavior of their subordinates; and second, the expectations of various other groups. The relevant role-sets and thus the reference groups differed for the occupants of different offices.[28] For the local chairman, for instance, they included his board, the members of his local, chairmen of other locals, and various District-level officials. Expectations from any and all of these sources might incorporate and support, enlarge upon and supplement, or modify and contradict formal norms. Expectations from these sources might be well integrated and compatible, strongly held or slightly emphasized, highly general or quite specific. No systematic investigation was made of extraconstitutional behavioral expectations, so the evidence is mostly incidental and indirect. Nonetheless, some examples can be cited that will illustrate the variety and character of the norms involved.

Some of the expectations concerning a leader's behavior related specifically to his office and functions, while others were more generally applicable. Among the latter, the observer often heard expressed the norms of party loyalty and a partisan attitude, of personal loyalty to elected officials, of "doing something" for other party members if the particular job permitted. This last was definitely expected of a leader, especially if he had got his job with the party organization's help. Compliance with these and similar general norms was not only widely expected in the District, but was "policed" by various informal methods, ranging from criticism to political nonsupport. These sanctions were applied to persons who deviated markedly from the norm in question.

Task-related expectations, for most party officials, were generally rather loose, lacking in specificity, and occasionally involved contradictions. The result was that District party leaders were left with considerable discretion. Incumbents in such loosely defined roles behaved according to personality needs and private role conceptions to a greater extent than would have been possible were their roles more clearly defined in the minds of others. The idiosyncratic element in their private role conceptions must especially affect that part of the organizational structure with which they regularly interact and, of course, the party members whom they lead.[29] These generalizations can be illustrated for different categories of office-holders.

The expectations regarding local chairmen reflected the constitutional task definitions for this office. A chairman's performance was evaluated according to how regularly he held meetings, the attractiveness of his speakers, his membership's attendance, how he kept his records, the carefulness of his monthly reports, how regularly he got members to pay dues, and his ability in maintaining or enlarging his local.

Most of these facts were recorded at the District secretary's office; some of them were compiled and passed around at regular intervals among local chairmen and among the District assembly members, thereby stimulating comparison. Other activities which might characterize a good chairman, such as getting his local to send resolutions or informal proposals for action to higher party levels, were occasionally mentioned, but no shared expectation existed that a local chairman should devote special efforts to these activities. Nor was a chairman expected to extend his activities beyond his unit's members to the population in his precinct. Of course, in the election campaign that took place every four years, each local was supposed to share in the effort to reach citizens with the party message. This task was accepted because it directly related to the goal of political power. Aside from this, contact with the general population was not consciously sought; it was in fact exceedingly slight. A few personally introduced guests might be seen at monthly meetings of the party locals. Occasionally, propaganda material was distributed in a neighborhood, usually following a demand by a higher party unit. But as a general rule neither the local board nor ordinary members sought to establish personal contact with the voters in their territory. The informal expectations concerning a local chairman served, then, to bolster that side of his formal job which referred to organizational maintenance. Individual party members sometimes expected more than usual of a local chairman. If so, their expectations, not being widely shared, created only slight pressure for conformity.

With some variation in individual emphasis, local chairmen performed according to these expectations. They, too, perceived their role in these terms. However, one important variation in the behavior of local chairmen was related to differences in subjective role perception and motivation. The chairmen differed in their interest in registering the views of their local in the policy-formulation process at higher levels. During 1956-57, the chairmen of a few locals got several resolutions passed about organizational matters, intraparty problems, even legislative and administrative policy, while in other locals this did not occur at all. Variation was also found in the attempted use of more informal channels for communicating opinions, wishes, and proposals to higher level personnel. This had little to do with whether ordinary members of a local were disposed to become active; rather, it was most clearly the reflection of a particular chairman's motivational pattern. The unambitious chairman, motivated largely by personal commitment to his local, might easily be less intent on being heard at a higher party level than a chairman who aspired to advancement and personal influence in the CDU.

Local chairmen varied, secondly, in "leadership style," which ranged from permissive and democratic to directive and authoritarian.[30] The various district locals furnished examples of each leadership style. In the largest local, the highly active and ambitious chairman urged members constantly and quite successfully to participate in party affairs. He demanded that his board fulfill many tasks that other locals neglected, and his board usually complied. He instructed local delegates, occasionally even committee representatives, in their official duties and behavior. While directive, this chairman was not "undemocratic." On the contrary, he put many questions to a vote which other local chairmen typically decided for themselves. He tried also to involve members in as many activities as possible. His leadership behavior reflected his view of his own functions.

The chairman of another local ran his board like an informal friendship circle, discussing local matters while playing cards. He made few demands for group activity, but his laissez-faire leadership was not necessarily democratic. This particular chairman sometimes pursued ideas or made proposals to higher officials without troubling to have his board or local unit consider the proposition.

Opinions differed widely in the District concerning the "best" leadership style, occasionally giving rise to conflict. The CDU as a whole is rather strongly committed to personal freedom and the associated principle of voluntariness. For many, this implied the liberty either to give or withhold co-operation in party work and called for permissive leadership. Leaders should not direct, but only ask, members to volunteer for certain tasks. However, when a task was seen as urgent, and members were, as usual, reluctant to volunteer, some leaders and members felt that the principle of voluntariness was detrimental to the party's efficiency and success. Thus, in one case, a District board member was charged with organizing a distribution of special propaganda leaflets. It had to be done at a certain day, place, and time, and he requested each local by letter to send a stated number of helpers. Most local chairmen tried to do so, but some failed because they relied on volunteers. One, however, refused the request because "it sounded like an order." There was even a hinted comparison with "Nazi methods." A heated discussion ensued, in which most office-holders tended to agree with the board member under attack. Few of them, however, came out openly in his support, because they felt his behavior conflicted with the principle of voluntariness to which they also subscribed.

Consider also the behavior typically expected from the chairmen of District-level committees. They were expected to call meetings regularly and to secure good attendance at them, usually by selecting "interesting" topics and "attractive" speakers. Expectations were not nearly as widely shared or strong regarding a chairman's activity in fulfilling his committee's advisory function or in strengthening its impact upon higher-level policy-formation. Lateral consultation at the District level seemed rather pointless, since most problems discussed in the committees were of city-wide if not national concern, rather than borough-wide problems. The ordinary member of a District committee possessed very little of the specialized knowledge, experience with subject matter, and insight into legislative and administrative processes required to form judicious judgments and proposals. Any real expert appearing among the committee's new members was soon co-opted by a higher level committee searching for able additions. The ordinary committee member, observed on numerous occasions, revealed himself as receptive and interested, willing to learn, but showed no initiative to work out solutions. This orientation was reflected also in what he expected of his chairman. In part, it was due to the haphazard way in which most locals chose their committee representatives. Willingness to take the assignment and minimum interest in subject matter were often considered sufficient qualifications.

With these expectations in mind, it was difficult to do more in a committee than hold informative discussions. It is interesting to see how committee chairmen perceived their role. None of the chairmen, when interviewed, felt that their committee should give advice to another body at the District level. All expressed the felt obligation to inform their own committee members of current issues and new legislative developments.

Aside from showing how personal orientation influenced behavior, comparisons of committee chairmen indicated the extent and limits of the activating effect a chairman could have on his committee. Actual conditions in the District left much to be desired. However, a properly oriented and qualified chairman could involve his committee in the formulation of policy proposals. One limit to his effectiveness lay in the insufficient insight and knowledge of committee members. Of course, a qualified chairman could help his group make a well-considered and potentially effective judgment, although this might easily be more of an expression of his own views than a product of group deliberation. Probably a more severe limit to a committee's effectiveness was organizational; the participation of District committees in policy-formation was not institutionalized and not formally requested by other party organs. Thus, these committees were rarely able to deliberate on matters not already decided. The effectiveness of their unsolicited proposals apparently depended largely on the personal influence of their chairman.

The decisive influence of a group leader's behavior upon the functioning of a party organ and the behavior of its members is illustrated by the following example. The District board chairman of 1957 saw his role as co-ordinator and non-directive figure. He saw to it that the District board collectively discharged all of its organizational maintenance and co-ordination duties. He did not, however, seek to define more carefully the tasks of his board members. The constitution provided for four board members dealing respectively with organization, information and education, recruitment and propaganda, and social work; and these members were left to fulfill those special tasks delegated from the Land level in their own way. They were also free to set themselves additional tasks according to their own initiative and desire for action. Some reacted by fulfilling only the delegated tasks; others developed their own action programs. Similarly, the District chairman did not involve his board in attempts to influence higher-level policy-formation, although he gladly received suggestions and formal proposals from locals or board members, and he was willing to act on them or pass them on to higher levels, as the case might be.

Some of the various board members liked his leadership style; others criticized it. His non-directive attitude and his lack of interest in using the District board as a springboard for launching his own policy views was partly due to the fact that he had high organizational status and considerable influence at the Land level. He was, moreover, strongly oriented toward his higher offices. He also had a pronounced liberal democratic philosophy; it was for him appropriate to prefer non-directive leadership behavior. A third contributing factor might well have been his realistic assessment of his board's internal structure: it was characterized by low cohesion, with latent tensions along generational, religious, and ideological lines. Attempts to force agreement on matters other than routine organizational business, District-oriented problems, or delegated tasks might have brought these tensions into the open, precipitating conflicts. As it was, the other board members hardly thought of themselves as "we, the District board," but were oriented autonomously to the special tasks and other groups to which they separately belonged. This situation is not true in general of district boards, however. Informal reports about other CDU districts, obtained during the field work, indicate that in some instances a chairman dominated his board, or that small cliques within a board ran affairs rather jealously, occasionally using manipulative techniques.

In the District studied, the chairman had the closest co-operation with his secretary, the only paid functionary in the District. The functions of this secretary, who ran the District office, included routine co-ordinating and bureaucratic tasks, and special tasks of a similar nature which the Land or District board occasionally assigned. This secretary, in office for more than ten years by 1957 and therefore intimately familiar with the District and borough administration, was on the job every day, constantly available to everyone seeking advice or information or just wanting to talk. He was in a position to learn quickly of almost every important happening in the district; he occupied a focal position which might easily have enabled him to exert more influence than he was supposed to have. His personal orientation, however, was curiously nonpolitical. Without political activity or interests until 1945, his interests even in 1957 did not touch on policy formulation or the content of politics. His identification was organizational rather than ideological, and it was directed to the District rather than to the CDU as a whole.

This orientation made him forego opportunities to exert influence over policy-making within the party. He conceived his role much as it was formally defined, as directed almost exclusively to organizational administration. While the power goal was a strong guiding standard for him, he wanted power for the organization, without much thought about what policies this power should support. He had no higher office and desired none above the District level. He had no ambition to advance in the party. What influence he exerted was limited to organizational questions and personnel matters in the District. This was by no means the case for secretaries in all CDU districts. In this District, the secretary's conduct contributed much to the effective working of the CDU apparatus.

4. SANCTIONS SUPPORTING NORMS

The main sanction available to force office-holders to meet shared expectations is the threat of withdrawing support in the next election. This sanction rests, of course, with the appropriate group of legitimate electors and applies only to those leaders interested in keeping or achieving an office. The constitution provides a more generally applicable sanction, namely, expulsion from the party. This extreme measure is, however, only to be used if a member's behavior is "harmful to the party," including damaging its public prestige. Expulsion can be requested by any member, but it must be initiated formally by a local, district, or the Land board. It is finally decided by the latter. The procedure, which involves party arbitration courts, is tedious. Not only is it painful for the accused but also undesirable for the party, since it forces formal recognition of shameful occurrences. The District's records showed only five expulsion procedures initiated during its eleven-year history. Two of the persons involved were expelled; two other voluntary left the party before expulsion procedures were completed. In one case the charge was withdrawn.

Of course, behavior harmful to the party occurred more often, even in pronounced degree, than this suggests. In most cases, an open or implied threat to start expulsion procedures was used, usually by a superior official, to suggest that the culprit resign his membership "voluntarily," which he usually did. In a few cases, he left the party even before such a threat could be made. In other cases, it was possible simply to strike his name from the membership list, since the constitution permitted this whenever a member failed to pay his dues over a certain time or had hidden a fact that would have precluded his admission. From observation and information about such cases, it would appear that in this District, a considerable offense was involved before the attempt was made to get rid of a member. Some offenses involved no deviation from party rules or standards; they referred instead to private conduct or legal offenses which affected the CDU's reputation.

The widely shared desire to keep shameful occurrences secret in order to protect the party's reputation and its officials' prestige and authority strongly motivated people to cover up irregularities. Office-holders, being more visible and with more influence, can do more damage than a misbehaving ordinary member. At higher echelons, norms are more frequently evoked and sanctions advocated due to the competition for offices and personal rivalry. The desire to have the party appear in a favorable light is balanced by the protection which higher organizational status gives. Retrospectively, this observer marvels at how long the offensive behavior of a higher official was condoned and ignored before sanctions were finally applied. The line was generally drawn, however, where a public scandal could not be prevented and where fast action was needed to safeguard the party's reputation, especially when election chances hung in the balance.

Besides expelling or striking a member from the list, the constitution contains one other sanction. Local party units which are several months behind in their dues payments lose their votes in the district assembly. Similarly, delinquent districts lose seats in the Land assembly. If inability and not negligence is the reason dues were not payed, the assembly itself may make an exception. Such exceptions were not commonly made, however, since this would have created bad precedents. No constitutional sanctions enforce the fulfillment of any other tasks set forth as the responsibility of a local or district-level party unit. In consequence, while formal and informal sanctions can prevent or punish extreme departure from rules or norms, they can hardly insure optimal fulfillment of tasks. There is a connection between this lack of specific sanctions and the often vague definition of organizational tasks. Nonperformance of something which is not generally expected can hardly be punished as an extreme departure from norms.

Ultimately, of course, only limited normative consensus can reasonably be expected in an organization that is not strongly cohesive. Taking frequency of interaction, degree of personal involvement, dependence, and the need for acceptance as important conditions of cohesiveness, none of these were very strong for the District membership at large. For the most part, only the active minority, and among it largely the office-holders who interacted frequently, were strongly committed to the party and depended on it for important personal gratifications. The consensus among this minority in turn is impeded by different subunit identifications, rivalries, and the formation of factions along generational, religious, and ideological lines.

The District selection-processes did not guarantee that the person best suited to an office was the one elected. The main standard guiding the electors in their choice was the performance requirements of the office. Party members, however, did have certain expectations about the behavior of office-holders; while they did not deliberately select persons who would best fulfill these expectations, they applied the norms to those who were elected. Insofar as these performance norms directly reflected the functions which seem necessary for a democratically run and organizationally strong party apparatus, even a less-than-ideally-suited office-holder who responded to them may be said to have performed well. At local and District party levels, it is unlikely that many office-holders were willing but unable to fulfill such expectations. However, formal as well as widely shared informal expectations concentrated heavily on maintenance activities, and neglected such functions as citizen interaction and lower-level policy-making participation. In some cases, the personal orientation and role perception of an office-holder made up for this; some chairmen of local boards and committees tried to fulfill tasks not specifically requested of them. Here again, they were not selected because of their personal initiative. Where office-holders, whatever their inherent abilities, responded only to the minimal requirements of the formal and informal expectations, their performances reinforced these shortcomings, which are due not only to deficiencies in the selection process but even more so to deficiencies in the institutionalized role structures.

Characteristics of the Leadership Cadre

A composite picture of the leadership cadre must consider the combined effect of selective and self-selective tendencies, the latter being determined by the personal motivations and orientations of those willing to assume office.

The District offices form a differentiated hierarchy. In describing the selection processes by which various categories were filled, no explicit attention has been paid to connections between different types of offices which might constitute a patterned system of advancement. However, it is important to note where leaders come from within the party apparatus. Any structured limitations on eligibility would constitute additional selection factors; differences between the incumbents at different office levels might thus be partly determined.

1. ROADS OF ADVANCEMENT

A higher position in most organizations can be reached either by moving up to it through the hierarchy or by entering it directly, from within the ranks or from outside. Organizations differ in the formal prescriptions as well as the actual practices followed when filling positions at a given level. The German civil service, for instance, includes several hierarchically arranged subsystems, each of which is open to persons with a stipulated amount of formal education and professional training. A person entering a specific subsystem can hope to advance within it up to a ceiling established by his ability and training. Usually, however, he cannot look forward to moving into the next higher subsystem.

This compartmentalizing pattern is generally found also in military organizations. In industrial and business organizations, advancement roads, ceilings and the requirements of education and training are not as formally fixed; nevertheless, a rather similar situation often exists. In voluntary organizations fashioned after democratic models, on the other hand, there are typically no formal rules of this sort. The whole hierarchy of offices is, in theory, open to every member and can be reached from any starting point. This is the formal model of the CDU in West Berlin. However, we have already indicated how the permissiveness of such formal rules is habitually restricted in reality.

An attempt to spell out the typical roads of advancement to various types of party or public offices faces several difficulties. First, the absence of rules governing advancement makes every higher office accessible from a variety of starting points: movement may be upward, downward, and lateral. Vertical movement may be in steps as well as jumps. Second, the advancement pattern is complicated immensely by the practice of multiple office-holding. Hardly a District officer did not occupy several positions, the range of his organizational roles often including several levels. Furthermore, an officer might have held a lower office either before or after or at the same time as he held a higher office. Then, too, it was difficult to think of the District party organization as a simple hierarchy. It was not clear, for example, whether a District-level committee chairman occupied a higher position than a local chairman. Nor was it clear whether a District board member was on a par with a borough assembly member. Finally, this case study investigated only one district, which inevitably left the pattern partly unexplored.

In each local party unit, some subsidiary positions did not count as local board offices. Usually there were three to four times as many subsidiary posts as positions on the local board. A considerable number were held by board members, mostly because of the shortage of those willing to do the work, partly because board members were often interested in the particular tasks. Members elected to a local board for the first time often had been initiated into party work by serving in one or several of these subordinate posts. Of the newly elected board members in the District's largest local over a three-year period, 56 per cent had previously held one subsidiary post—if not more—for at least a year.

Positions on a local board, then, were often filled by members with some party experience. For all other types of party and public offices in the District, the situation was very different. The higher an office, the more exceptional were cases of direct access without prior experience. This was particularly true where an office required specific knowledge of party politics, as on the local, district, or Land boards. On some committees, to be sure, nonpolitical expertise might make up in part for a lack of party organizational background. However, even where committee and legislative work was concerned, direct access was rare, although in getting to such posts the aspirant might more easily jump over intermediate levels.

Between 1946, when the first CDU intraparty elections took place in the District, and 1957, 49 different persons had been elected local chairmen, while 43 persons had occupied positions on the District board itself. A comparison of the party-experience records of these two groups failed to indicate any clear advancement or office-mobility pattern.

Of the 49 local chairmen since 1946, practically all had previously served in some minor position, if not on the local board. For about half of them, the local chairmanship was the highest office held before or since. A somewhat larger group of 26 persons either had held or later did hold a position on the District level or higher. About one in four of these had already held the higher-level position at the time they assumed the local chairmanship; a similar proportion were simultaneously elected to the local chairmanship and to a higher office. The remainder, 12 persons, achieved higher office only after they had been elected local chairmen. In about twelve out of twenty-nine cases, then, the local chairmanship was part of a road to advancement in the party hierarchy. The proportion not following this simple progressive pattern is thus rather large.

Considering next the 43 persons who had been sometime District board members, we can distinguish several groupings, each characterized by the specific way in which membership was obtained. Nearly a third had belonged to the first District board; they constituted that group of leaders who had been instrumental in starting CDU activity after the war. Another one in every four came to the District board as nominees of one of the District-level "work-group committees" previously discussed; this meant they had held a committee office before coming to the District board. A third group, accounting for somewhat less than a third, may truly be said to have worked themselves "up" to the District board, having been local chairmen, members of the borough assembly, or occupants of some other lesser office before election. The remainder were persons who, because of special qualifications, had simultaneously been elected to positions on the District board and to some other important office. In one or two cases, a person was elected in a spontaneous manner by the District assembly, after having made an un-usually favorable impression during a debate, and without having previously held any consequential office, so far as is known.[31]

These data, while they fail to indicate any clear advancement pattern or even office-mobility pattern in the party, do illustrate rather clearly the complex tangle of roads leading to particular offices. They also support the general statement that a direct jump from the status of a rank-and-file local member to any office beyond the lowest CDU level is indeed rare.

2. SOCIAL CHARACTERISTICS OF THE LEADERSHIP CADRE

In most voluntary organizations, leaders differ from the ordinary members in a number of social characteristics; they are usually males with higher socio-economic status. This was also true in the CDU District. The previous discussion of selection criteria and personal motivations to assume office indicates the difficulties in predicting the extent and nature of the differences between leaders and ordinary members, much less between occupants of different types of offices.

Within the party hierarchy, only a limited number of offices, usually having special functions, were easily accessible to women. In 1957, all local chairmen were men; among the forty-nine persons who at some time had been local chairmen, there was only one woman. On the local boards, representation for women was more adequate; in 1957, 23 per cent of the local board members were women. In part, however, this was because of the constitutional requirement that every local board include at least one woman, as a representative of the female party members. Aside from this, women sometimes held the office of secretary, or more rarely, other special-ized offices; there was seldom a female treasurer.

On the District board, women were less adequately represented than on the local boards: Of all forty-three persons serving as District board members since 1946, only 14 per cent were women. Some of these were representatives of the "work group" committee for women; the rest were board members for social work. Of the ten committee chairmen at the district level in 1957, two were women; of the sixteen CDU members in the borough assembly of that year, four.

While women were less frequently CDU members than men, an even smaller proportion were found among the office-holders. However, less discrimination was involved than one might suppose. Female aspirants with the requisite skills, particularly for higher party offices, were very rare. It was sometimes difficult, indeed, to find even the small number of women needed to "balance the ticket" when the party nominated its borough assembly list.

As for religious affiliation, the major tendency seems to have been proportional representation. However, this was the result of conscious selectivity only in a limited degree. Some Protestant officers contended, and it was not possible to verify or rebut them, that there had recently been an expressly Catholic drive for more influence in the District. Catholics were about proportionately represented among the local chairmen and borough assembly members in 1957 (with 31 per cent and 37 per cent respectively, compared with 35 per cent of the party membership in the district). At the District level, both the committee chairmanships and the board membership itself were, in 1957, half Protestant and half Catholic. So far as the committee chairmanships were concerned, this overrepresentation of Catholics was probably a matter of chance, since religion was not a selection criterion for those offices. As for the overrepresentation on the District board itself, this appeared to be a fairly recent phenomenon. Seen as an average over the years since 1946, only 36 per cent of the board members had been Catholics.

An interesting feature can be observed when the religious composition of local boards is analyzed. In every District local, Protestants were in the majority, although in varying degrees. Locals which were disproportionately Catholic, however, were no more likely than other locals to have Catholic chairmen. But there was a distinct tendency for a local board to include more than a proportionate number of members having the chairman's religion, whichever that was. This was hardly due to conscious manipulation. A chairman usually succeeded in activating his personal friends to take local board positions; these friends were probably more often of his religion than of another.

Other groups of District office-holders fell somewhat short of the District board average in occupational status and formal educational attainments. But they, too, were of distinctly higher status than the average party member. Borough assembly delegates in 1957, for instance, included only 24 per cent who came from the highest occupational groups, while most of the rest were white-collar workers and civil servants. The occupational composition of local boards in 1957, excluding chairmen, corresponded quite closely to that of the District's over-all party membership; of all categories of officers, these local board members included the largest proportion of lower white-collar persons, and even some workers.

Among local board members was also found the highest proportion of persons who had no occupation, i.e., housewives, pensioned people, and unemployed. They were, so to speak, "set free" for party work. Since they belonged mainly to lower social strata, they were very different from the older type of *honoratioren*. The next higher percentage of persons without occupation was found, in 1957, among borough assembly members, whose time commitment in holding office is particularly high. On the other hand, the committee chairmen at the District level, in 1957, were all employed. So were the overwhelming majority of District board members and local board chairmen.

Socio-economic selectivity thus became more pronounced, the higher the party office. This was the result of two factors: first, the greater likelihood that persons of higher educational and occupational status would possess valued expertise and organizational skill; second, the tendency among many party members to defer to influential people and to presume that, simply because they have higher occupational and educational status, they have leadership ability and should, therefore, be elected.

If institutionalized training facilities for party members existed, some of these factors would very probably have less weight in the leadership-selection process. Independent of their occupation and education, party members could, through such training facilities, learn the requisite skills and achieve the necessary expert knowledge, which would give them organizational status, increase their visibility to the electors, and command the latter's trust in their ability. But such training facilities do not at present exist.

3. POLITICAL EXPERIENCE OF THE LEADERSHIP CADRE

Earlier, personal motivation was shown to have played an important role in determining who sought party office, and even which type of office was most desired. The personal orientation of an office-holder was not, however, an important criterion in the deliberations of electors, except insofar as it attested to a candidate's partisan dedication and readiness to work. The influence of personal orientation upon behavior after assuming office has also been highlighted; it has been possible to link specific orientations, e.g., professional interest versus political-career aspirations, with specific modes of performance. Next it will be shown how the motivational factor, resulting in a self-selective tendency, conferred a distinguishing characteristic upon the whole group of leaders in the District when compared to the rank and file. The starting point for this observation is in the fact that the District office-holders, and particularly higher office-holders, differed impressively from ordinary members in their length of party membership.

All local board chairmen and all borough assembly members, in 1957, had been CDU members at least since the end of 1947; the same was true for all but two of the District board members and for the great majority of the committee chairmen at the District level. By way of contrast, fully 60 per cent of the local board members in 1957 had entered the CDU after 1947, and one-third had joined the party since 1952. No comparison is possible with the rank-and-file members, but, if anything, their average length of membership was certainly even lower.

Of course, these differences are partly explained because it usually takes some time for a person to become known and work up to a higher office. Age as such, however, has no influence: District leaders turned out not to be older, but on the average younger than rank-and-file members. One might imagine that length of party membership, by strengthening party identification, would lead to greater activity and willingness to assume office;

available data do not bear out this expectation. Analysis of the attendance records of the largest local showed that length of membership was linked only slightly to attendance at meetings. If anything, those who had been members longer were less likely to attend. Since attendance was positively correlated with other measures of party activity, including office-holding and willingness to hold office at some later time, it may be inferred that length of membership in itself had little relationship to the time and effort put forth for the party.

In fact, the participation patterns for most party members seemed to be determined largely by their motivations in joining. For most party members, these motivations and their related participation levels remained rather constant over prolonged periods. Thus practically all holders of higher District offices in 1957 had been particularly active ever since they became members, usually some ten years before. What, then, were the present leaders' motivations for joining the party?

A specific type of political-ideological commitment, combined with professional or political career ambitions, was the modal motivation pattern of a CDU member striving for higher office. Indeed, the life histories of the 1957 office-holders show that, controlling for age possibilities, a majority in each of the four higher District office groups had been politically active during the Weimar Republic, either in a party, union, or political youth organization. After 1945, it was natural for them once again to engage in political activity; it was an opportunity they had clearly been waiting for. For many, perhaps most of them, there were additional motives. Moreover, their decision to join the CDU instead of another party implied special considerations. In general, however, the older office-holders gave a strikingly similar response to the question of why they had joined the CDU: given their former political activity and enduring political interest, it was "a matter of course."

For those who were too young to have been politically active before 1933 and who had attained higher District offices in the postwar years, the motivations that led them to join the CDU included, by their own testimony, a reaction to the catastrophe of 1945 and the threat of communism in the postwar period. In a very few cases, family tradition was involved. Most of them joined at the earliest postwar opportunity, although some were detained by wartime captivity or the need to finish their formal education. Among these younger party leaders, some had belonged to a political youth group before joining the CDU. It was in large part the leaders' own motivations that led to their party activity and that sustained it over many years.

One revealing difference illustrated the differential attractiveness of specific offices to persons with particular motivations. All older members of the 1957 District board and nearly all older local board chairmen of 1957 could point to some political activity before 1933. These were the people holding offices basic to the party hierarchy. Controlling for age, the percentage of District-level committee chairmen and borough assembly members in 1957 who had similar records was not as high, although a majority had records of prior political activity. Some of these leaders said they were not interested in politics at all before 1945. Some held also that their present orientation was not toward party politics or a political career, but was of a more professional nature, directed to the specific content of their work, e.g., some phase of borough administration, or cultural and school policy.

4. MULTIPLE INVOLVEMENT IN ORGANIZATIONAL ACTIVITY

One of the most important distinguishing characteristics of party leaders is their generally higher participation in formally organized social life. Among the adult population of the Federal Republic, only 53 per cent belong to formal organizations.[32] Compared to this population average, even the rank-and-file party members had a higher participation record. This would have been true had they belonged to no other organization than the CDU. Party officers were even more prone to formal affiliation, having a variety of social groupings and interests. If membership in formal organizations is a sign of a personality integrated into modern social life in ways peculiarly appropriate to it,[33] then the evidence is that party leaders were, to an impressive degree, representative of the most active citizens (see Table 1).

Table 1

Membership in Other Organizations, and Multiple Party Offices, 1957

	Members of Largest Local	Chairmen of locals	Committee District Chairmen	Members of District Board	Members of Borough Assembly*
Number:	(153)	(13)	(10)	(16)	(16)
Organizational Ties					
Church groups	35	6	9	13	13
Leisure-time groups	23	3	4	4	4
Union, professional associations	48	13	16	21	11
Interest groups	23	4	5	18	7
Other organizations	11	4	4	9	4
Average per person:	0.9	2.3	3.8	4.0	2.4
Party Offices					
Local Board, including chairmanship	13	13	7	13	10
District board	1	6	5	16	5
District committees	41	16	13	21	40
Borough Assembly	—	4	2	4	16
Land Assembly delegate	1	4	2	7	2
Land Committee	4	16	16	27	17
Land Board	—	—	—	1	1
Parliament, West Berlin	—	1	—	1	—
Other, including honorary positions	6	10	8	15	16
Average per person:	0.4	5.4	5.3	6.6	6.7

*The number of party offices for borough-assembly members is swelled by the high frequency of their District committee memberships, which are mostly **ex officio** and very often do not lead to much participation. District Board members hold more higher party offices, e.g., memberships in Land committees, which are usually not **ex officio** and correspond to a higher level of participation.

The importance of multiple memberships and organizational overlapping for the governmental process in a democratic society has often been pointed out and discussed in detail.[34] Multiple membership linkages with outside organizations on *all* levels of a party hierarchy are particularly necessary where party leaders have strong influence in the legislative phase of government and where parties are firmly structured, cohesive, formal organizations, as in Germany.

Members of the District board showed the highest average of memberships in other formal organizations of any leadership category studied. The figure for committee chairmen was nearly as high. Surprisingly, the District members of the borough assembly averaged far fewer memberships with organized interest groups.[35] Interest groups rarely tried, however, to influence District-level party leaders; their efforts were aimed at gaining access at the Land level of the party, where policy decisions relevant to their interests were more often made. In only a few cases was the outside organizational membership of a party official ever used by that group to exercise influence. In the few instances where this was tried, without exception the subject was of very minor importance. Occasionally, an official's implicit personal identification with an outside organization seemed to be reflected in his views and possibly influenced his stand on issues and decisions, without any request being made to him. Even this kind of indirect influence was limited; most group identifications were quite irrelevant for the kinds of decisions made on local and District boards.

Practically every leading person in the District party hierarchy held offices on more than one level, and not rarely on all three levels. This fact was of great importance, since personal union is perhaps the most effective type of interlinkage between organizational levels. This interlinkage allowed each lower level to participate most directly in the decisions made at the one above it; it afforded a direct channel of communication, both upward and downward. By increasing the insight and experience of individual leaders, multiple office-holding also improved performance.

Multiple office-holding had very serious drawbacks as well as these positive aspects. The accumulation of functions in a few hands limited the opportunities for active participation available to other party members. It also deprived them of opportunities for training in important work. These two considerations reinforced each other: the lower the number of trained personnel, the more accumulation of functions in the hand of the few. Moreover, the more offices one individual occupied, the thinner he had to spread his time and energy and the sooner, therefore, did he neglect some of his functions. This last disadvantage was hardly balanced by the accompanying increase in experience and insight which an accumulation of official functions brought.

A number of reasons accounted for the tendency of party leaders to accumulate offices. First, party rules make the occupants of certain offices ex officio members of other party organs. All borough assembly members, by virtue of that office, belonged to several District-level committees; the same was true for the holders of certain local board positions. Some District-level chairmen of special committees, in turn, by virtue of that position, belonged to the corresponding organ on the Land level. The District board chairman was an ex officio member of the Land board. Second, the electors considered certain combinations of offices desirable. Thus, it was held by many that local delegates to the District assembly should be persons from the local board or other important local office-holders; similarly, it was held that leading District board members should at the same time be delegates to the Land assembly. Again, it was thought that those chairmen of the District-level committees who do not belong to the corresponding committee on the Land level by constitutional provision should be sent as delegates on the initiative of the District committee. Third, even when such specific combinations were not consciously considered desirable by the electors, they tended to give their votes to persons whose visibility—or current organizational status and presumed experience—stemmed from the fact that they already held party offices. Those who succumbed to this selective bias were by no means always conscious that they did so. In fact, despite continued tendencies toward accumulation of offices, there was sometimes openly expressed opposition to it. Ordinary members and holders of minor offices, who might themselves aspire to more influence in the party apparatus, were most likely to be critical. The extent and strength of this criticism was, however, effectively curbed by a lack of knowledge of the real extent of office accumulation. Since a given office-holder received his several positions from different groups of electors, who did not often see him perform in more than one of his official capacities during his incumbency, office-accumulation was commonly underestimated.

From the offices-holder's point of view, he had consented to occupy more and more functions. Often, moreover, he was actively interested in seeking additional posts. More offices increased his experience and his influence, which might be desired in itself or as a means to some ulterior goal. When this desire for influence was satisfied by achieving a higher office, why did the incumbent retain his lower-level positions? Why did he sometimes even assume additional lower-level offices? To some degree, office-holders did cast off lower-level duties when they moved upward. When they did, it was sometimes criticized at the lower level in question. In part, it was deplored as a loss of a direct-influence channel to a higher level and as a loss of an officer with new-found prestige and experience. It was also interpreted by lower-level critics as a lack of devotion to them and a sign of personal ambition overriding subunit loyalty. To avoid such criticisms and still retain direct influence and personal following at the lower level, many higher party officials let themselves be elected and re-elected to lower-level offices. There was, then, a considerable contradiction in the attitudes of party members toward multiple office-holding. In fact, the apparent contradictions reflect the complexity and the various important aspects of the problem itself.

5. CONTINUITY AND THE CHANGE IN THE LEADERSHIP

The continuity of leadership in the different party organs is remarkably similar, considering either the average length of service for officers of a given category or average rates of re-election. Thus, the average length of service as local chairman of all 49 persons who at some time held this office was 3.3 years, while for the 43 sometime District board members it was 3.5 years.[36] These averages hide great differences: individual local chairmen, for instance, served anywhere from 6 months to 12 years.

Each year, between 70 and 80 per cent of the incumbents of each category were re-elected. This held not only for District board members, committee chairmen, and local chairmen, but also for local board members (judging from figures for the District's largest local) and even for committee members. These averages ignore annual variations, which, however, showed no trend. One might have expected stronger differences between the different kinds of offices. Apparently the stronger competition for higher offices, which should have led to higher rates of turnover, was offset by stronger tendencies and personal desires for re-election where these offices were concerned. Although only about one-fourth of each year's incumbents failed to return the following year, it was not true that as many as three-fourths of each year's District leadership group were carry-overs, since the various party organs have gradually grown in size.

The high continuity in office-holding reflected less the incumbents' desire to keep their positions than the frequent lack of contestants. In most cases where an office did change hands, the former occupant had not run for re-election, either because he no longer wanted to hold office or because he was unable to run—due to sickness, old age, death, or movement out of the District. These reasons definitely prevailed when lower-level offices changed hands. They accounted for the majority of changes in higher offices, but the stronger competition for these offices resulted in a somewhat greater frequency of political reasons for the changes. Table 2 illustrates this difference: it shows the reasons for the offices of local chairman and District board member changing hands from the time of the District's founding to the

Table 2
Reasons for Change in Office Occupant

Reasons	Local Chairmen (per cent)	District Board Members (per cent)
Voluntary Reasons:	28	7
Own wish was not to run again		
Circumstantial Reasons:	40	52
Death or moving away from the district	(24)	(30)
Sickness or old age	(16)	(22)
Political Reasons:	32	41
Defeated by rival or pressured to resign		
	100	100
Number of cases:	(37)*	(27)

*The reasons for 5 of the total of 42 changes are unknown.

present. Where an incumbent was pressured to resign during his term or urged to refrain from running for re-election, the candidate had sometimes been involved in an open scandal or could not be supported by the CDU for other reasons.

A comparison of the percentages who left office for voluntary reasons at the two levels suggests the basic difference in the character of these two kinds of party posts. Somewhat more than one in every four local chairmen relinquished office voluntarily: sometimes for lack of time combined with weariness at the tiresome tasks; in two cases because they assumed an important higher office. Only 7 per cent of the changes in District board membership during these years were instances of voluntary retirement. The two District board members so classified were individuals who became openly opposed to CDU policy and eventually left the party.

As a group, the District leaders presented a more positive picture in many respects than might be expected, considering the selection processes and criteria described. Regarding their motivations, their general activity in organized social life, their enduring commitment to party activity, their age, and their occupational and educational level (permitting some inferences as to general ability), the leaders were a select group among the party membership. This partly explains and partly justifies the high degree of continuity in office-holding.

It may seem, then, that a positive self-recruitment makes up for certain deficiencies in the selection procedures. Indeed, overstating the case, one might argue that if only qualified persons aspire to leadership, the electors are relieved of the need to apply rigid qualitative standards and to screen the motivations and orientations of office aspirants closely. Party members did not, of course, hold such a view. They did consider, among other things, the personal qualities of candidates; the more so, the higher the office. The progressive selectivity in some of the characteristics attests to this.

Nevertheless, the prevailing situation harbors a potential danger. To the extent that the quality of the leadership group depends upon tendencies of self-selection rather than upon a deliberate screening in the elections, the party electorate is no safeguard against the possibility that persons with motives and values ultimately detrimental to an efficiently functioning political democracy will assume leadership. Many of the present leaders came either from that group of older persons whose democratic political commitment had been tested and had survived the counterinfluence of the Nazi regime, or from those younger persons whose reaction to the breakdown and to the dangers and fresh hopes of the immediate postwar years was an equally earnest commitment to democratic political activity. With the passage of time, this leadership reservoir becomes exhausted.

One further point. If the character of the present leadership group is indeed as positive as these data imply, why was it necessary to point to deficiencies in the actual functioning of this party organization? The answer has already been indicated: given a certain easily achieved level of ability, factors operating upon the leader after his selection are of greater importance for behavior. With the same persons in office, the District could probably have performed significantly better its organizational functions—interacting with the population, activating the rank and file, and encouraging participation in policy-formation—had these functions been explicitly expected and institutionalized in the organization.

Summary and Outlook

Measured against realistic expectations, the picture presented by the District as of 1957 is favorable. From the viewpoint of an observer committed to the ideal of an efficiently functioning political democracy, however, there exist a number of more or less serious shortcomings and points of potential danger. Without repeating the arguments in detail, these points may now be summarized briefly.

There is a high degree of self-containment, not to say insulation, in the District. The lowest-level units of the CDU do not constitute a region of high mutual permeability and interaction between the organization and the public. Furthermore, organized interest groups hardly interacted with the party at this level, although they surely did so at higher levels. Analysis of the activity of the borough assembly *Fraktion* and the party's city councilors in the District, not reported here, revealed some instances of such interaction; but, even there, much less was found than expected and less than would seem healthy in a pluralist power system where the parties play integrative roles. Finally, selection of party officers and candidates for general election was purely a party affair in the District, intraorganizational in scope. The participation of the electorate, organized or unorganized, was limited to deciding, every four years, how many of the party's nominees were to achieve office.

A second point of criticism is that through neither a deliberate recruitment of potential leaders, nor a corresponding orientation in intraparty elections, nor systematic training did the party purposefully insure having leaders and candidates of the highest possible ability or personal and political quality. If the present District leadership nevertheless displays positive characteristics, the credit goes only in part to the District's elective bodies. Some of the present qualified leaders at the local and District level received their positions with the help and upon the suggestion of other qualified leaders, i.e., through their urging, informal advice upon candidacies, personal campaigning, and so forth. The effects of the preplanning practice in local elections should be recalled.

The observed facts might be interpreted in part as evidence of a District leadership markedly oligarchical in character. Closer inspection, however, shows that this criticism hardly applied. Some factors ordinarily assumed to strengthen oligarchical tendencies were little in evidence at this organizational level. While there is much emphasis on organizational maintenance and its problems, there is no overbureaucratization that would strengthen the position of the "apparatus." Again, the District leaders, best informed and most frequently interacting among themselves, have no monopoly on communication media. Indeed, in 1957, no such media were relied upon in the District. Thirdly, most offices were not sufficiently attractive to motivate their incumbents to hold to them tenaciously merely to preserve status or material gratifications. Finally, the skills required, at least in the local and in several District-level offices, were not so rare that many ordinary members, far more than actually did so, could not reasonably aspire to these positions. At least at this lower party level, willingness to assume office was a more crucial factor than possession of special abilities.

A low turnover rate among office holders is another feature usually indicative of oligarchical leadership. In the District, however, this was in large part the result of tendencies among members and delegates to re-elect incumbents. Elections in the District, except for local elections, were not manipulated in an oligarchic fashion, i.e., from above or by incumbents, and preplanning in the locals hardly deprived office to any interested persons. That delegates decided among themselves how to vote, rather than executing wishes of their parent bodies, did not violate the constitution—which gives no rules on this matter—and in fact corresponded to the actual level of limited interest and insight prevailing in the units from which the delegates came. Nor were the limited interest, low participation, and low involvement of large portions of the rank and file due to an entrenched leadership group deliberately usurping all responsibility and important functions, thus causing the remaining members to fall into apathy. Rather, this state of affairs was the consequence of the recruitment and admission standards, which permitted persons to join who never intended to participate actively. Nor should one evaluate this only negatively; even passive members may serve important functions in the larger context of a political system.

The District leadership was not oligarchic in the usual sense, yet it did display a high degree of independence as the result of several conditions, none of which these leaders had purposefully created. (1) Higher officeholders were insulated from lower-level control by the step-wise structuring of the election process. (2) The elected higher leaders were only limitedly visible to the lower levels, making assessment of their performance difficult by anyone outside of the small interaction group. Given the hierarchical structure of the organization, these two conditions may be unavoidable. The same was not true for two remaining conditions. (3) A large margin existed for self-definition of leadership tasks, because the norms and sanctions guiding leader behavior applied only to limited areas of their performance. (4) There was an absence of institutionalized participation by lower levels in matters of policy-formation dealing with programmatic value decisions (rather than the implementation of policy goals). The function of higher and intermediate ranks of party officials was presumably in part to translate general expectations relating to upward processes of policy-formation— and other neglected functions such as the interaction with the public—into specific tasks allocated to specific office-holders, and to institute, for instance, procedures by which certain kinds of higher-level decisions could be presented to lower-level bodies with requests for their opinion. While it was not true that the divorce between higher decision-making bodies and lower party levels had been created by a deliberate usurpation of functions, the lower levels could have been activated more than they were.

The danger implied in the prevailing situation is potential more than actual; it lies less in the conditions of the District itself than in the fact that the decision-making bodies at the Land level were apparently as independent of District officials as the latter were of the local rank and file. If the lower party level is habitually only a resonating body for the decisions of leaders, it will presumably lack the disposition and the organizational instruments to assert its control, if, at some future time, these higher leaders should act against the latent wishes of the membership or in a way detrimental to the democratic political system. The danger, then, refers to a certain structured weakness in the substance of the democratic process. As such, it applies first of all to the German scene, but the same problem is posed in principle for all democracies.

The above problem may be rephrased, for the sake of added clarity. We have noted that the District membership at large accepted wholeheartedly the goal of political power for the CDU, as manifested in electoral success, and that any activity seen as directly related to electoral success was performed with particular willingness. However, instead of consciously perceiving power as a means for implementing a specific program, the membership received it as an end in itself. This left the elected leaders and representatives free to decide which policies should be pursued. Naturally, the leaders could not go directly against the general attitudes of the party membership, by pushing, for instance, the nationalization of industries. But the extent of the margin for independent decision-making at the highest level was seen, for example, in the event of the CDU's espousal of atomic armament in the famous parliamentary debate early in 1958. This issue had not been previously debated, at least at the District level in Berlin. It is by no means certain that the party rank and file, if consulted before any higher-level decisions had prejudged their opinion, would have supported the action. As it was, the District membership was simply presented with the decision, and many then felt called upon to defend it, as an action of their party, against outside criticism and particularly against that of the rival SPD.

This observation leads to a final point. Participant observation made it clear that the membership opinions voiced in discussions in local, committee, and assembly meetings in the District aimed primarily at creating consensus and support for the party's actions and legislative policy. While this may be important for maintaining organizational cohesion, it inhibits the development of independent political opinions among members. If the discussion of future policy were carried down to the lowest party level, intraorganizational conflict would be sharpened. A certain measure of such conflict seems essential for a vital democracy.

Notes

1. See, for instance, the publications in the series, *Parteien, Fraktionen, Regierungen*, under the general editorship of Dolf Sternberger, and the publications

in the "Schriften des Instituts fuer politische Wissenschaft", Berlin.

2. Bernard R. Berelson, Paul F. Lazarsfeld, and William N. McPhee, *Voting* (Chicago: University of Chicago Press, 1954), chap. ix.

3. For this conception of the political party, see Otto Stammer, "Politische Soziologie," in H. Schelsky and A. Gehlen (eds.), *Soziologie* (Düsseldorf and Köln, 1955).

4. The project was financed by a grant of the Deutsche Forschungsgemeinschaft. The research profited from the advice of Otto Stammer, professor at the Freie Universitat in Berlin. The full German report is now available: Renate Mayntz, *Parteigruppen in der Grosstadt* ("Schriften des Instituts fuer politische Wissenschaft," Vol. XVI [Koeln and Opladen, 1959]). For an earlier study, see R. Mayntz, "Die Funktionen der Lokalen Parteigruppe in der kleinen Gemeinde," *Zeitschrift für Politik*, No. 1, 1955.

5. See Gerhard Schulz, "Die CDU—Merkmale ihres Aufbaus," in *Parteien in der Bundesrepublik* ("Schriften des Instituts für Politisch Wissenschaft," Vol. VI [Stuttgart and Duesseldorf, 1955]).

6. *Ibid.*

7. See "Berlin—Kampf um Freiheit und Selbstverwaltun 1945-46," *Schriftenreihe zur Berliner Zeitgeschichte*, Vol. I (Berlin, 1957); and Gerhard Schulz, *op. cit.*

8. See Wolfgan Leonhard, *Die Revolution entlasst ihre Kinder* (Köln and Berlin, 1955).

9. William Wright, in connection with the Institut für Politische Wissenschaft in Berlin, has conducted a comparative investigation into the activities of a district organization of the Social Democratic party in Berlin. At this writing, his study is still in the process of evaluation.

10. *Satzung des Landesverbandes Berlin der Christlich-Demokratischen Union Deutschlands vom 23 April 1955*, and *Satzung des Kreisverbandes . . . der Christlich-Demokratischen Union Deutschlands*. The latter restates and elaborates the former in some respects; they will be considered as if they formed an entity.

11. The local unit retains for its own purposes the dues it collects minus a sum per member it has to deliver to the District.

12. See Arnold J. Heidenheimer, "German Party Finance: The CDU," *American Political Science Review*, Vol. LI, No. 2 (1957).

13. This is a general characteristic of a certain type of voluntary organization. See David L. Sills, *The Volunteers: Means and Ends in a National Organization* (Glencoe, Ill.: The Free Press, 1957), pp. 79 ff. He found 10 per cent of the members joining on their own initiative, which is significantly higher than for the CDU District, though quite small in itself.

14. The importance of recruiting standards is illustrated by the results of a study of a voluntary organization: "Participation in Voluntary Committees" (Survey Research Center, University of Michigan, February, 1956, mimeo.). Members of the more active units were "selected because they have jobs and skills which are useful. . . . Activity committees [did not] select members merely because they are available or because they are not likely to be in a position to refuse to join" (p. 4).

15. Sills, *op. cit.*, pp. 109 ff., found it an important factor that joining is interpreted as fulfillment of obligations which derive from some role relationship. The same conclusion was drawn from the Survey Research Center study, "Participation in Voluntary Committees," pp. 4-5.

16. See "Rechtliche Ordnung des Parteiwesens: Probleme eines Parteiengesetzes," *Bericht der vom Bundesminister des Inneren eingesetzen Parteienrechtskommission* (Frankfurt and Berlin, 1957), p. 43.

17. Erich Reigrotzki, *Soziale Verflechtungen in der Bundesrepublik* (Tübingen, 1956), p. 59.

18. Attention to different personal orientations of members or of leaders in an organization has been paid in several recent studies. See Sills, *op. cit.*, pp. 102 ff; Harold L. Wilensky, *Intellectuals in Labor Unions* (Glencoe, Ill.: The Free Press, 1956) whose types are the missionary, careerist, professional, and politico; and S. M. Lipset, "The Political Process in Trade Unions," in M. Berger *et al.* (eds.), *Freedom and Control in*

Modern Society (New York: Van Nostrand, 1954). Lipset distinguishes the career-oriented from the calling-oriented leader).

19. Of the rarely attending half of the largest local's members, 45 per cent said they had no relatives, friends, neighbors, or colleagues in their local. The large majority of the more frequently attending half reported some such ties.

20. This has also been pointed out by A. S. Tannenbaum, "Mechanisms of Control in Local Trade Unions," *British Journal of Sociology*, VII (December, 1956), 312.

21. The constitution itself makes provision to ensure that certain party organs are represented on the District board. It stipulates that the three "work-group" committees—for women, young members, and work-place groups—each have the right to nominate a representative. The assembly has only the option of confirming or rejecting these individual nominees. Again, the *ex officio* memberships on the District board of the speaker of the CDU *Fraktion* in the borough assembly and of a member of the Berlin House of Representatives also link the District board rather closely to the legislative process, borough-wide and city-wide.

22. The work group for young members is a full-fledged, separate organization within the CDU. It includes all members under thirty-five years of age, although they may also belong to a regular party local. It also is open to interested young people who are not formal party members. This organization, the "Junge Union" or youth union, has its own three-level hierarchy in West Berlin, complete with a Land board, District board, and even some local units. The way in which it fits into, and works with, the more inclusive party structure is a complex matter. It will not be discussed here, nor will the election of the youth union's District chairman, who is usually its District board representative as well.

23. These remarks refer to the situation in 1954; for the 1958 election, a new election law brought about certain changes.

24. Clear task specification was found to be positively correlated with amount of activity in the Survey Research Center study, *Participation in Voluntary Committees*, p. 8.

25. For a pertinent discussion, see Otto Stammer in Wolfgang Hirsch-Weber (ed.), *Gewerkschaften im Staat, Drittes Europaisches Gespräch*, pp. 238-39.

26. This problem is more or less common to all parties in the Federal Republic. See F. A. Von Der Heydte and K. Sacherl, *Soziologie der deutschen Parteien* (Munich: Isar Verlag, 1955), pp. 41-44.

27. See S. M. Lipset, M. A. Trow, J. S. Coleman, *Union Democracy* (Glencoe, Ill.: The Free Press, 1956), p. 10.

28. See R. K. Merton, "The Role-Set: Problems in Sociological Theory," *British Journal of Sociology*, VIII (June, 1957), pp. 106-20. Also E. Jacobson, W. W. Charters, and S. Liebermann, "The Use of the Role Concept in the Study of Complex Organizations," *Journal of Social Issues*, Vol. VII, No. 3, (1951).

29. This has repeatedly been demonstrated in an industrial or occupational setting; see, for instance, R. Kahn and D. Katz, "Leadership Practices in Relation to Productivity and Morale," in D. Cartwright and A. Zander (eds.), *Group Dynamics: Research and Theory* (Evanston: Row, Peterson, 1953). Robert D. Weiss, *Processes of Organization* ("Survey Research Center Monograph Series," No. 17 [Ann Arbor, 1956]), shows that in a professional context, too, part of the learning of a new job comes from colleagues rather than the rule book; this serves to transmit habitualized deviations from formal role definitions. This same pattern applies in the District, although formal definitions were not very detailed in the first place.

30. The importance of leadership style for group performance has been a favorite topic for research in group dynamics and industrial human relations; two examples of its significance in voluntary organizations are A. S. Tannenbaum and R. Kahn, *Participation in Union Locals* (Evanston: Row, Peterson, 1958), and "Participation in Voluntary Committees."

31. A similar kind of analysis can be made of the ten persons who served as committee chairmen at the District level in 1957. All had held some other party office before assuming this position. But, as in the case of the local chairmen, they

did not all reach the committee chairmanship from below; some held offices of at least equal, if not higher, party rank beforehand.

Again, the complex tangle of mobility is illustrated by an analysis of delegates to the Land committees in 1957; more than half of whom occupied other high posts (a local chairmanship, a District-level office, or higher), while the rest had at least an additional functional position in their respective local units.

32. Erich Reigrotzki, *op. cit.,* p. 164.

33. This statement, which comes close to sounding like a tautology, actually points to a highly important and complex problem on which very little research has been done. Some incidental evidence pointing to a connection between psychological make-up and active participation in formal organizations may be found in Emory John Brown "Elements Associated with Activity and Inactivity in Formal Organizations" (Ph.D. dissertation, Michigan State College, 1952); in H. H. Plambeck as quoted in Brown, and in "A Study of the League of Women Voters of the United States" (Survey Research Center, University of Michigan, 1957, mimeo).

34. See D. B. Truman, *The Governmental Process* (New York: Knopf, 1951).

35. Considered in terms of the proportion of party officials who held important offices as well in outside organizations, 54 per cent of the local chairmen, half of the District board members, half of the chairmen of District-level committees, and 44 per cent of the borough assembly members in 1957 could be so characterized.

36. For the ten committee chairmen of 1957 the figure was likewise 3.5 years.

v

Recruitment Contrasts in Rival Campaign Groups

by DWAINE MARVICK

and

CHARLES NIXON*

SYSTEMATIC research into the patterns and bases of political behavior has added much to the understanding of "democracy" as a political method. Although auxiliary mechanisms can be identified, the electoral process is central to the functioning of a democratic political order. The indispensable rule of political parties is being explicitly acknowledged.[1] The various and diverse viewpoints and interests among the citizenry are abundantly documented.[2] Behavioral research has contributed to the identification of conditions sustaining democracy,[3] as well as to the delineation of conceptual models of what it is and how it works.[4] This, in turn, has meant that forthright defense of democracy—that is, of popular control and direction over government—need not be superficial or unrealistic.[5] It is now possible to buttress a justification of political democracy with a recital of relevant fact about voters, political leaders, and other component types whose actions make the system work or fail.[6] In talking about democracy or doing

*The study reported here has been supported by a grant to us from the Political Behavior Committee of the Social Science Research Council. This aid and that given at earlier phases of the study by the Faculty Research Committee, University of California, and the Bureau of Governmental Research, UCLA, are gratefully acknowledged.

research on problems of democratic order, the pivotal and distinctive role of active campaign-workers is not often denied, but it is easily blurred. This is, perhaps, because our attention focuses upon two essential categories, namely, the public and the leaders. The particular role played by each and the character of the relationships between them are seen differently by different theorists. But the tendency toward a dichotomy is persistent: politicians and voters, office-seekers and citizens, elite and mass.

There is little in either the literature of democratic theory or in empirical studies of politics that provides a systematic typology of active campaign-workers in free election settings. Yet, active workers are essential components in modern election processes. They are the rank-and-file personnel of politics. They man the precinct posts, sustain the activities of political clubs, and form the link by which the political process is integrated with other social and community worlds. Established patterns of analysis might suggest that they are adequately thought of as either more interested voters or less advanced political leaders. Either approach is plausible, both have difficulties.

One might reason, by extrapolating from findings about voting behavior, that an active campaign-worker is simply a more interested citizen.[7] This would assume a continuum of political behavior and the motivations behind it. The factors distinguishing barely interested, passive voters from highly interested, strongly partisan voters are presumed to be the same factors distinguishing the latter type from deeply involved, active campaign-workers. In significant ways, however, an active worker's behavior and orientation to politics differs from a voter's, however active and partisan he is. The campaign-worker has joined an organization; the voter has not. This provides the worker with new sources of gratification and imposes loyalties not present for the voter. The campaign-worker is engaged in activities that focus his attention upon influencing the electorate; the voter is intent largely upon the candidates and issues from which he must choose.

On the other hand, because the campaign-worker seeks to win votes, he may conceal his political convictions if they seem likely to alienate voters. In this minimum sense, he is plausibly classified as a type of politician. However, while many political leaders began their careers as campaign-workers, not all campaign-workers seek positions of political leadership and power. In fact, their organizational work may provide satisfactions that positions of greater responsibility and public leadership would not. It is at least questionable, then, that we can adequately view campaign-workers as having the same motivations as political leaders, although with lesser intensity, or as having the same qualities, although with lesser skills.

Findings are needed in order to clarify how campaign-workers differ from either voters or political leaders. Such findings would direct attention to a complex aspect of the political order that is too often slighted, both in describing and evaluating electoral mechanisms and the decision-making processes of modern democracy. What leads to active political participation, beyond voting or nominal party affiliation, is a question that can be raised in all communities. It is of particular interest in the Los Angeles area, however, because of the open character of political organizations and the largely voluntary nature of campaign work. There is little in the way of spoils of office or material reward with which to build a disciplined political machine. The motivation, attitudes, types of rewards received, and general characteristics of *voluntary* participants are, therefore, of primary concern.

In any democratic system, there are functional reasons why rival party organizations in the same locality are likely to present essentially the same appearance, at least "in profile." There are grounds for expecting symmetry. First, those who "manage" political affairs tend to become "professionals," whose skills and other characteristics are much the same, regardless of the interests or principles that attract supporters to the party banner.[8] Secondly, the basic conditions of competition existing between party organizations tend to lead one party's workers to be preoccupied with much the same electoral considerations as are the rival party-workers.

Although, for these functional reasons, party organizations in the same area may look somewhat alike, where the party apparatus is manned by voluntary participants it seems likely that the differences between rival parties will be important. It is necessary to search for asymmetry, especially in comparing the segments of the community from which volunteers are recruited to the rival party structures. Different segments of the community probably tend to nourish and sustain the Republican and Democratic parties respectively. The pool of experience and social contacts available among active Democrats in a given locality is correspondingly likely to differ from the pool of resources available among active Republicans.

If rival political organizations in the same localities do *not* reflect social and economic disparity in their composition, politics is probably not a very meaningful part of the way in which values are distributed in that community. Asymmetry in the composition of rival political organizations is, in this view, an index of the seriousness of the issues that the political arena is asked to solve. On the other hand, the extent of symmetry indicates the presence of a frame of reference common to those active in politics, suggesting what *they* "take for granted" about the struggle. Depending upon the task that politics is called upon to perform, the extent to which rival organizations are symmetrical in their social composition thus sets the limits within which those problems are likely to be solved.

In examining the place of campaign-workers in the electoral process, as revealed by the findings of the Los Angeles study, the ensuing agenda will be followed: After a discussion of the instrumentation necessary for our analysis, we will analyze the data of the Los Angeles study for the light they throw on problems of rival organizational strength, of the social origin of rival party-workers at different power levels, and of the familial and ideological processes that affect enlistment in campaign work for different types of party-workers.

Sampling Campaign Processes and Measuring Power Positions Simultaneously

The data presented here were collected by a series of interviews and reinterviews in successive campaigns with active campaign-workers in three state-assembly districts in the Los Angeles area. These districts were chosen so that workers from both political parties were drawn in identical proportion from "sure," "doubtful," and "lost" areas of party control. The main focus of attention and the major body of attitudinal data in this report relates to the 1956 general-election campaign.[9] In sampling these districts, our procedure provided a basis for sketching the opposing organizational structure and for specifying each participant's power position. Respondents were chosen according to two rules. First, we selected those holding official or semi-official positions in the formal party structure—persons such as members of the state and county central committees, heads of political clubs, and campaign managers. Second, each person interviewed was asked to name key figures or steady workers in the campaign organization of his area. Anyone so named by two respondents during the same campaign was eligible and interviewed if possible.

The result of the selection technique was to provide a panel of respondents that gave neither a random sample of the population in the assembly district, nor a random cross-section of all those, in some way, actively involved in the campaign universe in the assembly districts in question. If the campaign apparatus is thought of as a pyramid, this method of selecting a panel resulted in securing a large portion of those at the top of the pyramid and a smaller proportion of those at the middle and bottom. If the campaign structure is thought of as a series of concentric circles, this sampling method secured a large proportion of those in the central orbits of campaign activity and communication, and lesser proportions of those in the middle and peripheral regions of party campaign work. Of those named to us, we succeeded in interviewing 90 per cent of the 20 per cent most frequently named, 50 per cent of the 30 per cent least often named, and 65 per cent of the balance. Their responses, in short, sketched the outlines of the campaign structure, and at the same time, located one another in terms of the central or peripheral position each was seen as occupying.

In sampling campaign participation, data were gathered that permitted one gauge of a participant's power position, a measure of his "organizational prominence." At the same time, our informants were asked how much of a personal voice they had in party decisions regarding two basic campaign problems—what kind of campaign appeals the party organization should express, and what kind of organized activities the party should conduct. From their answers, a measure of "weight in campaign decisions" was developed. This was a second gauge of a participant's power position. Table 1 shows the close correlation of these two measures, one based upon the views of fellow campaign-workers, and the other based upon the informant's account of himself. While only 31 per cent of the least prominent were classed as having "much to say" about campaign decisions, fully 59 per cent of those most prominent in the campaign organization were rated as workers with "much to say." The intermediate rank of the campaign organization scored, appropriately enough, at the intermediate figure of 44 per cent.

Stratum for stratum, the Democratic Party structure appeared to be the more "democratic," in the specific sense that a higher proportion in each

Table 1

Weight in Campaign Decisions Claimed by Party-Workers in Different Organizational Strata*

| | REPUBLICANS | | DEMOCRATS | | TOTAL | |
	Per cent	No.	Per cent	No.	Per cent	No.
Most prominent	48	(38)	68	(47)	59	(85)
Intermediate	37	(59)	50	(70)	44	(129)
Least prominent	21	(34)	37	(51)	31	(85)
Total:	36	(131)	51	(168)	44	(229)

*Per cent rated as having "much to say" about various campaign decisions.

stratum were scored as having a considerable voice in campaign decisions. Over-all, 36 per cent of the Republicans and 51 per cent of the Democrats rated "much to say" descriptions.

In light of the close correlation shown in Table 1, it is clear that informants were naming as "key figures" and "steady workers" the same people who, when asked how much voice they personally had in campaign decisions, indicated they had quite a bit. The reasoning that leads to combining these two measures into a single index of power position is as follows: An individual's power depends partly on his being at the center of things. One of the measures locates each campaign-worker in an appropriate organizational stratum because of the concurrence of several other people as to how prominent he is. It is also necessary to have a gauge of the extent to which he has taken advantage of his decision-making opportunities; this is provided by the measure of each worker's "weight in campaign decisions."

An active worker's score on the composite index of "party power position" is the sum of his rating on each of the two component measures. The limited size of our sample necessitates treating power positions as a dichotomous variable. In Table 2, the composition in each party of the "powerful" portion of the campaign structure is shown. Four out of every five most prominent workers were rated as powerful, while only one out of every five

Table 2

Composition of the Index of Party Power Positions*

| | REPUBLICANS | | DEMOCRATS | | TOTAL | |
	Per cent	No.	Per cent	No.	Per cent	No.
Organizational Strata:						
Most prominent	82	(38)	87	(47)	85	(85)
Intermediate	39	(59)	51	(70)	46	(129)
Least prominent	15	(34)	24	(51)	20	(85)
Weight in Campaign Decisions:						
Much to say	100	(34)	100	(53)	100	(87)
Some to say	45	(56)	49	(73)	47	(129)
Little to say	0	(41)	0	(42)	0	(83)

*Per cent classified as "powerful" in their party.

of the least prominent were classed that way; all of those rated as having "much to say" and none of those classed as having "little to say" were so classified. On each count, roughly half of the middle category were classed in the powerful bracket.

These variables of "party affiliation" and "campaign power position" are basic to an analysis of campaign organizational strength. When the behavior, attitudes, or status characteristics of campaign-workers are studied, the distinction between Democrat and Republican permits analysis of how well matched in terms of manpower reserves rival parties are for an impending electoral struggle. On the other hand, if analysis proceeds by contrasting the characteristics of the "powerful" and "non-powerful" echelons of a campaign organization (without regard to the party in question), one can gauge how well staffed that organization is to perform its specialized campaign tasks. When analysis proceeds by combining these two variables, one can examine what kind of campaign organizations tend to *face* one another in electoral contests. This more intricate analysis of the way in which talent, energy, experience, and skill are distributed in one campaign apparatus, when contrasted with its immediate rival, would seem necessary for a more meaningful examination of our election contest.

Perhaps the most important fact about a political campaign organization is the formidability of the rival organization confronting it. An analysis that ignores this element of competition, and that seeks to treat party organizations as though they were much like churches, lodges, or clubs, so far as participation and power are concerned, is likely to miss a vital determinant of the organizational dynamics of modern electoral politics. How formidable is the rival? It seems necessary to keep this question in mind throughout our analysis.

The Organizational Strength of Rival Parties

An organization's effectiveness in large measure is the result of the resources it can draw upon for financial support, access to major communications media, and backing from powerful persons and groups in the community. Another major factor in the stability of a party and the continued viability of a two-party system, nonetheless, is the composition of the organization itself and the elements that determine its internal strength. Does it command the continued support of an experienced group of workers who are available to carry on the major campaign tasks year after year? Or is the campaign apparatus a temporary structure, good for one campaign only, so that in each successive campaign the recruitment and organization of workers must begin anew? Is the organization's work carried on largely by a well-co-ordinated team, whose members uniformly devote nearly full time to the campaign, or must it depend for its achievements on a loosely knit group which makes only a limited contribution of time or effort? Are the major kinds of work to be done specialized, with different workers doing rather distinctive jobs, or are the tasks spread broadly among the whole group of workers?

These elements of experience, of time devoted to party work, and of the particular pattern of campaign tasks are basic in determining an organization's strength and stability. How these factors are distributed between the powerful and the non-powerful within an organization will largely determine the organization's style of operations.

Examining these factors for the party organizations that faced each other

Table 3
Participation in Past Presidential Campaigns, 1948 and 1952

| | PARTICIPATION LEVEL, 1948 AND 1952 ELECTIONS | | | |
	Active in both	Active in one	Not active	(No. of cases)
Party Affiliation				
Democrat	24%	27%	49%	150
Republican	16	42	42	124
Power Position				
Powerful	28	35	37	137
Non-powerful	14	32	54	137
Rival Party Power Structure				
Democrat				
Powerful	35	27	38	82
Non-powerful	13	23	64	68
Republican				
Powerful	18	47	35	55
Non-powerful	14	39	47	69

in Los Angeles communities in the 1956 presidential campaign, we see that, although the tasks to be done were fundamentally alike, there were significant differences in experience and effort. The Republican and Democratic parties thus had quite different organizational characters.

Although at least half of the workers in each party had previous experience either in the presidential campaign of 1948 or 1952, there were marked differences in the distribution of this experience within the party structures (see Table 3). Almost two-thirds of the non-powerful Democrats were neophytes in presidential campaign work; fewer than half the Republican non-powerful workers were entirely lacking in such experience (64 per cent and 47 per cent, respectively). In either party those who held the more powerful positions had more experience than the non-powerful. Only about one in every three powerful campaign-workers—Democrats and Republicans alike— were entirely without previous presidential campaign experience (38 per cent and 35 per cent respectively). But the proportion of powerful Democrats who had participated in both of the campaigns of 1948 and 1952 was twice that of the powerful Republicans (35 per cent and 18 per cent, respectively). Thus, in the Republican ranks previous experience was fairly well distributed between powerful and non-powerful levels. In the Democratic Party, however, a powerful group with considerable experience was running a campaign in which nearly two-thirds of the non-powerful could claim no previous presidential campaign experience.

Not only were the Republican rank and file more experienced than the Democrats, but they also put more time and effort into it. Table 4 shows the amount of time workers gave. The Republicans got more from their workers; fully 61 per cent of the Republicans worked at least half-time, while 48 per cent of the Democrats did so. When party differences are

Table 4

Participation in the General Election Campaign, 1956

| | PARTICIPATION LEVEL, 1956 | | | |
	Full time	Half time	Part time	(No. of cases)
Party Affiliation				
Democrat	16%	32%	52%	168
Republican	25	38	37	131
Power Position				
Powerful	30	41	29	148
Non-powerful	8	28	64	151
Rival Party Power Structure				
Democrat				
Powerful	25	41	34	89
Non-powerful	6	22	72	79
Republican				
Powerful	39	41	20	59
Non-powerful	10	36	54	72

compared at the powerful and non-powerful levels, however, these disparities are seen to be much greater. Among the Democratic powerfuls, only two in every three worked half-time or more during the fall campaign, while four in every five Republican powerfuls did so. Among the non-powerful, three out of every four Democrats gave less than half-time, while only about half of the Republican non-powerfuls contributed so nominally.

The differences in the distribution of experience and effort between the two party structures suggest that they are quite different organizations. It was to be expected that most of the powerful would have had some active campaign experience. Organizational continuity is also sustained, however, by the experience and effort of non-powerful workers. In the Democratic Party, active participation in campaign after campaign came largely from a solid core of top-level workers. Their energies were given to the recruitment, training and co-ordination of successive groups of non-powerful, who dropped out when power positions were not attained. The Republican organization on the other hand was able to command the perennial service of substantial numbers who did not demand a prominent or weighty position in decision-making. It was able to maintain a balance between "chiefs" and "Indians." Thus, it was the kind of campaign group that could begin to develop the efficiency and momentum of the classic "political machine."

Differences between the rival organizations are found not only in the loci of experience and effort. There are also differences between the Republicans and Democrats in the way that particular campaign tasks were distributed between the powerful and non-powerful workers. These patterns are shown in Table 5.

Table 5

Kinds of Work Done in the General Election Campaign of 1956

	Speeches	Strategy	Co-ordination	Fund-raising	Canvassing	No. of Cases
		KINDS OF WORK DONE, 1956				
Party Affiliation						
Democrat	32%	51%	52%	64%	57%	168
Republican	24	44	58	44	52	131
Power Position						
Powerful	39	66	66	63	56	148
Non-Powerful	18	30	43	48	54	151
Rival Party Power Structure						
Democrats						
Powerful	41	67	68	68	63	89
Non-powerful	20	32	33	60	51	79
Republicans						
Powerful	34	66	63	55	45	59
Non-powerful	16	27	54	36	57	72

The Democrats were somewhat more likely to make speeches and feel that they helped to make campaign strategy. In both parties, however, twice as many speech-makers and strategy-planners were found among the powerful.

Another striking difference was in the distribution of the task of co-ordinating campaign activities. Although two out of every three among the powerful in each party did co-ordinating work, the Republican non-powerful did considerably more than the Democratic non-powerful (54 per cent and 33 per cent respectively).

Conversely, fund-raising among Democrats tended to be done almost as often by the non-powerful as by the powerful workers (60 per cent and 68 per cent, respectively); while among Republicans this task was carried on primarily by the powerful (55 per cent, compared with 36 per cent among the non-powerful).

Finally, doorstep-canvassing appears to have been disproportionately shouldered by the powerful in the Democratic Party and by the non-powerful in the Republican organizations. However, somewhat more than half of the volunteer workers of each party did some canvassing work.

In the over-all picture, neither party could be said to have a marked advantage over its rival in the combined resources of experience, time worked, or persons available to carry out basic campaign tasks. Yet, the two parties differed markedly in the way these resources were distributed between the powerful and non-powerful levels of the organization. This, in turn, created different styles of operation and different bases for stability and continuity. When inquiry turns to the social origins of those who are differently located in the rival party power structures, the contrasts between the Republican and Democratic campaign organizations begin to reflect the tensions within the local social structures.

The Social Origins of Rival Parties

The analysis of social origins brings out clearly the differential manner in which the two parties drew upon the social structures of the localities in which they operated. The Republican Party in the Los Angeles communities studied was the party of dominant-status people; that is, the majority religious groups, the middle-aged parents, and the upper-level social-economic groupings. Conversely, the Democratic organizations were sustained disproportionately by people with somewhat less status in the community. Table 6 demonstrates the manner in which the two parties rested upon different social bases.

First, the Republican camp was overwhelmingly drawn from the dominant Protestant element in these communities, while the Democratic organizations had disproportionate numbers of people with minority religious and ethnic status. Within the Democratic Party, there was no apparent tendency for minority-status workers to have any worse or any better chance of becoming "powerful" than their Protestant fellow-Democrats. This was not the case among the Republicans. There, not only were relatively few Catholics and Jews to be found, but those who were active in virtually all cases confined their efforts to the "non-powerful level" of campaign activity.

Second, the Republicans relied more upon married couples whose children were already in their teens. By contrast, the Democrats drew more heavily upon young married couples whose children were still at an age requiring baby-sitters. The Democratic organization had to accommodate itself to a greater family drain on the time and energy of these parents. Perhaps, therefore, the earlier findings (in Table 4) showing that at each power level there were fewer Democratic workers able to give as much as half-time during the fall campaign weeks of 1956, reflect the life-cycle composition of the Democratic cadre.

Thirdly, in terms of socio-economic status, the Republicans and Democrats rather clearly came from different sectors of the community.[10] Half of the Republican workers had high SES scores, the non-powerful only slightly less so than the powerful. By contrast, only a third of the Democrats had high SES scores; again, the powerful and non-powerful were much alike.

At each organizational level the Republican workers tended to have higher incomes and to possess fuller educational backgrounds (Table 6). In other findings not presented here, the Democrats appeared as less well-rooted in their communities. The Republicans had lived for longer periods in the

Table 6
Social Profile of Rival Parties

	Party Affiliation		Power Position		Rival Party Power Structure			
					DEMOCRATS		REPUBLICANS	
			POWER-FUL	NON P'RFUL	Power-ful	Non-p'rful	Power-ful	Non-p'rful
	D	R						
Religious Affiliation:								
Church-going Protestants	15%	45%	30%	27%	16%	13%	49%	42%
Nominal Protestants	41	43	41	43	38	45	46	40
Catholics	13	8	9	12	14	13	2	13
Jews	22	2	14	12	23	20	0	4
None	9	2	6	6	9	9	3	1
	100	100	100	100	100	100	100	100
CASES:	160	131	145	146	86	74	59	72
Life-Cycle Stage:								
Young, no dependents	12	12	15	10	14	11	15	10
Married, youngsters	43	25	33	37	39	47	24	26
Married, teenagers	32	48	42	36	35	28	53	44
Older, no dependents	13	15	10	17	12	14	8	20
	100	100	100	100	100	100	100	100
CASES:	160	131	145	146	86	74	59	72
Socio-Economic Status:								
Highest level	32	51	43	38	34	29	56	46
Middle level	19	15	19	15	22	15	14	15
Lowest level	49	34	38	47	44	56	30	39
	100	100	100	100	100	100	100	100
CASES:	149	122	136	135	81	68	55	67
Income:								
Over $9000	39	56	51	42	44	34	61	51
Under $9000	61	44	49	58	56	66	39	49
	100	100	100	100	100	100	100	100
CASES:	168	131	148	151	89	79	59	79
Education:								
College graduate	33	40	41	32	36	30	48	35
Some college	33	33	34	32	40	24	25	39
No college	34	27	25	36	24	46	27	26
	100	100	100	100	100	100	100	100
CASES:	159	131	144	146	85	74	59	72

locality, and had done less shifting of residences than the Democrats. The Republicans also were more active in non-political community organizations.

The findings in Table 6 indicate the asymmetrical manner in which the rival party power structures drew upon the social and economic resources of their communities. Further findings presented below indicate not only the differential *appeal* of the rival party banners, but also the contrasting *style* of operations by which human resources were used for campaign purposes in the Republican and Democratic parties (Tables 7 and 8).

Table 7
Family Socio-Economic Status in R's Youth

| Party Affiliation | FAMILY SES | | |
	High	Low	(No. of cases)
Democrats	58%	42%	134
Republicans	75	25	111
Power Position			
Powerful	68	32	130
Non-powerful	64	36	117
Rival Party Power Position			
Democrat			
Powerful	66	34	70
Non-powerful	50	50	64
Republican			
Powerful	69	31	47
Non-powerful	78	22	64

Two general findings of some importance emerge from this analysis of the social origins of campaign workers in the rival parties in Los Angeles areas. First, parties draw from different, though somewhat overlapping, strata of the communities in which they operate. The Republican workers were more advantageously situated on one count after another. When compared with the Democrats, they were more likely to come from the majority religious groups, to be further along in their life cycle, to be drawn from the upper socio-economic status levels, to come from family backgrounds that were higher in the social scale, to be in prestige occupations, and to have had longer residences, higher incomes, fuller educations, and deeper roots in their communities.

Despite these differences, both parties were basically middle class in character. Neither really presented a representative cross section of the class structures of their communities.

Probably, campaign organizations that depend primarily upon volunteers for their personnel tend to draw more heavily from the middle class than do campaign organizations that operate primarily upon a spoils basis, such as the older Eastern political machines. Early studies[11] of Chicago, down-state Illinois, and up-state New York organizations indicated that party-workers were uniformly drawn much more heavily from lower sections in

Table 8

Sex and Occupational Resources of Rival Parties

| | Party Affiliation | | Power Position | | Rival Party Power Positions | | | |
| | | | | | DEMOCRATS | | REPUBLICANS | |
	D	R	POWER-FUL	NON-P'RFUL	Power-ful	Non-p'rful	Power-ful	Non-p'rful
Sex:								
Men	59%	44%	58%	47%	61%	57%	54%	36%
Women	41	56	42	53	39	43	46	64
	100	100	100	100	100	100	100	100
CASES:	168	131	148	151	89	79	59	72
Occupation of Women:								
Housewife	38%	64%	42%	59%	23%	53%	67%	63%
Working	62	36	58	41	77	47	33	37
	100	100	100	100	100	100	100	100
CASES:	69	73	62	80	35	34	27	46
Occupation of Men:								
Business	33%	57%	46%	28%	43%	22%	53%	62%
Professional	28	24	26	37	24	33	28	19
Other	39	19	28	35	33	45	19	19
	100	100	100	100	100	100	100	100
CASES:	99	58	86	71	54	45	32	26

the social structure. Recent West Coast studies in Seattle, the San Francisco area, or Los Angeles reverse this.[12] In Detroit, however, the current contrast between the class compositions of the rival parties is dramatic and great.[13]

That the two party organizations should draw from somewhat different sections of the social structure for their campaign-workers is not surprising, of course, in light of previous work on the relationship of political interest and activity to one's social circumstances. It would presumably not occur, however, if politics were only a game with little or no relationship to the continuing social struggle among various segments of a modern community.

The second major finding is that parties also differ in the ways in which their campaign power structures are related to the social-status factors. Nearly all the Republicans who were Catholics or Jews were found at non-powerful levels of the campaign organization; no such differential was found among the Democrats. While 79 per cent of the Democratic workers who had the highest SES ratings were lifted to the ranks of the powerful in their party, only 51 per cent of the highest-rated SES figures in the Republican party participated as powerful campaign-workers. Among the Democrats, people with ascendant family backgrounds were found much more frequently at the powerful than at the non-powerful level; whereas the Republican organization relegated a much larger share of such people of high family-background status to the non-powerful group. Although women constituted a smaller percentage of the campaign-workers among the Democrats than among the Republicans (41 per cent and 56 per cent), the Democratic women had nearly as good a chance as the men to belong to the powerful group in the campaign organization; while in the Republican Party, women were much less likely than men to belong to the powerful group. Even the status of businessmen in the parties was different, for although the Republicans had more businessmen, businessmen were more frequently at the non-powerful levels; among the Democrats, they were almost twice as likely to be found among the "powerful."

What implications do these findings have for the dynamics of local party organization and political participation? There are two major possibilities, depending on whether the findings are judged in terms of the needs of the party organization, or whether they are evaluated as reflections of the character and needs of the volunteer campaign-workers themselves. Each line of inquiry merits attention.

Both parties may engage in similar sorts of campaign tasks, such as organizing meetings, preparing and distributing literature, carrying on precinct work, giving speeches, raising money, co-ordinating the activities of various party groups, and makng contacts within the community. Yet, the differences in the social standing of the groups attracted to the two parties probably produce differences in the problems a party must solve if it is to be successful in a campaign. Since the Republican Party is the party of higher-status people, it presumably has no special problems of gaining respectability within the community. It can thus direct the allocation of its personnel resources according to functional criteria of skill and experience. It is relatively free to ignore questions of social standing in the use of its own personnel. The Democratic Party, however, is in a somewhat different position. As the party with more subordinate-status people, it faces the electioneering problem of gaining respectability. It must husband more carefully the resources of prestige and social standing that are at its disposal. Social status thus becomes one of the criteria it must use in allocating personnel between the powerful and non-powerful echelons of its organizational structure. Viewed in this way, it appears that however similar the activities of rival campaign organizations in a particular community, the problems they have to meet in gaining community acceptance will be different; and the choice of personnel for playing various roles in the party will rest on different criteria, with the party manned by people of subordinate status being especially conscious of the need to use its high-status members in ways that will help it to gain acceptance within the community.

If we view the differential relationship between party power position and social status as a phenomenon related to the interests of the campaign-workers, rather than to the needs of the organization, a different set of dynamics is suggested. In examining previous campaign experience, it was found that the Republican Party had a substantial group of experienced workers in their non-powerful ranks, whereas the experienced Democratic workers were more heavily concentrated at the powerful level. These differences may be viewed as related to an individual's concern with affirming or improving his own sense of social status. Active work in the Republican

Party may tend to affirm one's high status. Indeed, the larger percentage of Republican housewives suggest the phenomenon to which Veblen called attention, the concern among a locality's dominant status groups with "conspicuous leisure." Among higher-status people, it may be inappropriate for the wife to earn a wage, but she may appropriately further her husband's career by using her leisure time in social and community activities that redound to the family credit. Republican housewives as higher-status people may thus continue to work at the non-powerful levels of the party organization in campaign after campaign, because their reputation for working even at this level serves to affirm their status in the dominant and leisured section of the community.

For the Democrats, however, the picture is different. Work in the Democratic Party does not usually enhance or affirm one's high status in the community at large. If one is to obtain status rewards by work in the Democratic Party, they must come in part from one's reputation *within* the party organization itself. People already having some prestige in the community, in this view, might fear damage to their social position because of Democratic Party work unless they could become known as powerful figures in it. On the other hand those without high status in the community who work in the party may continue only if their status strivings are satisfied within the apparatus itself.

According to this interpretation, among the Democrats, status must be gained in, or through, party activity. Becoming powerful is a preoccupying concern. Among the Republicans, one's status is affirmed merely by working in the party. A powerful position within the party is therefore not usually a pressing concern.

The evidence obtained in the Los Angeles study supports both of the views presented here, although of course, our limited evidence does not establish their generality. The differential relationship of the rival party power structures to the social structure of the community appears to reflect the different needs of the parties. Those same links between power position and social attributes suggest the different role which the parties play in satisfying the status needs of their volunteer workers.

To argue that status strivings may often lead Democrats to volunteer only when they can gain status through their position in the party, while Republicans will volunteer more commonly because of the status affirmed through mere identification with the party, does not imply that status striving is the sole explanation of active campaign participation. The evidence presented here suggests that it certainly may be an important latent factor in predisposing a number of workers to make the commitments of time and energy that the campaign entails.

Political Socialization and Active Campaign Participation

What other factors operated to draw particular individuals into the web of party campaign work? Party-workers were asked a battery of direct questions about the satisfactions received from political activity. Table 9 shows the relative importance that Los Angeles volunteer workers attached to ten commonly mentioned reasons for active campaign participation. The rank order of emphases given to different explanations is virtually the same for Democrats and Republicans.

Considered as "justifications" for involvement in active campaign work, those reasons dealing with the substance of politics are generally acceptable; those reasons indicating private gain as a motive are not. The use of reasons having a social and relatively non-political content to explain participation is acceptable to sizeable minorities in each party's ranks. Concern with public issues, strong party loyalty, and feelings of community obligation were the explanations widely said to be "very important" by Democrats and Re-

Table 9

Importance of Different Motivational Aims in Explaining Active Campaign Participation

	Democrats	Republicans	Composite
Concern with public issues	83%	71%	74%
Strong party loyalty	61	78	69
Sense of community obligation	56	61	59
Politics part of a way of life	48	37	43
Fun and excitement of campaign	30	38	33
Making social contacts and friends	30	34	32
Personal friend of candidate	21	19	20
Furthering political ambitions	10	13	11
Being close to influential people	6	9	7
Making business contacts	4	7	5
Cases:	132	105	237

Per cent saying each factor was "very important" to him.

publicans alike; making business contacts, being close to influential people, and furthering personal political ambition were the explanations least acceptable. Sizeable groups included being a friend of the candidate, making social contacts and friendships, enjoying the fun and excitement of campaigns, and feeling that politics was a part of their way of life.

What is the nature of the personal backgrounds that predisposed some people to use active campaign work as a channel for satisfying these various goals? One important facet of this inquiry focuses on the role of the family and particularly the importance of a parental model of political activity, in forming the desire and intent of campaign-workers to participate as purposefully as they did.

Empirical studies of political socialization give the family a central role in developing both political orientation and political participation.[14] Families in which both parents agree politically have more impact on the children than those where parental examples are at odds with one another. However, family influence is not uniform; it is stronger in determining party preferences than in shaping political ideology.

This evidence suggested the importance of examining the extent to which not only parental interest but parental activity in politics shaped the interest and activity of the Los Angeles sample of active campaign-workers. Table 10 shows the results of this inquiry into the importance of parental example.

Table 10

Political Activity and Interest of Parents

	Parent (s) Active	Parent (s) Interested	Neither	(No. of cases)
Party Affiliation				
Democrat	36%	41%	23%	142
Republican	39	39	22	122
Power Position				
Powerful	47	31	22	129
Non-powerful	28	49	23	135
Rival Party Power Structure				
Democrats				
Powerful	45	30	25	76
Non-powerful	26	54	20	66
Republicans				
Powerful	51	32	17	53
Non-powerful	30	44	26	69

Nearly two out of every five campaign-workers in each party came from families in which at least one parent was *active* in politics. Only about one in five, on the other hand, came from families where the parents were neither interested nor active in political affairs. National estimates indicate that approximately one in ten in the adult American population may be said to be "active" during a general election campaign.[15] It appears that family backgrounds of active campaign-workers in Los Angeles were considerably more "politicized" than is the case for a random selection of American families. Moreover, in both parties, campaign-workers with politically active parents were much more likely to be in the ranks of the powerful than were workers whose parents were not active. The inference, of course, is that for volunteer politics the politicized family may be a crucial training ground for future campaign-workers.

The conception of the "politicized family" needs to be more fully developed. It is not simply a family wherein parents manifest a casual interest in politics, confined to viewing political events on television or talking about late campaign developments. Rather, it is a family in which political matters receive both substantial and sustained attention, and in which skills in the analysis of public issues are supplemented by examples of adult political participation as well. In this way, the possibility is opened of developing a sense of civic responsibility that will cause each generation to "act out" its family heritage on the political stage, and, in turn, inculcate the same activist example and sense of duty in the succeeding generation.

Heretofore, the notion of a politicized family, a family in which the tradition of leadership and civic responsibility was nurtured and sustained, generation after generation, has largely been applied to families who have supplied, in an unusual degree, the leadership of a nation or a state.[16] Families such as the Adams, Roosevelts, La Follettes, Lodges, and others have distinctive records of supplying political leadership in our national political life over many generations. Evidence from the Los Angeles study suggests that this same process operates also at less widely publicized levels in American political life. Of course, the relatively modest investment of time and energy made by those who were active during the campaign weeks of 1956 may not have been as onerous a charge on the children of politically active parents as the often difficult task of following in the footsteps of a famous political father. But it was a considerably more substantial contribution than was made by millions of American adults. Analysis suggests that the politicized family and politically active parents are peculiarly important in accounting for the nucleus that sustains a voluntary party apparatus in campaign after campaign; thus, they are important in maintaining the continuity of talent and skill, experience and conviction, essential at this level of a democratic political order.

Ideological Conflict and Party Rivalry

People do not become active in campaign work merely because they seek to gain or affirm social status, or because their parents wanted them to. Their interest in the substance of politics is reflected in their concern with the issues of the day. It is one of the distinctive features of American politics that we have maintained a two-party system despite the many changes in our social and economic order and the political issues thrown up by it. Nonetheless, the role of ideology in maintaining the identity of parties and sparking competition between them, which in turn makes election-day choices meaningful, is still understood imperfectly.

For a long time, American political parties have been characterized as basically non-ideological in character. The cartoons of Tweedle-dum or Tweedle-dee, or the pictures of two wine bottles with the same liquid bearing different labels, have received considerable currency. Support for this view has also come from work done by serious scholars examining the American party system. Enduring special interests, rather than political convictions about complex issues; emotional attachments to symbols of regional or ethnic origin, rather than concern with principles or philosophies—these have been the primary party characteristics seen by academic students of American politics. Edmund Burke's definition of party is often quoted to show what the American party system is not. Maurice Duverger, in his comparative study of *Political Parties,* discusses the non-principled character of American parties. "The two parties are rival teams, one occupying office and the other seeking to dislodge it. It is a struggle between the ins and the outs, which never becomes fanatical, and creates no deep cleavage in the country."[17] The result, he argues, is to take from the election any validity as a choice between policies.

Duverger reflects a view that is common to many political scientists and observers of the American party system. This view, however, bears little relationship to the findings in the Los Angeles study. When active workers were asked why they belonged to their parties and what differences they saw between parties, they consistently answered in rudimentary ideological terms. Just as empirical political-behavior research has demolished the view that the support in the electorate at large comes with equal emphasis for the Republican and Democratic parties from the working class and the middle class, so also it now casts serious doubt on the view that those active in politics are mere self-seeking individuals who are in no meaningful degree the exponents of alternative sets of principles in Burke's sense. Campaign-workers—whether Democrats or Republicans—had a strong feeling that there *were* meaningful differences of principle between political parties, and that these principles were important in explaining their own personal adherence to their particular party.

Ideological determinants of activity in politics were studied in two ways: first, in terms of some measure of the *content* of the ideologies held by active party-workers; second, by reference to the sense of ideological *harmony* felt with their daily associates, on the one hand, and with their fellow campaign-workers, on the other.

Respondents were presented with a pair of statements regarding the proper role the American government should play—interventionist or not—first, in foreign affairs and, second, in domestic matters. Each respondent was asked to indicate which statement he wholly or partly agreed with, and was scored accordingly on a four-point scale.

From the responses, an index was developed of rudimentary ideology, in terms of preferences concerning governmental intervention. Analysis of this data in Table 11 shows that two out of every three Democrats were interventionists both at home and abroad. Only one in every four Republican workers showed this wholehearted willingness to use government to solve both foreign and domestic problems. A very substantial group of Republicans, roughly two out of every five, were unwilling to see intervention by the national government abroad, or with few exceptions, at home.

Among Democrats, there was little connection between ideological viewpoints and power positions; among Republicans, however, the connection was substantial. Democrats at both powerful and non-powerful levels were heavily committed to intervention by government both at home and abroad. Only slightly less enthusiasm was manifested by non-powerful Democrats than by their powerful colleagues. Among the Republicans, however, the situation was more complex. Only among non-powerful Republicans was there a substantial group who felt that intervention both at home and abroad was an acceptable policy—31 per cent among Republican non-powerfuls, compared to 16 per cent among powerfuls.

Table 11

Rudimentary Ideology

| | Party Affiliation | | Power Position | | Rival Party Power Structures | | | |
| | | | | | DEMOCRATS | | REPUBLICANS | |
	D	R	POWER-FUL	NON P'RFUL	Power-ful	Non-p'rful	Power-ful	Non-p'rful
Intervene both abroad and home	67%	24%	49%	47%	72%	62%	16%	31%
Intervene abroad but not at home	15	33	22	23	12	18	37	30
Don't intervene either abroad or (with possible exceptions) at home	18	43	29	30	16	20	47	39
	100	100	100	100	100	100	100	100
CASES:	156	124	140	141	84	73	56	68

It is when Republican and Democratic powerful workers are contrasted that the ideological cleavage is most sharply drawn. This suggests that political power is likely to go to those who most effectively express the ideological positions current for their party.

In a political system where parties draw from different but overlapping sections of the social structure, these ideological factors may well play significant roles in separating persons of roughly the same social status into defenders of the dominant interests, on the one hand, and champions of subordinate status groups, on the other. There is some evidence that ideological convictions were important in activating people, especially when they felt a sense of ideological *disharmony* with their daily associates. Respondents were asked to think of particular individuals with whom they were close friends, with whom they worked, and who they saw frequently in their daily routines. They were asked also to think of particular individuals with whom they worked closely in their campaign activities. Each respondent was asked if he felt himself more liberal or conservative than the daily associate or fellow campaigner he was at that moment thinking about. Respondents were not asked to define "liberal" or "conservative," but almost never did they manifest any sense of doubt as to what was meant or in any way hesitate to make such comparative judgments.

From these responses, measures were developed of the ideological harmony that a given campaign-worker felt with his daily associates, and again, with his fellow campaign-workers. Table 12 reports the results of this inquiry.

Fully 64 per cent of the Democrats and only 27 per cent of the Republicans considered themselves to be more liberal than their friends and associates. Conversely, only 13 per cent of the Democrats compared with 47 per cent of the Republicans considered themselves more conservative than

Table 12

Ideological Harmony

| | Party Affiliation | | Power Position | | Rival Party Power Structures | | | |
| | | | | | DEMOCRATS | | REPUBLICANS | |
	D	R	POWER-FUL	NON-P'RFUL	Power-ful	Non-p'rful	Power-ful	Non-p'rful
With Friends and Associates								
R more liberal	64%	27%	52%	43%	62%	66%	38%	18%
R about same	23	26	25	24	26	20	23	29
R more conservative	13	47	23	33	12	14	39	53
	100	100	100	100	100	100	100	100
With Fellow Campaign-Workers								
R more liberal	37%	23%	28%	33%	32%	42%	23%	22%
R about same	40	54	50	44	46	34	54	56
R more conservative	23	23	22	23	22	24	23	22
	100	100	100	100	100	100	100	100
CASES:	124	104	114	115	66	59	48	56

their friends and associates. The contrast in the ideological composition of the two parties in the Los Angeles area is thus clear.

Having found that Republican and Democratic workers are drawn from somewhat different strata of the community, this degree of ideological *disharmony* with daily associates is perhaps surprising. It suggests the complexity of the recruitment process. The earlier finding of ideological differences between parties concerned the proper extent of governmental intervention. It might have been explained by noting the different strata from which Republicans and Democrats were drawn. But it would have been consistent with that finding for workers to report a sense of harmony with their daily associates in a given segment of the community. Only one in four active campaign-workers reported such harmony.

This pattern suggests that a distinct factor leading people to become active workers is their desire to find a group with whom they are in ideological accord, thus relieving the tension they feel with their daily associates. Table 12 shows that in both parties the percentage of those reporting ideological harmony with fellow campaign-workers is nearly double the percentage reporting such harmony with daily associates. Harmony is greater in the Republican organization than in the Democratic one (54 per cent and 40 per cent, respectively), and is differently distributed within the parties. The Republican powerful and non-powerful attain about equal degrees of harmony within the party (54 per cent and 56 per cent, respectively), although the character of their disharmony with daily associates is markedly different. Only 18 per cent of the Republican non-powerful went so far as to say they felt themselves more liberal than their friends and associates, compared with 53 per cent who felt themselves more conservative. This contrasts rather markedly with the report from the Republican powerful, equal proportions of whom—38 per cent in each case—felt themselves to be more liberal and conservative respectively than their friends and associates. Those who become powerful in the Republican Party apparently possessed ideological views that led them to temper and moderate the opinions of their associates in the higher status level from which they largely came.

For the Democrats, the pattern is different, yet the factors related to positions of power are similar. The Democratic powerful and non-powerful were nearly equal in their feeling of being more liberal than their daily associates (62 per cent and 66 per cent respectively), and less than 15 per cent of either group felt more conservative. But nearly half the powerful Democrats attained a sense of ideological accord with their fellow campaign-workers, while only a third of the non-powerful Democrats did so. It would appear that volunteers with relatively moderate views were able to gain power in the Democratic party organization.

The importance of finding an ideologically compatible group, as a factor in leading people to take an active part in political campaigns, is highlighted when the picture of previous campaign experience is recalled (Table 4). Many more of the Republican non-powerful had had previous campaign experience than was true for the Democratic non-powerful. This suggests that the ideological compatibility may have kept many Republican workers on the job at non-powerful levels, whereas many of the Democratic non-powerful, being less successful in finding ideological harmony within the campaign group, did not return for a second round.

There is more ideological tension within Democratic campaign structures than there is within the Republican ones. This is partly because of the greater diversity of social economic groups that play a part in the Democratic Party, compared with those that nourish and sustain Republican activities. How the Democratic Party is able to survive in the light of this inner tension is indicated by the previous findings concerning the character of the Democratic campaign apparatus, notably that it tends to feature a small and experienced corps of powerful and intensely active partisans, surrounded by a much looser, more inexperienced, less reliable, and ideologically more diverse group of workers.

The Campaign-Worker in a Democratic Polity

What are the implications for contemporary democratic political theory to be drawn from this study of active campaign-workers in the Los Angeles area? Without attempting an extended statement of a working theory of democracy, it is desirable to note the nature of the contributions that this particular study seeks to make.

First, the findings support the approach that views the prerequisites of democracy not in terms of characteristics or qualities that should be shared by *all* its citizens, but in terms of the diversity of characteristics and roles together forming the democratic political order. The research began with the assumption that one type of political person—the active campaign-worker—was important and that the characteristics and roles of such a person needed to be identified. What is evident, however, is that there are several different types of campaign-workers, and that different characteristics lead to different positions in the power structure of campaign organizations. The development of a modern democratic theory must proceed by exploring the ways in which a great multiplicity of personalities, skills, attitudes, predispositions, and general characteristics are employed in the intricate web of relationships that constitutes the working political order.

Second, the findings about the campaign-workers in Los Angeles serve to reaffirm, in a new political and social context, the observations often made about the big-city machines of the past. Political organizations at the local level are closely related to the social structures of the communities in which they operate. Furthermore, these organizations may serve the latent functions of aiding people to attain a social identity or a social advancement, as well as serving the explicit political functions of carrying on campaigns. In the volunteer politics of Los Angeles, it is chiefly the middle class that provides the personnel for campaign work, in contrast to the support that the early eastern city machines drew from the lower classes. Yet, within this middle-class group, there are differences in status, which characterize those attracted to the rival parties. These differences in status are related both to the use that the parties make of their personnel and to the social functions that party work fulfills for its volunteers. Volunteer politics in an affluent society may not build strength by sending out food baskets on Thanksgiving day or helping the immigrant worker obtain his citizenship papers. However, to people with only modest claims to social status, it may provide a satisfying sense of position and power. The decline of the old type of machine should not lead us to assume that the social function of the campaign organization has disappeared. Rather, the details of its social functioning may have changed, in order to suit the status-conferring needs of the middle-class group from which it now draws its strength.

Third, this study has pointed up the role of the family as a major channel through which the attitudes and skills essential for the grass-roots management of our democratic political processes are transmitted. Understanding the extent to which the family serves as an agency for developing various political attitudes and skills may provide a key for solving the problem of stability and change in political life. Stability and continuity with the past may come through having a large proportion of active political workers drawn from families in which the parents played a similar role. Change, on the other hand, may come through the continual incorporation of active workers who do not have such ties to past standards of political behavior. There are a series of problems in democratic theory—such as the transformation of elites, the creation of democratic political structures in new states, and the transformation of authoritarian political structures into democratic ones—which may be illuminated by further explorations of the family as an instrument for transmitting the appropriate skills and attitudes. This study seeks to show that such explorations can fruitfully be made, not only at the levels of national leadership, but also at the grass-root level of the campaign organizations.

Finally, the findings suggest that active campaign-workers, and the organizations to which they are recruited, play important roles in both the crystallization and the mediation of ideological conflict in our communities. The crystallization of differences is important if our elections are to involve meaningful choices; yet it is also necessary to mediate these differences in order to maintain the essential unity, continuity, and stability. Voluntary campaign-workers apparently have ideological conceptions that sharply distinguish those of one party from those of the other. Positions of power within an organization are more likely to go to those who express the characteristic party position. Yet, within each party group, there is considerable diversity on ideological questions; although ideology is a factor in attracting workers to a party, it is clearly not the sole factor. When ideology is measured, not in terms of policy positions, but in terms of the accord or lack of accord with one's fellows, it further appears that leadership tends to go to those who can effect a balance of different tendencies, rather than to those who are more extreme.

It is the virtue of a democratic political system that it is able to achieve a voluntary unity in the face of great diversities. To understand how this is done will require extended study of those who play crucial roles in bringing about such a synthesis.

Notes

1. See the valuable chapter on the intellectual history of the concept of political party in Austin Ranney and Willmoore Kendall, *Democracy and the American Party System* (New York: Harcourt Brace and o., 1956), chap. vi.

2. See the chapter on "Democratic Theory and Democratic Practice," in Bernard Berelson *et al., Voting* (Chicago: University of Chicago Press, 1954), where older presumptions of citizen homogeneity are brought into juxtaposition with the evidence of heterogeneity.

3. For a valuable codification of the external circumstances necessary for maintaining democratic institutions, see Seymour Lipset, "Some Social Requisites of Democracy: Economic Developments and Political Legitimacy," *American Political Science Review,* March, 1959, pp. 69-105. For an attempt to specify some of the internally operative dimensions that determine whether an election is based upon "consent" or "manipulation," see Morris Janowitz and Dwaine Marvick, *Competitive Pressure and Democratic Consent* (Bureau of Government, Michigan Governmental Studies No. 32;

University of Michigan, 1956).

4. Two recent examples of the growing attention to the conceptual task are Anthony Downs, *An Economic Theory of Democracy* (New York: Harper and Bros., 1957), and Robert Dahl, *A Preface to Democratic Theory* (Chicago: University of Chicago Press, 1956).

5. In his *Capitalism, Socialism and Democracy* (3d. ed.; New York: Harper and Bros., 1950), Joseph A. Schumpeter attacked the premises and presumptions in so-called "classical" theories of democracy for just these reasons. In a subsequent chapter, he suggested the importance of a conceptual model of democracy that would permit relevant empirical dimensions, such as leadership, organizational activity, apathy and inconsistency among the citizenry, and conscious efforts to manipulate by political campaign propagandists all to be "brought in on the ground floor," as integral parts of the conceptual scheme.

6. One useful example has been the degree to which cumulative research on the characteristics and performance of "opinion leaders," as evidenced in the

works of Paul Lazarsfeld and his associates, give empirical warrant for confidence in the processes of popular judgment, similar to that asserted by A. D. Lindsay, in *The Modern Democratic State* (London: Oxford University Press, 1943), pp. 276-79, in which the essential defense of democracy is made in terms of the ability of the common man to find among his own associates someone whose guidance is a little more balanced and a little more sensible than his own.

7. Dahl, *op. cit.* This would seem to be the inference from Dahl's discussion of the problem of intensity, although he does not explicitly discuss campaign-workers. Similarly, it represents the emphasis in the Michigan studies. See A. Campbell, G. Gurin, and W. Miller, *The Voter Decides* (Evanton, Ill.: Row, Peterson and Co., 1954).

8. Max Weber, "Politics as a Vocation," in A. Gerth and C. W. Mills (ed.), *From Max Weber, Essays in Sociology* (New York: Oxford University Press, 1946), pp. 77-128.

9. An earlier wave of interviews took place during the June primaries, 1956; a subsequent wave of interviews took place during the spring nonpartisan city elections of 1957; and a follow-up mail questionnaire was administered in October, 1958. Findings from these data are not discussed in this report.

10. The index of socio-economic status here used gives equal weight to home ownership, car ownership, occupational prestige (whether manual or nonmanual, whether business, professional or other), and income levels; for convenience it is presented in the tabulation only in a trichotomy distinguishing high, medium, and low SES levels.

11. Harold F. Gosnell, *Machine Politics: Chicago Model* (Chicago: University of Chicago Press, 1937); Sonya Forthal, *Cogwheels of Democracy: A Study of the Precinct Captain* (1946); Leon Weaver, "Some Soundings in the Party System: Rural Precinct Committeemen," *American Political Science Review*, February, 1940, pp. 76-84; William E. Mosher, "Party and Government

Control at the Grass Roots," *National Municipal Review,* January, 1935.

12. See Hugh Bone, *Grass Roots Party Leadership,* (Seattle: University of Washington Press, 1952), and Glenn West, Jr. "The Precinct Workers of Santa Clara County" (Dittoed, 1955).

13. See the forthcoming study of Detroit by Samuel Eldersveld and Daniel Katz. An advance report in the *New York Times,* July 26, 1959, p. 70, stated: "Fifty-four per cent among Democratic party workers were laborers and machine operators and only three per cent had managerial or professional jobs. Among Republican party workers, sixty per cent had professional or managerial backgrounds and only twelve per cent had routine jobs."

14. Herbert Hyman, *Political Socialization* (Glencoe, Ill.: The Free Press, 1959).

15. Julian L. Woodward and Elmo Roper, "Political Activity of American Citizens," *American Political Science Review,* December, 1950, pp. 872-85.

16. W. J. Guttsman, "The Changing Social Structure of the British Political Elite," *British Journal of Sociology,* June, 1951, and "Aristocracy and the Middle Class in the British Political Elite, 1886-1916," *British Journal of Sociology,* March, 1954.

17. Maurice Duverger, *Political Parties* (New York: John Wiley and Sons, 1954), p. 418.

18. Regarding foreign affairs, the statements were: "America must assert leadership in finding solutions in the major world trouble spots." Alternatively, "America should leave the solution of the major international disputes to the nations most directly concerned."

With respect to domestic affairs, the statements were: "The national government should leave the solution of major problems in our economic and social life largely to the people most directly affected." Alternatively, "The national government should assert leadership in working out solutions to the major problems affecting various segments of our population."

Career Perspectives
of American State Legislators

by HEINZ EULAU,

WILLIAM BUCHANAN,

LeROY C. FERGUSON,

and JOHN C. WAHLKE

A POLITICAL career, like other careers, is a more or less typical sequence of events, a pattern in the life histories of men moving into positions made available by the framework of institutions. Political careers, therefore, can tell us a great deal about governmental institutions, which in turn are formalized and regularized patterns of action that shape and are shaped by political behavior. But political mobility is not simply determined by the politician's skill in occupying available offices. It may be facilitated or impeded by his position in the social structure at the time he enters politics. It may be furthered or limited by the ways in which the political system is structured.

The ways in which social structure and the politician's social attributes promote or obstruct the recruitment and mobility of political elites have been studied extensively.[2] The literature, if not saturated, is at least adequately served by a variety of studies that seek to discover the class origin, occupational status, educational level, religious or ethnic character, and other socially relevant attributes of public office-holders.[3] Even though many of these studies may largely be exercises in fact-gathering, they suggest and sometimes answer important questions about the social bases of politics.[4]

This type of research has shown that social origin may be linked to significant avenues of political mobility, enabling those favorably situated to advance and impeding or preventing a political career for those less favored. Moreover, by using appropriate data as indices of the distribution of power in a given political system, some of these studies have related transformations of elites to changing patterns of politics in diverse systems and to changes of whole systems themselves.[5]

In view of the continued research on political recruitment and its effect on political ascent, it is surprising that research on the effect of political structure on the development of political careers has been neglected.[6] There are available, of course, many excellent case histories of the careers of politicians, usually in the form of biographies or autobiographies of outstanding men.[7] They afford much insight into particular political careers but they are essentially nontypical and do not permit generalization. To our knowledge, there exist no systematic studies that trace the effect of different political structures on the career patterns of politicians, especially elective office-holders, from the point of entry into politics to the point of departure; or that are concerned with the career perspectives of politicians at a particular point in their life history.[8] As a result, questionable accounts of political-career patterns may find their way into the textbooks: for example, it is often said that political mobility follows a regular series of steps from local to state to national levels.[9]

The notion of a career *line* in politics, of a more or less typical sequence of successive office-holding within a determinate institutional setting, does not imply that political careers follow a regular series of steps from lower to higher positions. It is theoretically difficult and empirically impossible to specify such a series; there are no agreed-upon criteria by which to determine "higher" or "lower" office, particularly in a political system like the American, with its horizontal, federal structure cutting across vertical hierarchies. Nor is the assumption of a career line meant to imply that the politician invariably seeks "higher" office. Contemporary career perspectives may be symptomatic of aspirations, but no motivational hypotheses need be advanced, especially for democratic societies where a large sector of the community participates in determining who shall fill governmental positions.[10]

Tentatively suspending any assumption about regular ascent and the task of motivational analysis, does not mean that careers cannot be examined as realities in their causes and consequences.[11] Everett C. Hughes has said: "A career is the moving perspective in which a person sees his life as a whole and interprets the meaning of his various attributes, actions, and the things which happen to him."[12] Indeed, as a career is a sequence linking past with present and future,[13] a complete portrayal of political careers will have to include recollections of the past, present orientations, and expectations concerning the future.

A distinction may be made, then, between the recruitment patterns of political elites and their career patterns and perspectives. Recruitment patterns constitute conditions of political mobility, but they do not necessarily determine the development of political careers. Regardless of recruitment patterns, political careers are probably less dependent on recruitment than they are on the structure of the political system. Recruitment and career patterns may, of course, overlap, as in patrician societies, where the identity of social and political structures makes for stable expectations of public service, and where preparation for a political career is part and parcel of the training of those who, by birth and status, are destined to become political leaders.[14] On the other hand, recruitment and career patterns may diverge quite widely, as in bureaucratic systems. The promotional process in a bureaucracy is relatively rigid. Social origin and training are less likely to determine the career pattern and more likely to determine the level of entry into the hierarchy and the level at which a career will probably terminate.[15]

No such fairly simple models can be constructed for the career patterns of elective politicians in a democratic and pluralistic system as found in the United States. While recruitment patterns are certainly relevant, factors other than social attributes are likely to influence the career patterns of politicians. Given the fact that in the United States politicians are recruited from a great variety of social levels, it may be assumed that the structure of the political system, and notably of the party system, will significantly influence political career patterns and perspectives.

It would be a mistake, of course, to think of a single, invariable political system in the United States. The American political system, if it is permissible to use this conception at all, is inordinately complex and composed of many subsystems. These subsystems differ a good deal in their degrees of popular participation in the choice of office-holders and in political competition, ranging from areas where the struggle between the parties is intense to areas where it is almost nonexistent.

It may be assumed, therefore, that in the United States politicians will give varying emphases to different aspects of their careers, and that these emphases will vary with the structure of party politics in different jurisdictions. For instance, as one moves from highly competitive to noncompetitive party systems, there may be differences in regard to the level of office first entered, the sponsorship of political careers, the skills deemed appropriate for politics, the political goals sought, the opportunities considered relevant for political mobility, and the expectations and aspirations entertained for the future. Research along these lines, it has been suggested, "may be another way of describing and analyzing the political process itself."[16]

As the party is central in the political nominating and promotional process, the relationship between the two major parties in any particular jurisdiction—i.e., the character of the party system—may be expected to be of great interest to politicians intent on gauging their political opportunities. While bright or dim career perspectives are partly rooted in the components of personality, politicians are particularly skilled in reality-testing. They are likely, therefore, to be especially sensitive to those political conditions that either facilitate or obstruct their careers. Among these conditions, the structure of the particular party system is likely to be perceptually salient, though by no means alone determinative. Other considerations may affect career patterns and perspectives. Yet, even these considerations may differ from one structural context to the next. Just how career orientations and expectations are likely to be formulated in differently structured party systems is difficult to predict; there exist neither a theory of political-career patterns nor a body of empirical data about political careers that could serve as sources of viable hypotheses.[17] For this reason, this study is not a test of the hypothesis that different political-career patterns are a function of differences in the structure of party systems. Rather, it is the purpose of the study to explore the feasibility of using the structure of party systems found in different jurisdictions as an interpretative variable in analyzing career patterns and perspectives of American state legislators.

Research Design

The possibility of examining systematically, at one point in their development at least, the career patterns and perspectives of the state legislator was given in connection with a larger project of research on legislative roles.[18] During the legislative sessions of 1957, 100 per cent of the New Jersey legislators, 94 per cent of those of Ohio and California, and 91 per cent of the Tennessee legislators were asked the following questions:[19]

1) What governmental or party positions—local, state, or federal—had you held before going into the legislature?
2) Just how did it come about that you became a legislator?[20]
3) Do you expect to continue to run for the legislature?
4) Are there any other political or governmental positions—local, state, or federal—which you would like to seek?

The open-ended character of some of these questions makes it mandatory to consider the results of this study as suggestive rather than definitive. While open-ended questions have the advantage of leading to spontaneous and widely ranging responses, and of allowing the respondent himself to formulate or "structure" the topic under investigation, there are certain drawbacks that limit their usefulness for systematic treatment. For instance, many respondents gave more than one answer, thus preventing the possibility of assigning priorities within a particular response pattern. Secondly, the respondents differed a great deal in a number of personal characteristics significant in answering open-ended questions. A few were suspicious of the interview and gave minimum, if not evasive, answers. Others were more candid. Some were genuinely pressed for time and failed to elaborate as fully as those who were willing to devote a great deal of time to the interview. Still others—especially those with relatively little education—were unable to articulate answers to questions about which they had evidently thought little prior to the interview. Fluctuations in mood, in attitude toward the interview, in verbal facility, or in self-consciousness lent considerable variability to the answer patterns.

These differences are inherent in the open-ended interview question and in the interview situation. They do not allow us to make categorical statements about possible distributions in answers, which we might have found if we had asked only direct, closed questions about particular aspects of career patterns or perspectives. For instance, the fact that a certain proportion of the respondents mentioned the political party as a sponsor of their political careers does not mean that others, who did not mention this, were not sponsored by a party or, on second thought, might not have recalled the party as a sponsor.

Because of the heterogeneity of answer patterns, we used as the base for computing percentages only those respondents whose answers could be coded in a particular category. As we are unable to ascertain whether these "effective" respondents constitute a random sample of all possible respondents, i.e., of all those interviewed, we have not subjected the distributions to the familiar tests of statistical significance. Instead, we relied on patterns in the percentage distributions in interpreting the findings.

The four states included in this study represent different regions of the country, different ratios of metropolitan and other population, and, most significantly from the point of view pursued in the analysis, different degrees of party competition and party discipline. New Jersey, at the time of the interview, had the most competitive party system and well-organized parties. Ohio had a somewhat less competitive party system, in which the Republicans, at least on the state legislative level, were more often dominant than the faction-ridden Democrats. California was characterized by a system in transition toward partisanship with the Democrats better organized and more united than the dominant Republicans. Tennessee was, for all practical purposes, a one-party system heavily favorable to the Democrats, who, however, were not held together by much party discipline.

The character of a party system in a state may differ, of course, from one electoral context to the next. It may be highly competitive in presidential elections, less competitive in gubernatorial contests, and almost noncompetitive in a district election for the state legislature. The index to be used in classifying a state's party system would seem to depend on the research objective in mind. For the purpose of this research, it seemed most appropriate to use legislative election returns, over a number of years, as the criteria for determining the character of the state party systems at the time of the interview. Therefore, all state legislators, including the few not interviewed, were classified in terms of the degree of party competition in the districts from which they were elected.[21] As Table 1 indicates, 49 per cent of

Table 1

Distribution of State Legislators by Degree of Party Competition in Electoral Districts

District	New Jersey N=79	Ohio N=173	California N=120	Tennessee N=132
Competitive	49%	31%	21%	8%
Semicompetitive	25	30	32	10
One-party	26	39	47	82
Total:	100%	100%	100%	100%
Index of Competition:	+23	—8	—26	—74

the New Jersey, 31 per cent of the Ohio, 21 per cent of the California, and only 8 per cent of the Tennessee legislators came from competitive districts. It may be added that in the semicompetitive districts the Republicans fared better than the Democrats in all states except, of course, Tennessee. The one-party districts were about equally distributed among the two parties in New Jersey and California, but more Republicans came from one-party areas in Ohio.

It is possible to construct a rough measure of party competition in a state's legislative electoral system by subtracting the percentage of legislators elected in one-party districts from the percentage of those elected in competitive districts. This index allows us to place the four legislative party systems on a continuum from most competitive to least competitive. The state's location on this continuum may then serve as a yardstick in interpreting similarities or differences in the career patterns and perspectives of legislators in the four states (Figure 1).

Figure 1

Location of States by Party Competition

+100	+23	−8	−26	−74	−100
	New Jersey	Ohio	California	Tennessee	

The location of the four states on the index of party competition suggests that, insofar as the index can be used as an interpretative device, New Jersey and Tennessee legislators should differ most from each other in regard to career patterns and perspectives; that both should also differ respectively, if less so, from Ohio and California legislators; that the latter two groups should resemble each other; but that, under certain conditions, Ohio legislators should be more similar to New Jersey legislators, and California legislators should resemble legislators in Tennessee. In general, state percentage distributions should follow a consistent pattern, as ordered by the location of the states on the party-competition continuum.

Prelegislative Career

A study of political career *lines* would, of course, trace the order of succession in which governmental or party offices are held by politicians as they move from one institutional context into the next. Our data tell us only *what* positions had been occupied by the respondents before they entered the state legislature. This limits us to examining two questions about the prelegislative career: (1) Is some sort of governmental or political experience a necessary pre-requisite for a career in the state legislature, or does the state legislature serve as a port of entry into politics? (2) What kind of previous governmental or political experience is particularly conducive to a career in the state legislature?

Table 2 presents the data concerning prelegislative governmental experience. From a third, in the case of New Jersey legislators, to a half, in the

Table 2
Prelegislative Career: Level of Government

Career	New Jersey N=79	Ohio N=162	California N=113	Tennessee N=120
No government job	34%	43%	51%	51%
Local job alone, or local and/or state, national	62	50	41	39
State and/or national job	4	7	8	10
Total:	100%	100%	100%	100%

case of California and Tennessee legislators, had not held any governmental
office before entering the legislature. It seems that an apprenticeship in some
other governmental office is by no means a necessary condition for a state
legislative career; the state legislature may serve as a direct gateway into
elective office. However, whether or not the state legislature can be a direct
port of entry, without a previous apprenticeship in some other office, seems
to differ somewhat from state to state. It appears that the more competitive
the state's party system, the more likely it is for legislators to have had some
prior governmental experience.

Furthermore, it seems that the more competitive the system, the greater
the likelihood that the apprenticeship has included service on the local level
of government. On the other hand, the less competitive the system, the
more likely it seems that prelegislative service, if any, was had on the
state and/or national levels alone. While the number of respondents in this
category is small, the pattern is consistent. In other words, if an "escalator
model" of political ascent is valid, it seems more likely to be valid in the
more competitive systems, although in both more and less competitive systems
the political escalator may be boarded at different governmental levels.[22]
These findings are not surprising. Because in competitive systems party
organization is more likely to be effective and the party is more likely to
participate actively in the nominating process, state legislative office is likely
to be regarded as a reward for service on the local level. The party will throw
its support behind candidates who have had some experience and who have
demonstrated a willingness to serve in local jobs—control of which is of
utmost importance to the party in competitive political systems.

What kind of prior governmental experience will state legislators have
had that may be preparation for holding legislative office? Our data indicate
that about a fifth of the respondents in all four states had held only executive
and/or judicial jobs before entering the legislature. Greater proportions had
held other legislative or quasi-legislative jobs, such as service on city councils,
county boards, school boards, and so on. Of course, this may be due simply
to the availability of more legislative-type offices than executive or judicial
positions. Still, the data suggest differences from state to state, which may

be related to the degree of competition in the state's party sysem. Of the New Jersey respondents, 48 per cent had legislative-type experience; of Ohio respondents, 36 per cent; of California respondents, 32 per cent; and of the Tennesseeans, 30 per cent. Except for New Jersey, the differences among the states are small but the pattern is consistent.

Prelegislative governmental experience seems to vary from one state to the next in a pattern anticipated by ordering the four states on the index of competition. Holding party office or being active in party work as a condition for a legislative career seems to follow a similar pattern. As Table 3 shows, fewer respondents in all four states had held party office or done party work than had held governmental office, but considerably fewer legislators in New Jersey than legislators in the less competitive states—especially in one-party

Table 3

Prelegislative Career: Party Activity

Career	New Jersey N=79	Ohio N=162	California N=113	Tennessee N=120
No party office or work	41%	62%	52%	66%
Local party alone, or local and/or state, national	41	30	29	19
State and/or national party	18	8	19	15
Total:	100%	100%	100%	100%

Tennessee—had no party record at all. Again, local party activity seems to be more highly valued in New Jersey than elsewhere, and the interstate pattern is consistent.

However, we note a break in the pattern in the cases of Ohio and California. More respondents in the less competitive California than in the more competitive Ohio system reported some prelegislative party activity. Speculation leads us to believe that this is due to the California Democratic party's organizational revival, spurred on in recent years by the local Democratic club movement, of which Democratic legislators are members in many cases.[23] In order to pin this down with our data, California and Ohio legislators were examined in terms of their party affiliation. It now appears, as Table 4 indicates, that the California Democrats in fact had been far more active in party work than the California Republicans, while Ohio Democrats and Republicans differed little in this respect. Quite clearly, the break in the

Table 4

Party Actives in California and Ohio

CALIFORNIA		OHIO	
Democrats N=54	Republicans N=59	Democrats N=51	Republicans N=111
59%	37%	35%	40%

pattern between Ohio and California is due to the amazingly high level of party activity on the part of the California Democrats.

We may tentatively infer from the data reported in this section that in competitive party systems political careers are likely to be more professionalized than in less competitive systems. There seems to be greater emphasis in competitive systems on entry into politics at the local level of government or party organization, and on having had some governmental and especially legislative-type experience before running for the state legislature. State legislative service is more likely to be a step on the political escalator that must be boarded early and, if the party is well organized, as the "deviant" case of the California Democrats suggests, under the auspices of the party. The following section will shed further light on the role of the party in molding political careers.

Career Sponsorship

If the structure of the party system is a critical factor in the unfolding of political careers, we should expect that politicians in more competitive systems would be more likely to see the party as a necessary vehicle for a career than would politicians in less competitive systems, and that they would regard party sponsorship essential for electoral success. Indeed, in response to the question of how they became state legislators, a number of respondents in all four states mentioned their party. But, as the totals in Table 5 show, only in competitive New Jersey did great proportions of our respondents spontaneously refer to their party as sponsoring their legislative career. That only 18 per cent would mention the party in noncompetitive Tennessee was to be expected, but that so few Ohio and California respondents mentioned it is rather surprising.

Table 5

Party Sponsorship of Legislative Career

State	DEMOCRATS		REPUBLICANS	
	Per Cent	Number	Per Cent	Number
New Jersey	74	(27)	66	(44)
Ohio	12	(49)	24	(108)
California	42	(48)	22	(55)
Tennessee	15	(68)	28	(18)

Table 5 also suggests that whether or not party sponsorship of the legislative career is considered salient may be a function of a party's discipline and morale. In New Jersey, where the parties are well organized, great majorities in both mentioned their party as sponsor. In Ohio, where the Democrats were organizationally weak, the Republicans referred to their party twice as frequently as the Democrats. The result is reversed in California, where, in line with the greater party activity of the Democratic legislators, Democrats mentioned their party almost twice as frequently as the Republicans. In Tennessee, more of the greatly outnumbered Republicans acknowledged their party as the sponsor of their career than did the Democrats. Party support seems to be seen as essential by members of a minority party in a system where the minority ever struggles for survival in the face of the overwhelming majority.

The party may not only be perceived as the sponsor of one's political career, but as the vehicle which makes available the "opportunity" for being promoted as a candidate, particularly by those already active in party work. In other words, service in the legislature will be seen as a "next step" in a political career already begun, and the legislator will attribute his position to having come up through the ranks. Again, we might expect that this will differ from the more competitive to the less competitive party systems. As Table 6 shows, regardless of party affiliation, New Jersey legislators were

Table 6

Party Promotion as Opportunity for Legislative Career

STATE	DEMOCRATS		REPUBLICANS	
	Per Cent	Number	Per Cent	Number
New Jersey	72	(18)	59	(39)
Ohio	11	(28)	30	(73)
California	23	(47)	21	(47)
Tennessee	3	(34)	0	(7)

the most likely to mention the opportunity given them by their parties, while in Tennessee hardly any of the respondents mentioned it. The only break in the pattern is, again, due to the reversal of the Ohio and California Democrats. The latter were more likely to attribute their career to the opportunity offered them by their party than were the former.

Just how legislators perceived the party's role in promoting their career may be illustrated by the following comments from the interview protocols:

After I was president of the Young Republicans, I became secretary-treasurer of the executive committee for ten years with the idea in mind of becoming a legislator. You might say that I came up through the ranks.

I was endorsed by the county central committee and I abided by their decision. . . . I hadn't sought it but as a member of the central committee myself I had indicated an interest in politics and they made this opportunity available to me.

Our county has a strong chairman whose endorsement you need for nomination. I waited for the blessing of the Republican Party organization. Twice I backed down to avoid a split in the party. You can't buck the county organization, you have to play ball. You get no place without the organization's endorsement. This avoids conflicts in primaries. A strong organization is a good thing.

There are different ways in which the party seems to enter the nominating process. When an incumbent decides not to run again, he may be the party's agent in approaching a possible successor. Quite a few respondents placed a high value on getting the nomination without having to contest it in the primary. The following comment is typical: "The representative who preceded me had enough. We were well acquainted. We decided that he would withdraw and I would run. I was unopposed in the primary."

At times, the party may be hard put to find suitable candidates, and it may go so far as to nominate a candidate without his prior consent:

The Republican committee, after many years of not even filing a candidate for the office, wrote my name in without my knowing it. I was elected. At first I was mad because they had done it without asking me. But I'm the first Republican to hold that office and the only Republican in office in the entire county at the present time.

On the other hand, some legislative careers may be said to have been "self-started." Fifty-five per cent of the Ohio legislators, 33 per cent of the California respondents, 31 per cent in New Jersey, and 23 per cent of the Tennesseeans made this claim. However, a closer look at the interview protocols may reveal the party in the background, these self-serving declarations notwithstanding. Whether actually true or not, these self-images may be quite genuine and behaviorally relevant aspects of the legislator's career perspective. Two from among many remarks must suffice to illustrate what are evidently considered prestige-giving self-conceptions:

I was county treasurer. Well, I left the office in————, and it wasn't very long that I found that my expenses were the same whether I had a job or not. I sat in the office one day, and a fellow politician came in. He asked me who we Democrats were going to run for the Assembly. My predecessor had been a six-termer and was running for the Senate. I said to this fellow: "Do you know who we are going to run? You look right at him."

Twenty years ago I developed the desire of becoming a legislator after practicing law awhile. . . . Nobody told me to run. One of my associates is Democratic county chairman; he didn't know until I told him. . . . It was a long-planned thing. I was very active in club work, local politics, had extensive acquaintances. I was in a position to run and win.

If the party is the major agency facilitating a legislative career in competitive systems or when it is especially well organized, one may ask whether there are functional equivalents in the less competitive systems that take over the role of sponsoring legislative candidates. Our interviews revealed that either interest groups or "friends" or "associates" may sponsor a candidate. Interest groups are usually not thought to cherish the task of sponsoring political careers. Yet, if the party is not active as a sponsor, interest groups may serve this function, if only to a very limited extent. As Table 7 shows, 16 per cent of the Tennessee respondents and 9 per cent of the Californians referred to interest groups as sponsors; they were scarcely mentioned in the more competitive states of New Jersey and Ohio. Apparently, the less competitive the party system, the more likely it is that interest groups will serve as functional equivalents of party in promoting political careers.

Table 7
Interest Groups and Friends as Sponsors of Legislative Career

State	Interest Groups (per cent)	Friends and Associates (per cent)
New Jersey (N=71)	1	8
Ohio (N=157)	2	19
California (N=103)	9	24
Tennessee (N=86)	16	54

Friends or associates were mentioned somewhat more often as sponsors of a political or legislative career. As in the case of interest groups, the interstate pattern noted in connection with party sponsorship is reversed. As Table 7 indicates, friends or associates were more likely to be mentioned as sponsors in the less competitive than in the more competitive systems, and especially in Tennessee. It seems that in the absence of party interest in nominating candidates, friends or associates sponsor political careers. As the interview protocols suggest, however, the choice of a legislative career has an evidently accidental quality when the suggestion to run for legislative office comes from this source. For example:

A good friend of the family suggested it to me. I was home on leave at Christmas time a few months before I was to be discharged from the army, and this friend told me that there were two vacancies in the legislature and that I ought to run. This friend has always given me good advice; he's been more or less my mentor.

There may be hidden behind the naming of friends, especially in California and Tennessee, the struggle of factions whose identity is thereby concealed. The following remarks in one of the interviews is suggestive in this respect:

I attribute that to about four close friends—a member of the legislature, a member of the county central committee, the county superintendent of schools, and the secretary of the election board. They said to me, "Hell, why don't you throw in your hat?" So I got my petition and away I went. I got entangled with the political leader in the county. He had a candidate he could dictate to. He knew he couldn't get to first base with me. He got his candidate to oppose me in the primary, but I won. The same thing happened with the second term.

Career Skills

Talents or skills are important considerations in the choice of a career. The more specialized and technical the tasks, the more clearly defined are appropriate qualifications likely to be. The surgeon, the watchmaker, the chemist, or the jet pilot are expected to possess highly specific skills. In governmental administration, civil servants take examinations geared to particular levels of expertise. In politics, the skills presumably necessary for professional success are much less specific. In many respects, politicians are generalizers rather than specialists. Their careers involve so wide a range of activities that speaking of skills seems almost paradoxical. Nevertheless, politicians themselves are likely to insist that certain qualifications, talents, or skills—broadly conceived as including certain personal characteristics—are necessary and desirable requisites for a career in politics.

That this is the case appears quite clearly from our data. The question we asked in no way directed the respondent to appraise his skills or qualifications as a candidate or politician; nevertheless, quite a few legislators made it an opportunity to discuss the matter. At least 75 per cent or more did so in New Jersey, Ohio, and California; but in one-party Tennessee only 40 per cent of the respondents made spontaneous comments about career skills or qualifications. Whatever skills they may actually possess, it would seem that in one-party systems politicians place relatively little value on specific qualifications as requisites of professional success.

A great variety of skills, experiences, or attributes were offered in this spontaneous self-assessment, but three main categories emerged: personal, occupational, and political qualifications.

A few legislators—no more than 13 per cent in any state—emphasized such attributes as a "sense of sociability" or "general ability" for political or legislative work. The differences from state to state were small and insignificant. But these personal qualifications were somewhat more frequently mentioned in the less competitive systems.

Those referring to their sociability would simply say that they went into politics because they liked people—"I like people and being here you get to meet all kinds"; or because they were good mixers—"the ability I have of being able to mix with people. I have always enjoyed mixing with people and getting along with them." Another respondent would say, "well, I'm gregarious at heart." Those who mentioned their general ability would identify it as being "smart," "well-equipped," or having "broad experience." The following two illustrations are typical:

That I picked the legislature? I had attended sessions in other states accidentally. I was impressed. And I did have experience. I felt that a smart man like I would stand out like a sore thumb. But I wasn't a member long before I found out they weren't so dumb.

Damned if I know! I liked the idea of writing the laws that I'd have to live under. I also feel that there is need, not to be boastful, for better-equipped people here in the House. I thought I could do a better job than some of the fellows I'd seen around here.

Somewhat larger proportions in all four states—but nowhere more than 15 per cent—mentioned nonpolitical occupational skills or experiences in assessing their careers. Although the differences were again very small, there was a slight tendency for legislators in the more competitive systems to stress legal skills or previous experiences with the legislature in some non-legislative capacity.

Politics as a career coincides with many other vocational roles in business, unions, real estate, insurance, and so on. Law, in particular, has long been noted as the one vocation most prominently connected with politics.

If, as we have reason to believe, the political career is more professionalized in competitive political systems, we should expect to find there more lawyer-legislators than in less competitive systems. In fact, 52 per cent of all legislators in New Jersey were lawyers; 36 per cent of all Ohioans were likewise members of the legal profession, followed by 30 per cent of all the legislators in California and in Tennessee. Of course, some lawyers will pick a political career for nonpolitical objectives, for example, as an avenue of advancement in their main profession. Others may look on their legal training as a qualification for legislative service:

I don't consider myself a politician. I just availed myself of the opportunity because I was interested in legislative law in my capacity as a lawyer. It was an opportunity to expand my knowledge of the law. Also good during the lean years of practice.

The fact that the legislature is the most important political office in the state, next to the executive. It is a position which would not interfere with my profession because it is only in session six months. And the law-making branch is the most compatible with the profession of law.

Previous service with the legislature in appointive positions may be considered a suitable experience for a legislative career. A former secretary to a congressman claimed to have learned about the nature and demands of legislative work in Congress. A former congressional assistant valued the opportunity he had "to watch the House and Senate in action." Another respondent had been counsel to a congressional committee, and the experience had stimulated him to seek elective office.

Similarly, local elective office—such as county commissioner, county treasurer, or probate judge—may acquaint politicians with the legislature, and this experience will be perceived as relevant in choosing a legislative career:

For eight years I served on the county treasurers' legislative committee. During the course of that time I came down to the legislature often. While on the committee, I worked on bills such as the County Officials Pay Bill. I decided that I had some good experience and that I should run for the legislature.

When I served on the probate bench, I was often required to appear before legislative committees to testify as to the legality of certain bills. That experience caused me to become interested in the legislature, and I decided that I would rather make up the bills than have to come afterwards to decide if it was legal.

Political skills or qualifications proper were mentioned by much larger proportions of legislators in the four states. Here the differences from state to state, as Table 8 shows, were more marked, but a consistent pattern is difficult to discern. As the bold face proportions indicate, the pattern may be obscured by the somewhat different emphases given in the four states to what we lumped together as "political skills and qualifications." The pattern is present in the diagonal and, as we shall suggest, the diagonal pattern is by no means arbitrary.

For instance, we are not surprised to find that New Jersey legislators

Table 8

Political Career Skills and Qualifications

Political Skills	New Jersey N=61	Ohio N=122	California N=94	Tennessee N=48
Political "Know-How"	59%	3%	25%	2%
Involvement in Politics	13	34	19	25
Civic Commitment	13	15	34	15
Political Ambition	23	24	27	13
Political "Availability"	13	7	12	21

were most inclined to stress political "know-how"—including such things as experience in local government, wide previous political contacts, demonstrated vote-getting ability, experience in campaigning, and so on. This again is an indication of the greater professionalization of politics in that state:

What helped me is that everyone knew me. All of the farmers knew that I was for them. I was lenient to the poor people when I owned a bakery, so they remembered me when I ran for the legislature.

I had a certain amount of success in the county court, getting done what people wanted done.

Where local and state politics are apparently less professionalized than in New Jersey, yet less amateurish than in one-party Tennessee, respondents were more likely to express themselves in appropriate attitudinal terms. Ohio legislators, in particular, emphasized their involvement in and fascination with politics as an important attribute of the successful political careerist. Politics appears as a game, a challenge, or sheer fun. By implication, persons who don't like the game are not qualified to be politicians. The politician sees himself as a fighter who is not discouraged by opposition or even repeated defeat:

Oh, I just think it's a lot of fun. Election time isn't too much fun, matter of fact it's a pain in the neck. But the legislature is fascinating business.

It was more or less a challenge. No Democrat ever was elected to county or state office from our area except on rare occasions. I used the direct approach in running. I represent what was once, if not still now, the strongest Republican county in the state. I went right direct to the people while running. I met with small groups and went to see individuals in every nook and cranny of the county.

There is special gusto in the statements of those whose career was begun in defiance of the party organization. The following comment is typical:

Mainly wanting to get my feet wet, to see what it's like. I did it just through campaigning. I had one endorsement, a newspaper. I never solicited organization support. I just did it on my own. It was a lot of fun that way. They wouldn't let me speak at some meetings, but the harder they kicked, the harder I tried. I'm not a party politician, yet.

Interest in government as a requisite for seeking a political career—in the sense of being civic-minded and devoted to the public interest—was more often mentioned in California than elsewhere. This may be, of course, a stereotypic response, designed either to camouflage lack of thought on the subject, or to portray oneself in a favorable light. But politicians may take their stereotypes of themselves seriously, seek to live up to them, and have a genuine commitment to the public welfare:

I felt it is a civic duty to run. The people weren't being well represented. The first time I wasn't elected. That encouraged me to run again. I ran for the good of the people of the county.

Politics is a means rather than an end. It is a means to an active interest in government. It is a vehicle for doing something. . . . How did I decide to go into it? Well, I liked the legislative job and you know you have to figure out how to get it, to wit, run.

Somewhat more respondents in New Jersey, Ohio, and California than in Tennessee pointed to their ambitions as requisite qualifications, and a few suggested "power" as a desirable aspiration. Yet, interestingly, power is a concept only very rarely used by politicians themselves, who prefer terms like "urge" or "ambition" to denote what is evidently considered a positive career requisite. As a first-termer put it: "I just wanted to be a legislator. I just had the urge. I thought of it all the time, and I just wanted to become one." Frequently, politicians seem to find it difficult to articulate this orientation. As another respondent said: "I don't know quite how to answer that; there was just the fact that I always felt that I might like politics." Even after initial expectations have been chastened by experience, ambition may remain central: "In the beginning I had political ambition; after you serve awhile you lose the ambition, but then there are lots of things you want to accomplish before you quit." Finally, legislative office may be viewed as a good jumping-off place for a career, a testing ground for the ambitious to acquire political skills. The following two comments are illustrative:

Well, there is a broader knowledge of things that I wanted than I could have gotten in the city. I know that if I had run for city council, you get only problems that concern the city, while here in the state legislature there are more complex problems ranging from city to county, state and federal level. I think any young man should start on the state level, that is, in the legislature. This is a proving ground for young politicians.

I came back from————and I wanted to run for some office, either prosecutor or legislator. I talked it over with my father, and we decided that the state legislature was better because it would lead some place more than being the prosecutor of a small county. A prosecutor of a city might go some place, but a small county man isn't likely to go far; he usually ends up pleading property claims, and whereas I don't mind property claims, that isn't my ambition.

A few legislators—but, as Table 8 shows, more in Tennessee than elsewhere—ascribed their career to the fact that they had been "available." That this rather passive qualification is most frequently mentioned in the least professionalized system is not surprising. In a one-party system political recruitment lags, and candidates are likely to be selected to attract supporters of competing factions, just as in competitive systems this consideration may determine the choice of party candidates. The fact that "availability" was more frequently mentioned in Tennessee only underlines the fact that in competitive systems more is required of a candidate than a "right" name or religion.

In spite of its wide use, both in political circles and the academic literature, the concept of "availability" is poorly defined. Its most frequent connotation seems to be that a candidate must have certain qualities or characteristics and that he must lack certain others, in such combination that he is more acceptable to diverse interests than another candidate who possesses these characteristics or lacks others in a less fortunate combination. Part of one's availability is to be widely known and to have cultivated wide contacts, but this is not enough. *Not* having been a controversial figure may facilitate one's availability. As one respondent put it: "I had no political scars, so I guess somebody thought they could use me." *Not* being identified with a particular interest may mean availability. This was expressed by a non-labor legislator who comes from a strongly unionized metropolitan area: "When a vacancy in the Senate occurred, the incumbent, who's a CIO leader, asked me to run, and I was endorsed by the CIO. I guess they asked me to run because they did not want another labor man."

On the other hand, availability may mean that the candidate has a single quality which, it is assumed, will attract a particular clientele. For instance, being a woman may be seen as a condition of being picked for the ticket —"there is usually one woman on our county ticket." That a "right" name may be a qualification for candidacy is familiar enough, and voting studies have shown that this is not simply political folklore. State legislators seem to share this criterion of availability:

You need a good name in politics, a simple name that appeals to the people. Mine is a good name, which helped me. Other good names are those like Marshall and Brown. Funny names are a handicap. Several people have changed their names when they went into politics. Funny names would appeal downstate. We often get funny names from————, you can notice them in the Senate, names like Bacigalupi or Radzinsky.

Finally, a few respondents who appraised their skills or qualifications —2 per cent in Ohio, 13 per cent in Tennessee, and 17 per cent in California—characterized themselves as essentially "nonpolitical," at least at the time of their candidacy: "I ran and won without knowledge of the election process or a machine of any kind to back me"; or "I was asked to run for the legislature. I talked it over with my wife. I was never really interested in it until then." Perhaps the most candid remark of a "nonpolitical" was this: "I don't consider myself in, very deep, very permanent, or very long."

Career Opportunities

Relevant skills and experiences are likely to be of little avail in politics unless those who have them can seize appropriate opportunities to apply them. By "opportunity," we mean the particular sets of circumstances which must be harnessed as they arise, whether accidentally or not, and not advantageous location in the social structure. In some respects, of course, recognition and seizure of opportunities are themselves skills which distinguish the politician from the average citizen. But opportunity as here conceived is essentially a matter of the situation in which a political career is pursued.

Our data suggest a number of ways in which would-be politicians can define political opportunities. Recollecting the circumstances of their entry into politics, our respondents tended to mention two types: (1) a relatively small proportion—31 per cent in California, 21 per cent in Tennessee, 17 per cent in Ohio, and 9 per cent in New Jersey—described the broad social or political context of their entry; and (2) much larger proportions of those giving relevant answers—83 per cent in California, 72 per cent in New Jersey, 62 per cent in Ohio, and 34 per cent in Tennessee—referred to more directly personal conditions.

Because the number of respondents in the first category is so small, and because no meaningful interstate pattern was apparent, we prefer to aggregate the data for descriptive purposes. For instance, only 3 per cent of the 95 legislators in all states who dealt with the broad context of their career choice mentioned the Depression or economically difficult times, and 6 per cent mentioned war. It would seem that for the great majority of politicians active at the state level, and few of whom are likely to advance much further in their political career, the "great issues" are relatively devoid of salience. Moreover, those who came to politics in time of depression fell into two quite distinct groups: some entered politics to help others, and some did so to help themselves. As one of the former group put it:

In Harding and Coolidge's times it seemed as though democratic government was to fall apart because of lack of good leaders. They were taking gold out of this country and that is the life blood of this country. Roosevelt called a bank holiday and knew where he was going. The miners and underprivileged people felt that they needed representation. They talked me into it. I've been elected five times, mostly by these people.

For the second group, politics was an alternative to unemployment. The context was to be exploited for personal interest rather than to be changed by political means:

The only job it was possible for one to get during the Depression years was some sort of political one. I was just starting to work, had to make some money to get back to school. It seemed like the politics business was all that was open.

Politics, in this statement, is perceived as "business," and politics as a remunerative alternative to business was also articulated by others.

Respondents who mentioned war and war's aftermath as conditioning their career choice also seem to fall into two groups. An "idealistic" view appears in this comment:

Getting out of the service for the second time and feeling that as long as the world is in turmoil young lives are affected. Feeling that young people should get into politics and do something about it, possibly correct previous mistakes of our elders.

The more directly personal consequences of war, as they relate to the political career, were expressed by one respondent as follows:

> The second World War had put me out of business. We couldn't get any merchandise. When I came out of the Navy, I was wholly free; nothing to do, absolutely nothing. At that time the man who represented our district in the Senate was retiring. I remember being in a restaurant with a friend. He said, "There goes the Senator, he isn't running anymore. Why don't you run for the Senate?" I thought it over and decided to run.

Much greater proportions—32 per cent and 43 per cent, respectively— mentioned "dissatisfaction" with general or specific situations or politicians as the context of their career choice. Squabbles over village zoning or water-works, fights over local sales taxes or public school expenditures, struggles with local political machines or special interests dominating local govern-ment are the kinds of context in which political careers may be initiated. The failure of a politician to respond to local demands may serve as the stimulus:

> I'd say that what triggered it was that we wanted two judges here. The man in the legislature would not introduce it. I threatened to run against him. So he introduced the bill and I was told that I could have one of the legislative jobs.

Or there may be a feeling that the incumbent has been in office too long. How dissatisfaction with an incumbent may start a political career is described in some detail:

> After serving as a page in the legislature, I attended the Republican caucus in the Spring of————. There was some discussion or comments made that perhaps a Republican should run against the incumbent. The incumbent was a solid Republican, but some people had some gripes against him. I went to a member of the precinct committee, who was also vice-chairman of the party, and said I was interested in running. A few months later there was a party picnic and from several comments made I felt that I would have some support. Starting around the first of September, I went around the county talking to members of various precinct committees. I talked to these people about running and found that I would have some support; enough support so that it seemed possible to win.

How local situations can serve to mobilize a political career was explained by another legislator:

> I was disturbed and disgusted by the very corrupt conditions in my home town. The city government had surrendered to, and was in collusion with, the illegal rackets. That was in the twenties. Prostitution and gambling and so on were protected. I knew some members of the city council and approached them, but they shrugged their shoulders. I told them that if I were on the council.... Well, this was the germ of an idea, and I ran and was elected.

More often, the local context was factional squabbles in the party and dis-satisfaction with the party organization:

I was cat's-paw for my party leaders. I didn't know it was my party. I ran for the city council, but the incumbent made amends, the leaders double-crossed me and I lost by twelve votes. I started campaigning on my own for the next term.

We formed a Young Men's club in the party to get young people elected. We felt the situation was such that the younger men were not properly treated. I was one of the first candidates they suggested to the older organization.

I was let out of a political job for no good reason and decided I had been pushing other people's wagons long enough, and that it was about time I started pushing my own. I was getting no place campaigning for other people. I wanted to campaign for myself.

Finally, the fact that certain well-known national leaders were running could serve as a stimulus—the hope evidently being, though not expressed, that the leader's coat tails might be helpful:

Bob Taft was running and labor was opposing him. Personally, I thought he should get in. When some labor people asked me if I would run with him, I accepted, hoping to do anything I could to get him elected.

Well, actually on my own initiative. F. D. R. was running for his fourth term. Nobody thought he had a chance. The regular Democrat didn't run. I ran to show my belief in F. D. R. and I was willing to fight even if the ship was sinking.

In contrast, a national figure could serve as a negative symbol stimulating a career:

F. D. R.—I hated his guts, and I still do. He did more goddamned harm to the country. I was in business then. Some guy named Isidore Lubin sent forms all the time wanting to know what I was doing. I was peed off.

A majority of the legislators in all states except Tennessee indicated some sensitivity to the more personal-chance or opportunity aspects of their political or legislative career. This sensitivity could be expressed with varying degrees of specificity. Some might simply say that there was an "opportunity" for them to begin a career without being more specific, while others would explain in more detail just what they considered this "opportunity" to be. Analysis reveals that some response categories do not follow any pattern from state to state, but others suggest that the findings are not necessarily random. In particular, as we already noted, there seems to be a direct relationship between perceiving the party as the promoter of a political career and the political structure reflected in the competition between the parties or the role that parties play in competitive systems. On the other hand, there seems to be an inverse relationship between an emphasis on combining political office with private occupation and the structure of the party system as patterned by competition. As Table 9 shows, regardless of whether they are Democrats or Republicans, legislators in the less competitive states were more likely to say that the possibility of combining their political career with their private employment led them into politics. Although the differences between the states may also be due to other factors, they seem to

Table 9

Opportunity to Combine Career with Employment

STATE	DEMOCRATS		REPUBLICANS	
	Per cent	Number	Per cent	Number
New Jersey	0	(18)	5	(39)
Ohio	7	(28)	12	(73)
California	11	(47)	17	(47)
Tennessee	24	(34)	43	(7)

indicate the greater professionalization of the political career in the states where party competition is keen. Occupations most likely to be paired with a legislative career were real estate and insurance—which permit the legislator to have control over his own hours—or law. Retirement was also mentioned as an opportunity to enter politics.

Opportunity in general, or specific opportunities, were more frequently cited by legislators in the less competitive states. Once again, however, Tennessee seems to represent a special case, as Table 10 indicates. This

Table 10

Opportunity and Political Career

STATE	DEMOCRATS		REPUBLICANS	
	Per cent	Number	Per cent	Number
New Jersey	17	(18)	49	(39)
Ohio	50	(28)	54	(73)
California	71	(47)	85	(47)
Tennessee	50	(34)	43	(7)

deviation may be explained, in part at least, by the fact that Tennessee legislators—like Californians—reported that they entered politics because there were no other candidates available (see Table 11, below). However, the data seem to support the notion that career "opportunities" in politics are more conspicuous in the less competitive systems than in the more competitive systems.

The interview protocols may throw some light on the dynamics of political or legislative career choices as they are a function of "opportunity." Although there is much lore and some evidence to the effect that politicians cherish the combat and challenge involved in campaigning, it may be that just the opposite is preferred. Few legislators, it seems, like to run against incumbents:

A vacancy came up and I had been building up towards it when the opening came. Then I made the move. All politics contains a certain amount of *opportunity*. If opportunities don't come, like in anything else, you don't go any place. One has to be at the right spot at the right time. I happened to be.

Opportunity more than anything else. I had some hours left in college and returned to my hometown to try some business. There was an opening and I didn't have to run against the incumbent. My father suggested that I run, for the education involved in it as much as anything.

If the candidate comes from a district in which his party is traditionally in the minority, the advantage of not having to oppose the majority party incumbent is all the more crucial. As a legislator said:

In———, the representative of my county resigned from his office, leaving a vacancy and allowing an open field. Since I am from a traditionally and historically Democratic county, and since I'm a Republican, this let me gain office without opposing my predecessor. I was the second Republican in 131 years to be elected from his county. If this event had not happened, I probably wouldn't have been a candidate at all.

The strength of the parties at the local level may also determine the level at which a political career is begun. While it may not be possible to succeed locally, the attempt may be made to enter politics at a higher level:

Well, it's the first step for a politician in politics. For me, it's probably the last step. As a Democrat, it was the only thing I could do. At the county level, although there are Democrats elected, all the incumbents were running again and I would not have had a good chance. There was more chance on the state level.

Even the choice of party may be dictated by exigency: "I went to the county chairmen of both parties and offered my services. The Democratic Party took more interest in me, and therefore I became a Democrat."

If politics is "opportunistic" and politicians are "opportunists," these attributes may not be so much a matter of personality, but a result of the structuring of politics. For example, the fact that only three candidates entered a primary for two available seats, a legislator said, "made a good climate for me to run in." On the other hand, a large number of candidates may favor the candidate with the best-known name. As a legislator from a one-party area whose father had been a well-known state and national figure pointed out:

A fellow with the name of———had five terms; he died after the May primary in———. So the committee had to meet to nominate a candidate. Some people didn't know my father was dead. So I put my hat in the ring. There were 12 or 13 wanting the nomination. They started the process of elimination 'til three were left. One fellow then swung to me and I was selected by the committee.

Finally, the opportunity for political office may present itself under very particular conditions. As a respondent who admitted to having "the political bug" pointed out. "we had a fellow here who went bad and took money. I ran on my own hook." On the other hand, having to run against others one respects may make the career decision difficult:

Mr.———, the previous legislator from my county, accepted employment as———, thus resigning and leaving what we term in political circles an open race for his successor. I was opposed in the primary by a very close friend, a respected and enviable person of whom I have always had great respect and regard. It was my own decision to run. In our county, the party never endorses a candidate in the primary. I was also opposed by the opposition party in the general election by a gentleman for whom I have the greatest respect.

Another set of responses involved more immediately personal circumstances which legislators perceived as salient in molding their careers. As Table 11 shows, the percentages are small and no consistent pattern can be discerned. However, it may be noteworthy that more respondents in the less competitive states of California and Tennessee attributed the opportunity to enter on a political career to the fact that nobody else was available for taking office. This is in line, of course, with other findings concerning

Table 11

Miscellaneous Opportunities for Political Career

Type of Opportunity	New Jersey N=57	Ohio N=101	California N=94	Tennessee N=41
Nobody else available	2%	2%	16%	15%
Reputation from other pursuit	11	8	12	10
Family conditions favorable		5	4	2
Earlier defeat encouraging	7	14	13	2

differences in the political vitality of the more and the less competitive systems. As a respondent pointed out:

I became actively interested in politics as a committeeman. I got on the executive committee, I was encouraged to run for the job. It was a rural area and kind of hard to get anyone to run. Older members dropped out and it was hard to get anyone to move into their place.

A reputation in some other pursuit enhances the candidate's chances to enter political life. As the following comments suggest, some would-be politicians had cultivated wide contacts for many years:

I've occupied a position for some years in which I've been well known: I've been active in veterans' affairs, retail merchandising and financial interests, as well as in the educational system, having taught for several years in the district school. The local party chairman figured I was a likely candidate and asked me to run. I hadn't been at all politically active until then.

My experience in organized labor, fighting for union hours and working conditions. I joined the ITU in———. I was 23 then. We had to serve six years of apprenticeship. It was a democratic union. Then I was active in social work, on the boards of the TB and health organizations in———, and one of the organizers of the United Fund and on the original March of Dimes committee in 1937.

On the other hand, rather recently gained notoriety may precipitate a political career which had not been previously anticipated:

I was drafted into politics. In———, the member of the House here was drafted into the army after he had been nominated. He, of course, had to with-draw and the Republican executive committee asked me to run in his stead, which I did and was elected. Now, here's what happened. It was about that time that a law was passed requiring a license for selling real estate. About that time Congress gave money to build an airport. I was employed to buy the property for the site of the airport. The publicity I got from this is the reason I think that the Republican committee picked me. I'd never been active in party politics before. It was a lot of publicity.

A few respondents mentioned family conditions as favoring their entering on a political career. One legislator reported that although he had always been interested in politics, he had not sought office because his father was in it, and he waited until his father had died. Others would mention the fact that their children had to leave home before they could consider politics:

> What clinched my taking a political position was that my children were grown up, and my wife is a school teacher, so when they came to ask me I felt that I could do it. Since my financial responsibilities to my family weren't great, I was able to take them up on their request.

Having been defeated in a first try may encourage rather than discourage a political career. As one respondent put it, "the first time I wasn't elected. That encouraged me to run again." Another reported that he had been defeated, but had come back in the next election to lead his party ticket. Even several defeats, as the following comment suggests, may be seen as an opportunity rather than as a handicap:

> About the time I was deciding to run, I was quite active in the union. I had held some pretty important positions. So they knew me pretty well. Didn't do me much good, though, because although they were on my side, no one else seemed to be. I was defeated for the first times I ran, for three successive times. I got a larger percentage of the votes each time, though. Finally, all of organized labor and the newspapers gave me some support which I guess must have finally helped because on my fourth try I finally got in. Been here ever since.

Career Goals

As politics involves the allocation of values, a political career may be chosen because the possession of public office is likely to facilitate achieving personal goals. One cannot simply assume, of course, that the choice of a political career is invariably related to well-conceived objectives. Entry into politics, as we have seen, is a matter of many circumstances and conditions —of family tradition, recruitment by a party, appropriate skills and particular opportunities. Yet, regardless of the varying individual "ports of entry" to political careers, politicians as a whole differ from their fellow citizens in the value they place on active political participation. No simple formula is possible, but it is plausible to assume that they do so because an active political career promises the attainment of certain goals they may cherish. The fact that a number of legislators, in all four states, voluntarily referred to goals in explaining why they entered politics or the legislature suggests an awareness of the connection between politics and the allocation of values.

The responses fell into two major categories: (1) goals that may be called altruistic or contributive, and (2) goals that are essentially selfish and exploitative. Table 12 reveals an interesting, but not fully satisfying, pattern— for, once again, at least in the first category, the Tennessee respondents defy the pattern. In general, it appears that the more competitive the political system, the smaller the proportion of legislators who perceive their career

Table 12

Major Types of Goals in Career Choice

Goals	New Jersey N=79	Ohio N=162	California N=113	Tennessee N=120
Altruistic-Contributive	27%	37%	47%	29%
Selfish-Exploitative	12	16	23	23

as an avenue of goal achievement. This is to be expected. Party discipline is greater in competitive systems, and the goals of politics are likely to be party-determined objectives. The legislator, therefore, not only has less leeway in what, as an individual, he can or cannot do, but as a consequence he also need not concern himself too much with the problem of goals. Indeed, he is quite realistic if he does not overestimate what he, the individual, can accomplish as a politician. On the other hand, the less competitive the political system, the more freedom there is likely to be for the individual politician to select among alternate objectives; his greater concern with goals may reflect the more free-wheeling political style made possible by the absence of party discipline and programs.

The politician, as Max Weber has suggested, in addition to enjoying the possession of power, is conscious that "his life has meaning in the service of a cause."[24] It is a commonplace that politicians, when asked what brought them to, and keeps them in, politics, will express noble sentiments about their devotion to "public service." But "service" is so widely held as the stereotypic response of politicians that it is difficult to discriminate between those who really mean it—who are characterized by that "inner balance and self-feeling" which Weber noted as a condition of living for politics—and those for whom it is only a convenient cliche. Nevertheless, whatever their commitment to public service, more detailed inspection of politicians' responses may be helpful in interpreting this aspect of political-career perspectives.

Table 13 presents three types of response that could be meaningfully coded in the interviews of those who expressed an altruistic-contributive orientation. Some respondents indicated "service" as a goal in the most general terms; others mentioned particular problems they hoped to solve by public service; still others stated more remote ideals as the goals of their political or legislative career. Although no consistent pattern is apparent, some aspects of the distributions in Table 13 may be noted. Tennessee

Table 13

Service and Ideals as Political Goals

Service or Ideals	New Jersey N=21	Ohio N=61	California N=53	Tennessee N=35
Service: general	24%	51%	28%	37%
Service: special	5	5	15	37
Ideals	24	18	30	6

legislators mentioned particular problems as a source of their service more frequently than respondents elsewhere. Possibly the legislator in a one-party system has more opportunities to concern himself with, and do something about, special objectives. California legislators, on the other hand, mentioned ideals somewhat more often than did the other legislators. This finding is in line with an earlier report, that California legislators, in recalling what first attracted them to politics, emphasized ideological beliefs.[25] It may be that political beliefs and ideals play a somewhat more important role in political systems where stable patterns, either of the competitive or one-party type, have not yet crystallized.

Those who mentioned service in general terms would simply say: "I like the idea of service to the people"; or, "well, I don't know what to say, I wanted to be of public service"; or, "there's no use in just arguing about politics, you got to do something about it"; etc. Those interested in serving for the purpose of solving special problems mentioned things like hospital construction, mental health, county roads, revision of welfare laws, child welfare, taxation, school financing, and a miscellany of other matters. A variety of "ideal causes"—liberalism, conservatism, fighting socialism or corruption, doing something about a world in turmoil, and so on—were professed by some respondents as career objectives.

A second category of altruistic-contributive responses referred to the struggle of group interests in the legislature. As Table 14 indicates, only very small proportions of legislators in the four states mentioned "group interests" as central concerns of their legislative-career goals. Business, labor, farmers, and ethnic or religious groups were cited as focuses of career objectives. The following quotations from the interviews convey some of the flavor of this approach:

Table 14

Group Interests as Career Goals

	NEW JERSEY		OHIO		CALIFORNIA		TENNESSEE	
	Dem. N=7	Rep. N=14	Dem. N=25	Rep. N=36	Dem. N=25	Rep. N=28	Dem. N=29	Rep. N=6
Business		7		6		14		
Labor	29	14	20	3	12			
Farmers		7	4	3		7	7	
Ethnic/Religious		7		6	4			

PERCENTAGE DISTRIBUTION OF GROUP INTEREST

A good many people urged me to run, with the argument that the *business* point of view represented in the legislature might be in the public interest. Many problems of legislation are identical with those of business—such as judicious spending of public funds, efficient administration, a clear philosophy of government.

They need people down here—laymen—that will represent the average viewpoint. The legislature needs people that aren't lawyers, that are for the common man. With my training and background in *labor,* I felt I could represent the average viewpoint, I mean the viewpoint of the people that work for a living. I thought I could do something that could better the position of the working man. I had no fancy slogans when I ran; this one thing was all I wanted.

I naturally have a desire to make advances beneficial to my *race.* Money isn't everything, and I'm not here for that. I wanted to make a contribution to this cause. Some must bend their shoulders to bring others up. Whatever I can do to help will be my satisfaction as my reason for being in politics.

I was also interested in maintaining the place of a person of the *Jewish faith,* there are so few of them in public life. . . . The man who held this position before me became a judge. He was of the Jewish faith also, the only one in the legislature. When he resigned there was a vacancy. The head of the Republican Party was looking around, and he suggested that I run. If I hadn't, we would have lost the Jewish seat, and we never would have been able to get it back.

Table 14, which controls the data by party as well as state, sheds light on the possible relationship between party membership and career goals. In the first place, it will be noted that no Democrat in any one of the four states mentioned business interests, while Republicans in New Jersey, Ohio, and California did. Second, more Democrats than Republicans mentioned the interests of labor as a career focus; the few Republicans who did came from New Jersey and Ohio, the two more competitive states. Of course, the numbers are so small that these results must be treated with great caution— although they do correspond to what is generally known about the connection between business and Republicanism and between labor and Democracy.

Finally, service to party or district was mentioned by a number of legislators as a career goal. The following two comments illustrate this orientation:

I wanted to protect the interests of local government.

I wanted to present local views in the legislature, and I don't necessarily mean rural views, to keep local government strong and stable.

I was in some of the local offices and active in the Young Republicans. We decided that no elected position should be lost through default. So I ran for the state legislature.

Table 15 presents the relevant data. No definite pattern emerges, but some aspects of the distributions are suggestive. In the first place, regardless of party affiliation, no New Jersey respondent mentioned service to his district as a career goal. This is somewhat anomalous, since representatives in competitive systems are expected to be particularly sensitive to their constituencies. However, it may be that the interests of district and party are perceived as

Table 15
Service to Party or District as Career Goals

| | NEW JERSEY | | OHIO | | CALIFORNIA | | TENNESSEE | |
| | Dem. | Rep. | Dem. | Rep. | Dem. | Rep. | Dem. | Rep. |
Service to:	N=7	N=14	N=25	N=36	N=25	N=28	N=29	N=6
Party	29%	14%	4%	11%	24%	4%	7%	17%
District			12	11	16	25	10	33

identical. Second, whether or not service to the party is seen as a career goal may depend on the morale of the party. In California, as noted in other connections, the Democratic Party seems to loom much larger in the career perspective of Democrats than the Republican Party does among Republicans. Moreover, where little value is placed on service to party, the district seems to serve as a focus of career goals. California Republicans and Ohio Democrats, both weakly organized at the time, bear this out. Finally, where a party is greatly outnumbered, as in Tennessee, the members of the minority are inclined to place relatively high value on service to their district as a career goal, possibly because their survival as politicians depends on retaining the loyalty of the district. The data suggest that career goals may be related to the roles which the parties play in diffferently structured systems, but they are not reliable enough to support this proposition.

Even fewer respondents in all four states mentioned selfish, exploiting goals. Table 16 presents the distribution of responses according to the categories in which they were coded. Although no pattern is evident, some figures stand out: New Jersey legislators, characteristically, felt that a political or legislative career would enhance, or at least maintain, their political influence; Ohio legislators thought they could gain experience from being in politics; and Tennesseeans were particularly prone to view politics as a pastime or as a way to advance their personal interests. These particular

Table 16
Selfish-Exploitative Career Goals

Percentage Distribution of Goals	New Jersey N=10	Ohio N=27	California N=26	Tennessee N=18
To make money:	20	19	4	
To occupy time—enjoyment:	10	15	31	44
To make useful contacts, get publicity:		22	4	22
To get away from previous occupation:			19	6
To find out about legislature:		7	15	22
To gain experience:		33	8	22
To gain by combining legislative service with occupation, secure laws for personal interest::	20	11	15	56
To maintain/improve own political standing/influence:	50	4	35	6
To meet people, make acquaintances:			4	11

responses are not surprising in terms of what we know about the different states, but they should not obscure the great variety of other selfish-exploitative goals that are apparently linked to the choice of a political career. Some of the interview material will illustrate this diversity.

Some of the respondents who mentioned "living off politics" were quite frank:

Well, the legislature meant income. If you start in the————business from scratch, and I was strictly on commission, the legislative salary helped.

It's getting to be kind of a matter of necessity. I like the income, and this is my only source. I'm dead set against the idea of looking forward to retirement and getting a check from the government. I expect to remain active for quite awhile for I'm completely opposed to the government supporting people.

For the first legislator, the legislative salary is a temporary, supplemental source of income. For the second respondent, it is the sole source. Although coded similarly, their orientations are quite dissimilar.

Another group simply stated that they came to politics or entered the legislature because they had nothing else to do. One respondent said, "when I came out of the navy, I was wholly free; nothing to do, absolutely nothing." These legislators do not seem to have a real commitment to politics as a career. In fact, the political career appears as a last resort to avoid a feeling of social uselessness.

It is widely assumed that for some people politics is an avenue of social or occupational mobility. Those respondents who said that they had sought a political career to make useful contacts or to get publicity—many of them young attorneys—were quite candid:

It was not so much for the political aspect of it. I went into politics really for selfish reasons. I'd been practicing law for less than a year and this is a very good way to become better known in the community. Consequently, that was my initial reason for going into politics.

Well, real frankly, I graduated from law school and couldn't take the bar examination 'til spring. I had no practice to go to. Running for political office seemed expedient. Once again, selfishly speaking, an attorney is prohibited from advertising. I thought it was better to go around meeting people through politics.

Few remarks are worth quoting from those who said they chose a political career because it promised to get them away from their occupation. A number of these respondents echoed the doctor who felt that "politics is a hobby to get relief from the rut of medical practice." Another small group indicated that they became legislators simply because they were curious about the legislature. As one of them put it: "mainly wanting to get my feet wet, to see what it's like." Those who said they chose a legislative career to gain experience were more explicit:

You can learn more of the ground work of politics here than anywhere else except the governorship.

Here you get an idea of problems in all fields, taxes, judiciary. Every young person should have a broad knowledge of all phases. This is a proving ground for young politicians.

Another reason for choosing a legislative career was in order to further one's business interests. One legislator wanted to protect his fishing business; another admitted to a personal interest in a sales-tax refund to service-station operators; a third was particularly interested in legislation affecting the automotive industry. Again, the close connection between law practice and politics was articulated in this connection, as follows:

> While in law partnership, it was decided that I would be the first one in the firm to run for office. I also felt that it would help the firm in general and me in particular to be in the legislative process. . . . So I was then chosen by the senior partners in the firm as having the best chance. . . . I appeared before the county screening committee at a late date, but I was not given full consideration for party backing because they had already chosen a candidate. So I ran as a Democrat, keeping opposition to party candidates at a minimum, and was nominated and elected.

Finally, a few legislators stated that they chose a legislative career because the legislature seemed a promising step to political influence. Some of the relevant remarks have been cited earlier in other connections, but one further comment may illustrate this orientation: "I thought this is a good place to start; it would be beneficial to me personally more than any other political job."

Career Commitment

For most state legislators, the political career is only a part-time occupation. Whatever their reasons for being in politics, neither the time demands of legislative service nor the remuneration for this service are sufficent to exact that degree of commitment which occupational choice usually calls for. Since politics is a sideline, the decision to run for legislative office is not a "big decision," comparable to choosing a nonpolitical occupation or profession.[26] Under certain favorable circumstances it may turn out to have been an important career step, as when it leads to a full-time political or governmental position. However, for most, the state legislature is likely to be a terminal point in their political career.

These observations are commonplace, but they have never been based on solid empirical data. Studies of tenure and turnover of state legislative personnel have been suggestive, but they do not reveal the character of the commitment that is involved in political-career choices.[27] In order to determine just how committed our respondents were to the legislative office they were occupying, we asked them whether they expected to run again for the state legislature.

Table 17 presents the findings. With the single exception, once again, of the California Democrats, the data show a consistent interstate pattern. The more competitive the party system of a state, the greater is the percentage of legislators who expect to run again for their legislative seat. The fact that

Table 17

Expectation to Run for the Legislature

EXPECTATION TO RUN	DEMOCRATS				REPUBLICANS			
	N. J. N=27	Ohio N=51	Cal. N=54	Tenn. N=97	N. J. N=52	Ohio N=111	Cal. N=59	Tenn. N=23
Yes	78%	57%	78%	36%	75%	62%	56%	26%
Don't know, perhaps	15	27	15	42	12	30	36	39
No	7	16	7	22	13	8	8	35
Total:	100%	100%	100%	100%	100%	100%	100%	100%

a relatively large proportion of California Democrats indicated continued commitment to their present office probably reflects their party's organizational strength and morale, already noted earlier. In general, however, the data suggest that politicians in more competitive situations are more inclined to see their legislative career as a continuing enterprise than do legislators in less competitive situations. As the structure of the political system assumes a one-party character, as in Tennessee, the proportion of legislators with a continued commitment is significantly smaller than anywhere else.

If we look at the differences between the two parties in each of the states, another interesting result is apparent. In highly competitive New Jersey, although outnumbered by a ratio of almost two to one, the Democrats do not seem discouraged from seeking the same office again. In fact, a slightly larger percentage of New Jersey Democrats than of Republicans expect to run again. Similarly, Ohio Democrats do not appear to be very much discouraged by their minority status in the legislature. In Tennessee, on the other hand, where the status of the minority party in the legislature is permanent, only a fourth of the Republicans, as against somewhat more than a third of the Democrats, expect to run again, and over a third definitely do not expect to run. In other words, the data suggest that a party's minority status may tend to work against continued candidacy only in a system where its political effectiveness is severely limited. However, as we will later demonstrate, minority status on one level of government—such as the state level—may encourage politicians to seek office on another level, where their party may enjoy more favorable prospects.

Comments spontaneously made by respondents who were not sure that they wanted to run again illustrate the effect of minority status on their commitment. "I don't know," said one legislator; "I consider that prospect with mixed emotions. It's very tough to be elected in my county as a Republican. The breakdown is about 65:35, and I'm a member of the 35 group. That makes it very difficult." Another said: "I'm from a tough district. Right now most of the court houses are Democratic. One county is Republican, but it's too small; you must carry the metropolitan county to win."

One may speculate on the consequences of different career commitments. The degree of commitment is certainly likely to affect legislative deliberation and action. In a state where only about a third of all incumbents expect to return—and regardless of the further possibility that some of these may be defeated in the primaries or election—every session of the legislature will include an inordinately large number of new members with no or little legislative experience. It is likely that the legislature will be dominated by a few old hands with almost oligarchical control over legislative action. On the other hand, a legislature such as that of New Jersey, where three-fourths of the members expect to run again, can more readily be expected to be both a democratic and well-functioning institution.

In spite of the fact that legislative career commitment seems to be related to the competitive or noncompetitive character of the political system and the varying roles played by the parties in different systems, only relatively few respondents in all four states saw their continued incumbency in a political frame of reference. Of the 252 legislators who gave "reasons" for their intention to run again, only 15 per cent mentioned political contingencies, 13 per cent referred to status considerations connected with holding office, and a bare 2 per cent acknowledged a responsibility to their party. The great majority expressed themselves in highly personal terms. Fifty-eight per cent spoke of their "personal involvement" in the legislative job, and 33 per cent indicated a commitment to "public service." Strictly private reasons, economic considerations of a personal character, service to special groups, and what we coded as "apathy" were mentioned by less than 10 per cent.

Moreover, the variations between the states in most of these response categories were very marginal (probably due to the very small number of cases in the categories), and they revealed neither meaningful patterns nor significant differences. Only interstate comparison of respondents who attributed their intention to run again to their "personal involvement" indicates that this consideration may be more salient in the more competitive systems. While 76 per cent of the New Jersey respondents, 63 per cent of the Ohioans, and 58 per cent of the Californians reported "personal involvement," only 35 per cent of the Tennessee legislators did likewise. Evidently, a competitive system calls for greater personal commitment to politics than a less competitive system.

"Involvement" in the legislative office or in politics generally may, of course, mean different things to different legislators. Many would simply say that they enjoy the work or experience in the legislature, that they like the people they come in contact with, or that they feel they are doing a good job. Some of them would like to be legislators full-time or would serve without compensation: "I'd say that this is the service I prefer; I dearly love it. If I had independent means, I'd run without compensation. It's entirely possible that I'll run again." The same sense of personal involvement was expressed by others in more picturesque language:

What else is there that's so nice to do? It gets into your blood and you like it.

I didn't intend to run the last time, but then the bell rings and the old fire horse wants to go.

When the whistle blows I get carried away and decide to run.

I read the other day, "there's nothing lonelier than a retired politician."

Other respondents emphasized the feeling of achievement their office gives them or their increasing experience as sources of their involvement:

It takes more than one term to make yourself felt. The first term seems to be a training period in spite of your familiarity with the routine. I felt that in my position as a————I would have time to do it, but am convinced that I would be better off financially if I had stayed at home. But selfishly I enjoy the work. Now salary helps to soften the financial loss. Before it was so low.

Oh, as I become more familiar with the work and have more experience, it becomes easier for me and I feel more capable. I realize from my experience what it means to the constituents to have a new man on the job. I feel more valuable to my constituents; of course, everyone feels that way. Seniority, for one, and experience are quite a thing.

Interestingly, a few legislators frankly admitted that their commitment to a legislative career was due to their having nothing else to do. These "apathetics" commented:

I'm too old to have aspirations for anything else, too old to step up. Maybe I'm too old to be here now. My aspirations end right here.

I like it. I have nothing else to do. As long as I can serve my county and the state I will continue to run. I'm not doing it for the money, for there was a time when I served here and got only $1,000 and met eight months a year.

You might say that I'm sort of unemployed now and am here for lack of a better job. If I was offered a good appointment that could change my mind. Naturally, then I'd give up the legislature. Any legislator would.

"Public service" is, of course, the rationale by which the politician publicly justifies his devotion to politics. Nevertheless, a deep sense of social responsibility may be a genuine concomitant of the politician's career commitment:

You'd be surprised at the things you can do as a representative. So many people come to you and ask for your help, and then you help your district to get home industry and highways. I find it very satisfying helping all these people.

Because I think I'm doing all right. I represent the people, I have experience, and I'm learning. I should use the experience I have acquired. The people were good to me. They paid for my training, and I should continue to use this training to their advantage by giving service.

Of course, the service motive need not be unrelated to a fascination with the political game. As a financially independent respondent pointed out, "I like to be in on it—each bill is a crossword puzzle and has something wrong with it. I like to find out what's wrong with it." Another said in this connection:

I enjoy being a legislator. I am interested in government and politics. Maybe because I'm a freshman; what may be old stuff to the others is not old to me. I like solving problems with people both at home and here. I feel that I have a job that I like and I want to keep it. I'm certainly not here for the money; but I'm not complaining about the money.

For others, the financial reward of "public service" may not be irrelevant: "I need the money. No, take that out. I have continued interest. I do have an interest in industrial relations and education. I'm interested in all that junk that goes on." In spite of this respondent's disclaimer, the money rather than the "junk" seems to be the more conspicuous motive. Others mentioned particular projects which made them want to seek office again, such as a twelve-month school schedule, strip-mining legislation, a mental-health program, natural-resources conservation, and so on. Continued representation of some group interest was cited by a few respondents as the reason for seeking re-election:

There's a lot to do for the working men. Normally he doesn't have representation. There's a better chance now, having someone who's in the majority party. Usually labor is Democrat. I can do more for them, being a Republican.

There is a need for business people serving in the legislature. The trend is away from professional politicians.

For another group of legislators, career commitment was closely linked with an appreciation of the influence, prestige, or status which they attributed to the legislative role. In particular, seniority was recognized as something worth preserving by seeking re-election:

It would be illogical to stop running now, as in government work it's seniority that counts. Your responsibility increases as the duration of your service is extended. There is no substitute for experience in the legislature, and that's recognized by seniority.

In the following interview, influence derived from politics is seen as committing the politician to his career:

I swear off every year. When you see the possible things that can be done, you always hope that next time you can get rid of your frustrations, that something can be accomplished. When———became governor, we could do things. I have a very strong feeling that in politics you have to take it on your own terms, otherwise you become a hack. There must be standards of accomplishment and goals, not just handshaking. I like being in the main stream of things.

Finally, returning for another term is a "must" for those politicians who view the legislative job as a way station to some more influential political position: "Well, not necessarily in a legislative capacity . . . either in a judicial capacity or a legislative capacity. This may be a springboard for some other office."

A number of respondents made their commitment dependent on such personal matters as the condition of their business, their health, or family considerations. If the legislative career can be harmonized with the incumbent's business affiairs, the commitment may be all the stronger:

I'm interested in it; I enjoy it. I commute from north of here, so there's an opportunity to carry on my practice in the morning at home. It doesn't interfere and probably helps my private business, if anything.

In fact, legislative tenure may be seen as a way of directly safeguarding one's private interest, e.g., the respondent who frankly stated, "I have to protect my fishing business." Finally, the salary itself may be attractive enough to maintain the commitment of some:

> I'll run one more term or as long as the people want me. You know a man of seventy can't find a $5,000-a-year job so easy. It's a good pastime; its educational and interesting.

One should expect that sensitivity to the emerging political situation would be an important factor in legislators' career expectations. Yet, only 15 per cent of our respondents articulated such "political contingencies." As the following comments will suggest, some took a rather passive view, making their own commitment dependent on their being drafted by party committees or guaranteed support by voters. Some of these statements suggest a healthy respect for grass-roots approval. As one respondent said, "it depends on the people. I now have the intention to run, but I can change my mind and will the minute I have an indication the people don't want me"; or another, "well, that's a question. . . . It depends a great deal on the political picture. If I feel people are satisfied. . . ." A third stated:

> I don't know where I stand. My county gets changes of ideas every year. My constituency is becoming more liberal in their thinking. A public office-holder who was doing a good job, they would insist on running for more than two terms.

Some others would make their continued career dependent on the decision of their party to support them again:

> I promised myself that I would stay in the legislature for ten years if I could keep getting elected. This was the only way in which I felt I could do a truly effective job. My ten years will be up at the end of this term. It is up to the party. They may want a younger man to run for the office.

> As long as I'm nominated by the nominating committee of my county, I will run. That is, I don't want to run forever, but I think I would like another term or two.

Just as no meaningful state-to-state pattern characterized the responses of those intending to seek their legislative office again, so no regular pattern was evident in the reasons given for not running again. Moreover, of the 220 respondents, at most a fifth would agree on a particular reason for not running: 20 per cent gave economic considerations; 18 per cent, personal reasons; 13 per cent found the job too demanding; and 12 per cent thought they had served long enough. Some 13 per cent intended not to run again because they were planning to seek another office; 12 per cent mentioned political circumstances. A few felt inadequate in the legislative job, and another few simply said they were bored with it.

The noteworthy aspect of these results is, again, how very few of these state politicians appraised their career in political terms. Most sensitive to political circumstances were, of course, those who were seeking another political office and who felt that another term in the state legislature might show a lack of political ambition:

That is difficult to answer. In five terms I have been presiding officer twice. To my knowledge this honor has been granted to only one other person in the history of this chamber. This office has tremendous responsibility and is very time-consuming. I don't know whether I'll go back. I would like to sit in Congress, but I wouldn't run against the incumbent representative from my district. He is a personal friend. Politics depend on circumstances.

I have been urged to run for Congress, and I must decide whether to stay here or go. I wouldn't have any trouble in getting the Democratic nomination. The congressional and the state senate districts are almost identical and I can get lots of votes. Last time I didn't campaign much, just went to two picnics. I wanted to see if I could get votes without campaigning. But there's one ethic of politics you must always live up to. That is to be a true friend. The present congressman is a very close friend of mine, and if he wants to run, I won't. But he is on the fence, he might be interested in running for governor. If so, I'll probably run for congressman.

One important factor in not seeking re-election, then, is the availability of another position. If a friend occupies a coveted office, the politician is unlikely to seek it, even if he would like to get it. Re-election is also out of question if the legislative seat is subject to rotation in office:[28] "I'm running now, but I doubt that I'll do it again. They usually limit you to two terms. In such a large county it has to be spread around." Some other respondents explained that they were not expecting to run again because they would not receive the necessary electoral support.

As already mentioned, a fifth of the respondents who were not planning to run again suggested that their legislative work adversely affected their private business affairs. The following comments are typical:

I think it's time I devoted myself to my law practice. Being in the legislature has hurt my practice and cost me money. Also, I don't think anyone should make a career of serving in the legislature. You do your part and then make room for the next guy.

Anyway you look at it, the job means a sacrifice to you, your home, and your business. Most people don't realize that there are continual demands on your time outside the legislative sessions as well. I don't intend to make a career of politics.

It depends on business. If it gets bad I won't be able to run. That's the way it is for a businessman. It's different for a lawyer. I can't depend on the pay up here. It doesn't even pay the food bill. I have four children. And the expenses are high—hotel bills and everything.

Apart from losing financially, these legislators find the demands of the legislative job greater than they had perhaps anticipated when they first ran for office. The irritations of politics are expressed in this comment:

It's a big problem. It's a problem of time. Legislative duties are bad enough, but handshaking, dinners, and speeches are the worst part. My phone rang 68 times yesterday. Politicians get a bad break from most newspapers and political scientists. A guy in his right mind wouldn't continue. I'm not going to worry if I get knocked out like these guys who make a complete career of it.

A few legislators felt that they had served long enough and expected not to run again for this reason. But, next to economic reasons, personal —usually family—considerations were given as obstacles to a continuing political career in the legislature:

I recently got married and I'd like to be home. I don't know if I'll ever be a candidate again, but I know I'll always be interested in politics, maybe on the local level.

I don't think I should stay too long. The law is my career. And there are family considerations—being away from them. A political career is too uncertain and hazardous.

Others tended to express unease, discomfort, disappointment, and similar feelings with the legislative career:

You have to take a beating. We have great problems in the party which affects my disposition. This is a very difficult area in which to be humble. That's the worst feature of the whole business.

One gets in the middle of a lot. The more service a man has, the more enemies he makes.

It's a nervous life. Some can just sit it out—maybe they are wise. If somebody awful good ran against me, I'm afraid he wouldn't have much trouble.

We live in strange times. Politics is my avocation, but frustration comes from modern problems—especially modern Republicanism.

Less than a handful of respondents were simply bored with the legislative process. "You can spend too much time here and get stale," said one of them. "There are three types of legislators up here. First, the young fellows who are here to use this position as a stepping stone. Second, the old, semi-retired men who like to be active. And third, those incapable of doing anything else." Another put it this way: "I'm going to retire, I think. I might come back, but I doubt it. After so many years it all becomes routine." Finally, two legislators, both from California, gave "ethical" reasons for their decision to terminate their political career. As one of them put it, "If you want to stay on you have to play footsie with the lobbies and say 'yes' to everybody."

Career Aspirations

At any one point in his career, the politician's perspective consists not only of past recollections, current orientations, and immediate expectations, but also of those more distant aspirations which probably mold a good deal of political behavior. We noted previously that a legislator may not expect to retain his seat due to an intention to seek some other public office. In order to gain a more systematic picture of all respondents' career aspirations—at least as they had crystallized at the time of the interview—we

asked them whether they would like to seek any other political or governmental position at the local, state, or national levels.

On theoretical grounds, we had no reason to expect that aspirations
would follow a pattern geared to the degree of competition in the structure
of the state legislative party system. Aspirations must necessarily refer to
offices in other political subsystems where the party system may be differently
structured. In fact, as Table 18 demonstrates, no clear-cut interstate pattern
predicated on an ordering of the state legislative systems from most to least
competitive structure is discernible. The results, however, are quite explicable.

Table 18

Aspiration for Other Office

	DEMOCRATS				REPUBLICANS			
	N. J. N=27	Ohio N=51	Cal. N=54	Tenn. N=97	N. J. N=52	Ohio N=111	Cal. N=59	Tenn. N=23
Yes	37%	45%	39%	27%	42%	31%	36%	35%
Don't know, perhaps	22	31	24	21	35	25	18	30
No	41	24	37	52	23	44	46	35
Total:	100%	100%	100%	100%	100%	100%	100%	100%

While Ohio Democrats or Tennessee Republicans, by virtue of their minority
status, may be discouraged from returning to the state legislature, they may
be encouraged to seek office at a level where they can expect to feel less
frustrated. For example, they may stand for election in congressional districts,
counties, or municipalities controlled by their parties, or in areas where they
can count on administrative appointments—Tennessee Republicans from
a Republican federal administration, Ohio Democrats from state or local
Democratic executives. But just why the proportion of New Jersey Democrats
with no aspirations differ so markedly from their Republican colleagues with
no aspirations we cannot say.

More insight can be gained from a glance at the kinds of office—i.e., level
of government—that were sought. As Table 19 shows, Ohio Democrats with
career aspirations looked toward federal legislative office (Congress) almost
as much as Ohio Republicans, and Tennessee Republicans did so slightly
more than Tennessee Democrats. Ohio Democrats and Tennessee Republicans
(but also Tennessee Democrats) had their eyes on local executive office, and
Tennessee Republicans apparently felt that local judicial office was not
beyond their reach. Both California Democrats and Republicans, more than
legislators elsewhere, saw state executive office as a goal—which may reflect
the more competitive structure of the gubernatorial and other state-office
subsystems in California. Finally, New Jersey respondents, regardless of party,
seemed to place high value on service in the New Jersey Senate. Reasons for
this were given in the interviews:

Being state senator is as good as you can do in New Jersey in elective office—
better than Congress. I would like to be in Congress if the district were safer. But

Table 19

Kinds of Office and Levels of Aspiration*

PERCENTAGE DISTRI-BUTION OF ASPIRATION	DEMOCRATS				REPUBLICANS			
	N. J. N=15	Ohio N=34	Cal. N=29	Tenn. N=41	N. J. N=32	Ohio N=49	Cal. N=24	Tenn. N=14
Local executive		12	3	17	6	2	4	14
Local legislative	7	9	3	2	13		13	
Local judicial	7	6		12	3	27		21
State executive	13	9	24	10	19	8	25	7
State legislative (other House)	33	18	17	29	34	12	21	21
State judicial	7		17	5	6	4	8	
Federal executive	7		3		3	2		
Federal legislative	40	62	45	32	28	59	42	36
Federal judicial		3						
Mention level but not office; or office but not level	7	15	7	20	13		13	29

*Percentages total more than 100 per cent, since some respondents mentioned more than one office.

you have to be away in Washington and it would not be easy to keep in office.

A lot of people have asked me about Congress, but I don't know. Congress is not a good job. The terms are too short. When you come back you are out of work. You can have more influence as a state senator.

It is not worthwhile to go to Congress for two years unless you are from a safe area. I would be more interested in Congress if it was for a four-year term.

Of the 474 respondents, 155 spontaneously volunteered some explanation of why they might seek another office. Almost half of these—46 per cent—expressed some desire for personal advancement or simply admitted to being ambitious. Almost as many—42 per cent—pointed out that political mobility depended a great deal on the availability of positions, on the kind of competition that could be expected, or on particular circumstances, such as the retirement or death of incumbents—in short, on "opportunities." Ten per cent indicated some sensitivity to political difficulties that might prevent them from fulfilling their ambitions, and 8 per cent referred to their ability or experience as grounds of their aspirations. Only 2 legislators out of the 155 mentioned a special goal they hoped to reach by running for another office. And there were, of course, a miscellany of other comments (10 per cent).

Comparison of these explanations with those given for legislators' commitment to their state legislative career reveals the greater sensitivity of these politically ambitious men to the complexities of political life. Many of the remarks suggest that in a democratic society political aspirations are severely circumscribed by the exigencies of political circumstance. The politically ambitious must be able to seize the "breaks" and adjust to the discontinuities of the political process. There must be the "right opportunity" or "right situation"; there must not be too much opposition; money and backing are requisites of success; the incumbent's plans must be taken into account; even God may enter the picture. The following interview remarks elaborate these points:

I'd say that about 90 per cent of political decisions depend on circumstances. Some have the opportunity. You don't altogether make an opportunity, you avail yourself of it.

There's one thing in politics—you have to take advantage of opportunities. The timing is important. But unless you have the money or backing you have difficulty to make your own opportunity.

It would depend on the possibility of getting the job at the particular time. If the other fellow I'd be running against seemed to have most of the backing from the people and the press, then I'd by-pass it for a time.

None are open in the present set-up, as the state senator and the congressman are Republicans. I would run if the opportunity presented itself. Politics, like a business, is run on seniority. It is very difficult to upset an incumbent. With the endorsement system, even if you think you are better than some in the higher echelon, there's not much you can do.

Oh, I keep an open mind. If the opportunity comes, I wouldn't be averse to it. You should be ready to meet the breaks. I don't beat the drums, but I believe that if one is qualified, the opportunity comes.

I'd like to be—I'm interested in the judicial branch, federal judge. You can't sit down and make out a schedule; people and time enter into it. You can't plan your whole life; God enters into it.

A number of respondents further emphasized some of the political difficulties that they anticipated: the strength of the opposition party, factionalism in one's own party, troubles in finding financial support, and the qualities of the immediate opponent were cited as obstructions to a smooth political career:

I plan to try for a county office when I'm through here. Of course I'd like to serve in Congress, but there's no chance of that with all the Republicans in my district. That is the same reason why I've never aimed for anything like mayor or governor, and they have too much strain anyhow.

I'd like to run for Congress. But I'll stay here until the time is ripe. The difficulty is that I'm a Republican from a Democratic congressional district. It will be difficult to win. I have to wait for the right time and the right opposition. Maybe next year. If I were a Democrat I could win now, I think.

Well, Congress is a vague possibility. At present I'm not too much interested in the congressional picture as things look in my district. As you get into larger positions, you got to have support. If you can't get it, it's foolish to try on your own. You have got to know how the cards are played. A fellow named————in my district has run every time and never has won a primary. When it comes to the votes, he just can't make it. Most men who run for Congress have quite a bit of finance or moneyed interests that support them. Since our congressional district has changed, considerable division has developed in the Republican ranks. There are old factions, and until some of the old-timers die out, regardless of peace overtures, underlying feelings have not yet healed.

On the other hand, some respondents would ignore political opportunities or difficulties altogether, simply stating their ambitions or justifying their aspirations by referring to their abilities and experience:

I'm conceited enough to think that I could fill another job better than some of the people now in them. There's nothing at the moment that I'm considering, but it has been suggested to me that I run for the state senatorship from my district. The job pays exactly the same, but you have the additional advantage of being called a senator.

I have the hope, I would like to be, mayor of my home town. I have served on the national and state level, and now I would like the challenge of local affairs. I have no desire for federal office now.

Some day I'd like to think about the governor's cabinet. Before this time I was in the army, I worked for the Division of Motor Vehicles, and so I have some experience in that line.

How little policy goals apparently enter the aspiring politician's frame of reference as he contemplates the future is especially noteworthy. That objectives could be related to career aspirations is illustrated by this comment:

The counties are getting so big that they'll have to consolidate many of their township departments under one county head. For example, all the sewage and water supply departments will have to come under one county commissioner. I'd like to run for that position.

Ninety-three respondents gave some explanations of why they intended to terminate their political career with their present job. Of these, 37 per cent said they simply preferred their state legislative seat to anything else. Twenty-three per cent denied having any political aspirations. Others gave business or occupational and personal reasons. Some 11 per cent referred to political difficulties. A few—only three, in fact—gave strictly political reasons: they said they preferred their current office because it could best serve their political interests. The following excerpts from the interview protocols illustrate why service in the state legislature may be preferred:

Operating a newspaper and being in the state legislature is as close to the people as you can get. I wouldn't take two seats in Washington for my position here.

In fact, the state senatorship is better than Congress—if you are interested in legislation and not in doing errand-boy work. You get a greater sense of accomplishment. Congressmen, at least many of them, live a dog's life in running errands.

Those respondents who frankly admitted that they did not have any political ambitions generally settled the matter in a few words: "I don't want anything but this"; or, "I have no political ambition whatever"; or, "politics is a hobby, not a career." Those who felt that another office would interfere with their private career in business or occupation were somewhat more explicit:

To hold any other political office would mean either giving up, or making a radical change in, my practice, which I am unwilling, and cannot afford, to do.

I have been with my firm seventeen years. I'd lose the job because it wouldn't allow for a full-time political job.

I feel like I would like to run some day for something higher, such as Congress. But I have to weigh what it would do to my law practice. I have a problem, I'm not in a good law association. I might lose a lot of professional fees. I might have to get out on my own. It would be wonderful to go into politics if I had a good partner. I hate to give up my law practice. I'll try to work things out. The next step may be running for the [state] senate. It all depends on circumstances.

Others mentioned age, ill health, or family problems as reasons for their lack of further political aspirations. Those who referred to political difficulties did not differ much from those who were not constrained on that account from aspiring to another office.

Conclusion

The data concerning state legislator's career patterns and perspectives reported in this study were ordered on the basis of a hunch: that while, in democratic pluralistic societies, political recruitment patterns are related to social stratification, political career patterns and accompanying career perspectives are likely to be shaped by the structure of the political system—the structural index employed being the particular degree of party competition. This hunch was not translated into particular research hypotheses; at the time the study was designed, neither appropriate theory nor empirical data were available to formulate such hypotheses. Rather, the notion that career patterns and perspectives will vary with the degree and kind of competition between the parties was used as a device to arrange and interpret the data in a meaningful fashion. The open-ended character of some of the questions resulted in a great variety of responses and reduced the number of cases in the analytical categories so that statistical analysis is difficult; nevertheless, the over-all patterns show enough internal consistency to support at least the plausibility of the guiding assumption.

It seems desirable, therefore, to pull together, if only as *post facto* hypotheses, those findings that suggest viable propositions. Hopefully, future research will test these propositions more fully and systematically, as well as integrate them into a more complete theoretical schema. There is enough reason to believe that they constitute a theoretical cluster of considerable significance for political behavior.

The more competitive the structure of the political-party system, the more likely it is that:

1) state legislators will have had some prior governmental experience,

on the local level and in a legislative or quasi-legislative capacity;

2) state legislators will have held party office or done party work at the local level;

3) state legislators will view the political party as a sponsor of their legislative careers;

4) state legislators will appreciate the opportunity given them by the political party in promoting their candidacies;

5) state legislators will not perceive interest groups and/or friends as agents sponsoring their careers;

6) state legislators will value the possession of particular skills thought relevant to a political career;

7) state legislators will have legal training and skills;

8) state legislators will not see opportunities to combine their private and political careers;

9) state legislators will not stress "opportunity" in general as a factor facilitating their careers;

10) state legislators will not look upon their political careers as a means for achieving personal—selfish and/or altruistic—goals;

11) state legislators will be committed to their legislative careers insofar as they plan to run for their seat again;

12) state legislators will attribute their continued commitment to their legislative careers to their "personal involvement" in the legislative job.

In addition, our data have suggested that varying degrees of a particular party's organizational strength and morale—apart from the structure of the party system as such—may be an important factor affecting career patterns and perspectives. The better organized the party, the more prominent it is likely to be in legislators' careers and outlooks. Party organizational strength and morale is probably related to the degree of competition between the parties, but, as the case of the California Democrats indicates, it may also operate independent of it.

Underlying our study was, of course, the assumption that the politician's career course and perspectives are circumscribed by his sense of reality, i.e., his cognitive sensitivity to political circumstances as they really are. Although a good many respondents referred directly to those political conditions and contingencies that might affect their careers, the data are not altogether satisfactory in this respect. In their spontaneous answers to our questions, respondents were more likely to mention aspects of their careers which were either wholly nonpolitical, or those which could be interpreted as politically relevant only indirectly in connection with the major analytical theme of this study. We do not know what questions that were more directly political might yield. It is likely that this line of investigation would prove fruitful.

Finally, it must be pointed out that the structure of a party system, measured by aggregated election results, constitutes a very gross variable; in consequence, deviations from hypothetical patterns may be a function of the raw character of the interstate analysis undertaken here. Tentative as the findings are, even this type of relatively macro-cosmic analysis suggests the worthiness of further research along more detailed lines, making use of more directed questions and of improved indexes for measuring party competition and discipline in given political systems.

Notes

1. This study was made possible by grants from the Political Behavior Committee of the Social Science Research Council. Neither the Committee nor the Council is responsible for the study. The senior author also wishes to express his gratitude to the Center for Advanced Study in the Behavioral Sciences, whose superb facilities he enjoyed during a year's residence in 1957-58, and again as a visitor in 1959-60. Aid for the study was also received from the other authors' institutions and connected agencies: Mr. Buchanan, University of Southern California and Legislative Internship Program, University of California (Berkeley); Mr. Ferguson, Bureau of Social and Political Research and All-University Research Fund, Michigan State University; Mr. Wahlke, Institute for Research in the Social Sciences, Vanderbilt University. In expressing our gratitude to these institutions for their support, we wish also to absolve them from responsibility for the findings and interpretation.

2. Donald R. Matthews, *The Social Background of Political Decision-Makers* (Garden City: Doubleday and Company, 1954), examines some of the theoretical assumptions and empirical implications of speculative and research writings that are concerned with the relationship between political institutions and the structure of society.

3. One could list here a great many studies; an excellent bibliography is available in Harold D. Lasswell, Daniel Lerner, and C. Easton Rothwell, *The Comparative Study of Elites* (Stanford: Stanford University Press, 1952), pp. 43-72.

4. Richard C. Snyder, in his introduction to Matthews, *op. cit.,* p. iv, has summarized these questions: "Does the decision-maker's socio-economic status and previous life experience make any difference in the way he looks at policy problems? in the social groups he will listen to and agree with? Are certain strata of the population over-represented or under-represented because decision-makers do or do not share their basic characteristics? What kinds of people enter politics? What kinds are predominantly successful? Are everyone's chances of a political career roughly equal? Are decision-makers recruited from all citizens who have the requisite ability, or are some excluded? Is the balance of power and influence among various groups reflected in the social composition of the decision-makers? Do the most high-ranking social groups dominate the decision-maker roles? Does the social status of the government official have anything to do with who has access to him?"

5. See, for instance, the Hoover Institute Studies by Robert C. North, *Kuomintang and Chinese Communist Elites* (1952); George K. Schueller, *The Politbureau* (1951); Maxwell E. Knight, *The German Executive, 1890-1933* (1952); and Daniel Lerner, *The Nazi Elite* (1951).

6. This lack was recently noted by Avery Leiserson, who comments that "there are few satisfactory, systematic studies of political career patterns," and who, generously, refers to the familiar elite studies as "approximations." *Parties and Politics* (New York: Alfred A. Knopf, 1958), p. 200, fn. 3.

7. See Morris Janowitz, "The Systematic Analysis of Political Biography," *World Politics,* VI (1954), 405-12.

8. See, however, a recent study by Robert M. Rosenzweig, "The Politician and the Career in Politics," *Midwest Journal of Political Science,* I (1957), 163-72. The data in this study come from interviews with only sixteen candidates for public office in western Massachusetts and are hardly systematic.

9. See, for instance, the model presented by Hugh A. Bone, *American Politics and the Party System* (New York: McGraw-Hill, 1949), p. 740. After

pointing out that political careers do not follow as definite patterns as careers in the professions or even in business or farming, Bone writes: "There are fairly definite steps, however, which the great majority of persons in politics today have taken. It becomes essential in most communities for the citizen to be an active party member, a ward or district leader, or a committee member. From here the individual may work up through the ranks to obtain a nomination for a lesser local office, the state legislature, and so on, possibly to Congress." Most other recent texts are more cautious: a survey of some ten books in the field of parties and politics, published in the last ten years, shows that they simply and, in view of the lack of research evidence, rightly ignore the matter of political careers.

10. See Harold D. Lasswell, "The Selective Effect of Personality on Political Participation," in Richard Christie and Marie Jahoda (eds.), *Studies in the Scope and Method of "The Authoritarian Personality"* (Glencoe, Ill.: The Free Press, 1954), p. 221: "Consider the United States, which can be described as a great (indeed a giant) power in the arena of world politics, possessing relatively democratic institutions so that the active decision making elite in government is selected by procedures in which a large part of the community is involved and must be taken into account."

11. See Edmund H. Volkart (ed.), *Social Behavior and Personality—Contributions of W. I. Thomas to Theory and Social Research* (New York: Social Science Research Council, 1951), esp. pp. 1-32.

12. Everett C. Hughes, "Institutional Office and the Person," in *Men and Their Work* (Glencoe, Ill.: The Free Press, 1958), p. 63.

13. For the notion of developmental pattern, see Heinz Eulau, "H. D. Lasswell's Development Analysis," *Western Political Quarterly*, XI (1958), pp. 229-42.

14. See the classic study by Sir Lewis Namier, *The Structure of Politics at the Accession of George III* (2d ed.; London: Macmillan & Co., 1957), pp. 2-4: "Predestination: The Inevitable Parliament Men."

15. There can, of course, be significant exceptions: additional training, excellent performances, and cumulative experience may facilitate promotion beyond originally anticipated limits of bureaucratic advancement. See Arthur W. MacMahon and John D. Millett, *Federal Administrators* (New York: Columbia University Press, 1939).

16. These are the words of Joseph A. Schlesinger, in a research proposal entitled "A Description and Analysis of Movement between Political Offices in the States."

17. Matthews, *op. cit.,* p. 59, comments: "Curiously enough, a major gap in the facts concerns the *political career patterns* of decision-makers. For the United States, especially, it would be useful to know the usual pattern or sequence of public offices leading to the Presidency or Congress and whether or not there are differences between political career patterns in one-party or two-party areas, between the career patterns of Democrats and Republicans, and so on. Questions such as these have yet to be systematically explored."

18. It should be pointed out that the problem of legislators' career patterns and perspectives was only peripheral to our main research interest—the analysis of state legislatures as political role systems. We did not intend to collect as full a set of data as might be desirable in a comprehensive study. The study of political careers could be the subject of a full-scale research project in its own right.

19. The following questions were preceded by another: "How did you become interested in politics? What is your earliest recollection of being interested in it?" The findings have been reported in Heinz Eulau, William Buchanan, LeRoy Ferguson, and John C. Wahlke, "The Political Socialization of American State Legislators," *Midwest Journal of Political Science, III* (1959), 188-206.

20. This question was preceded by another: "Just what clinched your decision to go into politics yourself?"

21. Because of technical difficulties, "competition in district" had to be *severally* defined in the four states on the basis of past election returns. Space limitations prevent us from reporting here

the criteria that were used. They may be obtained from the authors.

22. For the conception of the "political escalator," which may be boarded or left at various levels, see Lester G. Seligman, "Recruitment in Politics," *PROD*, I (1958), 14-17. Seligman believes that "though points of entry are multiple, the state legislature is the most common port of entry." Our data suggest that the model may be most appropriate in the less competitive systems.

23. See Francis Carney, *The Rise of the Democratic Clubs in California* (New York: Henry Holt and Company, 1958), p. 16: "The Democrats function now more effectively as a party within the legislature. Assemblyman William Munnell of Los Angeles, minority floor leader and chairman of the assembly Democratic caucus, and other CDC leaders agree that Democratic legislators elected after 1952 are more party conscious, vote together as a group, and appear willing to make the caucus a binding agency. These legislators are CDC and club men more often than not. Many owe their nominations and elections to CDC endorsement. They are committed to the idea of party responsibility in the legislature and some of the younger ones are willing to devote time to party work."

24. Max Weber, "Politics as a Vocation," in H. H. Gerth and C. Wright Mills (eds.), *From Max Weber: Essays in Sociology* (New York: Oxford University Press, 1946), p. 84.

25. Eulau *et al., op. cit.,* p. 205.

26. For the notion of occupational choice as a "big decision," see Morris Rosenberg, *Occupations and Values* (Glencoe, Ill.: The Free Press, 1957), pp. 1-9.

27. These studies have been pioneered by Charles S. Hyneman. See his "Tenure and Turnover of Legislative Personnel," *Annals of American Academy of Political Science,* CVC (1938), 21-31.

28. These rotational arrangements should be distinguished from the "floterial" agreements characteristic of some Tennessee politics: these are agreements among the county party leaders (now almost exclusively within the Democratic Party), whereby the nomination for representative or senator in multi-county districts is rotated from one county to another by some fixed schedule. Where such agreements apply, voters in only one county (the county whose turn it is to make the nomination) vote for nominations to the seat in the primaries. Party leaders in the other counties live up to the agreement by seeing to it that no names appear for nomination to the seat on their county's primary ballot. Obviously, the value of such an agreement depends on the extent of party competition in the district, and these agreements are found only in one-party districts.

Agenda for the Study of Political Elites

by HAROLD D. LASSWELL

CONTEMPORARY studies of elite phenomena in politics are enormously diversified in conception and procedure. The field has abounding intellectual vigor, despite, or because of, its conspicuous lack of elegant intellectual unity. The present review of recent developments is selective rather than exhaustive and emphasizes variety. After glancing at the literature having to do with the history of elite studies themselves, we will move to developmental constructs which envisage the past-future sequence of elite transformation. We next examine systematic investigations of elite systems, and conclude by considering studies that deal with the strategies by which elites are protected or broken up. The latter section is directly pertinent to the policy problems confronting the defenders or the enemies of any particular elite structure.

Precursors of Elite Analysis

Perhaps the outstanding contribution to the study of texts of historical importance is Franz Rosenthal's translation from the Arabic of Ibn Khaldun's *The Muquaddimah, an Introduction to History*.[1] Ibn Khaldun (1332-1406) was a scholar and statesman who came from a long line of scholars and statesmen. Toynbee's praise for the *Muquaddimah* has given new prominence to a thinker who deliberately made the transition from history to science. The treatise is full of general propositions that are pertinent to the political and social science of any epoch or that can be stripped of localisms and readily generalized. Modern investigators will be struck by the stress upon "group feeling" as a factor in power. Ibn Khaldun is sensitive to styles of civilization—especially of desert nomads and sedentary city dwellers—and examines royal power in detail. His propositions include the following samples:

Royal authority and large dynastic power are attained only through a group and group feeling.[2]

Religious propaganda gives a dynasty at its beginning another power in addition to that of the group feeling it possessed as the result of the number of its supporters.[3]

When the natural tendencies of the royal authority to claim all glory for itself and to obtain luxury and tranquillity have been firmly established, the dynasty approaches senility.[4]

Prestige lasts four generations in one lineage.[5]

The vanquished always want to imitate the victor in his distinctive mark[s], his dress, his occupation, and all other conditions and customs.[6]

Ibn Khaldun covers a tremendous range of topics, including the role of various skill groups. For instance, he offers useful generalizations about men of "the pen" and "the sword." It would be worthwhile to take systematic inventory of Ibn Khaldun's hypotheses and to prepare a guide to available evidence confirming, disproving, or limiting their application. So far as that goes, similar inventories need to be made of Kautilya and many other scholars whose work is studded with general propositions that are amenable to inquiry.

Among recent monographic studies of landmark figures is James H. Meisel's *The Myth of the Ruling Class: Gaetano Mosca and the "Elite."*[7] Meisel traces three versions of Mosca's theory and translates the final statement into English.[8] Mosca wrote: "Today, a whole new method of political analysis . . . stud[ies] the formation and organization of that ruling stratum which in Italy is by now generally known by the name of *political class*—an expression which together with the term *elite,* used by Pareto, begins to find international acceptance."[9]

Mosca's conception is not difficult to apply to social systems where great differences of rank prevail, or to regimes that are ascendant by the overt use of force. However, when the attempt is made to identify an elite in a highly diversified modern nation where the tradition of popular government is strong, political scientists frequently disagree.

Shall we say, with C. Wright Mills,[10] that the power class of the United States is composed of the top decision-makers of civil government, the military, and business? Shall we agree with the many writers who deny that the United States possesses a ruling class on one or more of the following grounds? (a) Important decisions are not, in fact, made or executed by a sufficiently restricted body of decision-makers to justify the use of the term "elite." (b) Top decision-makers do not stay in control positions long enough to justify the designation. (c) Top figures do not share a common consciousness of identity. (d) They do not act together with sufficient cohesion to protect their current position or to control the selection of successors. (e) They do not act covertly (conspiratorially) to maintain and extend their control. (f) They compete with one another for the popular support which they are not able to obtain by traditional obedience or by the use of coercion. (The many pressure groups and other private-interest associations are strong enough to prevent any one version of the past or future from monopolizing the mass and special media of communication.) (g) The members of the body politic, no matter how indifferent or critical they may be at any given moment, expect to be able to make themselves effective in the decision-making process whenever they become genuinely involved, which is frequently enough to keep the expectation alive.[11]

When we turn to Mosca for guidance, it is with disappointing results. In common with other elite analysts of his generation and earlier, Mosca did not consider it his obligation to specify the indexes of his key terms in the detail required for contemporary research on great administrative structures, public and private. Today, we are in the midst of hammering out agreement, or agreed-upon differences, in all these matters.

Developmental Constructs[12]

Contemporary research has been visibly affected by hypotheses concerning the possible sequence of significant past-future elite developments.

Stripped of dogmatic affirmations, Marx and Engels remain the progenitors of the most influential hypotheses about the "from what—toward what" of our historical epoch. In elite terms, the past was dominated by elites selected on a narrow social basis; the future is to be a free man's commonwealth, where social mobility prevails and the whole community participates in politics on equal terms. More specifically, the elites of the land-holding nobility or the owners of industrial instruments of production are to be superceded by elites chosen on a democratic basis by electorates no longer divided by great discrepancies in their control over the means of production. During the transition, of course, the proletariat seizes power and, exercising a monopoly of coercion, liquidates the survivors of past classes, while defending and advancing the socialist cause against foreign counterrevolutionaries. Today, it is apparent that the dictatorship at the world revolutionary center —Moscow—has not passed away, as was the early expectation. At the same time, the unanticipated vitality of capitalistic systems has kept private ownership and management alive, while enlarging the governmental sector of the economy to whatever degree has seemed opportunistically necessary. Absorption of the older nation-states by the projected universal system of socialist states—and societies—has not occurred.

Alternative constructs owe much to Marx and Engels. In some ways the most challenging is the hypothesis originated by a Polish revolutionary many decades ago:[13] that the key to our epoch is the rise of the intellectual whose capital is his knowledge and who appeals to whatever disaffected elements are present in the social context. The intellectual organizes civil bureaucracies or professionally educated officers' corps or trade union bureaucracies; through them he subtly conquers all in the name of merit, as attested by schooling and administrative service.[14] The recent rise of the scientist and engineer[15] and of the managerial type,[16] coupled with changes in technology, has tended to confirm the idea that manual toilers are obsolete social formations, alongside large estate-holders or absolute owners of industrial property.[17] The intellectuals—educated specialists on symbols relating to nature and society—are unmistakably forging ahead.

An indirect indication of the potency of the elite of knowledge is the growth of tension among intellectual skill groups and the attention given to developmental constructs foreseeing the rise and relative dominance of this or that formation. Continued international and internal crises have provided favorable conditions for specialists on violence, whether belonging to the armed services or the political police.[18] Crisis also works to the advantage of agitators—the demagogues stressed by Pareto[19]—in conjunction with the organizers of mass parties, pressure associations, and official administration. The hypotheses mentioned earlier that relate to scientists, engineers, and managers are expressions of the same implicit sense.

In broadest outline, the "garrison state" construct is simply that specialists on violence will be favored by the chronic expectation of large-scale violence, and by the demands of all who are identified with world-power units to maintain or extend their positions. Rising armament expenditure carries with it centralization, governmentalization, and increased consultation of the military in reference to a widening range of decision. Apprehension of foreign subversion leads to an expanded political police, who begin by reporting intelligence concerning the "loyalty" of actual or potential occupants of positions regarded as important. Security considerations cut down popular access to key facts and interpretations needed to form an intelligent public judgment of national policy. Despite many oscillations, the trend is toward concentrating more effective control and formal authority in the hands of professionally trained specialists on military and political police skills.

This is a long-run construct; investigators have directed attention to several relevant trends which appear to confirm or disconfirm the projected line to date.[20] In the United States, the tremendous rise in national productivity has made it possible to carry huge military expenditures without cutting consumption or reducing outlays for housing, public health and education, highways, and "civilian" activities generally. No doubt potential outlays have suffered, but in dollar terms expenditures have not gone down. Although the international crisis has continued, it has not culminated in drastic peaks of military control. A continuing stream of information about trends in the Soviet world keeps alive the hope that as the Soviet Union becomes industrialized and creates more "middle-income-skill" formations, world tension will be abated by consent.

Among the many factors pointing directly toward militarization are the emergence of new technologies—missiles, space flight—that require vast outlays, and the imminent prospect that nuclear weapons will cease to be monopolized by Moscow and Washington. Whatever the affirmations of the desirability of ending the present armament race, however, the race is still on.

An important point related to the "garrison" hypothesis is that the modern scientific and technological revolution is abolishing the forms of training that created a distinctively "military" or "political policeman's mentality."[21] Hence, even if we grant the likelihood that professionally trained officers will play a decisive role, we must evaluate the possibility that the transformation in their value demands, expectations, and identifications will be so far-reaching that they will bear no resemblance to the traditional stereotype of a soldier or a policeman. Possibly, the man of the sword will be civilized and humanized in outlook; he may even discover a humanistic element in his own tradition that confirms his self-sacrificial and blood-conserving responsibility as a professional man.

The Systematic Study of Elite Systems

We turn now from the direct consideration of developmental constructs to studies which attempt to discover the important variables composing an elite system and the patterns by which they are interrelated.

FOLK-SOCIETY ELITE ADJUSTMENTS TO CIVILIZATIONS

Two closely connected sets of facts have influenced the course of research upon elite-formation within what have historically been known as savage or primitive or tribal societies, but which are now known more commonly among social scientists as folk societies. One great fact is the restless self-assertion exhibited among the folk peoples everywhere—notably in Asia, Africa, and the Pacific. The other is the rapid upsurge of social anthropology, which is itself an expression by the civilizations of their sense of being threatened.

Modern research has been provided with a timely map of the history of man's culture, a map that makes it possible to put specific investigations into fruitful relation to all others. Contemporary archeologists, working closely with anthropologists and historians, have focused upon the crucial significance of the urban revolution that can be dated from about 5000 B.C., notably in the valley of the Tigris-Euphrates. I shall select only a few of the points made by V. Gordon Childe in his theoretical image of the civilized life made possible by the invention of cities:[22]

(a) great increase in the size of settlement since material equipment for human association became far larger; (b) the institution of tribute or taxation with resulting central accumulation of capital; (c) monumental public works;

(d) the art of writing; (e) the beginnings of exact and predictive sciences, such as arithmetic, geometry, and astronomy; (f) the growth of economic institutions and the expansion of foreign trade; (g) full-time technical specialists, notably in metal working; (h) a privileged ruling class; (i) the invention of the State, defined as the organization of society on the basis of residence in place of, or even on top of, a basis of kinship.

What was man like before civilization? To some extent we can learn this by direct observation of the isolated folk societies least affected by the great innovation:

(a) the community was small; (b) communities were isolated from one another; (c) only one mould of culture was permitted in any community; (d) the members had a strong sense of group solidarity; (e) on the whole, men shared in the same essential knowledge, practiced the same arts of life, had the same interests and experiences; (f) the relationships among people were primarily those of personal status; (g) the groupings of people depended on status and role, and were by no means in terms of practical usefulness; (h) the original human society was one of kinsmen.

The late Robert Redfield generalized the foregoing contrast by saying that civilizations are technical orders; folk societies are moral orders. "It is the urban community that rests upon mutual usefulness. The primitive and precivilized communities are held together essentially by common understandings as to the ultimate nature and purpose of life."[23]

Political scientists are especially concerned with the changes in legal and political systems that have come about during typical phases in the relationship between folk societies and the encircling environment of civilizations. Leaving to one side the total demolition of folk units that has frequently occurred and referring only to those transitions made with minimum disruption of personnel, we observe several gradations. At one end, the peasant village can be recognized as a distinct new form of social life. The essential feature is that it is incorporated within a larger social whole of which it is aware, however fantastic the image may be. At the other end, which lies near the self-absorption of the "perfect type" of folk society, we can distinguish the communities that do not permit outsiders to stay overnight but which develop an external accommodation elite. Typically, as among the Pueblo villages of the southwestern United States, a "governor" *(cacique)* is named at the demand of outside authorities. The effective power-holders usually do not, at least at first, perform the contact role, since they feel least vulnerable when invisible as targets of outside pressure.

During the interplay with the surrounding civilized environment, a conflict almost invariably develops between members of a folk society who do, and those who do not, have enough outside contacts to acquire sentimental or calculated interests in modernization. The outcome depends especially upon the degree of support that "progressives" or "conservatives" are able to get from outsiders. In the United States, we have adopted a policy intended to preserve what is left of the folk societies. The result is to turn the scales against the younger generation of returned veterans who preferred progress.[24]

ELITE ADJUSTMENTS AMONG PREINDUSTRIAL CIVILIZATIONS

Ancient civilizations such as China and India, had been in long contact with one another prior to the appearance of modern science and technology, with its disrupting accompaniment of nationalism and democracy and related doctrine, formulae, and folklore. Some ancient civilizations have been in advance of others in adopting new modes of life, and immigrants from a relatively modern area carry the new into the precincts of the old. Presently, however, the people may "wake up" as a result of partially incorporating the modern pattern, and conflicts occur.

A study of such a situation has been made with exemplary skill in elite analysis by G. William Skinner, in *Leadership and Power in the Chinese Community of Thailand.*[25] This part of Skinner's research called for a detailed examination of the changes internal to the Chinese population of Bangkok. During the first six months in the field, a file was begun which included any Chinese who appeared to have a claim to leader or elite status. Newspapers, business directories, and publications by private associations were utilized. Informants—especially staff members of organizations—were interviewed. A provisional list was then drawn up and submitted individually to Chinese judges, balanced primarily by political leaning and speech group. The top 135 in the original list were chosen, and all but five were interviewed directly. The leaders were classified primarily according to the base values on which they depended for leadership.

Thus, leaders may depend upon: (1) all-around influence; (2) political mandate; (3) economic control—commensurate prestige, wealth, and politico-economic power, but significantly less political authority; (4) economic political authority—banking prestige and political control commensurate with wealth; (5) standing—commensurate wealth and prestige, with low political authority and politico-economic power; (6) prestige—respect disproportionate to all other values; (7) wealth alone; or (8) formal power—wealth and prestige not commensurate with number and importance of offices. It was found "that leaders classed together according to the comparative possession of different aspects of the key values are likely to be similar in social characteristics."[26]

As a means of exhibiting power structure, the interlocking officerships of all associations in the Chinese community were analyzed. An examination was also made of the interlocking directorates uniting Chinese business corporations. "The fact is that Chinese political and business structures in Bangkok, when defined in terms of leader positions, are not only interdependent but virtually inseparable."[27]

Skinner goes on to discuss the group of leaders who,

by virtue of their interrelations in commercial enterprises and nonprofit community organizations constitute important loci or clusters of influence. On the basis of common memberships, these clusters of leaders are then shown to be related more or less closely to one another and are grouped in blocks, each held together by a 'key leader.' The blocs in turn are tested for structural interrelatedness and, on the basis of formal criteria, are shown to be either isolated or united with one another to form one or more structures descriptive of power positions and potential in the Chinese leadership corps.[28]

Not only was it possible to study the structure of the community in 1952, but a follow-up in 1955 exposed the dynamic shifts during a period in which substantial deprivations were inflicted upon the Chinese by the Thailanders, who were using their new political initiative to advance themselves by curbing the Chinese. Leadership turnover rates were computed for the three-year period and annually.

Skinner's conclusions include the following:

... it is extremely noteworthy that for the 1955 series of 185 influential leaders, as for the 1952 series, each part of the hypothesis of value agglutination ... was proved.[29]

The very logic of population dynamics and leader recruitment promises a Chinese leadership corps in Thailand increasingly weighted with 'leaders from the periphery.' If present trends are continued, these leaders and their families will eventually be entirely lost to Chinese society in Thailand. Following the example of their leaders, and weakened by their defection, the entire Chinese community will inevitably move more rapidly toward complete assimilation to Thai society.[30]

ORIENTAL DESPOTISMS

Karl A. Wittfogel's *Oriental Despotism: A Comparative Study of Total Power*[31] is one of the most exhaustive investigations ever made of elite formation. The fundamental hypothesis is broadly Marxist: it connects, on the one side, control of the large aggregates of fixed and specialized capital required to achieve the productive potential of a given technology with, on the other side, the formation of a narrow ruling class which is largely self-perpetuating and relies upon coercive strategies of control. The particular question is one of an agrarian economy largely dependent upon water control. The productivity of the hydraulic economy depends primarily upon the skill with which irrigation and flood control installations are assembled, kept up, and managed. Central control has the advantage of enabling accumulation of the knowledge and capital needed for original investment, maintenance, and protection. Based upon productivity, great administrative hierarchies proliferate, evolving a technique that relies upon comprehensive and rapid influx of intelligence and rapid execution of central decisions. The surpluses, above the minimum requirements to maintain the labor force and the engineering works, are available for the embellishment of capital cities. They are also used to encourage craftsmen and other skill specialists for the edification of a top elite. The following captions selected from the table of contents indicate many of the points developed which link the refinements of elite structure with the society as a whole:

A State Stronger Than Society ...
Despotic Power—Total and Not Benevolent
Total Terror—Total Submission—Total Loneliness
The Rulers

1. The Men of the Apparatus
   A. The Basic Vertical Structure
      The Ruler and the Court
      The Ranking Officials
      The Underlings
   B. Horizontal Developments
      Satraps
      Subordinate Princes, *Curacas,* Rajas
2. Subclasses Attached to the Men of the Apparatus
   A. Attachments Based on Kinship
      The Ruling House
      The Bureaucratic Gentry
      The Relatives of Civil Underlings and Rank-and-File Soldiers
   B. Attachments Based on Semi-, Quasi-, or Pre-official Status
      Secular Semi-officials (commercial and fiscal agents)
      Religious Quasi-officials (functionaries of dominant religion)
      Persons occupying a Pre-official Status (Trainees and degree-hold-
        ing candidates for office)
   C. Subdivided but Still an Entity
The Ruled
1. Property-based Subsections of Commoners
2. Slaves

As a distinguished specialist on China, it is to be expected that Wittfogel should rely upon Chinese data. But this is amplified by studies of India and the Near East, of the Great Empires of pre-Columbus America, and of many other situations.[32]

THE ELITE SYSTEM IN FEUDAL SOCIETIES

There's renewed curiosity today about the dynamics of feudal obligations, stemming from the appearance of great nongovernmental organizations in the industrial world. A contributing factor is the apprehension that science and technology will presently put nuclear weapons in many hands, transforming the character of modern world politics without bringing security.[33]

Rushton Coulborn edited a symposium on *Feudalism in History,*[34] which, despite variations in detail, provides a more helpful set of elite conceptions than had previous literature in this vast and scattered field. In Chapter I, Joseph R. Strayer and Coulborn formulate the following working "description" which is here abbreviated:

Feudalism ... is a method of government in which the essential relation is not that between ruler and subject, nor State and citizen, but between lord and vassal.

... The performance of political functions depends on personal agreements between a limited number of individuals, and ... political authority is treated as a private possession.

Military functions are prominent in most feudal societies, especially in their beginnings.

The existence of private armies in the service of great men is a sign that the growth of feudal institutions is becoming possible. . . .

The men who discharge political functions in a feudal society are not necessarily aristocrats when they first begin to gain power, but . . . they are soon recognized as an aristocracy.

. . . It seems likely that in a fully feudal society there will be an almost equal development of both vassalage and the fief, whereas in a proto-feudal or partly feudal society the growth of one or the other will be stunted.

The chapter also calls attention to conditions favorable to the rise of feudalism: (a) where government is unable to protect its subjects against either internal oppressors or external marauders; (b) where military power has fallen into the hands of a relatively small part of the population; (c) where a former large economic unity has broken down; and (d) where a large political unit has been built up in the absence of economic unity. Furthermore, a monopoly or near-monopoly of military power in the lord-vassal group is most easily established when a new technique of fighting is introduced, especially if this technique involves expensive military equipment.

THE FORMATION OF TOTALITARIAN ELITE SYSTEMS

The largest body of contemporary research has been directed to the task of understanding the dynamics of the totalitarian regimes originally identified with Russia, Italy, and Germany. An important attempt to formulate a workable model is by C. J. Friedrich and Z. K. Brzezinsky,[35] *Totalitarian Dictatorship and Autocracy,* who select six traits as a means of distinguishing the new from older forms of autocracy: (a) a total ideology; (b) a single mass party; (c) a terroristic secret police; (d) a monopoly of mass communications; (e) a monopoly of weapons; and (f) a centrally-directed planned economy. The appearance of modern science and technology is a necessary condition for totalitarian regimes, partly because of the physical instruments provided and partly because of the "rationality" with which power processes are analyzed.

As defined, it is obvious that Bolshevik, Fascist, and Nazi regimes did not become fully totalitarian immediately upon the "seizure of power." The "totalitarian break-through" is said to have culminated in Soviet Russia in the year 1928; in Italy, 1934; and in Germany, 1936. Having located crucial dates in the strategy of handling the instruments of power, it is possible to examine the interaction between these adjustments and such factors as the origins of the elite, the methods of elite training and selection, and the perspectives exhibited at successive stages of rise or fall. The essential point is the stereotyping of the basic values, expectations, and identifications of all who survived, irrespective of their points of origin within the social context or their mode of ascent.

Research has disclosed a great deal about the source of the elite transformations, from the initial "take over" to the "totalitarian break-through" and later. The results may be arranged according to five categories of factors, which are involved in hypotheses put forward to explain the formation of new elites from old. The five groups are culture, class, interest, personality, and crisis.[36]

1. Culture.—At the agitation and consolidation phases of social revolution, the marginal affiliations and exposures of prominent figures are important. Standard instances are South Germans among the Nazis, Georgians around Stalin, and certain provincials among Mussolini's early followers. The later movement is toward more "representative" elites in terms of culture.[37]

2. Class.—Analysis according to class origin has long since discredited the "proletarian" myth that did such valiant service during decades of agitation. Bolsheviks and Mensheviks depended heavily upon students from upper-rank families under the old regime; and although the Fascists and Nazis drew rather more heavily from the middle strata, they were reflecting the structure of the societies where they took shape.[38]

3. Interest.—Interest analysis considers affiliations and exposures to groups that are smaller than classes or that cut across class boundaries. Investigations of this kind help to reveal the finer structure of elites. We shall glance briefly at some of the findings which result when an interest group is classified according to the dominant value-institution category.

Power.—Within revolutionary movements, struggles arose early: Interests created by contact abroad clashed with more parochial elements. Interests consistently affiliated with factions and leaders who eventually won conflicted with interests created by inconstant affiliation. Theorists and agitators contended with elements chiefly focused upon organizational routine. Interests springing from gang warfare and early military experience as a soldier in a defeated army collided with interests related to more elaborate training and a more satisfactory military role.[39]

Wealth.—Not even the Bolsheviks at once eliminated all the private enterprises currently operating in Russia; those that were abolished were given some hope of benefiting from new economic policies. Both Fascist and Nazi parties catered to many special economic interests—banks, heavy industry, etc. The new power elements insisted on being "cut in."[40]

Respect.—Initially, all parties were somewhat "parasitic," depending upon the prestige of families who occupied a significant place in the older social-class system, whether at the international, national, regional, or local levels. Subsequently, one notes the rise of "new" families connected with prominence at successive phases of the revolution.[41]

Skill.—At first, ideological purity is more important than special competence. During the change-over, total demoralization is avoided by retaining many of those possessing top skill until they can be replaced.[42]

Enlightenment.—The rise of the parochial element is one of the conspicuous features of any movement whose members have had to live abroad at some stage or which rejects the philosophic outlook of the old regime. Comprehensive and realistic perspectives are re-established rather slowly, owing to the acute sense of insecurity attending every seeming deviation.[43]

Rectitude—Religious leaders are recognized as dangerous rivals of the secular leadership of totalitarian regimes. If the new order cannot pre-empt religion, the new leaders can at least play willing "compromise" interests against others, and detach local organizations from full foreign contact and support. New regimes also draw regularly upon criminal elements from the old, including common criminals who are not simply "politicals." These elements are dispersed through police and military sources.[44]

Well-being.—Modern social revolutions make large promises of welfare and attract some social-workers, physicians, and others who are devoted to the interests of special groups of the diseased, defective, maimed, under-fed, and under-cared for. Cultivating sanitation, accident-prevention, and sport plays a significant part in elite-recruitment through time.[45]

Affection.—Every leader must learn to exploit not only the affection received from crowds but the loyalty and love of specific comrades and de-pendents. Elite-formation is profoundly influenced by these intimate com-patibilities or incompatibilities. Furthermore, the totalitarian regime is op-posed to every focal center of love outside itself; hence, family ties are under attack from the beginning, and resettle only when the regime feels relatively secure.[46]

4. Personality.—Perhaps the most challenging hypothesis about to-talitarian leaders is the deviational quality of the "carry-over" generation and the "realism" of the generation that comes to maturity when the great transformation is consolidated. In a police-type of regime, a position of top leadership is the outcome of a process of realistic adjustments to the ever present necessity of identifying and separating potential friend from foe; the survivors are not likely to suffer from inner distortions of perception. They are likely to have buried the failures.[47]

5. Crisis.—In political analysis, it is often convenient to consider *levels* of crisis as distinct categories and to consider culture, class, interest, and personality factors at each of the different levels. Friedrich and Brzezinsky suggest that older autocracies are structurally more committed to warfare that modern totalitarians[48]—which indicates how differently elite systems with highly concentrated power may relate themselves to external power crises.

We shall not carry the analysis further in this discussion; the principal point has been to call attention to categories of analysis and to those types of empirical inquiry that appear promising.

ELITE SYSTEMS IN INDUSTRIAL AND DEMOCRATIC POLITICS

It may seem paradoxical to find that theoretical models are less well developed to guide research upon democratic than upon totalitarian elites. To a degree this shows that scholars tend to focus upon threatening develop-ments. Perhaps the decisive factor is that the political process of industrialized and democratic societies is enormously complicated.

Current research work has tackled the study of the decision process in the United States at a great many points; it will be useful, therefore, to apply a more elaborate system of analysis to our review of results than we used for the studies of totalitarian, feudal, and other societies.

Non-specialists usually assume that any study of the political elite in the United States will deal with the organs of government. From the standpoint of the specialist on social and behavioral research, the task is not so simple.

The scientist is accustomed to think comparatively and to recognize the possibility that what is called "government" in one context may not correspond to the institutions that exercise effective power. The entire context must be investigated before final judgments are made.

Although the distinction between formal authority and effective control has long been recognized in political theory, it has gained new emphasis in modern times from Marx and the Marxists.

The most influential Marxist hypothesis has been that a positive relationship exists between a group's position in the production process and the position of the group in the political process. Marx's analysis was functional rather than conventional: he appraised conventional usages rather than adopting them for analytic and comparative purposes. Scholars trained in this tradition do not regard it as likely, or even probable, that the personnel of recognized agencies of government will make the most important decisions in a modern industrial community. In order to establish this proposition in any concrete case, it is essential to apply a consistent set of definitions to every social context. The definition of the most important decisions is often left implicit, but it appears to be that *decisions are important to the extent that they affect the value positions of the most people*. Explicit definitions were often narrower, specifying as important only those decisions that affect positions regarding production. The significant fact is that post-Marxist scholars have been directly or indirectly inspired to identify actual rather than nominal decision-makers.

1. *Elites in Community Context.*—As a matter of convenience, research studies often begin with the personnel of official organs of government found at a given community level—whether national, regional, state, or local. Within this setting, research may move to unofficial or semi-official organizations, notably to political-party and pressure-group networks.[49]

Other studies focus more narrowly upon subareas within the whole decision process. Here, too, it is convenient to take off from specialized organs within the official flow of decisions, such as the Congress, the presidency, the administrative departments and agencies, and the courts.[50] If these structures are to be compared with one another in detail, scientists must fix upon a set of categories to be applied to every structure. For example, my immediate colleagues and I have found it expedient to use a seven-fold breakdown of any decision process: intelligence (informing, planning), recommendation (promotion), prescription (legislation), invocation, application, appraisal, and termination.[51]

2. *Elite Perspectives.*—What do elites want? This delusively simple question is the point of departure for researches that make full use of interviewing and related methods of data-gathering which have become part of the armory of modern behavioral science.

The question refers to the outcomes and effects sought by the elites as a whole or individually. These preferred events are the values which elites seek to maximize by acting in and through the decision process. In order to put the governmental structures of a given community in correct relation to the context, we must examine all the official structures in reference to all other structures of a community. As a first step toward describing a concrete social process, therefore, all organizations must be assigned to a category in a comprehensive list of value terms. *(Random* category lists do not make it possible for comparisons to be made from one context to another, or through time.) Organizations are classified according to the degree in which the perspectives current in a community approximate the functional definition of the value category. The community perspectives may at first be described according to the testimony of a very limited number of informants. Later, as more intensive methods are used and the picture begins to appear in detail, the original classifications may be changed. Thus, in a given community, we may at first assign a "church" to the rectitude category. After further research illuminates the context, we may reassign the "church" to the power category. Similarly, a "business corporation" may be initially assigned to "wealth." On further study it may be reassigned, perhaps to "power" or even to "rectitude," if it is run not for profit but for charitable purposes, such as providing employment for the handicapped.

Elite studies in the United States, whether or not conducted by scholars who are conventionally called political scientists, have made at least preliminary coverage of organizations in every category. These include power,[52] wealth,[53] respect,[54] well-being,[55] rectitude,[56] skill,[57] enlightenment,[58] and affection.[59]

All value-shaping and value-sharing activities, although "patterned," are not "organized." Hence, some elite researches seek to discover elites in interaction contexts that have no overhead organization.[60]

The foregoing discussion has referred to studies of one component of elite perspectives, to wit, the "demand system"—scope values sought. Inquiry also emphasizes the role of conscious and unconscious identification. Do elites, compared with mid-elites or the rank and file, regard themselves as more or less identified with the activities—organized or unorganized—in which they play a role? Who perceives himself as a member of which culture, class interest, personality, or crisis grouping? Which categories are perceived, though excluded from the "self"? It is a question of examining "reference individuals and groups," whether perceived and introjected, or perceived and excluded from the self.[61]

A further component of elite perspectives is the "expectation system," which includes all matter-of-fact assumptions about past, present, and future events affecting one's value position. In particular, expectations concerning one's own influence (what Eulau calls "competence") are important. There are pertinent distinctions between expectations referring to "self-role as a whole" and to "specialized self-roles"—such as performance as members of culture, class, interest, personality, and crisis groupings.[62]

One objective of elite research is to ascertain the "perspective maps" of elites. What is the relative importance of value outcomes and effects (in terms of the eight value categories, for instance) for the self as a whole or for a component identity? How are specific demands within each broad value category appraised when compared with other demands within the same category, and within other categories? These questions call for data that will enable the construction of maps of elite demand-identification-expectation, which in turn allow predictions to be made (and verified) regarding which values will be pursued at what cost (calculated in terms of all values).[63]

Another dimension of perspective analysis concentrates upon the discovery of predispositions regarding the "attention-perception" that distinguishes one elite from another. Elites differ in the events to which they give attention and in the events which they perceive.[64]

The distinctions that have been made make it possible to integrate studies of elite perspectives with investigations whose principal orientation is the rise, diffusion, and restriction of political myths. The term myth is defined for such purposes as the relatively stable patterns of demand, identification, and expectation occurring in a body politic. Among the key questions in elite-myth research are the following: Under what circumstances do elite members fail to incorporate a prevailing ideological myth within their personality systems? What factors account for the acceptance or rejection of alternative myths among those who have but loosely incorporated the prevailing ideology? How elaborate is the grasp of political doctrine by an elite? Of the political formula? Of political folklore (miranda)?[65]

3. Base Values of Elites.—Many elite researches occupy themselves with the task of describing the assets and liabilities available to any elite in a given situation. An inventory of this kind deals with base values, that is, with the values at the disposal of participants for use in attempting to affect decision outcomes and effects. One fundamental question is how to explain eliteship. For instance, what base values are available to an elite group or individual for maintaining an elite position in the power process, assuming for the moment that this demand exists—with a specifiable degree of intensity—among the perspectives?

Comparative purposes can be served by classifying participants according to the primary values demanded—sought as scope values. An inventory can then be made of all the values available to each elite category. Among the researches oriented toward the base values of elites classifid by scope, are those dealing with power, wealth, respect, enlightenment, affection, skill, rectitude, and well-being.[66]

4. The Strategy of Elites.—We understand "strategy" to mean the employment of base values to affect outcomes and effects. When skillfully employed, strategy enables an elite whose members intially control fewer assets than their rivals to come out disproportionately well. Researches are often directed to the whole range of strategic alternatives open to an elite member or an elite group. Some investigations proceed to examine strategy as related to one base value, or to the characteristics of the outcome sought. In foreign affairs especially, it is common to classify strategies into four categories according to the instrumentalities used. Two categories stress the management of communication: diplomacy, or interelite communication; and propaganda (ideological management), or elite-mass communication. Two categories put the emphasis upon economic or military instruments, where resource management is more prominent than communication.[67] Some studies

are relatively more concerned with explaining the choice of strategy by an elite than with formulating principles of success.[68]

5. *Elites in Outcome and Preoutcome Alignments.*—As a means of estimating the power of elites and elite components, much attention is lavished upon the study of alignments at the phase in the decision process where the decision is perceived as being made. Typically, these researches focus upon a conventionally recognized outcome, such as a popular vote, a legislative vote, an administrative finding, a judicial decision, or a battle result.

It is generally understood among political investigators that the alignments occurring at the outcome phase of a conventional decision process do not necessarily give a satisfactory picture of the facts of life. This can be rectified to some extent by examining the preoutcome sequence of events and discovering who *initiated* the winning outcome. Studies of legislation frequently show that the initiative comes from administrative agencies or private pressure associations. In addition to initiators, studies of sequence look for *pivots,* that is, for participants whose change-over appears to anticipate the final result. In presidential elections this has long intrigued the professionals and the general public—"as Maine goes, so goes the nation." Sequence studies often go beyond official records to examine the informal interactions during or before formal confrontations. In any case, the aim is to identify the individual or individuals who initiate or pivot the ultimate result.[69]

6. *The Effects of Elite Policy.*—Outcomes are relatively clear-cut incidents in the unending stream of political events. The events following outcomes—whether immediately or at long remove—are less readily describable by research workers. Nevertheless, everybody recognizes the crucial importance of examining effects through time, since the rise or fall of elites, in terms of power or any other value, may not be "registered" in outcomes until they have cumulated for some time. At any given cross-section, "effects" can summarize the probable impact of past policies upon the realization of scope values; or "effects" can be estimates of the future.

Particular individuals or subgroups of an elite can be singled out for examination or aggregate impacts can be appraised. Effects are not appraised exclusively in terms of rising or falling value positions, since the rise or fall of institutional practices are also of great scientific and policy interest. Public-order studies are oriented in this direction.[70]

7. *Implications.*—In this review I shall not try to interpret the significance of the published research upon the power process in the United States. However, it is worth observing that the principal categories of much nineteenth-century thought on elites are of little relevance. Marx was inspired by the seeming clarity and validity of his bipolar image of society moving toward civil war. The bipolar conception does scant justice to societies in which value distributions are graduated and mobility is relatively high. The picture that emerges from the study of coalitions at various phases of preoutcome, outcome, and postoutcome sequences is sufficiently definite to reveal the multiplicity of participants in the total process, and the diversity

of the perspectives, base-value positions, strategies, and value-practice out-comes involved. Not bipolarity but pluri- and multi-polarities characterize the politics of Big Democracy among industrial peoples. Today we are liberating ourselves from one-sided concentration upon wealth and the in-tellectual impoverishment that resulted from de-emphasizing other values—such as power, respect, enlightenment, and skill. We live among high-frequency changes in the multiple coalitions that affect the outcome of decisions.

A Note on Policy

I conclude this review by drawing attention to the need of building special institutions for providing and disseminating information concerning the elite structure of the world.

Elite studies have not been properly integrated with one another or with the policy process as a whole. This is not to deny that U.S. programs of foreign military and economic aid have been guided to some extent by the growth of modern social and behavioral science.[71] Researches are underlining some "lessons" from these programs. Perhaps the principal "lessons" relate to the timing of transformation programs. If sudden improvements in health occur, population is likely to expand faster than the capital formation or loans needed to raise living standards. The resulting discontent exposes the current regime to spontaneous assault within and manipulated subver-sion from without. Furthermore, if an intellectual class is created far in advance of opportunities for productive employment, the result is to strengthen the elements hostile to the public order. Pertinent as these generalizations are, they offer incomplete characterizations of the main fea-tures of the context in which military- and economic-aid policies must operate. "Factor analysis" or "concept analysis" must be related to "time."

The most promising development among scholars, I think, is the appre-ciation that effective social and behavioral science depends upon perfecting a *continuing, comprehensive survey of world predispositions.* Such a survey must employ methods that range in intensiveness, from brief interviews to detailed local and regional investigations like Skinner's study in Bangkok. It should be possible to predict the results of relatively *extensive* methods from the results of relatively *intensive* methods.

Today, it is almost within the grasp of social science to employ machines to produce detailed simulations of social contexts. As simulation becomes feasible, a given pattern of predisposition can be exposed, in a machine exercise, to experimental changes. In principle, value costs and gains can be exhaustively assessed, and alternative policies chosen that maximize net ad-vantages in terms of postulated goal values and specifications.

Machine simulation can be combined, in varying degrees, with simulation by scholars or administrators. The human teams can be used to correct the current description of elite and non-elite predispositions.

The new facilities put heavy demands upon scientists to obtain trend and distribution data for the machines. But the challenge is especially acute to prepare theoretical models whose routines, when built into automatic processes, correctly prescribe the patterns of interaction among variables. It must not be forgotten that the basic commitments are of the mind, followed by the machine.[72]

The pressure for data and rules of interaction will establish closer connection between laboratories and the field. As new basic principles are demonstrated under the special conditions of the laboratory, they will be incorporated into the automatic system. In order to know the magnitude of the variables actually occurring in a field context, it will be necessary to transfer the measures developed in the laboratory to the context. For example, if involuntary muscle movements reveal the degree of involvement on the part of a respondent to a questionnaire, the procedure will be a valuable working tool of socio-political research.[73]

Conclusion

The foregoing summary has amply confirmed the assertion on the first page that elite studies are abounding in vigor and diversity. It is especially appropriate to ask how elite studies will affect elites, recognizing this as a special case of how science, and especially social science, affects society. The general proposition, I believe, is this: *To the extent that procedures and results are public and competitive, democratic tendencies are favored, since they foster the simultaneous improvement of insight and understanding.*

Notes

1. (3 vols.; London: Routledge and Kegan Paul, 1958). The title means "Introduction" in Arabic and was originally applied to the first volume.

2. *Ibid.*, Bk. I, chap. iii, sec. 1.

3. *Ibid.*, sec. 5.

4. *Ibid.*, sec. 11.

5. *Ibid.*, chap. ii, sec. 14.

6. *Ibid.*, sec. 22.

7. (Ann Arbor: University of Michigan, 1958).

8. Chap. xl of *Storia delle dottrine politiche* (1933).

9. Quoted in Meisel, *op. cit.*, p. 383.

10. *The Power Elite* (New York: Oxford University Press, 1956).

11. Among many others, consult C. J. Friedrich, *The New Image of the Common Man* (2d ed.; Boston: Little, Brown, 1950); J. A. Schumpeter, *Capitalism, Socialism and Democracy* (3d ed.; New York: Harper, 1950); R. Aron, "Note sur la stratification du pouvoir," *Revue*

francaise de sciences politiques, IV (1954), 469-83; D. Riesman, N. Glazer and R. Denney, *The Lonely Crowd* (New Haven: Yale University Press, 1950), chap. x; J. H. Meisel, *op. cit.*, esp. pp. 332-81.

12. See H. D. Lasswell, *World Politics and Personal Insecurity* (1935), chap. i (reprinted in H. Lasswell, C. Merriam and T. V. Smith, *A Study of Power* (Glencoe, Ill.: The Free Press, 1950); H. Eulau, "H. D. Lasswell's Developmental Analysis," *Western Political Quarterly,* XI, (June, 1958), 229-42.

13. MacLaw Machajski (A. Wolski), cited in Max Nomad, *Rebels and Renegades* (New York: Macmillan & Co., 1932).

14. Milovan Djilas has inadvertently provided rich confirmation in his first-hand account of Yugoslavia in *The New Class* (New York: Praeger, 1957).

15. Veblen remains one of the seminal

figures: *The Engineers and the Price System* (New York: B. W. Huebach, 1921). Nothing of comparable grasp has been put forward by or about physical scientists despite the upsurge of recent years resulting from nuclear advances.

16. J. Burnham, *The Managerial Revolution* (New York: John Day, 1941). See the critique by Donald R. Matthews. If Burnham asserts that people with the same relationship to the process of production will constitute a self-conscious class, his "error is even greater than Marx's, for he defines 'managers' on the basis of work-technique rather than on a relationship to the productive process." If Burnham does not assert conscious solidarity, then "conflicts of interest" within the managerial group will "appeal for popular support in their conflict with other managers" and the power is "no longer absolute" but "contingent upon popular approval." *The Social Background of Political Decision-Makers* (Garden City: Doubleday, 1954), p. 13. Further, Michael Young, *The Rise of the Meritocracy* (London: Thames and Hudson, 1958).

17. The owners of industrial property are subject to severe limitations in modern nation-states where private capitalism prevails. On the limited scope of the policy choices open, see D. M. Wright, *Capitalism* (New York: McGraw-Hill, 1951) and the papers on "Power Blocs and the Operation of Economic Forces," by B. W. Lewis and G. H. Hildebrand, with discussion by Calvin B. Hoover and E. H. Chamberlin, *American Economic Review,* XLIX (1959), 383-418. Commentary upon A. A. Berle, Galbraith, and others.

18. My "garrison state" hypothesis appeared originally in 1937 and in expanded form in 1941. The 1941 article is reprinted in *The Analysis of Political Behaviour* (London: Routledge and Kegan Paul, 1948), pp. 146-57.

19. Vilfredo Pareto, *The Mind and Society,* ed. and trans. A. Livingston (4 vols.; New York: Harcourt, Brace, 1935), esp. par. 2178 ff.

20. J. M. Smith and C. P. Cotter, "Freedom and Authority in the Amphibial State," *Midwest Journal of Political Science,* I (1957), 40-49.

21. It was Gaetano Mosca who emphasized the crucial role of professionalization in domesticating the soldier as an instrument of civil society. The most optimistic version of the potential of the military is found in S. P. Huntington, *The Soldier and the State: The Theory and Politics of Civil-Military Relations* (Cambridge: Harvard University Press, 1957). A careful formulation and critique of the "garrison state" hypothesis is given; the formulation itself is sought to be accounted for as part of the reactive despair of liberals. Should we extend the latter hypothesis to include glorifications of the military? One reaction formation consists in denial of "bad traits" in a strong figure, accompanied by positive identification with the re-edited source of threat. In any case, data pertinent to possible changes in the perspectives of the military are in J. W. Masland and L. I. Radway, *Soldiers and Scholars: Military Education and National Policy* (Princeton: Princeton University Press, 1957). See especially M. Janowitz, *The Professional Soldier: A Social and Political Portrait* (Glencoe, Ill.: The Free Press, 1960).

22. *Man Makes Himself* (London: Watts, 1936, 1941).

23. Robert Redfield, *The Primitive World and Its Transformations* (Ithaca: Cornell University Press, 1953), p. 12.

24. W. N. Fenton, "Factionalism at Taos Pueblo, New Mexico," Anthropolitical Papers, No. 56, *Bureau of American Ethnology Bulletin,* CLXIV (1957), 297-344; J. Adair and E. Vogt, "Navaho and Zuni Veterans: A Study of Contrasting Modes of Culture Change," *American Anthropologist,* LI (1949), 547-61; D. H. French, "Factionalism in Isleta Pueblo," Monographs of the American Ethnological Society, No. 14 (1948), 1-47.

25. (Ithaca: Cornell University Press, 1958).

26. *Ibid.,* p. 108.

27. *Ibid.,* p. 201.,

28. *Ibid.,* pp. 208-9

29. *Ibid.,* p. 268.

30. *Ibid.,* p. 319.

31. (New Haven: Yale University Press, 1957).

32. A pertinent and critical recent study is Sally Falk Moore, *Power and Property in Inca Peru* (New York: Columbia University Press, 1958). See also:

C. K. Yang, "Some Characteristics of Chinese Bureaucratic Behavior," in D. S. Nivison and A. F. Wright (eds.) *Confucianism in Action* (Stanford: Stanford University Press, 1959), pp. 134-68; J. T. S. Liu, "Some Classifications of Bureaucracy in Chinese Historiography," *ibid.*, pp. 165-81.

33. See A. Wholstetter, "The Delicate Balance of Terror," *Foreign Affairs* XXXVII (1959), 211-34; also A. M. Ross, "Do We Have a New Industrial Feudalism?" *American Economic Review*, XLVIII (1958), 903-20.

34. (Princeton: Princeton University Press, 1956). Contributions by J. R. Strayer, E. O. Reischauer, D. Bodde, B. C. Brundage, W. F. Edgerton, D. Thorner, E. H. Kantorowicz, M. Szeftel and R. Coulborn. Foreword by A. L. Kroeber.

35. (Cambridge: Harvard University Press, 1956).

36. These categories are not explicitly used in the Friedrich-Brzezinsky summary of research; nor were the studies to be mentioned necessarily cited in their book.

37. See Richard Pipes, *The Formation of the Soviet Union, Communism and Nationalism,* 1917-1923 (Cambridge: Harvard University Press, 1954); F. C. Barghoorn, *Soviet Russian Nationalism* (New York: Oxford University Press, 1956).

38. For example, a succinct bit of evidence from southeastern Europe brings out the "representative" character of the Greek Communist party. The data were obtained from imprisoned Communists. R. V. Burks, "Statistical Profile of the Greek Communist," *Journal of Modern History*, XXVII (1955), 153-58.

39. M. Fainsod, *How Russia Is Ruled* (Cambridge: Harvard University Press, 1955), and E. H. Carr's detailed history of the Russian revolution currently in publication. Also, V. K. Brzezinski, *The Permanent Purge: Politics in Soviet Totalitarianism* (Cambridge: Harvard University Press, 1955).

40. See especially the old but authoritative work of F. Neumann, *Behemoth* (New York: Oxford University Press, 1942, 1944).

41. Consult J. A. Armstrong, *The Soviet Bureaucratic Elite: A Case Study of the Ukranian Apparatus* (New York:

Praeger, 1959). See also *Schriften des Instituts fur politische Wissenschaft* (Berlin), Vols. III, V, VIII, XI.

42. See the Hoover Institute Studies on Comparative Elites, especially D. Lerner, *The Nazi Elite* (1951); also "Profiles of a Few Outstanding Propagandists," in W. E. Daugherty and M. Janowitz, *A Psychological Warfare Casebook* (Baltimore: Johns Hopkins University Press, 1958), pp. 231-57.

43. C. Milosz, *The Captive Mind* (New York: Alfred A. Knopf, 1953), is most penetrating.

44. S. Wolin and R. M. Slusser, *The Soviet Secret Police* (New York: Praeger, 1957).

45. For glimpses at various types, see F. Gross, *The Seizure of Power* (New York; Philosophical Library, 1958).

46. Many incidental indications of family relationships are in N. Leites and E. Bernaut, *Ritual of Liquidation. The Case of the Moscow Trials* (Glencoe, Ill.: The Free Press, 1954); W. W. Kulski, *The Soviet Regime, Communism in Practice* (Syracuse: Syracuse University Press, 1954).

47. See H. D. Lasswell, "The Selective Effect of Personality on Political Participation," in R. Christie and M. Jahoda (eds.), *Studies in the Scope and Method of "The Authoritarian Personality"* (Glencoe, Ill.: The Free Press, 1954); Bayle, *Psychologie et ethnique du national socialisme; étude anthropologique des divergents SS* (1953); H. V. Dicks, "Observations on Contemporary Russian Behavior," *Human Relations* V, (1952), 111-75.

48. C. Friedrich and Z. Brzezinsky, *op. cit.,* chap. vii. Also B. Moore, Jr., *Terror and Progress, USSR* (Cambridge: Harvard University Press, 1954); W. W. Rostow, *The Prospects for Chinese Communism* (Cambridge: Technology Press of MIT, 1954).

49. Perhaps the most concise investigation of the elite composition of a large-scale, non-autocratic nation-state is not of the United States. For Great Britain, see W. L. Guttsman, "The Changing Structure of the British Political Elite," *British Journal of Sociology*, II (1951), 122-34; W. L. Guttsman, "Aristocracy and the Middle Class in the British Political Elite, 1886-1916," *Brit-*

ish *Journal of Sociology*, V (1954), 12-32; K. H. Abshagen, *Kings, Lords and Gentlemen: Influence and Power of the English Upper Classes* (London: Heinemann, 1959). For Germany: K. W. Deutsch and L. J. Edinger, *Germany Rejoins the Powers: Mass Opinion, Interest Groups and Elites in Contemporary German Foreign Policy* (Stanford: Stanford University Press, 1959). C. Wright Mills has undertaken to identify the ruling elite of the United States, in *The Power Elite* (New York: Oxford University Press, 1956.) Among recent Investigations of local communities: W. Lloyd Warner *et al.*, *Democracy in Jonesville* (New York: Harper, 1949). Floyd Hunter, *Community Power Structure* (Chapel Hill: University of North Carolina Press, 1953); A. J. Vidich and J. Bensman, *Small Town in Mass Society* (Princeton: Princeton University Press, 1958).

50. Examples are R. Bendix, *Higher Civil Servants in American Society* (Boulder: University of Colorado Press, 1949); D. R. Matthews, "United States Senators; A Study of the Recruitment of Political Leaders" (Ph.D. diss., Princeton University, 1953); J. R. Schmidhauser, "The Justices of the Supreme Court," *Midwest Journal of Political Science*, III (1959), 1-57; J. L. McCamy, *The Administration of American Foreign Affairs* (New York: Alfred Knopf, 1950); W. B. Graves (ed.), "Our State Legislators," *Annals*, 195 (whole issue).

51. H. D. Lasswell, *The Decision Process; Seven Categories of Functional Analysis* (Bureau of Governmental Research, College Park, University of Maryland, 1956). Other category systems are put forward, for example, in the work of Herbert Simon and Richard C. Snyder.

52. Private organizations conventionally regarded as specialized to power include political parties and pressure groups. Sample studies: W. S. Sayre, "Personnel of Republican and Democratic National Committees," *American Political Science Review*, XXVI (1932), 360-63; C. R. Nixon and D. Marvick, "Active Campaign Workers: A Study of Self-Recruited Elites" (Paper, American Political Science Association Convention, 1956); D. Blaisdell (ed.), *Unofficial Government: Pressure Groups and Lobbies*

(Philadelphia: American Academy of Political and Social Studies, 1958).

53. C. Wright Mills, *The New Men of Power: America's Labor Leaders* (New York: Harcourt, Brace, 1948); W. Lloyd Warner and J. C. Abegglen, *Occupational Mobility in American Business and Industry, 1928-1952* (Minneapolis: University of Minnesota Press, 1955); M. Newcomer, *The Big Business Executive: The Factors that Made Him, 1900-1950* (New York: Columbia University Press, 1955).

54. R. Bendix and S. M. Lipset (eds.), *Class, Status and Power* (Glencoe, Ill.: The Free Press, 1953); E. D. Baltzell, *Philadelphia Gentlemen* (Glencoe, Ill.: The Free Press, 1958).

55. Some information on the internal structure of the AMA is in O. Garceau, *The Political Life of the American Medical Association* (Cambridge: Harvard University Press, 1941). See M. Greenblatt, D. J. Levinson, R. H. Williams, *The Patient and the Mental Hospital* (Glencoe, Ill.: The Free Press, 1957).

56. L. Ebersole, *Church Lobbying in the Nation's Capital* (New York: Macmillan & Co., 1951); and the scattered information in treatises on politics and criminology about the impact of organized counter-mores, interests, and especially the composition of the leadership of such elements.

57. W. Miller, "American Lawyers in Politics and Business," *Yale Law Review* LX (1951), 66-76; C. A. Horsky, *The Washington Lawyer* (Boston: Little, Brown, 1953); K. Krastin, "The Lawyer in Society—A Value Analysis," *Western Reserve Law Review*, VIII (1957), 409-55.

58. R. L. Jones and C. E. Swanson, "Small-City Daily Newspapermen: Their Abilities and Interests," *Journalism Quarterly*, XXXI (1954), 38-55; S. Kelley, Jr., *Professional Public Relations and Political Power* (Baltimore: Johns Hopkins University Press, 1956); H. P. Beck, *Men Who Control Our Universities* (New York: King's Crown Press, 1947).

59. Women's organizations and ecclesiastical groups are expected to be most active on behalf of the family and especially of children.

60. Ethnic groups—more broadly, community groups with distinctive culture—are but partly organized. Thus, the fol-

lowing report does not necessarily imply that highly articulate organizations are accountable for the members of Congress: M. G. Lawson, "The Foreign-Born in Congress, 1789-1949, a Statistical Summary," *American Political Science Review,* LI (1957), 1183-89. Upper, middle and lower classes are not necessarily organized in comprehensive structures. See G. Almond, for instance, "The Politics of Wealth," *Journal of Politics,* VII (1945), 213-55. Interests, too, do not invariably coincide with an organization: see the studies of sex and age groups in politics, such as F. L. Strodtbeck, "Sex-Role Differentiation in Jury Deliberation," *Sociometry,* XX (1956), 300-10. All persons having similar personalities are not brought together in a master organization. Nor are all survivors of a crisis situation brought together in a single structure. Veterans' associations do not include every eligible member of the armed forces, nor do they take in surviving civilians.

61. M. Janowitz and W. Delaney, "The Bureaucrat and the Public: A Study of Informational Perspectives," *Administrative Science Quarterly,* II (1957), 141-62; D. Marvick, *Career Perspectives in a Bureaucratic Setting* (Ann Arbor: University of Michigan, 1954); M. Janowitz and D. Wright, "The Prestige of Public Employment," *Public Administration Review,* XVI (1956), 15-21.

62. H. Eulau and P. Schneider, "Dimensions of Political Involvement," *Public Opinion Quarterly,* XX (1956), 128-42; H. Eulau, "Identification with Class and Political Perspective," *Journal of Politics,* XVIII (1956), 232-53; H. Eulau, "Perceptions of Class and Party in Voting Behavior: 1952," *American Political Science Review,* XLIX (1955), 364-84; R. E. Agger, "Independents and Party Identifiers: Characteristics and Behavior in 1952," in E. Burdick and A. J. Brodbeck, *American Voting Behavior* (Glencoe, Ill.: The Free Press, 1959), chap. xvii; A. Campbell, "The Political Implications of Community Identification," in R. Young (ed.), *Approaches to the Study of Politics* (Evanston, Ill: Northwestern University Press, 1958), pp. 318-28; S. Greer, "Individual Participation in Mass Society," in *ibid.,* pp. 329-42.

63. The maximization postulate can be interpreted with varying degrees of strictness. In some formalistic studies, participants are assumed to possess articulate, detailed demand and contingency perspectives. Herbert Simon introduces less exacting requirements. In general, see J. C. March, H. A. Simon, and H. Guetzkow, *Organizations* (New York: Wiley, 1958); A. Downs, *An Economic Theory of Democracy* (New York: Harper, 1957); W. Edwards, "The Theory of Decision-Making," *Psychological Bulletin,* LI (1954), 380-417; J. Buchanan, "Social Choice, Democracy and Free Markets," *Journal of Political Economy,* LXII (1954), 114-23.

64. E. Katz and P. F. Lazarsfeld, *Personal Influence* (Glencoe, Ill.: The Free Press, 1955); I. Pool (ed.), "Studies in Political Communication," *Public Opinion Quarterly,* Vol. XX (1956); G. Almond, *The American People and Foreign Policy* (New York: Harcourt, Brace, 1950); F. C. Barghoorn, *The Soviet Image of the U. S.: A Study in Distortion* (New York: Harcourt, Brace, 1950). See "Political Discussion: Who Listens to What? Who Talks to Whom?" chap. vi, and "Mass Media and Mass Politics," chap. xix of R. E. Lane, *Political Life: How People Get Involved in Politics* (Glencoe, Ill.: The Free Press, 1959); I. Pool, *"The Prestige Papers." A Survey of Their Editorials* (Stanford: Stanford University Press, 1952).

65. G. A. Almond, *The Appeals of Communism* (Princeton: Princeton University Press, 1954); R. E. Lane, *The Regulation of Business Men* (New Haven: Yale University Press, 1954); T. W. Adorno *et al., The Authoritarian Personality* (New York: Harper, 1950); F. X. Sutton, S. E. Harris, C. Kaysen, and J. Tobin, *The American Business Creed* (Cambridge: Harvard University Press, 1956); R. G. McCloskey, "American Political Thought and the Study of Politics," in R. Young (ed.), *Approaches to the Study of Politics* (Evanston, Ill.: Northwestern University Press, 1958), pp. 155-71.

66. Examples of research focused upon the extent to which a specific value is available as a base for influencing other values include Alexander Heard's studies of money in politics.

A summary of research concentrated

upon the base values of political elites in the world arena is H. and M. Sprout, *Foundations of National Power* (2d ed., New York: Van Nostrand, 1951).

Personality research deals with the value pattern of the individual and the practices and mechanisms by which he achieves various degrees of integration. The context of the individual in the social process conditions the degree to which his personality is a positive or negative asset (base value). Examples of recent studies of individuals and of the relation between a role or situation and personality: A. and J. George, *Woodrow Wilson and Colonel House: A Personality Study* (Evanston, Ill.: Row, Peterson, 1956); H. J. Eysenck, *The Psychology of Politics* (London: Routledge and Kegan Paul, 1956); R. Christie and H. J. Eysenck, *Psychological Bulletin,* III (1956), 411-51; J. B. McConaughy, "Certain Personality Factors of State Legislators in South Carolina," *American Political Science Review,* XLIV (1950), 897-903.

67. Examples are F. M. Keesing and M. M. Keesing, *Elite Communication in Samoa: A Study of Leadership* (Stanford: Stanford University Press, 1956); D. Lerner (ed.); *Propaganda in War and Crises* (New York: G. W. Stewart, 1951); E. Earle (ed.), *Makers of Modern Strategy* (Princeton: Princeton University Press, 1952); D. L. Gordon and R. Dangerfield, *The Hidden Weapon; The Story of Economic Warfare* (New York: Harper, 1947).

68. See especially Nathan Leites' investigations of political strategy in Russia and France. For instance, C. Melnik and N. Leites, *The House without Windows: France Selects a President* (Evanston, Ill.: Row, Peterson, 1958).

69. The theoretical discussion of power is characteristically concerned with alignment relations at outcome and preoutcome phases of the whole decision process, authoritative and controlling. Among recent discussions, see R. Bierstedt, "An Analysis of Social Power," *American Sociological Review,* XV (1950), 730-38; H. A. Simon, "Observation and Measurement of Political Power," *Journal of Politics,* XV (1953), 500-16; R. A. Dahl, "The Concept of Power," *Behavioral Science,* II (1957), 201-15; R.

A. Dahl, "A Critique of the Ruling Elite Model," *American Political Science Review,* LII (1958), 463-69; J. G. Marsh, "Measurement Concepts in the Theory of Influence," *Journal of Politics,* XIX (1957), 202-26; J. V. Kempski, "Wie ist Theorie der Politik Moglich?" *Zeitschrift fur die gesamte Staatwissenschaft,* CVI (1950), 447 ff; P. H. Rossi, "Community Decision-Making," in R. Young (ed.), *op. cit.,* pp. 363-82; L. H. Chamberlain, *The President, Congress and Legislation* (New York: Columbia University Press, 1946); M. Gluckman, *The Judicial Process among the Barotse of Northern Rhodesia* (Glencoe, Ill.: The Free Press, 1955); R. C. Snyder, "Game Theory and the Analysis of Political Behavior," in *Research Frontiers in Politics and Government* (Washington: Brookings Institution, 1955), 70-103; R. D. Luce and A. A. Rogow, "A Game Theoretic Analysis of Congressional Power Distributions for a Stable Two-Party System," *Behavioral Science,* I (1956), 83-95; T. C. Schelling, "The Strategy of Conflict: Perspectus for a Reorientation of Game Theory," *Conflict Resolution,* II (1958), 203-64; H. Guetzkow, "Building Models about Small Groups," R. Young (ed.), *op. cit.,* pp. 265-81; and the quantitative studies of court decisions by G. A. Schubert, Fred Kort, Herman Pritchett, and others.

70. By public order is meant the pattern of values and the basic institutional practices defended and fulfilled by the legal process (the authoritative and controlling patterns of the decision process). See M. S. McDougal and H. D. Lasswell, "The Identification and Appraisal of Diverse Systems of Public Order," *American Journal of International Law,* LIII (1959), 1-29; and the entire *Proceedings of the American Society of International Law, 1959,* devoted to "Diverse Systems of World Public Order Today." See also G. Dession and H. D. Lasswell, "Public Order under Law: The Role of the Advisor-Draftsman in the Formation of Code or Constitution," *Yale Law Journal,* LXV (1955), 174-95.

71. See Edward Shils, "Intellectuals, Public Opinion and Economic Development," in *World Politics,* X (1958), 232-55; D. Lerner with L. W. Pevsner, *The Passing of Traditional Society: Mod-*

ernizing the Middle East (Glencoe, Ill.: The Free Press, 1958); D. Lerner (ed.), "Attitude Research in Modernizing Areas," *Public Opinion Quarterly*, Vol. XXII (1958); W. A. Lewis, *The Theory of Economic Growth* (London: Allen & Unwin, 1955); R. E. Ward *et al.,* "Village Government in Eastern and Southern Asia: A Symposium," *Far Eastern Quarterly*, XV (1956), 175-237; E. C. Banfield, *The Moral Basis of a Backward Society* (Glencoe, Ill.: The Free Press, 1958); M. Mead, *New Lives for Old: Cultural Transformation-Manus, 1928-1953* (New York: Morrow, 1956); R. Redfield, *A Village That Chose Progress: Kom Revisited* (Chicago: University of Chicago Press, 1950); D. Apter, *The Gold Coast in Transition* (Princeton: Princeton University Press, 1955). An important historical and comparative study is R. Syme, *Colonial Elites: Rome, Spain and the Americas* (London: Oxford University Press, 1958).

72. On various new techniques: W. N. Locke and A. D. Booth (eds.), *Machine Translation of Languages* (New York: Wiley, 1953); B. F. Skinner, "Teaching Machines," *Science,* CXXVIII (1958), 969; J. W. Perry and A. Kent, *Tools for Machine Literature Searching* (New York: Interscience Publications, 1958); F. Rosenblatt, "The Design of an Intelligent Automaton," *Research Trends,* Vol. VI (1958), No. 2 (Cornell Aeronautical Laboratory, Buffalo, N. Y.); J. J. Gibson, *The Perception of the Visual World* (Boston: Houghton Mifflin, 1950); R. K. Potter, G. A. Kopp, and H. Green, *Visible Speech* (New York: Van Nostrand, 1947); H. Quastler (ed.), *Information Theory in Psychology* (Glencoe, Ill.: The Free Press, 1955); L. E. Allen, "Symbolic Logic: A Razor-Edged Tool for Drafting and Interpreting Legal Documents," *Yale Law Journal*, LXVI (1957), 833-79.

Reviews

Editorial note: The intensive study of outstanding political personalities by way of psychoanalytic concepts and methods, pioneered by Harold D. Lasswell almost thirty years ago, has remained, in spite of its rich promises, an ephemeral enterprise. Political scientists lack the training to undertake deep analyses of political personalities. Most psychoanalysts do not seem particularly interested in applying their skill to the study of public figures. Erik H. Erikson's *Young Man Luther: A Study in Psychoanalysis and History* (New York: W. W. Norton & Company, 1958) is a rare exception. Treatment of this book seemed particularly appropriate in a volume concerned with political decision-makers. Luther was a world revolutionary figure, in politics as well as religion. We therefore asked a political scientist and a practicing psychoanalyst to review the book for this volume.—H.E.

289

Personal Identity
and Political Ideology

By LUCIAN W. PYE

I

MUCH OF political science may be thought of as an attempt to understand the connections between individual and group behavior. While a statement may not provide the most satisfactory beginning for a definition of the discipline, it does accentuate the concern of political science with both the nature of the individual and the nature of society. Political theorists have traditionally been interested in the state and the statesman, the law and the lawmaker, the community and the citizen, and historical forces and individual choices. All political theories are premised on either explicit or implicit assumptions about the nature of man and of society; hence, the political scientist must be to some extent both a psychologist and a sociologist.

These were the qualities of the traditional political scientists. The most important forerunners of the discipline were also the leading authorities on questions about human nature and the structure of society. Thus, Aristotle, Machiavelli, Hobbes, Locke, and Rousseau were concerned not just with the traits and arts of political leaders but with the basic nature of man; and in Plato we have some remarkable anticipations of modern psychology. Similarly, traditional political theorists were concerned with more than just the polity: their interests usually covered the entire web of human associations. They were extraordinarily successful in building their systematic political theories out of the most advanced psychological and sociological knowledge available to them, producing syntheses that related the character of man and society to normative standards and judgments about the design of public institutions. For example, one strand of this Western tradition of political science can be summed up readily under the rubric of reason, an essentially psychological concept. The universe was conceived of as rational, and man, as having the rational power to understand it: given the right sort of institutions, men would act rationally according to their enlightened self-interest, and the result would be a happy and harmonious social order.[1] Other systems were erected on the premise that man's essential nature is brutal, selfish, and inherently evil. Clearly, the traditional political theorist did not shirk from psychological considerations. On the contrary, he often permitted them to color all aspects of his theories.

The contemporary political scientist wishing to follow in the tradition is confronted with an infinitely more difficult task. The first problem is the extraordinary rate of growth of specialized knowledge about psychological and sociological matters. Many political scientists have come to feel that it is hopeless to attempt to incorporate these intellectual developments into systematic political theories. Finding it impossible to follow the practices of the earlier political theorists, they have decided instead to examine systematically, and with reverence, the works of these earlier thinkers. Furthermore, a second and more fundamental problem is posed in our new understanding of the basic nature of man. In his insight into the full dimensions of man's inner nature, Freud made it embarrassingly clear that previous theories of political relationships were generally premised on impoverished and inadequate notions of human nature. The concept of the rational man has had to be altered. At the same time, Freud held out the promise of a deeper understanding of political phenomena—a promise that has not been fully realized.

It is one thing to suggest that all political theories depend upon some psychological view of man, and quite another matter to relate the insights of psychoanalysis to political analysis. In spite of the enthusiasm of those who are ready to try to enrich political science with Freud's psychoanalytic contributions, it must be acknowledged that the results are often awkward, and at times even grotesque. How can the political scientist significantly benefit from the contributions of those psychologists who have altered our image of man?

In performing the path-breaking task of applying psychoanalytical concepts to political analysis, Harold D. Lasswell focused on the relationship between private motivations and public acts. He suggested that the dynamics of political action were to be found in the configuration of the individual personality and not just in the grand issues of history. Lasswell suggested a formula for expressing the developmental aspects of political man: $p]d]r=P$, in which "p" stands for private motives; "d" is displacement onto a public object; "r" is rationalization in terms of public interest; "P" is the political man; and "$]$" symbolizes "transformed into."[2] Political man is characterized as being moved by private motives, which are displaced on public objects and rationalized as being in the national interest. By employing the assumption about the nature of man that dominated psychoanalytical thinking during the 1930's, Lasswell was led to believe that release of tension is fundamental to all political behavior and the key to human action in general. We find him writing that: "Nations, classes, tribes, and churches have been treated as collective symbols in the name of which the individual may indulge his elementary urges for supreme power, for omniscience, for amorality, for security."[3] Again, he stated that: "Indeed one of the principal functions of symbols of remote objects, like nations and classes, is to serve as targets for the relief of many of the tensions which might discharge disastrously in face-to-face relationships."[4]

Lasswell's efforts to trace the connections between private motivations and public acts were an attempt to deal systematically with the kinds of problems that political biographers have long sought to untangle: the relationship between the child and the man, between personal peculiarities and political preferences, between private frustrations and public ambitions. Lasswell's critics have charged that he exaggerated the importance of private and irrational considerations because he so undervalued the significance of political issues and rational choice. On the other hand, his critics have generally failed to appreciate that, despite the special attention he gave to psychological matters, he steadfastly maintained a remarkably rigid distinction between the psychological and the political, between the pattern of personality development and the logic of institutional change, between private motivations and public policy.

Thus, in advancing the view that the social process consists of people pursuing *values,* through *institutions,* by means of available *resources,* Lasswell implied that the individual and his value preferences are one thing, and social institutions another.[5] Some institutions may be more appropriate than others for maximizing particular values, but, in the final analysis, institutions are based on functions that involve more than individual preferences. Similarly, Lasswell pointed to the likelihood of certain personality types being more successful in particular political roles. However, he rigidly held that the basic character of any political role is determined by its functions in the political process and not by the personality. By posing the problem in these terms, Lasswell avoided the error, frequently made by psychologists, of seeing the *homo politicus* as a distinct personality type characterized by an inordinate craving for power. He defined instead a variety of political roles and political personality types. In particular, Lasswell identified personality types with the political roles of the administrator, the agitator, and the theorist.[7]

Lasswell's method of bringing psychoanalytical considerations to bear on political analysis opened the way for a tremendous growth in studies of factors traditionally considered to be "nonpolitical." (Indeed, some critics have held that "political behavior" studies are nothing more than studies of the nonpolitical, i.e., the social and personal aspects of group behavior.) For example, Lasswell's formulation of the relationship between personality and politics encouraged studies of the social backgrounds of political elites, the symbols of political identifications, and the informal factors influencing decisions.[8] The same assumptions about the relationships between personality and politics are usually present in the studies of voting behavior.[9] Implicit in most such studies is the notion that personality and "informal" considerations are largely "irrational" with respect to the logic of public institutions.

There have been numerous attempts to bridge the gap that Lasswell has left between the private and the public, between the dimension of personality and the sphere of politics. In general, these attempts may be divided into two categories. First, there are those efforts to find direct correlations between specific personality types and political behavior. These are attempts to see the political from the perspective of psychological insights, and they generally concentrated on the dynamics of personality formation during childhood.[10] The second category consists of those attempts to fill the gap between the psychological and the political with other social processes. Instead of moving directly from personality formation to political action, the psychological factor is related to all the other factors that might influence political behavior. The "psychological" dimension thus includes cognitive processes. In the main, this approach has centered on various aspects of the political socialization process.

Most studies in the first category are made by cultural anthropologists and others involved in work on personality and culture. In defining culture as the pattern of basic values reflected in all phases of life, the anthropologist has assumed a close and direct relationship between personality and political behavior. This approach has largely taken the form of national character studies; the names of Ralph Linton, Margaret Mead, Ruth Benedict, and Geoffrey Gorer come readily to mind. Historians have, of course, long employed unspecified notions concerning the characteristics of different nations and peoples.[11] Psychoanalytically oriented students of national character have been much more explicit; consequently, it has been easy for their critics to take exception to particular details.[12]

Within the category of attempts to relate directly personality and politics are those seeking to establish a connection between specific personality configurations and susceptibility to particular political ideological orientations. The outstanding example of this form of study is, of course, *The Authoritarian Personality*.[13] This monumental study, originally conceived as a search for the possible psychological sources of anti-Semitism, became an attempt to demonstrate congruence between personality type and political ideology. Despite its impressive reception in the social sciences, most students of political behavior have found it difficult to accept its suggestion of a direct correlation between authoritarian personality types and membership in authoritarian political movements.[14]

A common characteristic of such studies is that the methodological treatment of psychological matters has been considerably more sophisticated than the political analysis. Subtlety in psychological insights has not necessarily yielded significant knowledge about the political realm. Advances stemming from public-opinion research have further encouraged the study of social processes that intervene between personality formation and political behavior. These studies, which we have put in the second category, tend to be more influenced by orientations common to social psychology than by psychoanalysis. The shift has also been away from a central interest in childhood development and toward an appreciation of the immediate total social context within which action occurs.

For example, Gabriel Almond, in his study of the appeals of communism in four European countries, found it necessary to trace the total process of personality development from early determinants to the later cognitive developments.[15] By working in terms of political socialization, Almond developed the concept of "political culture." The process of political involvement is seen as similar to, but distinct from, the process by which an individual becomes a member of his culture. Out of the early childhood experiences, and later influenced by the way in which he is introduced to the political world, the individual finally assumes a specific political role.[16] Subjective psychological factors can be treated at all stages in the analysis. At the same time, objective factors relating to the social and political setting can be given their full weight. Other attempts to narrow the gap between personality and politics are to be found in the works of M. Brewster Smith, Jerome Bruner, and Robert W. White;[17] Herbert Hyman;[18] Daniel Katz and Charles McClintock; Irving Sarnoff;[19] and Harold R. Isaacs.[20] The rate of advances in political psychology is impressively demonstrated by the recent books of Robert E. Lane[21] and Seymour Martin Lipset[22] which systematically build upon the best of current research in the field.

There are two principal reasons why these various authors have been able to add the psychological dimensions to their studies without grossly oversimplifying basic political considerations. First, they have balanced their analysis of the shaping of the unconscious with explicit treatment of ego-functioning in the total development of the personality. Second, they have related personality factors to the social context of action and, wherever possible, to specific sociological variables. The link between "personality" and political behavior is established by recognizing that personality development depends upon the individual's perceptions of social reality, his emotionally conditioned responses to his environment, and his learned modes of evaluating reality. This approach has led some scholars to a rigorous search for relationships between attitudes, opinions, and "basic orientations," on the one hand, and social or demographic distinctions on the other. Others —like Erich Fromm[23] and David Riesman[24]—have related more broadly defined personality or character types to the main social or economic configurations of an historical period. A highly original and complex analysis has been Daniel Lerner's treatment of the connections between basic aspects of personality and the dynamics of social change in transitional societies.[25]

The use of this image of personality, largely derived from social psychology, has been extremely rewarding when combined with survey techniques. It focuses attention on the relationship between "personality type," basic social and political attitudes, and the distribution of each according to demographic and socio-economic categories.[26] But there is some concern among those who have worked with survey techniques that studies built largely upon a psychology of the cognitive processess will give too "flat" a picture, lacking in the nuances that depend upon the functions of the unconscious. In order to avoid this problem, it may become increasingly necessary to supplement social survey studies with "interviews in depth." These approaches all represent significant advances in the use of psychological theory for political analysis. It would seem, however, that political scientists have yet to arrive at satisfactory methods of realizing the full potentialities of psychoanalytical theory. Every now and then there is the rare work—such as that of Nathan Leites[27]—which taps this potential and demonstrates what may be accomplished if the new image of man is truly incorporated in a political analysis. Thus, although political science has been greatly enriched by the insights of modern psychology, we are still seeking new ways of bridging the gap between the dynamics of individual behavior and the forces of history.

II

It is from such a background of experience as we have just outlined that the political scientist looks for guidance to Erik H. Erikson's *Young Man Luther: A Study in Psychoanalysis and History*.[28] In what ways can the clinical analyst, who has made great contributions to ego psychology and cultural anthropology, assist the student of history?

Erikson is concerned in this volume with the problem of the great man in history, who creates the ideologies in which people find their beliefs. He is concerned with clarifying how the lone individual, in seeking to find himself and give meaning to his own character, can give shape and form to a period of history. More precisely, Erikson is interested in the relationship between the identity crisis in the personality development of the reformer and the ideology he creates. Erikson reduces the gap between the public and the private spheres, between the psychological and the political, by stressing the links between personal identity and public ideology.

It has not been fashionable for political scientists to grapple with the problem of the great man who tries to change the course of history. Modern political science grew up during a time when the notion of "science" was largely one of a quest for uniformities. This assumption encouraged political analysis oriented toward sociology and economics. Even when the pendulum began to swing back to a greater emphasis upon the individual—and, hence, upon psychological considerations—attention still centered largely on aggregates and not on the unique person. The search has been mainly for relationships between social and economic factors and personality types. Recent interest in the study of decision-making and of elite roles has centered primarily upon the webs of relationships through which individual decision-makers have to fight their way, and not upon the function of the leader's personality. One exception to this tendency is Alexander and Juliette George's provocative analysis of Woodrow Wilson's personality.[29]

Before discussing the content of Erikson's study, it is necessary to remark

on Erikson as a writer, for his style is a major clue to his method. His book
is more the product of a man than of a technique.

This study of Luther reveals Erik Erikson's profound and subtle qualities
of mind. His book reflects wisdom and a restless search for knowledge. It
bears no relationship to the kind of superficial and intellectually precious
"psychological interpretations of history" that confuse insight with the cute
or the grotesque. Throughout his book, Erikson warns against the danger
of shallow interpretation; he emphasizes the need "to differentiate psycho-
analysism from psychoanalysis, and to realize that the latter is not only a
profession recognized among professions, but also a system of thought subject
to fashionable manipulation by molders of public opinion" (p. 21). As we
shall note in detail, Erikson differs from the popularizers of psychoanalytical
theory, who he feels have distorted the meaning of Freud's insights.

Erikson is at home in the literary tradition; he knows the importance
of style. He is also unmistakably the product of a humanistic tradition, for
he communicates his fascination with the unique and the distinctive, with
the individual who must be different from all others even as he passes through
the common experiences of all men.

To the political scientist, Erikson seems the very soul of caution in
formulating generalizations. Only in the most tentative way will he suggest
possible patterns and universal tendencies. It is fascinating indeed for a
political scientist to observe the delicacy and care with which the master
clinician handles his data. One fact suggests not a conclusion but the need
for further facts. Only after the clinician has established a long-standing
acquaintanceship and a deep familiarity with his subject does he arrive at
his conclusions.[30]

Erikson's work is also a remarkable demonstration of the clinician's
concern with all the details of a case: in this sense he may be even more
conscious of the importance of the unique occurrences of life than the historian. Erikson explains this concern with the total situation by noting that
"we clinicians have learned in recent years that we cannot lift a case history
out of history, even as we suspect that historians, when they try to separate
the logic of the historic event from that of the life histories which intersect
in it, leave a number of vital historical problems unattended" (pp. 15-16).

On this score, Erikson's book is a direct repudiation of those who
criticize the behavioral sciences for ignoring reality and the logic of the
historical situation in favor of abstract generalization. Erikson has too much
respect for his audience to force upon them his own abstractions or theories,
and he has too much regard for his subject matter to try to force his data
into preconceived molds. Finally, he has too much respect for his own
creativity to make excessive commitments to his still evolving concepts.

As a writer and student of the subconscious, Erikson seems to have
tremendous confidence in the powers of subjective communication. He
refuses to make the explicit, the cold statement; yet he is confident the
reader will grasp the import of his thinking. In dealing with an admittedly
subtle subject, he employs subtle forms of communication. Above all else,
Erikson relies upon the total impact of his work and not upon the logic of

sentences. No doubt he would maintain that one must understand the whole problem and not just isolated parts; and, thus, it is impossible to take any sentence out of the context of the whole and find complete meaning in it. The result is a style of writing that the political scientist should be able to appreciate, for it is in that tradition of political theory that began wih the works of Plato. This also means, however, that it is often extremely difficult to tell exactly what Erikson has in mind. The reader may feel at one moment that he is missing something of significance, while at the next his mind may be led off in directions he is not sure Erikson intended him to take.

As a result, it is quite possible to misinterpret Erikson, or at least to arrive at multiple interpretations of his views. This reader of Erikson's writings, for example, has arrived at conclusions quite different from those of Helen Lynd.[31] It must be acknowledged, however, that writers who refuse to be explicit and rigorously systematic and who allow the suggestive power of words full play are likely to be misunderstood.

In Erikson's case, the dangers of misunderstanding are compounded, for he is not only the suggestive artist but also the psychoanalyst. As Erikson has noted, "psychoanalysis for historical reasons often occupies a position on the borderline of what is demonstrably true and of what demonstrably *feels* true" (p. 21). What "feels true" is a highly relative matter. Those insights that seem convincing to one person may seem strained, implausible, and even foolish to another; just as a metaphor or simile that seems forceful and illuminating to one reader may appear absurd or trite to another. In this reader's judgment, Erikson's concepts, in the main, ring true, and they open up new perspectives of great value in understanding political action.

It should also be noted that Erikson does not aim for shock effects by juxtaposing psychoanalytical—hence highly private—matters and historical and religious matters. He advances his psychological interpretations in a sober manner, but he does not pretend that intimate activities are not emotionally charged subjects; there are, as he notes, matters "which in our enlightened day can become conscious only on the level of the bawdy joke: as long as you smile when you say that" (p. 246).

III

In turning to the content of Erikson's analysis, we must begin with his key concept of the identity crisis. This is the crisis of late adolescence, when the young person, after having synthesized and resynthesized the experiences and reactions of each of the earlier stages of childhood, must move out of childhood and assume a place in the adult world.[32] Erikson finds significance in all the typical characteristics of this stage of life: the periods of moodiness and sentimentality; the restless spirit but lethargic body; the sense of ambition and the desire to explore and know all possibilities, but also the endless moping and hanging around; and the unexpected vacillations between excessive wordliness and unbelievable naivete—between trying to be more adult than adults, and then being more childish than children. Above all, it is the crisis of uncertainty when the youth must commit himself—usually after many fitful starts—to a definition of himself that he and others will recognize. Erikson says:

I have called the major crisis of adolescence the *identity crisis;* it occurs in that period of the life cycle when each youth must forge for himself some central perspective and direction, some working unity, out of the effective remnants of his childhood and the hopes of his anticipated adulthood; he must detect some meaningful resemblance between what he has come to see in himself and what his sharpened awareness tells him others judge and expect him to be [p. 14].

Erikson has emphasized elsewhere that the term "identity" expresses a "mutual relationship in that it connotes both a persistent sameness within oneself (self-sameness) and a persistent sharing of some kind of essential character with others."[33] Thus, *identity formation*

arises from the selective repudiation and mutual assimilation of childhood iden-tifications, and their absorption in a new configuration, which, in turn, is dependent on the process by which a *society* (often through subsocieties) *iden-tifies the young individual,* recognizing him as somebody who had to become the way he is, and who, being the way he is, is taken for granted. The community often not without some initial mistrust, gives such recognition with a (more or less institutionalized) display of surprise and pleasure in making the acquaintance of a newly emerging individual. For the community, in turn, feels recognized by the individual who cares to ask for recognition; it can, by the same token, feel deeply—and vengefully—rejected by the individual who does not seem to care.[34]

It becomes immediately apparent that Erikson's concept of ego-identity provides a far more complex and multi-faceted model of the human per-sonality than is customarily used in political analysis. His concept covers not only the individual's constitutional givens and his idiosyncratic libidinal needs, but also the nature of his cognitive processes and the historically specific quantities of information that he has stored in his memory. The concept goes beyond this. It implies that there are systematic relationships among not just these dimensions of the personality, but among the particular mental or physical faculty favored and best developed by the individual, his effective psychological defense mechanism, his successful sublimations, and even the degree of consistency with which circumstance has required him to assume particular roles.

The political scientist is not one to pass judgments on the technical aspects of Erikson's concept of ego identity.[35] In order to appreciate, however, the ways in which Erikson relates the great ideological reformer to his times and to history, it is necessary to understand the outlines of Erikson's theories about the development of the individual. Erikson assumes that the way in which the major problems of each stage in the development of the individual are met will be reflected in the evolving configuration of that individual's identity; in the case of the great man, this means that his peculiar pattern of development will be reflected in his political ideology. Erikson thus implies that there is a minimum but fundamental structure to any ideology, which is related to elemental aspects of personality develop-

STAGES OF DEVELOPMENT AND THE IDENTITY CRISIS

	1	2	3	4	5	6	7	8
I INFANCY	Trust vs. Mistrust				Unipolarity vs. Premature self-differentiation			
II EARLY CHILDHOOD		Autonomy vs. Shame, Doubt			Bipolarity vs. Autism			
III PLAY AGE			Initiative vs. Guilt		Play Identification vs. (Oedipal) Phantasy-Identities			
IV SCHOOL AGE				Industry vs. Inferiority	Work Identification vs. Identity Foreclosure			
V ADOLESCENCE	Time Perspective vs. Time Diffusion	Self-Certainty vs. Identity Consciousness	Role-Experimentation vs. Negative Identity	Anticipation of Achievement vs. Work-Paralysis	Identity vs. Identity Diffusion	Sexual Identity vs. Bisexual Diffusion	Leadership Polarization vs. Authority Diffusion	Ideological Polarization vs. Diffusion of Ideals
VI YOUNG ADULT					Solidarity vs. Social Isolation	Intimacy vs. Isolation		
VII ADULTHOOD							Generativity vs. Self-Absorption	
VIII MATURE AGE								Integrity vs. Disgust, Despair

ment. Therefore, in reviewing Erikson's theories about the development of the individual, we shall focus on those aspects that are most relevant in contributing to the tone and the spirit of ideologies.

It is only in the last chapter of Erikson's book on Luther that he sets forth his theory of the various stages of personality development. Indeed, those readers who have not previously been exposed to his views on the subject may find that they can get more out of his analysis of Luther if they read this chapter as an introduction. For our purpose of summarizing the stages of development and suggesting their relationship to the identity crisis, we may rely upon a diagram Erikson has devised.[36] It should be noted, however, that a diagram often suggests well-defined and rigorous relation-ships without actually articulating their precise nature. This is an important warning, and, as Erikson has remarked, such a diagram "can be recom-mended to the serious attention only of those who can take it *and* leave it."[37]

The diagram is so constructed that the diagonal line of squares reading from the upper left-hand corner to the lower right present the major crises in personality development for each of the stages of growth, which are listed in the left-hand margin from top to bottom. The basic pattern of personality development, from infancy to early childhood and on through to adolescence and the mature age, is outlined along this diagonal. Each crisis is of a dialectical nature. In the diagram, what would generally be considered as the more successful outcome of each crisis is stated first.

The diagram also shows the relationship of the other stages to the critical stage of the identity crisis. Vertical column 5 states the ways in which the identity crisis is foreshadowed during each of the earlier crises. In each of these earlier ages, there is some aspect of the identity crisis. Horizontal row V outlines the principal implications of the way in which the other crises may be resolved. Thus, horizontal row V should be matched up with the diagonal line of squares, while vertical column 5 should be related to the age categories.

If we begin with the beginning, we have the crisis of *basic trust* during infancy, which corresponds in large measure with Freud's oral stage. Out of this first social relationship between the mothering adult and the mothered child, the individual gains that first and most fundamental of all psychosocial traits—that original "optimism," that assumption that "somebody is there," the treasure of "basic trust." Or, denied the necessary security, he comes to a profound sense of mistrust which will color his entire existence. He will miss something others can take for granted most of the time, and, according to Erikson, only psychiatrists, priests, and born philosophers can appreciate how sorely he will miss it (p. 118). The question of identity at this age takes the paradoxical form of the "positive" development being the lack of differentiation or a sense of "unipolarity," while the "negative" development would be a premature sense of self-differentiation. Erikson's concept of a sense of unipolarity goes beyond the more traditional Freudian concept of narcissistic omnipotence, which is customarily associated with this age. The infant not only feels that he can command his world, but, more fun-damentally, he feels that the world is for him and he can be for the world.

If, on the other hand, the infant feels that in his first relationship he is un-related to the other, that the world can ignore him and he can have no control over it, then the consequence will be a sense of isolation, of premature self-differentiation, of basic mistrust.

Shifting next to the subsequent consequences for identity formation of the basic trust crisis (1, V), the main issue is that of the relationship of the individual to time. With trust comes a sense of time perspective, an optimism about the future, a feeling that good things will come with waiting, that stress will soon be relieved with pleasure. On the other hand, a failure of the ego function to maintain this perspective is related to an early inability to develop satisfactory expectations about need-tensions and their satisfac-tions. Time diffusion is a basic mistrusting of time: every delay appears as deceit; every need to wait becomes an experience of impatience; every hope, a signal of danger; every potential provider, a probable traitor.

Going beyond the level of individual identity to that of ideological for-mulations, the crisis of basic trust is related to the role of faith. With a perspective on time and a powerful sense of trust, Utopias become possible, planning and programming give hope and meaning, and loyalty is in itself rewarding. When the efficacy of faith must be denied, planning and policy must lose all meaning, and deceit is seen in all actions. Presumably, a political ideology might meet the needs of some who have not had the full measure of basic trust. But according to Erikson: "Of all the ideological systems, however, only religion restores the earliest sense of appeal to a Provider, a Providence. In the Judeo-Christian tradition, no prayer indicates this more clearly than 'The Lord make His Face to shine upon you and be gracious unto you. The Lord lift up His countenance upon you and give you peace' " (p. 118). What was to Freud the oral stage has become with Erikson that which also makes the "face" so important in human affairs: "face-to-face relationships," "face the facts," "face the future," "face up to life," "let's face it."

The next age of early childhood, comparable to Freud's anal stage, brings the crisis of autonomy as against shame and doubt. From this stage comes that element in the sense of autonomy "which can and does mean independence, but does and can also mean defiance, stubbornness, self-insistence" (p. 122). What is basic faith in the earlier age becomes human will, "in its variations of will power and willfulness" (p. 225). And what is basic mistrust in the oral stage becomes shame and doubt in the second stage. In Erikson's view, shame is different from, and quite as important as, guilt. Shame is "the loss of social innocence, the blushing awareness that one can 'lose face,' have 'too much cheek,' and suffer the wish to be invisible, to sink into the ground. Defiance obviously, is shame's dialectical opposite: and it makes sense that the willfull exposure of the behind came to mean a defiant gesture of shamelessness . . ." (p. 122). With respect to the later identity crises, the issue of autonomy versus shame will be resolved either in favor of a sense of self-certainty, a sense of autonomy with will and purpose, or with a crushing sense of self-consciousness and a defiant need to claim a self.

It is impossible to summarize accurately Erikson's extremely subtle interpretation of young Luther's experiences during these first two crises of his life. It must be recognized that we are doing Erikson an injustice when we reduce his analysis to the following bare statements: First, Luther obtained an extraordinary reservoir of basic faith from his mother, and thus always had a deep understanding of the dynamics of faith. However:

Martin was driven early out of the trust stage, out from under his mother's skirts by a jealously ambitious father who tried to make him precociously independent from women, and sober and reliable in his work. Hans succeeded but not without storing in the boy violent doubts of the father's justification and sincerity; a lifelong shame over the persisting gap between his own precocious conscience and his actual inner state; and a deep nostalgia for a situation of infantile trust. His theological solution—spiritual return to a faith which is there before all doubt, combined with a political submission to those who by necessity must wield the sword of secular law—seems to fit perfectly his personal need for compromise [pp. 255-56].

These are the origins, as Erikson sees it, of that combination of faith and wrath; of the belief that behind a God that shames and a God that is demanding, there is still the possibility of mutual recognition, of the face-to-face meeting of personal salvation. As Erikson puts it: "It would be much too easy (although some stalwart opponents of all interpretation would consider even this easiest and most obvious explanation far fetched) that Han's son was seeking in religion what he would not find in Hans" (p. 115).

We have gone into detail with these first two stages, in order to give some feeling of Erikson's mode of analysis. We must treat the other stages in more summary fashion.

The third crisis, that of initiative versus guilt, covers more than the Freudian concept of the Oedipus complex. Erikson reflects his personal values and, above all, his ability to be hard-headed yet sympathetic, without being precious and sentimental, when he writes of the Oedipus complex. For example, he says:

...we...most certainly...would ascribe to Luther an Oedipus complex, and not a trivial one at that. We would not wish to see any boy—much less an imaginative and forceful one—face the struggles of his youth and manhood without having experienced as a child the love and the hate which are encompassed in this complex: love for the maternal person who awakens his senses and his sensuality with her ministrations, and deep and angry rivalry with the male possessor of this maternal person. We would also wish him with their help to succeed, in his boyhood, in turning resolutely away from the protection of women to assume the fearless initiative of men [p. 73].

Clearly, Erikson does not minimize the Oedipus complex; yet it is not a dominant theme in his total analysis. The influence of the initiative versus guilt crisis on the subsequent identity crisis depends upon whether the individual resolves his Oedipus complex by turning outside of the family to seek his future development, thus envisioning the possibility of experimenting with other roles. The alternative would be a sense of *negative identity,* that is, a need to become what one has been warned not to become, which is something one can only do with a divided heart. Since there seems to be a need to protect one's wholeheartedness, those who have a sense of negative identity cannot even be steadfast rebels.

Erikson's analysis moves without interruption from this stage into the crisis of industry and inferiority. In this fourth stage, the individual's "budding will to phantasy, play, games and early work" are all related to the occupational and technological ideals that the child perceives in his environment. What for Freud was the phallic stage becomes with Erikson a period of systematic learning and of collaboration with others:

> The resolution of this stage decides much of the ratio between a sense of industry or work completion, and a sense of tool-inferiority, and prepares a man for the essential ingredients of the ethos as well as the rationale of his technology. ... In Martin's case, the tool was literacy, Latin literacy, and ... he was molded by it ... and later he remolded, with the help of printing, his nation's literary habits. With a vengeance he could claim to have taught German even to his enemies [pp. 258-59].

A major dimension of personality formation in Erikson's view is learning a craft or a skill and developing proficiency in manipulating particular tools, instruments, or symbols.

Next comes the identity crisis, the principal one in Erikson's analysis, in terms of which his book on Luther is written. The last three crises—those of intimacy versus isolation, generality versus self-absorption, and integrity versus despair—are fairly self-evident and need no further elaboration here. We need only note that, in Erikson's view:

> The integrity crisis, last in the lives of ordinary men, is a lifelong and chronic crisis in a *homo religiosus.* He is always older, or in early years suddenly becomes older, than his playmates or even his parents and teachers, and focuses in a precocious way on what it takes others a life-time to gain a mere inkling of: the question of how to escape corruption in living and how in death to give meaning to life [p. 261].

IV

It has been considerably easier to set forth Erikson's views on the "metabolism of generations" than it will be to state his theory about the dynamics of the great man in history. In this volume Erikson is still experimenting with his theory, and he is extremely reluctant to use any direct propositional statements. We can only outline what seems to be the direction of his explorations.

The story of the great man, ideologically speaking, is the story of an individual striving to find his own identity. By following the peculiar logic of that struggle, he gives, without necessarily intending to, a sense of identity and meaning to a people at a particular juncture of history. The individual pattern of development may be extremely complicated, but Erikson suggests that there are certain uniformities. In particular, he makes comparative references to the lives of Freud, Darwin, G. B. Shaw, and Hitler.

The beginning point—indeed, the central theme—of the development of the great man is his need to settle a personal account on a large scale and in a grand context. This involves far more than the idea that public life provides the opportunity for reducing psychic tensions. In Erikson's view, the great man must have some score to settle with others and the score must be of such grand proportion that it is appropriate to seek a public arena. The problem must be far more than just the sting of the Oedipus complex. Erikson elsewhere has commented: "Whoever has suffered under and identified with a stern father, must become a stern father himself, or else find an entirely different means of moral strength, an equal measure of strength. Young Martin Luther's religious crisis is a transcendent example of the heights and depths of this problem."[58]

This magnitude of the personal problem and the compelling need to resolve it seems to produce a deep sense of ambivalence: a feeling of sinfulness on the one hand, and a feeling of being chosen on the other. The great man may come to seek greatness, to believe in his own destiny, and yet he can be consumed with a fear of failure, a precocious fear that may arise at a very early age. Indeed, Erikson suggests that such men often fail as children, in that they are people with lost childhoods—people who place excessive demands upon themselves from a very early age. In their lives, the identity crisis is likely to involve a conflict between a sense of allness and a feeling of nothingness. The fear of failure becomes a dread of nonexistence, and the individual vacillates between a sense of nothingness and a sense of being everything. Erikson is convincing when discussing the thin line that separates the feelings of omnipotence and of insignificance.

A key element in the identity crisis—but something which may last through life—is the "moratorium." Erikson attaches considerable significance to the need of all individuals for a period of moratorium: a withdrawal from full involvement, a time of loneliness and uncertainty, a time during which psychic growth may catch up with physical development. Most societies have institutionalized, in varying degrees, this moratorium, in the sense that they withhold responsibility from young people who are physically as developed as adults. During the moratorium, the young person generally develops some skill or technique that will either subsequently become central to his identity or give him the necessary sense of discipline so that he will be able to employ more effectively some other faculty or skill. Luther's moratorium was spent in the monastery; Freud's "monastery" was his medical and scientific training; G. B. Shaw spent his moratorium in a business house; Darwin spent his in medical training and two years aboard the *Beagle;* for Winston Churchill, it was the Indian army. Erikson suggests that the common pattern of the ideological innovator is one of coming upon his life work without prior planning or design. Disciplined training is in one area, and creative innovation in another.

To achieve his sense of identity and break out of his moratorium, the great man must rely upon some dominant faculty, some special gift. In Erikson's reading of history, there is also likely to be at this juncture some technological innovation that can peculiarly complement the special qualities of the great man, becoming the bridge that links him to his times. In the case of Luther, it was his understanding of the Word and Gutenberg's invention of the printing press. Erikson has some subtle things to say about playing with words and about the importance people will attach to isolated words and characters, to doctrines and pronouncements, to the Word and to the Good Book. Even more important is Erikson's appreciation of the compulsions that lie behind the need of the great ideological innovators to talk, to manipulate words. Above all else, such people do not need simply to talk: they need to *talk back*. It is not at the level of the content of their words, but at a much deeper level, that they really mean what they say. This is the need to settle their score; this is the real "Meaning of Meaning It."

Once the reformer has found his identity and commands a medium through which he can act without conflict, the stage is set for a great moment in history. This is the moment of consummation, when both the reformer's search and the period's search for identities are mutually realized. Erikson suggests that this moment of success affects the ego of the leader and the ego of those reached by, and receptive to, his word. All who are involved know that they "mean it," and a historical force of great power is produced.

For the people, a long-needed shift in outlook has occurred; they will never be the same again. For the leader, this can only be a moment of balance and then the inner conflict must be resumed. While Luther was "in the cloister all three factors—his sense of identity, his potential for intimacy, and the discovery of his generative powers—were stubbornly engaged in the life-or-death struggle for that sense of total justification which both the father and The Father had denied him, and without which a *homo religiosus* has no identity at all" (p. 149). Once he did find the main executive of his identity, the Word, he was caught up again in the conflict between a sense of nothingness and an urge for fame.

This conflict can result in the collapse of the innovator and even in his becoming in time the very thing he fought. However, this is only part of the problem. The leader may also realize that he really did not intend to do what he did on the grand scale; he may come to recognize that it was only a private score he had to settle.

The crisis of an ideological leader naturally emerges when he must recognize what his rebellion—which began with the application of a more or less disciplined phantasy to the political world in the widest sense—has done to the imagination, the sense of reality, and the conscience of the masses. The fact is that all walks of life, revolutionized but essentially leaderless, exploited Luther's reformation in all directions at once. They refused to let him, and a few people like him, settle down in parsonages as the representatives of the praying orientation in life, and otherwise accept the estate and occupation in which, as he claimed, God had placed them. The princes became more absolute, the middle-class more mercantile, the lower classes more mystical and revolutionary; and the universal reign of faith envisaged in Luther's early teachings turned into an intolerant and cruel Bible-quoting bigotry such as history had never seen. As Tawney put it, "the rage of Luther . . . was sharpened by embarrassment at what seemed to him a hideous parody of truths which were both sacred and his own" [p. 242].

The final result is that the ideological leader produces consequences that are quite the opposite of those he intended.

Consider for a brief moment certain great names of our time, who pride themselves on a dominant identity enhanced by scientific truth. Darwin, Einstein, and Freud—omitting Marx, who was a conscious and deliberate ideological craftsman—would certainly deny that they had any intention of influencing, say, the editorials, or the vocabulary, or the scrupulosity of our time in the ways in which they undoubtedly did and do. They could, in fact, refute the bulk of the concepts popularly ascribed to them, or vaguely and anonymously derived from them, as utterly foreign to their original ideas, their methodology, and their personal philosophy and conduct. Darwin did not intend to debase man to an animal; Einstein did not preach relativism; Freud was neither a philosophical pansexualist nor a moral egotist. Freud pointed squarely to the psychohistorical problem involved when he said that the world apparently could not forgive him for having revised the image of man by demonstrating the dependence of man's will on unconscious motivation, just as Darwin had not been forgiven for demonstrating man's relationship to the animal world, or Copernicus for showing that our earth is off-center [pp.177-78].

In summary, the great man, in seeking to settle his own inner problem, strikes out against his environment. He is both destructive and constructive; indeed, without a capacity for destruction he cannot be truly constructive. It is through leveling blows against the existing system that the great man first wins his audience. His public must also feel some uncertainty over the times, some loss of identity. Then comes the role of charisma, the basis of a new mode of communication, and the beginnings of a new sense of identity for both the leader and the followers. The particular faculty and the particular technology provide the foundations for institutionalizing the relationship of charisma and for giving structure to the new sense of identity. Then come the extremist reactions: first the leader overdoes it, and then the followers overdo it.

V

What is Erikson's purpose in this book? What special value does the study have for political scientists? In making his point that the consequences of ideological leaders are often the opposite of their intended purposes, Erikson presents a penetrating comparison of Luther and Freud. There is considerable significance in each of the points he makes about Luther, who came at the end of the age of absolute faith, and Freud, who came at the end of the age of reason. I was particularly struck by the following:

Both men endeavored to increase the margin of man's inner freedom by introspective means applied to the very center of his conflicts; and this to the end of increased individuality, sanity, and service to men. Luther, at the beginning of ruthless mercantilism in Church and commerce, counterpoised praying man to the philosophy and practice of meritorious works. Subsequently, his justification by faith was absorbed into the patterns of mercantilism, and eventually turned into a justification of commercialism by faith. Freud, at the beginning of unrestricted industrialization, offered another method of introspection, psychoanalysis. With it, he obviously warned against the mechanical socialization of men into effective but neurotic robots. It is equally obvious that his work is about to be used in furtherance of that which he warned against: the glorification of "adjustment." Thus both Doctor Luther and Doctor Freud, called great by their respective ages, have been and are apt to be resisted not only by their enemies, but also by friends who subscribe to their ideas but lack what Kierkegaard called a certain strenuousness of mental and moral effort [p. 252].

Here and there throughout the book Erikson criticized the popularizers of Freudian analysis. At the surface level, he is particularly critical of their soft-headed and sentimental qualities and of their lack of appreciation for the high costs and the self-discipline that must go into any form of human excellence. Erikson repeatedly reminds us of a point that some popularizers of psychoanalysis ignore: Freud did not merely seek to help the individual adjust to his environment; he also demanded that the individual make the "environment" adapt to him. The difference is extremely important for political analysis. A peculiar set of biases, largely favoring static analysis and equilibrium concepts, is likely to predominate if it is assumed that the individual must either adjust to, and be molded by, "society" or revolt against society. A radically different outlook comes from picturing the individual as not only adapting to others, but in turn changing and controlling his surroundings. With such an orientation, initiative, creativity, and the basic dynamics for the system do not come from anything as abstract as "society," but rather from particular individuals. All people are to some extent creative, for all people must shape their worlds in finding their identities.

At a deeper level, Erikson's concern over what he considers to be the popular misinterpretations of Freud involves another problem, which is left largely unarticulated but which colors much of the analysis. This is the problem of the proper relationship of the disciple to his ideological father. How can one find one's own identity while remaining true to one's leader and mentor? This of course, is the dynamic element behind all controversies about who is perpetuating the true faith and who is deviating from it. This has been the problem of those who took their inspiration from Luther and of those who took theirs from Freud. Erikson is known as a Freudian; yet he has quite possibly done more original and innovational work than any of the neo-Freudians. (Freud only used the term "identity" once, and with a rather different meaning than that of Erikson's.) A clue to Erikson's method in becoming both the complete follower and the creative innovator is to be found in the following words, which he once used to sum up his appraisal of Freud:

Freud, before he went into medicine, wanted to become a lawyer and politician, a lawmaker, a *Gesetzgeber*. When, in 1938, he was exiled from his country, he carried under his arm a manuscript on Moses, the supreme law-giver of the people whose unique fate and whose unique gifts he had accepted as his own. With grim pride he had chosen the role of one who opens perspectives on fertile fields to be cultivated by others. As we look back to the beginnings of his work, and forward to its implications, we may well venture to say: Freud the physician in finding a method of healing himself in the very practice of emotional cure has given a new, a psychological rationale for man's laws. He has made the decisive step toward a true interpenetration of the psychological with the technological and the political in the human order.[39]

Erikson thus claims that Freud was centrally concerned with the larger order of human relationships, and that such historical studies as this one of Luther should belong at the heart of the intellectual revolution sparked by Freud. The insights of psychoanalysis should not be treated as marginal ideas that may add novelty to otherwise completed studies. Erikson would hold that these insights must be placed at the center of political analysis to become an integrated part of research. Erikson, however, is quick to recognize that this will be a difficult development because there is such widespread misconception about what Freud's contribution really was. This is why Erikson is so critical of the superficial popularizers of psychoanalysis. He also acknowledges that psychoanalysis has

... developed a kind of *originology* ... a habit of thinking which reduces every human situation to an analogy with an earlier one, and most of all to that earliest, simplest, and most infantile precursor which is assumed to be its "origin." Psychoanalysis has tended to subordinate the later stages of life to those of childhood. It has lifted to the rank of a cosmology the undeniable fact that man's adulthood contains a persistent childishness: that vistas of the future always reflect the mirage of a missed past, that apparent progression can harbor partial regression, and firm accomplishment, hidden childish fulfillment.... We must grudgingly admit that even as we were trying to devise, with scientific determinism, a therapy for the few, we were led to promote an ethical disease among the many [pp. 18-19].

Erikson's answer to this problem is that Freud's great contribution was not certain formulas about personality development, but a *technique of observation*. Throughout his book, Erikson says that if we are to understand, analyze, and appreciate those who shape history, we must really look at them and observe them as full individuals. Our ability to see others clearly depends, however, upon our readiness to take a hard introspective view of ourselves. This, of course, is where the argument becomes delicate and even sticky. Erikson, however, does not imply that only those who have, under the guidance of others, taken such a long introspective view are capable of sensitive and complete political analysis. Rather, he is warning us that we should be especially careful whenever we feel that we are being especially "honest," "objective," or "open-minded." We must recognize that some of our claims to being "objective" may be prompted by a desire to protect ourselves from an honest look at reality. We must be prepared, as Erikson says, "to relinquish the security of seemingly more objective methods."[40] There are times, of course, when the problem for the individual social scientist must become even more complex. In the words of Erikson:

An adult studying a child, an anthropologist studying a tribe, or a sociologist studying a riot sooner or later will be confronted with data of decisive importance for the welfare of those whom he is studying, while the strings of his own motivation will be touched, sometimes above and sometimes well below the threshold of awareness. He will not be able, for long, to escape the necessary conflict between his emotional participation in the observed events and the methodological rigor required to advance his field and human welfare. Thus, his studies will demand, in the long run, that he develop the ability to include in his observational field his human obligations, his methodological responsibilities, and his own motivations. In doing so, he will, in his own way, repeat that step in scientific conscience which Freud dared to make.[41]

Erikson's basic criticism of the popularizers of psychoanalytical concepts is that they have given to the social scientist a set of phrases that have become mechanical and wooden formulas, shielding those who use them from the painful tasks of introspection and of honestly viewing reality. It is not surprising that intelligent, sensitive, and knowing people have found dubious value in studies which seek to make a direct connection between the nursery and world affairs, between crib and cabinet.

The primary contribution of Erikson's work for the political scientist is the reminder that Freud's main contribution was a technique of observation, and that observation is the key to the study of human relationships as it is the key to all sciences.

What about the particular theories and concepts that Erikson has developed? He has created a model of personality development which can be of great interest to the political scientist. It is, however, so complicated and subtle that it can probably only be used to full effect by its creator. With this in mind, Erikson's contribution is primarily one of making us more sensitive to a wide range of emotional nuances and of subjective relationships in human development and behavior.

Erikson's concept of identity can have a more specific impact on political research. It becomes an exciting and illuminating concept when applied, for example, to the problem of political development in the emergent countries. These are societies whose peoples, in spite of their slogans of nationalism, lack a sense of identity. When old forms and customs lose their binding, their sustaining, and their reassuring powers, the people must restlessly search for new personal identities and for a new sense of collective identity. The arena is prepared for the ideological reformer—in Erikson's terms, the great man of history. In this setting, it is all too easy for the shallow charismatic leader to appear for a moment as a prophet. Those who are facile with words may have great appeal, for the people need the word to find a new way. It is a time in which words are fundamentally more important than actions. It is also a time in which words become cheap and action becomes impossible. The setting is right for the politically anxious to try out—possibly with enthusiasm, but certainly without true commitment—all manner of ideological forms. Before the nation can develop, leaders must emerge who have found integrity in their own quests for identity, and who can therefore speak in terms that will bring meaning to other people's search for identity. The need is for that set of shared orientations which force a people steadfastly to face reality, and which make it impossible for them to turn from reality. This is the meaning Erikson gives the ideology.

Erikson's concept of identity thus suggests that the problem of consensus in transitional societies runs deeper than mere agreement over political forms and over the appropriate ends and means of political action; it involves the creation of an inner coherence of values, theories, and actions for the entire polity. The implication is that in underdeveloped countries there is a vicious circle at the subjective level, which is more crucial to the problem of national development than the more manifest vicious circle of poverty, ill-health, and illiteracy. Those who hope that national identity can come from modernization cannot escape the depressing psychological fact that modernity, in the mind of these people, has always been the monopoly of those who were their former masters. If they hated their colonial rulers, then they cannot expect to find their identities by following the same path. If they did not hate their former rulers, there might still be the problem of preferring dependency to autonomy, which would confuse the quest for identity. National identity cannot be built upon doing less well what one's former master excelled at. Similar psychological roadblocks appear when identity is sought among the recorded but forgotten remnants of a distant history, for such a search becomes, psychologically, a constant reminder of national impotence in recent history. These are only some of the subjective problems that impede the solution of the more objective problems in the underdeveloped countries, and that cannot be resolved until a sense of national identity is achieved.

The readily apparent utility of Erikson's concept of identity to the problems of the underdeveloped countries suggests that it must have a much broader value. Specifically, his concept can give focus to all forms of study concerned with the development of the political actor. By stressing the individual's need to find coherence in his self-image, Erikson suggests that we should see the process of political socialization, not as a series of random experiences, but as a trend in development in which there is always a central theme, an element of unity. There is an inner logic or coherence in the way in which people come to their political orientations. Our search should thus be for more than connections between isolated attitudes and opinions on the one hand, and particular demographic characteristics on the other; it should be for the more complete pattern, the total configuration, the full style of political actors.

By demonstrating that the gap between the private and the political can be effectively bridged by the relationship between personal identity and political ideology, Erikson helps the political scientist with more than the problem of the psychological aspects of behavior. He also offers an approach for studying ideologies themselves. For some time, political scientists have known that the logic of ideologies is not encompassed by mere reason. However, there has remained the problem of a systematic method for treating the nonrational components. Erikson, in suggesting that political ideologies express the total character of the human personality, has provided us with an analytical framework to understand the inner structure of ideologies. Psychoanalytical theory can be a guide for comprehending more than just individual patterns of behavior. Nathan Leites has shown how extremely rewarding it can be to examine an ideology—or in his phrase, an operational code—according to the insights of psychoanalysis. Leites chose to leave his theory implicit; Erikson has stated his theory in more detail. Both have worked at the creative stage in the development of a promising approach; the next stage will have to be one of increased precision in stating propositions and increased rigor in empirical testing.

Erikson is able to challenge and stimulate the thinking of political scientists because he combines so effectively in himself the qualities of both the scientist and the artist. Like a great artist, he evokes in others an urge to imitate him. Also like a great artist, he makes us sensitive to the wonders of what we had taken to be mere commonplaces. In referring to his own youth, Erikson once noted, "I was an artist then, which is a European euphemism for a young man with some talent, but nowhere to go."[42] In going far since then, Erikson has not lost the genius of the true artist.

Notes

1. For an excellent outline of the psychological premises of classical political theory and of the problems posed by modern psychology see Thomas I. Cook, "Democratic Psychology and Democratic World Order," *World Politics,* I (July, 1949), 553-64.

2. Harold D. Lasswell, *Psychopathology and Politics* (Chicago: University of Chicago Press, 1930), pp. 74-76.

3. Harold D. Lasswell, *World Politics and Personal Insecurity* (New York: Whittlesey House, 1930), p. 39.

4. *Ibid.,* p. 73; quoted in Helen Merrell Lynd, *On Shame and the Search for Identity* (New York: Harcourt, Brace and Co., 1958), pp. 97-98.

5. Harold D. Lasswell, *Power and Personality* (New York: W. W. Norton & Co., 1948), pp. 16-17.

6. *Ibid.,* chaps. ii-iv.

7. Harold D. Lasswell, *Psychopathology and Politics* (Chicago: University of Chicago Press, 1930), pp. 53-55.

8. The most outstanding examples would be the Hoover Institute Studies in the RADIR project that were authored by Daniel Lerner, Ithiel deSola Pool, Robert North, and others.

9. Harold F. Gosnell, *Grass Roots Politics: National Voting Behavior of Typical States* (Washington: American Council on Public Affairs, 1942); Paul F. Lazarsfeld, Bernard Berelson, and Hazel Gaudet, *The Peoples' Choice* (New York: Columbia University Press, 1948); Bernard R. Berelson, Paul F. Lazarsfeld, and William N. McPhee, *Voting* (Chicago: University of Chicago Press, 1954); and Angus Campbell, Gerald Gurin, Warren E. Miller, *The Voter Decides* (Evanston, Ill.: Row, Peterson and Co., 1954).

10. Among the best statements of the methodology of this form of psychocultural analysis are: Nathan Leites, "Psycho-Cultural Hypotheses about Political Acts," *World Politics,* I (October, 1948), 102-19; Abram Kardiner, *The Psychological Frontiers of Society* (New York: Columbia University Press, 1945); Margaret Mead, "The Study of National Character," in Daniel Lerner and Harold D. Lasswell (eds.), *The Policy Sciences: Recent Developments in Scope and Method* (Stanford: Stanford University Press, 1951).

11. The advantages for historians of the newer insights of psychoanalysis are well stated by William L. Langer in his presidential address to the American Historical Association, "The Next Assignment," *The American Historical Review,* LXIII (January, 1958), 283-304.

12. David Potter, a historian, has written an excellent and sympathetic critique of much of the work on national character. See his *People of Plenty* (Chicago: University of Chicago Press, 1954).

13. T. W. Adorno, E. Frenkel-Brunswik, D. J. Levinson, R. N. Sanford, in collaboration with Betty Aron, Maria H. Levinson, and W. Morrow, *The Authoritarian Personality* (New York: Harper & Brothers, 1950); sponsored by the

American Jewish Committee, "Social Studies Series," publication No. 3.

14. Herbert McClosky has continued to search for correlations between political conservatism and a set personality type. See "Conservatism and Personality," *American Political Science Review,* LII (March, 1958), 27-45.

15. Gabriel Almond, *The Appeals of Communism* (Princeton: Princeton University Press, 1959).

16. Gabriel Almond, "Comparative Political Systems," *Journal of Politics, XVIII* (August, 1956), pp. 391-409; "Theoretical Introduction," in G. Almond and J. Coleman (eds.), *The Politics of Underdeveloped Areas* (Princeton: Princeton University Press, 1960).

17. M. Brewster Smith, Jerome Bruner, and Robert W. White, *Opinions and Personality* (New York: John Wiley & Sons, Inc., 1956).

18. Herbert Hyman, *Political Socialization* (Glencoe, Ill.: The Free Press, 1959).

19. Irving Sarnoff and Daniel Katz, "The Motivational Bases of Attitude Change," *Journal of Abnormal and Social Psychology,* XLIX (January, 1954), 115-24; Daniel Katz, Charles McClintock, and Irving Sarnoff, "The Measurement of Ego Defense as Related to Attitude Change," *Journal of Personality,* XXV (June, 1957), 465-74; Daniel Katz, Irving Sarnoff, and Charles McClintock, "Ego-Defense and Attitude Change," *Human Relations,* IX (January, 1956), 27-45.

20. Harold R. Isaacs, *Scratches on Our Minds: American Images of China and India* (New York: John Day Co., 1958).

21. Robert E. Lane, *Political Life: Why People Get Involved in Politics* (Glencoe, Ill.: The Free Press, 1959).

22. Seymour Martin Lipset, *Political Man: The Social Bases of Politics* (New York: Doubleday & Co., 1960).

23. *Escape From Freedom* (New York: Rinehart & Company, Inc., 1941).

24. *The Lonely Crowd* (New Haven: Yale University Press, 1950).

25. Daniel Lerner, *The Passing of Traditional Society* (Glencoe, Ill.: The Free Press, 1958).

26. An outstanding example of such a study is Alex Inkeles and Raymond A. Bauer, *The Soviet Citizen* (Cambridge: Harvard University Press, 1959).

27. *A Study of Bolshevism* (Glencoe, Ill.: The Free Press, 1953). For two excellent commentaries on Leites' methods and his analytical assumptions, see Daniel Bell, "Ten Theories in Search of Reality," *World Politics,* X (April, 1958), 327-65; and Clyde Kluckhohn, "Politics, History and Psychology," *World Politics,* VIII (October, 1955), 112-23.

28. (New York: W. W. Norton & Co., 1958).

29. Alexander L. George and Juliette L. George, *Woodrow Wilson and Colonel House* (New York: John Day Co., 1956).

30. For Erikson's own statement of the clinical method, see his Hayden Colloquium Lecture, "The Nature of Clinical Evidence," *Daedalus,* Fall, 1958, pp. 65-87. For a comparison of his methods with those of other investigators see Daniel Lerner, "Preface to the Issue 'On Evidence and Inference,'" *Daedalus, Fall,* 1958, pp. 3-10.

31. Helen Merrell Lynd, *On Shame and the Search for Identity* (New York: Harcourt, Brace and Co., 1958).

32. Erikson has developed his theories of ego-identity in numerous writings: *Childhood and Society* (New York: W. W. Norton & Co., 1950); "Ego Development and Historical Change," in *The Psychoanalytical Study of the Child* (New York: International University Press, 1946), Vol. II; "Growth and Crises in the 'Healthy Personality'" (For Fact-Finding Committee, Midcentury White House Conference; New York: Josiah Macy Jr. Foundation, 1950), and in Kluckhohn and Murray (eds.), *Personality in Nature, Culture and Society* (New York, Alfred A. Knopf, 1953); "On the Sense of Inner Identity," in *Health and Human Relations* (Report on the International Conference in Hiddesen, Germany, 1951; New York: The Blakiston Co., 1953); "The Problem of Ego Identity," *Journal of The American Psychoanalytic Association,* IV (January, 1956), 56-121.

33. Erik Erikson, "The Problem of Ego Identity," *Journal of the American Psychoanalytical Association,* IV (January, 1956), 57.

34. *Ibid.,* pp. 68-69.

35. The political scientist with cu-

riosity about ego psychology may want to read, in addition to Erikson's writings: Anna Freud, *The Ego and the Mechanisms of Defense* (New York: Basic Books, 1952); H. Hartmann, "Ego Psychology and the Problem of Adaptation," in D. Rapaport (ed.), *Organization and Pathology of Thought* (New York: Columbia University Press, 1951), chap. xiv; H. Hartman, "Comments on the Psychoanalytic Theory of the Ego," in *The Psychoanalytic Study of the Child* (New York: International Universities Press, 1950), V, 74-96.

36. Erikson, 'The Problem of Ego Identity," p. 75.

37. *Ibid.*, p. 76.

38. Erik Erikson, "The First Psychoanalyst," *Yale Review,* Autumn, 1956, p. 50.

39. Erikson, "The First Psychoanalyst," p. 62.

40. Erikson, "The First Psychoanalyst," p. 60.

41. *Ibid.*

42. *Ibid.*, p. 40.

Of Man, Magic, and Motives

by DARYL DeBELL, M.D.

I

It is difficult to respond in a consistent way to Erik Erikson's *Young Man Luther*. This is so for two reasons. In the first place, it is difficult to ascertain the intent of the book. Quite clearly, Erikson intended to describe in detail an identity crisis in an exceptionally gifted man, and to indicate the effect which this crisis and this man had on history. He does this admirably, but I cannot escape the feeling that I am missing something. It is as though there is something being said that I do not quite catch or understand. I feel that if I read it again quickly I will catch in the sweep what I have missed in the perusal. I also fail in this attempt, but I still trust my intuition. I believe Erikson must have had something in mind to which he was not yet ready to commit himself in print—something which if expressed now would sound mystical, or vague and inconclusive, and would be unconvincing, but which after further ripening would come out in Erikson's characteristically lucid and disarmingly simple style.

A second reason for difficulty is the wide range of the book. In addition to the main theme of identity crisis, Erikson has included extensive commentary on the interrelationship between individuals and their society, and he has done it without emphasizing the fact by a subtitle or a chapter heading. I have selected for comment two of these themes—the nature and function

of ideology and a consideration of the factors which make a "great" man—
Erikson makes other observations more difficult to catalogue. He makes
shrewd observation of facts, whose recognition alters our conceptions, and
intuitive analyses that are presented as speculative but that nevertheless
influence our subsequent views of the matter. All these are stimulating and
valuable, but they do not lend themselves readily to the kind of treatment
here employed.

It is popularly recognized that to avert intemperate disputes one should
avoid the discussion of sex, politics, and religion. Erikson has managed to
write a book composed almost entirely of just such explosive content. Even
the most detached scientific reader will doubtless find himself reacting emotionally to Erikson's treatment of one or another of these ideological sacred
cows. The problem posed by the assignment to write a critical essay about
such a book is therefore acute and unavoidable. In writing about a book that
discusses the nature and function of ideologies, one automatically invokes his
own. In this case, the problem is compounded by the fact that I am writing
about a fellow psychoanalyst's work, for an audience composed essentially
of non-analysts. Since it seems to me to be pointless for a critic to write a
series of "Amens" to the author's text and equally improper and patronizing,
to both the author and reader, to undertake to "explain" the author's meaning, I have chosen to deal extensively with some points of difference in
emphasis with Erikson. I take pains to mention this point, because I am
wary that this spark of difference in an ideological tinderbox might lead to
an explosion of disagreement from the mutual audience. I hope that such
differences as do appear will, rather, provide a sharp perspective for the
details of Erikson's theses as well as indicate the remaining problems that
both of us recognize.

It is easy, for example, to say that Erikson has achieved a brilliant
psychoanalytic exposition of Luther's conflicts, his identity crisis, and the
resolution of both. It is easy because it is true, and my agreement with his
exposition is virtually complete. It is also true, however, that a number of
other such analyses could have been made—and some have been—without
doing violence to the facts. It is a recognized principle that for validity to
be established, psychoanalysis depends on a constant feed-back of verifying
and orienting comment from the patient. That comment is not available from
Luther. The alternative is to observe carefully all the facts available and
correlate them intuitively with observed events in former patients and with
one's theoretical position. Erikson has remarked on the results obtained by
the psychiatrist and the "psychoanalyst" using this method. I think he is
entirely correct in believing that the psychiatrist is severely handicapped by
the limitations of his psychological theory, and that the "psychoanalytic"
evaluation is equally inadequate.

The conservative psychoanalyst will always be reluctant to apply his
method to anyone other than a spontaneously co-operative, communicative
patient. Freud warned against the pitfalls and felt that even the analysis of a
dream could only be carried out with the help of the dreamer's associations.
Still, he could not resist "analyzing" Michelangelo's statue of Moses as well

as Leonardo daVinci. I think there is a simple but compelling consideration that justifies such analyses. The validity of interpretations during psycho-analysis is established by the nature of the further associations of the patient. The usual neurotic problem exists because of the autoplastic activity of the patient. He has tried to change himself. With most public figures another condition obtains. Their conflicts and impulses have led them to action in-volving their surroundings. These actions are generally visible to all and have the same significance with respect to their conflicts as the symptoms of neurotics have to theirs. Thus, with the patient, if one has historical informa-tion and the symptoms, an educated guess can be made about the dynamics and the unconscious factors. A similar reconstruction may be based on the consistent action and behavior of any individual, particularly if such action has a symptomatic, irrational component. Since great men leave extensive records of their actions, a significant analysis of them is possible even with-out the desirable verifying feedback ideally required.

As a psychoanalyst, I can only applaud Erikson's careful development of themes. Luther becomes a powerful, gifted, tormented, sensitive human being, whose motivations, crises, and activities are intelligible and con-vincing. The remaining problem is whether this image is complete as well as valid. It almost certainly is not. Even if everyone would agree to this, it might well be that the necessary additions would not add anything to our understanding of Luther's *actions* and, even more likely, his effect on history. Every psychoanalyst who reads about Luther's life will develop his own tentative hypotheses about Luther—his conflicts, his motivation, and the nature of his pathology. Such is the nature of psychoanalysis: each sees the subject through his own glass; each measures him with his own rule. This does not change the subject, but it does change his image to those who hear of him at second hand. It would be easy, for example, for a psychoanalyst who was so inclined to emphasize Luther's unconscious homosexual conflict and his paranoid tendency. He would do so by collecting such material as the following: Luther's lifelong struggle with authority and the form of his conflict concerning passive wishes; the ubiquitous appearance of anal material in his thoughts; his entry into the monastery, the fact that he did not like to be looked in the eye; the letter to his friend who was to be married, which outlined the plan—and which Erikson discusses in terms of his need for intimacy—to think of each other during their intercourse with their wives. These and many other items could be marshaled as evidence for such a thesis. Other theses could be developed in a similar way; it is important to realize this before one can approach the problem of assessing Luther himself, or Erikson's assessment of him.

When I say that it is possible to construct alternative theses in such a relatively arbitrary way, I hope I have avoided creating a false impression that all such theses are arbitrary and hence dismissable as pipe dreams. Rather, I would say that such theses bear a relationship to the reality that is comparable to the relationship existing between statistical or graphic analysis and the total reality that they represent. Mischievous bias is possible, but, granting intelligence and good will to the author, the analysis will represent the reality in a meaningful and instructive way; yet, at the limits of its application, it can be appropriately challenged by an alternative analysis.

Before discussing Luther or Erikson's discussion of him, I should make clear certain assumptions of my own, which Erikson does not specify. I must assume that there are only two categories of influence to be considered as relevant in the shaping of Luther's development and career—his nature, and the culture of his time. To include a third influence—divine intervention—as, of course, most of his biographers do, would introduce too many wild cards into the deck and make all psychological and social theorizing fruitless.

I realize that a personal bias is operating to influence my view of the matter. I am impressed by what appears to me to be Erikson's sympathetic admiration for Luther, and I find myself moved to doubt the legitimacy of this admiration. Luther acquires the aura of a mythological hero emerging victorious over the forces of darkness; the twin dragons being his inner travail and the evil genius of the hierarchy. I see his inner travail pictured by Erikson as "Luther at the Eight Stages of Man," in much the same way as one might think of Ulysses on his Odyssey or Hercules performing his labors. It is the admiration which bothers me. I sympathize with the man's problems, and I cheer his efforts against his own devil and against the bigotry around him, but I am not convinced that the form of the resolution of his inner turmoil accounts for his effect on his world, for his greatness. It appears that it was the *force* rather than the form of the solution that accounts in part for his impact. Although Erikson at times appears to credit Luther with having created a new ideology with the resolution of his personal crises, it is open to question whether the nature of his solutions was new to his world. Erikson has given considerable evidence that it was not the newness of his ideas that shook the people of his world, but the extraordinary genius of their presentation. When Erikson establishes Luther as a master of the German language, whose range and power of expression parallels that of Shakespeare, he creates a conviction that with such a vehicle as Luther's language even a commonplace would find an audience. He thus makes it possible to question whether the idea contained in the language or the language itself was responsible for the reception it received.

Although I tax Erikson with writing a too-admiring biographical study of Luther, it is quite possible that my writing on the subject is relatively tendentious where his is relatively neutral. Erikson has, on the whole, and particularly in the Epilogue, presented Luther's successes as results of the interaction of many forces, the critical elements of which were often the dynamic balances achieved during the several life crises that Erikson has postulated. At other times, however, he has strayed slightly from the concept of dynamic balance and has used terms implying that these crises were solved; permitting the inference that it was Luther's *solution* of such crises that played the critical role in his theological and philosophical formulations and in making possible his impact on his civilization. These two subtle differences of approach create a polarity of opinion, to which I have reacted with that degree of energy characteristic of one who has been in search of a "cause" and has finally found one.

My own reaction to Luther's image presented by Erikson is one of disappointment. Instead of a triumphal fulfillment, I see a tragic miscarriage. It appears that Luther, trapped by his insoluble problem with father and authority, created a revolution whose full consequences he could not accept. One result, for example, was another peasant revolt, a revolt entirely in keeping with Luther's rebelliousness and at the same time remarkably compatible with a sense of true, emancipated identity. Nevertheless, Luther was not able to accept it; and on the basis of his failure to resolve a problem of personal identity, was as cruel and punitive towards it as he was toward himself on many an occasion. This same incompleteness of resolution of his inner problem is, I believe, responsible for the more tragic and far-reaching failure of the subsequent emancipation of the individual in some Germanic or "Lutheran" countries. This question is better left to the historians; however, in at least one aspect, a comment is in order. It is as though Luther's own ambivalence about independence were projected onto a whole people, and a terrible emphasis placed on righteousness and works and the relation to an implacable Judge, at the same time that one professes his independence from Papa. The result is not a true emancipation and independence, but an unstable alternation between servile docility, and passivity, and seeking after strong authority images, on the one hand, and an attitude of arrogance, pride, and the trappings of power whenever this attitude can safely be displayed to "inferiors." Combined with these features is the introjected image of the father, which is almost a stereotype of a "Lutheran" super-ego —strict, harsh, implacable, terrifyingly powerful, and not susceptible to reason.

It is particularly difficult to be convinced that Luther was ever able truly to resolve either his basic infantile conflicts or their later counterparts, his theological conflicts. I believe that this failure is reflected in his inability to countenance what might have been an enlightened, successful revolution of individuals asserting their own independence. It is true that Luther had a series of emotional experiences of a religious nature—all of which appear to be resolutions of such conflicts. His reflections on Romans 1:17, "For therein is the righteousness of God revealed from faith to faith: as it is written, The just shall live by faith," were accompanied by the feeling that they had "opened the door of paradise" to him. This, and the experience of "insight" about the phrase, "and deliver me in thy righteousness," in which he realizes that, as Erikson says, "he knew that *iustitia dei* meant the righteousness by which He justifies us through the free gift of Christ's justice, then I understood the *grammatica,* and I truly tasted the Psalms." I believe, as Erikson does, that these experiences were profound emotional crises. However, I believe that they were profound efforts to find within the word of God reassurances about God's attitude toward himself. They seem to reflect a deep and inner conviction that he is condemned, damned, and worthless. This hopelessness was never resolved. There was, from time to time, an effort to search God's face for a sign of mercy, and this effort was occasionally rewarded. Luther remembers these successes, and henceforth clings to them, but it does not seem that they truly resolved his sense of hopelessness.

II

In order to criticize Erikson's conclusions, I must engage in that most sincere form of flattery: I must follow Erikson's model of ego development. It must also be noted that Erikson has expressed his conclusions in an admirably temperate, cautious form, and his opinions are transmitted to his readers by means of an elegant, leisurely process of literary induction. Neither space nor talent affords me the same opportunity. I shall have to be blunt, and state my objections and differences with Erikson's conclusions briefly and essentially in summary form. Neither will I be able to marshal the extensive evidence that would be desirable. This may not be too serious, however, because the relevant evidence is entirely included in Erikson's argument; it merely leads him to a different emphasis of interpretation or conclusion.

The first crisis during early infancy determines whether the individual's prevailing mood will be influenced more by basic trust or by basic mistrust. Erikson concludes that Martin received from his mother sufficient quality and quantity of attention such that his sense of basic trust was well established. It seems quite clear that he received enough to make it possible for him to know of the existence of such a state of trust. His marvelous imagery about the sow makes this evident:

> For a sow lies in the gutter, or on the manure as if on the finest feather bed. She rests safely, snores tenderly, and sleeps sweetly, does not fear king nor master, death nor hell, devil or God's wrath, lives without worry, and does not even think where the clover may be. And if the Turkish Caesar arrived in all his might and anger, the sow would be much too proud to move a single whisker in his honor.... And if at last the butcher comes upon her, she thinks maybe a piece of wood is pinching her, or a stone.... The sow has not eaten from the apple, which in paradise has taught us wretched humans the difference between good and bad.

Still, it does not seem a perfect rendering of Luther's psychic state to conclude that he had a preponderance of basic trust. The very imagery of Genesis might describe his state more accurately. He had known the bliss of existence in the Garden, but was soon expelled. He had reason to know of faith, but perhaps even greater reason to doubt that it was justified. Three simple facts would argue that mistrust was a real and constant threat: first, his recurrent depressions; second, his almost paranoid fear of the Devil; and third, the pervasive questioning of his faith. When we speak of his frequent and intense doubt, we may seem to be anticipating an element of the second crisis, that of autonomy versus shame and doubt. This is more a semantic problem than a real one, however, because doubt in the present instance is doubt as opposed to trust. It relates to the question of faith, and Luther was never able to resolve this issue and comfortably trust in the Lord.

Erikson has said it too, but it is worth restating that the institutions of religion and the Church operate as very effective agents for the restitution or the shoring up of individuals whose sense of basic trust is marginally adequate for prevailing circumstances. That Luther chose the career of a man of God, concerned with matters of faith as a central issue of life, is presumptive evidence of his great concern with just this conflict. He chose this career, as Erikson points out, at a time when there must have been some doubt about his career in law and probably considerable conflict about conforming completely to his father's wishes. The actual statement—"I want to become a monk,"—came, however, during a moment of agonizing terror when he had been nearly struck by lightning. It is not unreasonable to suppose that the destruction of basic faith by agonizing terror was followed by a plea for mercy, and the equivalent of a promise to devote himself to God's works if he were spared.

This speculation is supported by his subsequent sense of commitment to the idea of becoming a monk, even though his words would not appear to have obligated him to do so. The shattering experience of the thunderstorm seems to have created a crisis in Luther at a time when he was especially susceptible. His susceptibility arose from his adolescent identity crisis, but the more primitive crisis of trust versus mistrust was evoked by the mortal danger. The reverberations of that thunderstorm echo throughout Luther's career, in the form of his agonies of doubt; they must reflect his earliest experience of fear that he was forsaken by those whom he had begun to trust.

The crisis of early childhood, in which the alternatives are the achievement of autonomy or the development of shame and doubt, was also of crucial importance for Luther. Again, in his more explicit conclusions, Erikson is less sanguine in his appraisal of the degree to which Luther achieved the more desirable alternative, autonomy. For one to question the autonomy of Martin Luther, whose simultaneous defiance of his Emperor and the Pope is an unparalleled autonomous gesture, would seem a rather foolish thing to do. It is not the existence of autonomy, but the means by which it existed that needs clarification. Over and above this, the simultaneous development of the alternative deserves mention. Luther's description of shame leaves no doubt that he experienced it with exquisite intensity. It is the same with doubt, although the following quotation used by Erikson to exemplify it could as well be used to illustrate the other kind of doubt, i.e., a kind of paranoid mistrust.

When he is tormented in *Anfechtung* it seems to him that he is alone: God is angry only with him and irreconcilably angry against him: that he alone is a sinner and all others are in the right, and they work against him at God's orders. There is nothing left for him but this unspeakable sighing through which, without knowing it, he is supported by the Spirit and cries, 'Why does God pick on me alone?'

Is it not somewhat misleading to speak of Luther as being truly autonomous? One might, and Erikson seems to, assume that the spirit of the times was such that all men found their lives inextricably bound up with the beliefs and customs of the Church, that religion was such an integral part of existence that independence from its philosophy and practice was not possible. This does not appear to be a completely invulnerable position. In terms of a true independence of spirit, Martin's father Hans, may have been more autonomous than his infinitely more powerful, historically more effective son. Hans himself was not demonstrably intimidated by the Church. It does not appear that he felt obliged either to defy it or to submit to its wishes. He stubbornly maintained his position of wanting Martin to follow a career of law, and he felt free to argue spiritedly with the monks at the banquet after Martin's first Mass. He did this with an easy familiarity toward God, saying, "God give that it (the thunderstorm) wasn't a devil's spook." Such a statement indicated that Hans took for granted the existence and action of God and devil, but to say it in those circumstances suggests complete lack of awe of the Church. Martin, on the other hand, appears to be truly a man supported by his ideology. It is true that he could act with great courage and independence of other men, but his freedom of action was only by virtue of the support he assumed he had from God himself. It is no wonder that he had his moments of terror. He was often convinced that God disapproved his actions or indeed had forsaken him. Luther's whole theological effort might be viewed as an effort to prove that each man can find the way to an omniscient and omnipotent ally, God. This may lead to acts of great audacity, power, and effectiveness, but the very derivation of the word autonomy, would argue against its application to such a condition of partnership.

These first two stages are deservedly given more space by Erikson than the others. Their influence on Martin's attitudes and behavior was preponderantly important. In particular, they had profound influence on the other critical crisis of Martin's life, the identity crisis. At the risk of being redundant, the point can be made that the incomplete resolution of these two crises kept Luther working at them all of his life, while the relatively more complete resolution of most of the others permitted him to proceed smoothly until the crisis of identity versus role diffusion reactivated the issues of the first two.

In its more direct form, the crisis of initiative versus guilt was not a crucial one for Luther. He was not free of guilt, to be sure, but although guilt is a common measure of the zeal of many religious figures, and is prominent in the Puritan derivatives of Lutheranism, it was by no means the prominent feature of Luther's relation to his God. While he suffered from that inevitable measure of guilt which would accrue from his earlier mistrust, shame and doubt, his guilt was not so readily demonstrable as a motivation for action or theological speculation. Even his belief that man was completely corrupted by original sin and his concept of predestination was to be overcome by his doctrine of saving faith. Luther was never troubled by lack of initiative; the only stricture on it being his recurrent doubt. One can only speculate that the great man might have become a titan, if the resolution of this and the preceding crises had not been incomplete in such a way that he was unable to follow through on his rebellion. As Erikson says, it is important to recognize that reaction and counterrevolution are possible for the most ardent revolutionary. This defect in both autonomy and, as Erikson construes it, a certain form of initiative, prevented Luther from pursuing his successful revolution to a successful, humanist conclusion.

In the next stage, Luther seems truly to have outdone himself. If we judge the degree of resolution by the quality of the product, then this issue must have been well-nigh perfectly resolved. Luther's capacity for work was prodigious; even in periods of emotional turmoil his production was outstanding. The other aspect of this stage, the acquisition and mastery of tools, was also carried out with great success. It would seem that if any single factor was responsible for Luther's impact on the men of his time, it was his eloquence and power with language. Certainly, if Martin did once identify himself with the "son which hath a dumb spirit . . ." he also considered himself truly cured by faith—and proved it. At the same time that we find such overwhelming evidence of the positive element in his masterful manipulation of the Word, we have difficulty detecting a significant degree of the negative element, a sense of inferiority. Even in his most depressed and hopeless moods, Luther did not consider himself inferior. He might feel damned, or forsaken, but never inconsequential.

When we come to the crisis of identity versus role diffusion, we deal with the central issue of Erikson's book. Erikson deals with this problem on so many levels, and so often by implication and allusion that it would be difficult or impossible to summarize his position explicitly and supply an adequate critique. It is possible that my reluctance to accept completely what I understand to be Erikson's position depends on a semantic problem. When Erikson speaks of the solution of a crisis, perhaps he only intends to imply a relative and temporary containment of the disturbing problem. A usage which might be considered preferable is that in which "solution" is understood to be substantially complete and permanent. A classical example from psychoanalytic literature would be the solution of conflict about sadistic impulses. If the conflict is "solved" by a reaction formation, the individual does not carry out sadistic acts; on the contrary, his behavior is characterized by the complete opposite. Great care is taken to avoid hurting anything. On no account will such a person exert authority in such a way that he or others could think of him as manipulative and hence sadistic. A great overconcern is expressed about the suffering of others, or the possible and frequently fantasied suffering of others. Such reaction formation is relatively unstable when exposed to "temptation," and requires the constant expenditure of psychic energy to maintain its operation. Under conditions of stress, the person is apt to develop symptoms, often obsessional thoughts about sadistic behavior, and a free and spontaneous participation in activities which might reawaken the conflict cannot occur. It is particularly common for such persons to betray the existence of the sadistic impulse by an "unintentional" and essentially unconsciously determined act. Such an act might take the form of good-natured teasing that deteriorates until the victim really suffers, or it might take the form of wit or sarcasm that hurts the object. It may take the form of a type of "consideration" that is painful, or of gift-giving or the doing of favors that make the recipient uncomfortable.

In contrast to reaction formation, a true resolution of the conflict about sadistic impulses may occur and is called sublimation. Such a solution involves an alteration of the aim so that it is acceptable both to the individual and to some important segment of his society. The range of possibilities is very wide, and probably includes nearly all of the complicated and intense impulses to master things (rather than people), to compete successfully, and to sway and mold others. Thus, the classical example of sublimation in choice of profession is the surgeon, and its opposite number in reaction formation would be the "anti-vivisectionist."

To return to the issue of Luther's solution of his identity crisis, Erikson seems to treat the matter as though Luther had solved this crisis in such a way that it could be compared to sublimation, in the sense that a transcendental change occurred. A more appropriate emphasis would indicate that Luther was forced to expend endless effort in order to maintain his precarious identity position.

Luther had to have a God. His psychological economy was incomplete without one, and if there had not already been a religious system with One in it, he would have had to create One. His sense of identity required the existence of an omnipotent agency to protect him from, and buttress him against, his own impulses. His problem was made more difficult because so many of his impulses involved rebellion against the very object upon which he was so dependent. (Luther had reason to fear God because of his blasphemous fantasies.) His identity was as a man *of* God, and yet he had reason to know that he had not always thought of God in such a way as to be welcomed by Him. Thus, he first emphasized predestination; this arrangement of the cosmos would remove one uncertainty, and at least the issue was settled primarily without reference to one's individual behavior. Still he was not reconciled, and his earliest crises of trust versus mistrust returned in the form of an affirmation of faith as the reconciling agent between him and a God whom he "knew" he had provoked.

Luther, therefore, was able to maintain his sense of identity only by invoking the alliance of another agency—God. Even after this, Luther had trouble maintaining himself on good terms with Him. His endless struggle to so maintain himself generated his ideology. This kind of activity is not to be called a reaction formation, of course, but its structure and function parallel reaction formations more closely than sublimations; hence, it seems preferable to consider that the basic conflict had never been truly solved.

Although Erikson puts it differently, Luther's identity crisis so occupied his life that the subsequent crises were delayed, and of relatively lesser importance. The crisis of intimacy versus isolation can hardly be traced. In spite of Luther's magnetic presence, and aptness of phrase, he does not come through to me as having had an extraordinary capacity for intimacy. Still, he was certainly not isolated, and it is probably more important that a great leader should lack this negative quality than that he have a great store of the positive one.

The crisis of generativity versus self-absorption was not of critical consequence either. Certainly Luther was a creator—one might consider that for him "necessity was the mother of invention." Still, it could be said that the shadow of inner failure pressed him onward in his creative theological efforts. This theme becomes repetitious, however; and, in any case, Luther's self-absorption was reprojected universally in the form of a consideration for the souls of mankind.

Integrity to his principles was absolutely characteristic of Luther if defined in the usual way—as honesty and unswerving devotion to principle. If defined more as I believe Erikson has used it, as the end result of an integration of the diverse impulses and agencies of the psyche into a coherent, consistent, and smoothly functioning whole, then the previous objections will appear again. Again, it was the effort to recreate the world according to his own needs that partly accounts for Luther's emerging as a great man; but the world was offered a Procrustean bed, one which was consistently the same, but not necessarily appropriate. Thus, the principle of freedom to approach God directly was championed, and virtual equality of man before God was established, but comparable secular freedom was not championed by Luther. This failure to apply generally a principle derived from the "resolution" of his specific and personal identity crisis is the strongest argument against Luther's having achieved a true psychological integrity.

III

My own supplementary reconstruction is as follows: In infancy, Luther perceived his father in a highly ambivalent way. Father was the source of strength and security and power, but at the same time he was feared because he could withhold these benefits and because of his anger and his violence. Which way father would be was unpredictable and, more important, uninfluenceable by Martin, who could only helplessly accept or endure whatever mood father was in. This would be a rather universally experienced state of affairs, but there is evidence that it was not limited to Martin's infancy, but continued throughout his childhood and to a degree throughout his life. With such an image for a model, it would not be surprising to find Luther's own introjected image of authority in much the same form. I think we may paraphrase the Scripture and say that indeed "Man made God in his own (father's) image." Luther made his own God a vengeful one, in the image described above. However, there was another image too, one that might be discovered even if it could not be either commanded to appear or made to appear by means of a prescribed course of behavior. That is, the favorably disposed image exists, but is capricious. It cannot be sought successfully by any preconceived plan; its favor cannot be earned, but it does exist and may appear according to its own inscrutable rules. There is but one rule that may be followed and that may favorably influence the desired image: to endure all things, have faith and trust, and patience. This magical formula will work, but not predictably, and Luther, in his theological investigations and his religious experience constantly sought to find and then to improve this formula. He found it and he used it, but true to his infantile and childhood experience, it was only partially effective, and he suffered throughout his life from the recurrent certainty that he was either forsaken or damned by God.

Erikson takes exception to the "psychiatrist" for expecting Luther to reach a "state of inner balance such as normal people are said to display." He proposes that Luther was a great man because of his particular resolution of his identity crisis. He thinks that Luther was able, to a unique degree, to *create* a new life-pattern, and not only follow it himself but persuade his civilization to adopt it. There is considerable evidence for this. However, there is another consideration. It would not be incorrect to call Luther a zealot, and I do not believe that all great men have been zealots, and certainly not all creative men are zealots. I would propose in fact what might amount to a counter thesis, that Luther became a great man not because he resolved his identity crisis, but because he failed to in a particular way. There is good evidence that Luther never fully resolved his conflict with his father. I cannot believe that his fear of God and his life-long preoccupation with the Devil were not prompted by an intense and complex relation to his father. His failure to resolve that part of his identity crisis that involved both intense libidinal and aggressive impulses toward his father left him with a festering wound, which drove him relentlessly to solve with action those problems that he could not solve intrapsychically.

History is the judge of Luther's greatness. I am merely trying to say that he suffered all his life under the pressure of a very significant degree of psychopathology; and, further, that it might well be this very psychopathology which accounted for his zealotry and his greatness. The trouble with this thesis, compared with Erikson's, is that it resembles the prosaic, common-sense opinion held by the man-in-the-street about scientists and "great men" in general—"they are all crazy geniuses."

The ego of the neurotic has had a trial by fire. It is proved by turmoils to which the complacent ego is never exposed. The circumstances which lead to conflict—great drive pressure, especially strong or selective environmental suppressive forces, and special circumstances in the environment that maximize one or the other of the first two—expose the ego to great stress. The defective ego, in the midst of such terrible conflict, needs muster all of its resources to regain or retain mastery. It often fails, and symptoms and suffering result. Yet the ego does not abandon its effort, and in the great man the struggle is titanic. Erikson mentions the current tendency to misguided application of the cliche of "adjustment" or "adaptiveness." The ego has two courses, autoplastic and alloplastic. Luther used both extensively. He changed himself with the help of a tremendously strong social instrument—the Augustinian monastic training. As Erikson says, this was effective only for a time. Luther then turned to the other course. He changed the world. It is perfectly clear that he did not change it to conform to an ideal image. He changed it in such a way that it conformed all too precisely with *both* elements of his conflicts and his ambivalence.

The old psychoanalytic adage about the return of the repressed is all too neatly born out by the righteous savagery of his attacks against the peasant revolt. It may be going too far to consider that Luther intended such revolution to take place. However, it seems certain that he was generally urging that men should be responsible for their own souls; that he was questioning the omniscience of the Catholic hierarchy. Yet, when the spark of this idea was caught by the spirit of the times and grew to the flame of a more general revolt. It may be going too far to consider that Luther intended such a revolu-directed against it.

Thus, in changing the world, Luther attempted to solve his terrible conflict with the authority of his father by overthrowing in his world generally the then prevailing attitude of unquestioning obedience. One might say that he was willing to go only halfway, and in only one direction. He could bear the thought of revolt against Papa, but not against Father in Heaven, and he was entirely unable to consider it against the more immediate civil authority. In summary of this point, it would seem that Luther was caught in the same kind of trap that the autoplastic neurotic is caught in. Even after he had succeeded in changing the world, he found his old conflicts facing him again; ironically, the solution was designed to afford both gratification of forbidden wishes and, at the same time, punishment for them.

I will violate my own dictum and attempt to "explain" a vital theme. I do this because I think Erikson has not been explicit about it, in spite of the fact that it constitutes the most central point supporting his contention that Luther was a great man, not only because of his acceptance by masses of people, but also because of a true contribution to a progressive evolution of society. Erikson says that Luther's contribution was the development of the ideal of personal, individual responsibility. He contends that this was, perforce, couched in the ideological framework of religion. The trappings of Protestantism—its dogma and ritual—are irrelevant to the basic issue, that henceforth each man should have the choice of deciding for himself the nature of his relationship to God. The equivalent decision in nonreligious, purely psychological terms would have been to say that each man should decide for himself the nature of his relationship to his conscience.

Erikson believes that the nature of the times was such that man could only conceive of himself in the context of the religious universe; consequently, any greater departure from the earlier concept of himself within a religious hierarchy would have been impossible. Since this is primarily an historical question, it is outside of my area of competence. One must acknowledge that others who had similar ideas and even some whose ideas had relatively wide circulation did not in consequence become great leaders. I believe that Erikson shows very clearly that Luther's efforts to deal with his own psycho-social crises led him to make his choice of profession and to formulate his theological arguments. They led him to oppose paternalistic interference, and to proclaim vigorously the right and responsibility of man to act psychically in behalf of his own self-determination. He also indicates that the acceptance of an ideology is governed by the fact that the gap between the current one and the new one must not be too great, and that even then the new one will soon be contaminated and its effects vitiated by reaction and counterrevolutionary trends. More will be said about ideology later.

IV

There is one dimension of character or personality that is not explicitly mentioned by Erikson, but that seems to have a bearing on Luther's greatness and on the relationship between leaders and their followers. It would be simplest to introduce it as a dimension involving "magic" versus "reality." As an issue, it may not rank with those mentioned by Erikson, in the sense that it commonly generates an identity crisis. As an attribute of greatness, however, much depends on whether the major emphasis of orientation is in one direction or the other. The reality-oriented person seldom becomes a "great" popular leader, while the magical-oriented person may do so through his appeal to the magical orientation of the population at large. To define "magic" and "reality" and develop the theme adequately is not easy, mainly because the shift from an objective to a subjective frame of reference is easy to overlook, and because reality may be used in a magical way and magic may be used with reality effects. To complicate it further, what is intended as one may become the other with little change in appearance.

Magic is first of all a state of mind within the individual. It is roughly equivalent to that neurotic state in which reality is misperceived. However, we need not think of this as a matter of "unreality" versus "reality," because there is something more positive about "magic" than that. In fact, the concept comes from the observation of the way people maintain *wishes* and fantasies of their fulfillment throughout their lives, in total disregard of the facts. With this observation, we will quickly see that we can by no means identify "magic" with "pathological"; it is clear that as far as we have gone this activity is an essential step in any creative activity. To dream is the essence of magical action. To loosen the bonds usually connecting cause and effect, or one sequence of events with another, and substitute connections of one's own choosing, this is magical thought. Invoking a God to solve problems we cannot solve and do things we cannot do but desperately want done—this is a related magical act. Luther's ideology was perceived by him and by many others as more appealing and effective than the ritualistic and indirect appeal made through the Church.

There is one large area of such thought that requires special mention. When an individual is faced with an insoluble problem in infancy or childhood, his capacity to manage the subsequent frustration is limited. The longing for gratification persists, and the effort to achieve substitute gratification may influence behavior to a surprising degree. I would call such behavior "magical" because of its marked resemblance to a ritual intended to accomplish the magical gratification of a wish. The activities of obsessive-compulsive persons would be classic illustrations of this behavior.

One might pose the issue differently and arrive at a better comprehension of the concept. Magic is essentially a type of action of the ego. The ego must deal with the reality of the external environment and the reality of inner needs. Some of these exigencies are more urgent than others. In the most urgent circumstances, there may be no choice. Immediate and appropriate action is necessary for survival. In other circumstances, the inner need is only pressing, and the failure of satisfaction has importance only in psychological terms. Sexual impulses, in the broadest psychoanalytic sense, fall into this category. So also do many aggressive impulses as well as the infantile wish for omnipotence and its later counterpart, the developing ego's wish for mastery. The process of achieving gratification of these wishes by means of hallucination or fantasy, I would call magical. Extensions of fantasy into action would also be magical, and would be best exemplified by magical gestures such as "body English" which billiard players, bowlers, and many other athletes use to attempt magically to change the course of a ball already released from their influence in reality. More complicated actions and beliefs may also be best understood as magical. For example, the fear of death—whatever its psychological origin—may lead to a belief in immortality. Such a belief, when based on the need to deny a greatly feared eventuality, has a psychological function that I would term magical. I would say this independently of what the reality might be. The magical nature of the psychological act depends on its form, not upon its verification in reality. The rain-making ceremony of the Hopi is a magical activity—whether it rains or not.

That the human psyche is susceptible to magic goes without saying. All popular leaders make use of this fact consciously or unconsciously, and demagogues invariably have a flair for determining and exploiting popular conflicts about the current issues. They promise gratification of deeply conflicting wishes, and they make it socially acceptable.

I would like to quote Erikson on a closely related point:

We will call what young people in their teens and early twenties look for in religion and in other dogmatic systems an *ideology*. At the most it is a militant system with uniformed members and uniform goals; at the least it is a "way of life," or what the Germans call a *Weltanschauung*, a world-view which is consonant with existing theory, available knowledge, and common sense, and yet is significantly more; an utopian outlook, a cosmic mood, or a doctrinal logic, all shared as self-evident beyond any need for demonstration. What is to be relinquished as "old" may be the individual's previous life; this usually means the perspectives intrinsic to the life-style of the parents, who are thus discarded contrary to all traditional safeguards of filial devotion. The "old" may be a part of himself, which must henceforth be subdued by some rigorous self-denial in a private life-style or through membership in a militant or military organization; or, it may be the world-view of other castes and classes, races and peoples: in this case, these people become not only expendable, but the appointed victims of the most righteous annihilation. The need for devotion, then, is one aspect of the identity crisis which we, as psychologists, make responsible for all these tendencies and susceptibilities. The need for repudiation is another aspect. In their late teens and early twenties, even when there is no explicit ideological commitment or even interest, young people offer devotion to individual leaders and to teams, to strenuous activities, and to difficult techniques; at the same time they show a sharp and intolerant readiness to discard and disavow people (including, at times, themselves). This repudiation is often snobbish, fitful, perverted, or simply thoughtless.

I believe that what Erikson calls "ideological" is entirely included in what I have called "magical." I think that Erikson's qualification, "a world-view consonant with existing theory, available knowledge, and common sense," is gratuitous. I do not believe that such a test is commonly applied to an ideology by the person who seeks one, and, if it is, it is not the factor determining the choice. I cannot agree too strongly with the implied purpose of the choice, however. These people choose such ideologies in order to achieve a personal sense of existence, fulfillment, and destiny. This is precisely what Luther did with religion and with God. They and he are forced to repudiate and even annihilate the "old," because the "old ones" are perceived as responsible for limiting or destroying their sense of individuality. I think that some degree of such rebellion will always occur when the child becomes an adult; no matter how perfect the performance of the parent as a parent, there will always have been some degree of intrusion and coercive modification of the child that must be repudiated. The compromise that must be effected between inner impulses and the demands of society requires that restrictions be imposed, and these are apt to be resented even when they are necessary.

The best thing that can be said for magical activity in an individual's character is that it exists, and, if defined in a certain way, that it is a part of creative thought; the best that can be said of adherence to an ideology is that it gives an individual time and acts as a bridge to a final identity. When it remains as a part of a functioning character I can only consider that it is pathological, or at best a kind of internal psychological splint, which may cause no pain, be invisible, and assist in achieving what appears to be normal or even supernormal function.

Luther's relation to religion was of this order. There was never a true resolution of inner drives for Luther—no personal channeling and control of drives that could be depended on, and that is necessary if dependence on external authority is to be discarded. Throughout his life, Luther was struggling with his concept of a vengeful God and his satanic counterpart, both of which were needed to help him maintain an uneasy balance of power in his struggle to control his impulses.

V

Erikson has compared Luther's effect on the ideology of his time with Freud's effect on that of his. I will graft my own concepts onto what I assume Erikson's to be, in order to proceed further with the consideration of the interrelationship between ideology and society. I believe that Erikson suggests the existence of a progressive evolution of society, which depends primarily for its movement on the relative resolution of societal crises that might be compared to the epigenetic series of personal psycho-social crises that he has postulated. (It might very well be that the "something in mind" to which I referred in my opening paragraph is just this thesis.) Whether or not such a series exists, I do not know. If it does, the segment with which we are presently concerned consists of the adoption by society at large of Luther's idea of individual responsibility. At the time of its adoption, it applied only to man's relationship to God; with the passage of time, the action of the idea itself has extended to include most of human behavior.

The comparison of Luther with Freud emphasizes that comparable emancipation became possible as a result of Freud's contribution of the concept of the unconscious, together with a method for "knowing" it and hence subjecting it to a measure of control.

I believe that the course of history can be sketched and perhaps extrapolated in the following way. Man progresses in a general way toward an increasing mastery over the inanimate universe, both in the sense of understanding its laws and in the sense of manipulating and altering its features and effects. He does the same with his social institutions, although at a later time. He may possibly be progressing in the same direction with respect to a true understanding and mastery of his own individual nature. Both social and personal mastery have always relied upon ideological tools for their effectiveness. Such control of the individual and society by ideologies is analogous to the most primitive efforts to control the physical universe by incantation and ritual—by magic. The analogy is imperfect, because, except by accident, magic does not influence physical events. On the other hand, it does have profound influence on social and individual psychological events. The step that Luther took effectively increased the chance for an individual to achieve freedom and independence of action. The achievement of this increment of emancipation can then be considered as a crucial step toward a true state of emancipation. *To free every individual from his need for magic* is a goal which, I freely predict, will never be reached, but it seems to me to be the one toward which all the efforts of science are directed.

What is it then that makes a great man and a great leader? It is more or less self-evident that it is not as we tend to think of it: that some inner quality of competence simply results in his achieving heroic stature. It depends, to be sure, on the nature of the greatness that we are considering. If it involves great leaders, greatness must be a product of the inner quality and its reception by an informed populace in some especially favorable circumstance. Erikson makes the point that for Luther the time was ripe, but considers it a mistake to overemphasize the importance of the economic factors, ascribing Luther's success to fortunate coincidence of his defiance with the already stirring rebellion of others. Quibbling over this issue would surely never settle it. The irreducible fact is that all three factors must be present in significant degree for a man to become a great leader, and the absence of any one dooms him to relative anonymity. I think it is easy to define these factors as the *necessary* ones for greatness. The difficult problem is that of determining how much of each is *sufficient*.

I have been talking about magic and reality, and I think that most great leaders have been so because of their ability to communicate to large numbers of people their own powerful magical belief. Most intense emotional appeals depend for their effectiveness upon a magical resolution of a strong inner conflict, or the equivalent, the promise of a magical satisfaction of an unsatisfied drive.

Doctor Schweitzer is a great man because he appears to have conquered aggression. He is the perfect altruist, and people revere him for it. Gandhi was likewise a great man, not because he conquered aggression—such an attribute is too cheap in India, but because he adapted nonagression as the most effective aggressive instrument of his time. Hatred and resentment of the British found the perfect outlet in Gandhi's activity. Gandhi's appeal was tremendous; it might have been so even without his political action, but the combination of saintliness and an effective political weapon was irresistable.

Hitler must be called a great leader, and the source of his greatness partakes of both Gandhi's and Luther's sources. He was a successful political activist, and he had power as an orator. It is generally agreed that his language and style were execrable. On the other hand, he had execrable things to say and to promote, so perhaps the style suited the task. He was, I believe, a deeply disturbed and pathologically re-"balanced" person whose degree of pathology would only be matched by a severely paranoid schizophrenic. His zeal, his terrible inner rage, and his promises of redemption fell on fertile soil in the German people of his time. He was able, by boasting and promising and threatening, to kindle hope in defeated, apathetic people, and to frighten moderate, "realistically oriented" ones. He was able to collect masses of aggressive and opportunistic followers, and to intimidate them by the intensity and single-mindedness of his zeal. He was in this respect, too, like Gandhi—not to be diverted from his purpose—in this sense he, too, was altruistic. At least there is no evidence that his drive was simply a personal drive for power. It was personal only in that he was the agent through which an identity of power and self-respect was to come to Germany.

If we attempt to summarize what has been said about the inner factors determining the emergence of a great man, we will recognize two things: first, that they are cursed or blessed by having an inner conflict that they are unable to resolve within themselves; and second, that they have a great store of aggression at their disposal. A third consideration would be that they are able to find, in the circumstances of their time, some important issue that can be fused successfully with their inner conflict and that, after fusion, can be communicated successfully to great numbers of people.

The concept of ideology now enters the picture. The great man usually creates an ideology or at least crystallizes one already loosely formed by others. The important thing about an ideology is that it fulfills a psychological need for those committed to it. It should be emphasized that ideology combines a world view *and* a plan of action and that, as Erikson has used it, it requires the rejection of many past commitments—at least those in conflict with it. It requires further sacrifice of its adherents: they must accept its methods and aims above all others, even if other methods might accomplish the stated aims more quickly or expeditiously. It is this feature of an ideology that betrays the neurotic basis of its adoption. The ideology gives strength to its devotee, but it is the strength of stereotypy.

Erikson has made an important contribution by emphasizing the inter-relationship between the search for identity, the great man, and the creation of ideology. The difference between the rabble-rouser and the great man, however, seems less than he implies. In each case, the member of the group seeks to piece out his own inadequate identity by accepting a prefabricated solution in the form of an ideology and membership in a powerful movement, with which he identifies and from which he extracts a spurious sense of power. In principle, this formula is not discernibly different from that which accounts for the success of General Motors, which, by building large, powerful, and impressive automobiles, permits the individual to indulge his fantasies that *he* has those attributes. In this case, too, it is not merely a fantasy which the purchaser indulges; when he hurtles along at ninety miles per hour, he is indeed a threatening and impressive juggernaut.

To say that the great man does no more than provide a vehicle for transporting the self-doubting populace from their feelings of inadequacy and incomplete identity to a state wherein they glory in a sense of power and fulfillment would be an oversimplification. However, that is the core of the matter. It is apparent that great leaders differ from rabble-rousers in general by virtue of the fact that their ideology is broader in scope, and includes a greater measure of positive, constructive elements.

I should like to close the discussion of the great-man concept with a brief comparison of two opposed figures, Hitler and Churchill. I have already discussed Hitler in part, but would add that without his sickness of soul it is inconceivable that he could have become the kind of leader he was. To press the point, it is equally inconceivable that he could ever have become a leader of the British people. He did, however, create an ideology that suited the times for a significant number of Germans, and he pursued the aims of that ideology with tremendous energy and tenacity of purpose. In contrast, Churchill cannot be said to have created any ideology at all. He *functioned* in a critical and demanding role, and he *embodied* characteristics which most Britons admired and with which they identified strongly. By his conduct and utterances, he assured each individual that he would conduct himself properly and according to the common need. Churchill did not create an ideology; he provided a rallying point at a critical time, and it is for this reason that he became a great man.

The difference between the ideological commitment in Germany and the commitment to the performance of a common task in Britain appears to me to cover the extreme range possible for the nature of a group's relation to its leader and his ideology. The difference between seizing an ideology as a crutch for one's sense of identity, on the one hand, and accepting necessary strictures on one's individuality because of a recognized necessity for group action, on the other, is a true measure of the difference in stability of the individual sense of identity in each instance. Leaders like Churchill would appear to be fundamentally different from what I have described as the "great man." Their greatness does not depend upon the formation of an ideology, but upon the reaffirmation of widely accepted ideals and upon their embodiment of them. Although the magic of an ideology is lacking, there is something magical about their greatness. Their public image is idealized, thereby providing a standard toward which the individuals in the group can strive. Whether such idealization is fostered or not, it occurs as a result of the need of the individuals in the group. Without this idealization, no leader would ever be "great." He would only be effective. Men become great in the same way that folk myths and legends are created—out of the need of the creators.

Erikson's penetrating resume of Luther's conflicts and their resolution is an interesting psychoanalytic exercise in the use of historical material. It is exercise conducted against the fearful odds of absence of validation and feed-back, but still done with considerable persuasiveness. If psychoanalysis is to be useful as a tool, it would be so as a background for understanding and perhaps predicting events, on the basis of a recognition of discrepancies between individual needs and the opportunities for satisfaction available in institutions of the moment. Another and related function might be as a method of studying the developing institutions in a society that, parallel to ego institutions, are recognizably pathological.

It has often been said that history cannot be written from an unbiased viewpoint. I believe that this is a truism that should not blind us to the fact that it can at least be studied in an unbiased way. More important, it should be acknowledged that political institutions can and must be studied. To measure social or political institutions by their success in reproducing their kind, their relative stability, their capacity to meet challenge, their ability to meet the needs of the participating individuals—these or related measures are necessary if the study of human institutions is to advance beyond partisan polemics, on the one hand, and statistical compilations, on the other. In a venture such as this I do believe psychoanalysis has something to offer.

A Selected Bibliography

Research Paraphernalia and Conceptual Tools

ABRAMSON, E., CUTLER, H. A., KAUTZ, R. W., and MENDELSON, M. "Social Power and Commitment: A Theoretical Statement," *American Sociological Review*, February, 1958.

BENDIX, R., and LIPSET, S. "Political Sociology," *Current Sociology*, Paris: UNESCO, Vol. VI, No. 2 (1957).

BONILLA, FRANK. "Elites and Public Opinion in Areas of High Social Stratification," *Public Opinion Quarterly*, Fall, 1958.

COSER, LEWIS A. *The Functions of Social Conflict*, Glencoe, Ill.: The Free Press, 1956.

DAVIES, JAMES C. "A Note on Political Motivation," *Western Political Quarterly*, June, 1959.

DION, LEON. "Political Ideology as a Tool of Functional Analysis in Socio-Political Dynamics," *Canadian Journal of Economics and Political Science*, February, 1959.

ETZIONI, A. "Authority Structure and Organizational Effectiveness," *Administrative Science Quarterly*, June, 1959.

EULAU, HEINZ. "H. D. Lasswell's Developmental Analysis," *Western Political Quarterly*, June, 1958.

EXLINE, R. V., and ZILLER, R. C. "Status Congruency and Interpersonal Conflict in Decision-Making Groups," *Human Relations*, Vol. XII, No. 2 (1959).

GORE, WILLIAM J., and SILANDER, FRED S. "A Bibliographical Essay on Decision-Making," *Administrative Science Quarterly*, June, 1959.

GUSFIELD, J. R. "Fieldwork Reciprocities in Studying a Social Movement," *Human Organization*, Fall, 1958.

HAMBLIN, R. C. "Leadership and Crises," *Sociometry*, December, 1958.

HUND, J. M. "Changing Role in the Interview Situation," *Public Opinion Quarterly*, Summer, 1959.

HYMAN, HERBERT. *Political Socialization*. Glencoe, Ill.: The Free Press, 1958.

JANIS, I. L. "Decisional Conflicts: A Theoretical Analysis," *Journal of Conflict Resolution*, Vol. III (1959).

JANOWITZ, MORRIS. "Social Stratification and the Comparative Analysis of Elites," *Explorations in Entrepreneurial History*, Winter Supplement, 1956.

KINCAID, H. V., and BRIGHT, M. "Interviewing the Business Elite," *American Journal of Sociology*, November, 1957.

NADEL, S. F. "The Concept of Social Elites," *International Social Science Bulletin*, Autumn, 1956.

"Factions in Indian and Overseas Indian Societies," *British Journal of Sociology*, December, 1957.

RIKER, WILLIAM H. *The Study of Local Politics*. New York: Random House, 1959.

———. "A Test of the Adequacy of the Power Index," *Behavioral Science*, April, 1959.

ROSSI, PETER H. "Community Decision-Making," in ROLAND YOUNG (ed.). *Approaches to the Study of Politics*. Evanston: Northwestern University Press, 1958.

SCHUTZ, WILLIAM. "On Categorizing Qualitative Data in Content Analysis," *Public Opinion Quarterly*, Winter, 1958-59.

SCODEL, A., RATOOSH, P., and MINAS, J. S. "Some Personality Correlates of Decision-Making under Conditions of Risk," *Behavioral Science*, January, 1959.

SELVIN, H. *The Effects of Leadership*. Glencoe, Ill.: The Free Press, 1960.

SIMON, HERBERT A. "Theories of Decision-Making in Economics and Behavioral Science," *American Economic Review*, June, 1959.

SMEGEL, ERWIN O. "Interviewing a Legal Elite: The Wall Street Lawyer," *American Journal of Sociology*, September, 1958.

SMITH, J. M., and COTTER, C. P. "Freedom and Authority in the Amphibial State," *Midwest Journal of Political Science*, May, 1957.

UNESCO. "African Elites," in *International Social Science Bulletin*, Paris, Autumn, 1956.

WASSERMAN, PAUL. *Decision-Making: An Annotated Bibliography*. Ithaca, N.Y.: Graduate School of Business and Public Administration, Cornell University, 1958.

Governmental Decision-Makers in Advanced Pluralist Societies

ATTLEE, EARL. "The Attitudes of M.P.'s and Active Peers," *Political Quarterly,* January-March, 1959.

BOLIN, B., and SVENSSON, O. "New Recruits in Parliament in Home-Guard Age Groups." *Tiden,* January, 1957. (English translation of Swedish title given here.)

BENNER, JEAN. "The Four Labor Cabinets," *Sociological Review,* July, 1958.

BUCK, PHILIP W. "Election Experience of Candidates for the House of Commons, 1918-1955," *Western Political Quarterly,* June, 1959.

CHAPMAN, BRIAN. *The Profession of Government.* New York: MacMillan Co., 1959.

COHEN, BERNARD C. *The Political Process and Foreign Policy.* Princeton: Princeton University Press, 1957.

COOLEY, RITA W. "Judicial Appointments in the Eisenhower Administration," *Social Science,* January, 1959.

DERGE, DAVID R. "The Lawyer as Decision-Maker in the American State Legislature," *Journal of Politics,* August, 1959.

ECKSTEIN, HARRY. *The English Health Service.* Cambridge: Harvard University Press, 1958.

EULAU, HEINZ, et. al. "The Role of the Representative: Some Empirical Observations on the Theory of Edmund Burke," *American Political Science Review,* September, 1959.

FELD, M. D. "Information and Authority: The Structure of Military Organization," *American Sociological Review,* February, 1959.

FULLER, MARGARET G. *Leadership in the Michigan Legislature.* East Lansing: Michigan State University, Department of Political Science, 1957.

FORDHAM, JEFFERSON B. *The State Legislative Institution.* Philadelphia: University of Pennsylvania Press, 1959.

GALLOWAY, GEORGE B. "Leadership in the House of Representatives," *Western Political Quarterly,* June, 1959.

GOODWIN, GEORGE, JR. "The Seniority System in Congress," *American Political Science Review,* June, 1959.

HADWIGER, DON F. "Representation in the Missouri General Assembly," *Missouri Law Review,* April, 1959.

HUNTER, FLOYD. *Top Leadership, U. S. A.,* Chapel Hill: North Carolina University Press, 1959.

HUNTINGTON, SAMUEL. *The Soldier and the State.* Cambridge: Belknap Press, 1957.

JANOWITZ, MORRIS. *The Professional Soldier.* Glencoe, Ill.: The Free Press, 1960.

————. "Changing Patterns of Organizational Authority: The Military Establishment," *Administrative Science Quarterly,* March, 1959.

KEEFE, WILLIAM J. "Judges and Politics: The Pennsylvania Plan of Judge Selection," *University of Pittsburgh Law Review,* March, 1959.

KIRCHHEIMER, OTTO. "Majorities and Minorities in Western European Governments," *Western Political Quarterly,* June, 1959.

LEITES, NATHAN. *On the Game of Politics in France.* Stanford: Stanford University Press, 1959.

LUPTON, T., and WILSON, C. S. "The Social Background and Connections of 'Top Decision-Makers,'" *Manchester School of Economic and Social Studies,* Vol. XXVII (1959).

LYONS, GENE M., and MASLAND, JOHN W. *Education and Military Leadership: A Study of the R. O. T. C.* Princeton: Princeton University Press, 1959.

MASLAND, J. W. *Soldiers and Scholars.* Princeton: Princeton University Press, 1957.

MATTHEWS, DONALD R. *U.S. Senators and their World.* Chapel Hill: University of North Carolina Press, 1960.

MELNIK, CONSTANTIN, and LEITES, NATHAN. *The House Without Windows: France Selects a President.* Evanston: Row, Peterson, 1958.

MITCHELL, WILLIAM C. "The Ambivalent Social Status of the American Politician," *Western Political Quarterly,* September, 1958.

NEUNREITHER, KARLHEINZ "Politics and Bureaucracy in the West German Bundesrat," *American Political Science Review,* September, 1959.

PATTERSON, SAMUEL C. "Patterns of Interpersonal Relations in a State Legislative Group," *Public Opinion Quarterly,* Spring, 1959.

RHODE, WILLIAM E. *Committee Clearance of Administrative Decisions.* East Lansing: Bureau of Social and Political Research, Michigan State University, 1959.

RICHARDS, PETER G. *Honourable Members: A Study of the British Backbencher.* London: Faber and Faber, 1959.

ROSENBERG, HANS. *Bureaucracy, Aristocracy and Autocracy: The Prussian Experience, 1660-1815.* Cambridge: Harvard University Press, 1958.

SCHLESINGER, JOSEPH A. *How They Became Governor.* East Lansing: Michigan State University Press, 1958.

————. "Lawyers and American Politics: A Clarified View," *Midwest Journal of Political Science,* May, 1957.

SCHUMM, SIEGFRIED. "Interest Representation in France and Germany," *Cahiers de Bruges,* Nos. 3-4, 1958.

STAUDE, WILLIAM L. *The Lawyer in Michigan State Government.* Institute of Public Administration, University of Michigan, 1959.

STROUP, HERBERT. "The Military as the Controlling Elite," *Fellowship,* May 1, 1959.

TRUMAN, DAVID B. *The Congressional Party: A Case Study.* New York: John Wiley and Sons, Inc., 1959.

TUBERVILLE, A.S. *The House of Lords in the Age of Reform, 1784-1837.* London: Faber and Faber, 1958.

URICH, THEODORE. "The Voting Behavior of Freshmen Congressmen," *Southwestern Social Science Quarterly,* March, 1959.

WALLACE, ROBERT ASH. "Congressional Control of the Budget," *Midwest Journal of Political Science*, May, 1959.
WESTERFIELD, H. B. *Foreign Policy and Party Politics*. New Haven: Yale University Press, 1957.
WHITE, WILLIAM S. *Citadel*. New York: Harper and Bros., 1957.

Political Decision-makers in Advanced Pluralist Societies

AGGER, ROBERT E., and GOLDRICH, DANIEL. "Community Power Structure and Partisanship." *American Sociological Review*, August, 1958.
ALLEN, V. L. "Trade Union Leadership." *British Journal of Sociology*, September, 1958.
BARTH, E. A. T., and ABU-LABAN, B. "Power Structure and the Negro Sub-community," *American Sociological Review*, February, 1959.
BAYLISS, F. J. "The Independent Members of British Wage Councils and Boards," *British Journal of Sociology*, March, 1957.
BEALEY, FRANK, and PELLING, HENRY. *Labour and Politics, 1900-1906: A History of the Labour Representation Committee*. London: Macmillan and Co., 1958.
BERDAHL, ROBERT O. *British Universities and the State*. Berkeley and Los Angeles: University of California Press, 1959.
BIRCH, A. H. *Small-Town Politics*. New York: Oxford University Press, 1959.
BONE, HUGH A. *Party Committees and National Politics*. Seattle: University of Washington Press, 1958.
CARNEY, FRANCIS. *The Rise of the Democratic Clubs in California*. Henry Holt and Co., 1958.
CARTER, ROY E., JR. "Newspaper 'Gatekeepers' and the Sources of News," *Public Opinion Quarterly*, Summer, 1958.
COHEN, BERNARD C. *The Influence of Non-Governmental Groups on Foreign-Policy Making*. Boston: World Peace Foundation, Studies in Citizen Participation in International Relations, Vol. II, 1959.
COMFORT, GEORGE O. *Professional Politicians: A Study of British Party Agents*. Washington: Public Affairs Press, 1959.
CUTRIGHT, P., and ROSSI, P. "Grass Roots Politicians and the Vote," *American Sociological Review*, April, 1958.
EPSTEIN, LEON D. *Politics in Wisconsin*. Madison: University of Wisconsin Press, 1958.
FOLKMAN, WILLIAM. "Board Members as Decision-Makers in Farmers' Co-operatives," *Rural Sociology*, September, 1958.
FORM, WILLIAM H. "Organized Labor's Place in the Community Power Structure," *Industrial and Labor Relations Review*, July, 1959.
FRANKENBERG, RONALD. *Village on the Border: A Social Study of Religion, Politics, and Football in a North Wales Community*. London, 1957.
FREEMAN, J. LEIPER. "Local Party Systems: Theoretical Considerations and a Case Analysis," *American Journal of Sociology*, November, 1958.

GRAINGER, G. W. "Oligarchy in the British Communist Party," *British Journal of Sociology,* June, 1958.

GROSS, NEAL. *Who Runs Our Schools?* New York: Wiley, 1958.

GUSFIELD, J. R. "The Problem of Generations in an Organizational Structure," *Social Forces,* May, 1957.

HALSEY, A. H. "Genetics, Social Structure, and Intelligence," *British Journal of Sociology,* March, 1958.

HERO, ALFRED O. *Americans in World Affairs.* Boston: World Peace Foundation, Studies in Citizen Participation in International Relations, Vol. I, 1959.

ISAACS, HAROLD R. *Scratches on Our Minds.* New York: Day, 1958.

KEISER, N. F. "Public Responsibility and Federal Advisory Groups," *Western Political Quarterly,* June, 1958.

KINNARD, WILLIAM N. JR. *Appointed by the Mayor: Inter-University Case Program, No. 36.* University, Alabama: University of Alabama Press, 1956.

LANE, ROBERT E. "Fathers and Sons: Foundations of Political Belief," *American Sociological Review,* August, 1959.

LA PALOMBARA, JOSEPH. *The Italian Labor Movement: Problems and Prospects,* Ithaca: Cornell University Press, 1957.

LIPSET, SEYMOUR M., and BENDIX, REINHARD. *Social Mobility in Industrial Society.* Berkeley: University of California Press, 1958.

LOWE, F. E., and McCORMICK, T. C. "A Study of the Influence of Formal and Informal Leaders in an Election Campaign," *Public Opinion Quarterly,* Winter, 1956-57.

MILLER, DELBERT C. "Decision-Making Cliques in Community Power Structures: A Comparative Study of an American and an English City," *American Journal of Sociology,* November, 1958.

MITCHELL, STEPHEN A. *Elm Street Politics.* New York: Oceana, 1959.

MORGAN, R. J. "Pressure Politics and Resource Administration," *Journal of Politics,* February, 1956.

OVERACKER, L. "The British and New Zealand Labor Parties: A Comparison," *Political Science Quarterly,* March, 1957.

PELLING, HENRY. *The British Communist Party.* New York: Macmillan Co., 1958.

PITCHELL, R. J. "Influence of Professional Campaign Management Firms in Partisan Elections in California," *Western Political Quarterly,* June, 1958.

POIRIER, PHILIP P. *The Advent of the British Labour Party.* New York: Columbia University Press, 1958.

POLSBY, N. W. "The Sociology of Community Power," *Social Forces,* March, 1959.

PORTER, JOHN. "The Economic Elite and the Social Structure in Canada," *Canadian Journal of Economics and Political Science,* August, 1957.

REISSMAN, LEONARD. "Life Careers, Power, and the Professions: The Retired Army General," *American Sociological Review,* April, 1956.

REMINI, ROBERT V. *Martin Van Buren and the Making of the Democratic Party.* New York: Columbia University Press, 1959.

RHYNE, E. H. "Political Parties and Decision Making in Three Southern Counties," *American Political Science Review,* December, 1958.

ROSENZWEIG, R. M. "The Politician and the Career in Politics," *Midwest Journal of Political Science,* August, 1957.

ROSS, A. D. "Control and Leadership in Women's Groups: An Analysis of Philanthropic Money-Raising Activity," *Social Forces,* December, 1958.

SCHULZE, ROBERT O. "The Role of Economic Dominants in Community Power Structure," *American Sociological Review,* February, 1958.

SCHULZE, ROBERT O., and BLUMBERG, L. U. "The Determination of Local Power Elites," *American Journal of Sociology,* November, 1957.

SEEMAN, MELVIN. "The Intellectual and the Language of Minorities," *American Journal of Sociology,* July, 1958.

SELIGMAN, LESTER G. "A Prefatory Study of Leadership Selection in Oregon," *Western Political Quarterly,* March, 1959.

SHILS, EDWARD A. "The Prospect for Intellectuals," *Soviet Survey,* July-September, 1959.

SILLS, D. L. "Voluntary Associations and Planned Change," *Human Organization,* Spring, 1959.

SNOW, C. P. "The Two Cultures and the Scientific Revolution," *Encounter,* June-July, 1959.

SWANSON, G. E. "Agitation through the Press: A Study of the Personalities of Publicists," *Public Opinion Quarterly,* Winter, 1956-57.

VIDICH, A. J., and BENSMAN, J. *Small Town in Mass Society.* Princeton: Princeton University Press, 1958.

WALTER, E. V. "The Politics of Decivilization," in Stein, Vidich, White (eds.). *Identity and Anxiety* (Glencoe, Ill.: The Free Press, 1960).

WESTERSTAHL, J., and JANSON, C .G. *The Political Press.* Sweden: Political Science Institute, University of Gothenburg, 1958.

WOOD, ROBERT C. *Suburbia: Its People and Their Politics.* Boston: Houghton Mifflin Co., 1959.

WYLLER, THOMAS CHR. *Nyordning og Motstand (The New Order and Resistance).* Oslo: Universitetsforlaget, 1958.

Political Decision-makers in Modernizing Societies

Anonymous, "The Soviet Intelligentsia," *Foreign Affairs,* October, 1957.

ARMSTRONG, JOHN A. *The Soviet Bureaucratic Elite: A Case Study of the Ukrainian Apparatus.* New York: Frederick A. Praeger, 1959.

AVAKUMOVIC, I. "A Statistical Approach to the Revolutionary Movement in Russia, 1878-1887," *American Slavic and East European Review,* April, 1959.

BELLINGTON, J. H. "The Renaissance of the Russian Intelligentsia," *Foreign Affairs,* April, 1957.

BERGER, M. *Bureaucracy and Society in Modern Egypt: A Study of the Higher Civil Service.* Princeton: Princeton University Press, 1957.

BILLING, M. G. "Tribal Rule and Modern Politics in Northern Rhodesia," *African Affairs*, April, 1959.

CARTER, GWENDOLYN M., and BROWN, WILLIAM O. (eds.). *Transition in Africa: Studies in Political Adaptation*. Boston: Boston University Press, 1958.

CHANG, CHUNG-LI, with Introduction by Franz Michael. *The Chinese Gentry: Studies on their Role in Nineteenth-Century Chinese Society*. Seattle: University of Washington Press, 1955.

COLE, ALLAN B. *Japanese Society and Politics: The Impact of Social Stratification and Mobility on Politics*. Boston University Studies No. 1, 1956.

COLEMAN, JAMES S. *Nigeria: Background to Nationalism*. Berkeley and Los Angeles: University of California Press, 1958.

DINERSTEIN, H. S. *War and the Soviet Union: Nuclear Weapons and the Revolution in Soviet Military and Political Thinking*. New York: Frederick A. Praeger, 1959.

DORE, R. P. *City Life in Japan: A Study of a Tokyo Ward*. Berkeley and Los Angeles: University of California Press, 1958.

EISENSTADT, S. N. "Political Struggle in Bureaucratic Societies," *World Politics*, October, 1956.

EPSTEIN, A. L. "Tribal Elders and Trade Unions," in P. Smith (ed.) *Africa in Transition*. London: Reinhardt, 1958.

EPSTEIN, A. L. *Politics in an Urban African Community*. New York: Humanities Press, 1958.

FEITH, HERBERT. *The Wilopo Cabinet, 1952-1953: A Turning Point in Post Revolutionary Indonesia*. Ithaca: Cornell University Southeast Asia Program; New York: Institute of Pacific Relations, 1958.

FISCHER, GEORGE. *Russian Liberalism: From Gentry to Intelligentsia*. Cambridge: Harvard University Press, 1958.

FITZGIBBON, RUSSELL H. "The Social Basis of Changing Political Structures in Latin America," *Social Science*, April, 1959.

FRANK VICTOR. "The Russian Radical Tradition," *Soviet Survey*, July-September, 1959.

FREE, LLOYD A. *Opinions of Parliamentarians in India and Japan*. Princeton: Institute for International Social Research, August, 1958.

GULLICK, J. M. *Indigenous Political Systems of Western Malaya*. New York: Humanities Press, 1959.

HAIMSON, LEOPOLD H. "Three Generations of the Soviet Intelligentsia," in Howard W. Winger (ed.). *Iron Curtains and Scholarship*. Chicago: University of Chicago Press, 1958.

HARE, RICHARD. *Portraits of Russian Personalities between Reform and Revolution*. New York, London: Oxford University Press, 1959.

HERSON, L. J. R. "China's Imperial Bureaucracy: Its Direction and Control," *Public Administration Review*, Winter, 1957.

HOUN, FRANKLIN W. "Chinese Communist Control of the Press," *Public Opinion Quarterly*, Winter, 1958-59.

HOUN, FRANKLIN W. "The Eighth Central Committee of the Chinese Communist Party: A Study of an Eite," *American Political Science Review,* June, 1957.

JALENSKI, K. A. "The Genealogy of the Polish Intelligentsia," *Soviet Survey,* July-September, 1959.

JOHNSON, JOHN J. *Political Change in Latin America.* Stanford: Stanford University Press, 1958.

KEESING, F. M., and KEESING, M. M. *Elite Communication in Samoa: A Study of Leadership.* Stanford: Stanford University Press, 1956.

KLING, M. "Toward a Theory of Power and Political Instability in Latin America," *Western Political Quarterly,* March, 1956.

KUO-CHUN, C. "Leadership in the Chinese Communist Party," *Annals,* January, 1959.

LABEDZ, LEOPOLD. "The New Soviet Intelligentsia," *Soviet Survey,* July-September, 1959.

LANPERT, E. *Studies in Rebellion.* New York: Frederick A. Praeger, 1957.

LERNER, DANIEL. *The Passing of Traditional Society.* Glencoe, Ill.: The Free Press, 1958.

LEWIS, OSCAR. "Medicine and Politics in a Mexican Village," in B. D. Paul (ed.). *Health, Culture and Community.* New York: Russell Sage Foundation, 1955.

LEWIS, OSCAR. *Village Life in Northwestern India.* Urbana: University of Illinois Press, 1958.

MANNONI, DOMINIQUE O. *Prospero and Caliban.* New York: Frederick A. Praeger, 1956.

MORRIS-JONES, W. H. "Recent Political Development in India: II.," *Parliamentary Affairs,* Winter, 1958-59.

MULLER, E. M. "Eine Zentral Afrikanische Herrschafts-institution in Idealtypologischer Betrachtung," *Archiv. Rechts-Soz Philos.,* Vol. XLIII, No. 2 (1957).

MUNDY, J. H. and RIESENBERG, P. *The Medieval Town.* Princeton, N. J.: Van Nostrand, 1958.

NAHIRNY, V. C. "Status Structure in Soviet Rural Communities," *American Catholic Sociological Review,* October, 1956.

OPLER, M. E., *et al.* "Indian National and State Elections in a Village," *Human Organization,* Spring, 1959.

PARK, RICHARD L., and TINKER, IRENE (eds.). *Leadership and Political Institutions in India.* Princeton: Princeton University Press, 1959.

PRESTHUS, ROBERT V., with EREM, SEVDA. *Statistical Analysis in Comparative Administration: The Turkish Conseil d'Etat.* Ithaca: Cornell University Press, 1958.

PYE, LUCIAN W. *The Policy Implications of Social Change in Non-Western Societies.* Cambridge: Massachusetts Institute of Technology Press, 1957.

———. "Communication Patterns and the Problems of Representative Government in Non-Western Societies," *Public Opinion Quarterly,* Vol. XXI, No. 1 (1956).

———. "Administrators, Agitators and Brokers," *Public Opinion Quarterly,* Fall, 1958.

RAMSAUR, E. E., JR. *The Young Turks: Prelude to the Revolution of 1908.* Princeton: Princeton University Press, 1957.

READ, K. E. "Leadership and Consensus in a New Guinea Society," *American Anthropologist,* June, 1959.

RICHERT, ERNST. *Macht ohne Mandat: Der Staatsapparat in der Sowjetischen Beaatzungszone Deutschlands.* Cologne and Opladen: Westdeutscher Verlag, 1958.

———. *Agitation und Propaganda: Das System der publizistischen Massenfuhrung in der Sowjetzone.* Berlin and Frankfurt: Verlag Franz Vahlen, 1958.

RUSH, MYRON. "Esoteric Communication in Soviet Politics," *World Politics,* July, 1959.

RUSTOW, D. A. "The Army and the Founding of the Turkish Republic," *World Politics,* July, 1959.

SETON-WATSON, HUGH. "Intelligentsia and Revolution," *Soviet Survey,* July-September, 1959.

SHILS, EDWARD. "The Culture of the Indian Intellectual," *Sewanee Review,* April-July, 1959.

SKINNER, G. WILLIAM. *Leadership and Power in the Chinese Community of Thailand.* Association for Asian Studies; Ithaca: Cornell University Press, 1958.

———. *Chinese Society in Thailand.* Ithaca: Cornell University Press, 1957.

SWARTZ, MARC J. "Leadership and Status Confliction Romonum, Truk," *Southwestern Journal of Anthropology,* Summer, 1959.

TABORSKY, E. "The Revolt of the Communist Intellectuals," *Review of Politics,* July, 1957.

TAIT, D., and MIDDLETON, J. (eds.). *Tribes without Rulers.* London: Kegan Paul, 1959.

VAN DER MEHDEN, FRED R. "Party Development in Newly Independent States," *Social Science,* June, 1959.

WASHINGTON, S. W. "Student Politics in Latin America: The Venezuelan Example," *Foreign Affairs,* April, 1959.

WEBER, MAX. *The City.* Translated by DON MARTINDALE and GERTRUD NEUWIRTH. Glencoe, Ill.: The Free Press, 1958.

WITTFOGEL, K. A. *Oriental Despotism and Hydraulic Society.* New Haven: Yale University Press, 1956.

WORSLEY, PETER. *The Trumpet Shall Sound: A Study of "Cargo" Cults in Melanesia.* London: MacGibbon and Kee, 1957.

Index